Globalization and Welfare

A Critical Reader

Edited by
Ritu Vij
School of Social Sciences, University of Aberdeen, UK

D1394137

First published 2007 by
PALGRAVE MACMILLAN
Houndmills, Basingstoke, Hampshire RG21 6XS and
175 Fifth Avenue, New York, N. Y. 10010
Companies and representatives throughout the world

PALGRAVE MACMILLAN is the global academic imprint of the Palgrave
Macmillan division of St. Martin's Press, LLC and of Palgrave Macmillan Ltd.
Macmillan® is a registered trademark in the United States, United Kingdom
and other countries. Palgrave is a registered trademark in the European Union
and other countries.

ISBN-13: 978–1–4039–0165–1   hardback
ISBN-10: 1–4039–0165–1   hardback
ISBN-13: 978–1–4039–0166–8   paperback
ISBN-10: 1–4039–0166–X   paperback

This book is printed on paper suitable for recycling and made from fully
managed and sustained forest sources.

A catalogue record for this book is available from the British Library.

Library of Congress Cataloging-in-Publication Data
Globalization and welfare: a critical reader / edited by Ritu Vij.
    p. cm. – (International political economy series)
Includes bibliographical references and index.
    Contents: Citizenship and global governance – Regulating global
capital – Re-politicizing the retreat of the state – Governmentality and the
micro-politics of welfare reform.
    ISBN-13: 978–1–4039–0165–1 (cloth)
    ISBN-10: 1–4039–0165–1 (cloth)
    ISBN-10: 978–1–4039–0166–8 (pbk.)
    ISBN-10: 1–4039–0166–X (pbk.)
    1. Welfare state. 2. Public welfare. 3. Globalization. I. Vij, Ritu, 1959-

JC479.G58 2007
361.6'5–dc22   2006050188

10   9   8   7   6   5   4   3   2   1
16   15 14 13 12 11 10 09 08 07

Printed and bound in Great Britain by
Antony Rowe Ltd, Chippenham and Eastbourne

Contents

**Part IV   Governmentality and the Micropolitics of
Welfare Reform**   **193**

Acknowledgments

Testimony to the displacements and possibilities of nomadic existence, work on this volume began in the comfort of 'home' in Takoma Park, Maryland, USA, continued briefly in India, and was completed in the cosmopolitan labyrinth of Nishi-Azabu and Mita in Tokyo, Japan. I have many people to thank: Tim Shaw, series editor at Palgrave, for commissioning this project, and for the faith and patience with which he, along with my editor, Phillipa Grand, have seen it through completion; for their help in navigating data bases, tracking down hard to locate sources and going beyond the call of duty to a *gaikokujin kenkyushya*, the library staff at Tokyo University (Hongo campus), Tokyo Metropolitan Library (Hiroo), and especially, Keio University, my institutional home in Japan; Shinichi Obayashi in Tokyo, David Bario and Frederico Umana in Washington D.C. for research and computer assistance; for their friendship, critical feedback, and sustained interest in this work, I am indebted to Matt Davies, David Levine, Michael Niemann, Magnus Ryner, Gigi Herbert, Itty Abraham and Lalitha Gopalan; Craig Murphy and Rob Walker I must thank for their enthusiastic encouragement at the early stages of this project. My deepest thanks, go to my fellow travelers: my children, Ayesha and Tariq – willing nomads both – for forgiving my absences from story and bed and bathtime; my parents and sister for extended stays with them, and for their support; but above all, Mustapha Kamal Pasha, fellow traveler *par excellence*, for much else, but especially his fortitude of will, intellectual generosity, and for making possible the luxury of time to complete work on this book.

Every effort has been made to trace copyright holders of material produced in this book, but if any have been inadvertently overlooked the publishers will be glad to make the necessary arrangements at the first opportunity. Teresa Brennan, 'Which third way', *Thesis Eleven* 64: 39–64, Sage Publications, 2001. Mitchell Dean, 'Governing the unemployed self in an active society', *Economy and Society*, 24(4) (1995): 559–83. Reprinted by permission of author and Routledge, Taylor and Francis. Gosta Esping-Andersen, 'The sustainability of welfare states into the twenty-first century,' *International Journal of Health Services* 30(1) (2000): 1–12. Reprinted by permission of author and Baywood Publishing Company. Geoffrey Garret, 'Shrinking states? Globalization and national autonomy in the OECD', *Oxford Development Studies* 26(1) (1998): 71–98. Reprinted by permission of author and Taylor and Francis Group. Colin Hay, 'The normalizing role of rationalist assumptions in the institutional embedding of neoliberalism', *Economy and Society* 44(4) (2004): 500–27. Permission to reprint granted by author and Routledge, Taylor and Francis Group. Bob Jessop, 'Towards a

Schumpeterian workfare state? Preliminary remarks on post-fordist political economy', *Studies in Political Economy* 4 (1993): 7–30. Permission to reprint granted by author and Studies in Political Economy (Carleton University). Claus Offe, 'Some contradictions of the welfare state', in *Contradictions of the Welfare State*, Cambridge, Mass.: The MIT Press (1984): 147–61. Reprinted by permission of the author and MIT Press. Jamie Peck, 'Political economies of scale: fast policy, interscalar relations, and Neoliberal Workfare', *Economic Geography* 78(2) (2002): 331–60. Permission to reprint granted by author and *Economic Geography Journal* (Clark University). Frances Fox Piven and Richard Cloward, 'Eras of power', *Monthly Review* 49(6) (1997): 11–23. Sanford F. Schram, 'Compliant Subjects for a new world order: globalization and the behavior modification regime of welfare reform', in *Praxis for the Poor: Piven and Cloward and the Future of Social Science in Social Welfare*, New York and London: New York University Press (2002): 201–40. Reprinted by permission of author and New York University Press. Paul Pierson, 'The New Politics of the Welfare State', *World Politics* 48(2) (1996) 143–79. Reprinted with permission of The Johns Hopkins University Press. Nikolas Rose, 'The death of the social? Re-figuring the territory of government', *Economy and Society* 25(3) (1996): 327–56. Reprint permission granted by author and Routledge. Elmar Rieger and Stephan Leibfried 'Welfare state limits to globalization', *Politics and Society* 26(3) (1998): 363–90. Permission to reprint granted by author and Sage Publications. Lynne Segal, 'Subject to suspicion: feminism and anti-statism in Britain' in *Social Text* 86(1), pp. 143–51. Used by permission of author and Duke University Press. Bryan S. Turner, 'The erosion of citizenship?' *British Journal of Sociologym* 52(2) (2001): 189–29. Permission to reprint granted by Routledge Journals, Taylor and Francis Ltd. Nicola Yeates, 'Social politics and policy in an era of globalization: critical reflections', *Social Policy & Administration* 33(4) (1999): 372–93. Permission to reprint granted by author and Blackwell Publishers Ltd.

The authors and publishers have made every attempt to contact copyright holders. If any have inadvertently been overlooked, the appropriate arrangements will be made at the first opportunity.

List of Contributors

Gosta Esping-Andersen is Professor at Universitat Pompeu Fabra in Barcelona. He has previously taught at Harvard University, the European University in Firenze, and at the Universita di Trento, and worked extensively for international organizations, including the UN, World Bank, and European Governments. His most recent books include *Why We Need a New Welfare State* (2002), *Why Deregulate Labour Markets* (2001), and Social Foundations of Postindustrial Economies (1999).

Teresa Brennan was Schmidt Distinguished Professor of Humanities at Florida Atlantic University when she was killed in a hit-and-run accident in 2003. She taught at several universities, including Cambridge, the University of Amsterdam, Brandeis University and the New School for Social Research. Professor Brennan's many publications include, *The Transmission Affect* (2004), *Globalization and its Terrors* (2003), *Exhausting Modernity: Ground for a New Economy* (2000), *History After Lacan* (1993), and *The Interpretation of the Flesh: Freud and Femininity* (1992).

Richard Cloward, a distinguished scholar and social activist, was a professor at Columbia University's School of Social Work until his death in 2001. A driving force (along with his partner and co-author, Frances Fox Piven) behind the National Voter Registration Act of 1993 (USA), Professor Cloward was a catalyst in numerous protest movements on behalf of the poor. He published numerous books, monographs and articles, including *The Breaking of the American Social Compact* (1997), *Poor People's Movements: Why they Succeed, How they Fail* (1977), and *Regulating the Poor: The Functions of Public Welfare* (1971) which was listed among the 40 Most Notable Books by the American Library Association.

Mitchell Dean is Dean, Division of Society Culture Media and Philosophy (SCMP), and Professor, Department of Sociology, at Macquaire University, Sydney, Australia. His many publications include *Governing Societies* (2006), *Governmentality: Power and Rule in Modern Society* (1999), *Critical and Effective Histories: Foucault's Methods and Historical Sociology* (1994), The *Constitution of Poverty: Toward a Geneology of Liberal Governance* (1991), and co-editor (with Barry Hindess) Governing Australia (1998).

Geoffrey Garrett is President of the Pacific Council on International Policy (PCIP) and a Professor of International Relations at the University of Southern California (USA). He was previously Vice-Provost and the founding Dean of the International Institute, and Professor of Political Science at the University of California, Los Angeles. He has also served on the faculties of Oxford, Stanford, and Yale universities as well as the Wharton School. An expert on globalization, Professor Garrett's publications include the widely cited *Partisan Politics in the Global Economy* (1998), and numerous articles in journals such as, *Annual Review of Political Science, Foreign Affairs, International Organization, Comparative Political Studies,* and *British Journal of Political Science.*

Colin Hay is Professor of Political Analysis and, currently, Head of the Department of Political Science and International Studies at the University of Birmingham, UK. He has previously held visiting position at the Harvard University and the Massachusetts Institute of Technology in the USA. He is the author of the award winning *Re-Stating Social and Political Change* (1996), *The Political Economy of New Labour: Labouring Under False Pretences* (1999), and, most recently *Political Analysis* (2002). His articles have appeared in journals such as *British Journal of Politics and International Relations, Cambridge Review of International Affairs, Economy and Society,* and *Review of International Political Economy.*

Bob Jessop is Professor and Director of the Institute for Advanced Studies at Lancaster University, UK. A prolific writer on corporatism, regulation theory, Fordism and Post-Fordism, social theory, political-economy and the welfare state, he is best known for his work on state theory, *The Capitalist State: Marxist Theories and Methods* (1982), *Nicos Poulantzas: Marxist Theory and Political Strategy* (1985). His current research focuses on the cultural political economy of the knowledge-based economy, an ambitious attempt to develop a post-disciplinary analysis of contemporary capitalism.

Stephan Leibfried is Professor at the Graduate School of Social Sciences, University of Bremen, Germany, where he teaches social policy and social administration. He is the co-author (with Elmar Rieger) of *Limits to Globalization in the Age of Welfare Democracies* (2002), and editor of *Welfare State Futures* (2001), and co-editor (with Paul Pierson) of *European Social Policy: between Fragmentation and Integration* (1995).

Claus Offe is a distinguished political sociologist who was based at Humboldt University, Berlin (1995–2005) until his recent retirement. He is the author of several ground-breaking essays and books in political sociology, social theory, and public policy, including *Modernity and the State* (1996), *Varieties of Transition* (1996), *Disorganised Capitalism* (1985), *Institutional Design in Post-Communist Societies*, co-authored with John Elster and Ulrich Preuss (1998) and the widely influential, *Contradictions of the Welfare State* (1984).

Jamie Peck is Professor of Geography at the University of Wisconsin, Madison, USA. He has published widely on a number of topics including, welfare, theories of economic regulation and governance, and labor geography. He is the author of a number of books including *Workfare States*

(2001), *Work-place: The Social Regulation of Labor Markets* (1996). His articles have appeared in journals such as *Antipode, Critical Social Policy, Journal of Economic Geography, International Journal of Urban and Regional Research* and *Transactions of the Institute of British Geographers.*

Paul Pierson is Professor of Political Science at the University of California, Berkeley, where he moved after teaching at Harvard University for a number of years. He is the author of a widely cited book, *Dismantling the Welfare State* (1994), and co-editor *The New Politics of the Welfare State* (1995, 2001). His articles have appeared in journals such as the *American Political Science Review, Comparative Political Studies* and *World Politics.*

Frances Fox Piven is Distinguished Professor of Political Science and Sociology at CUNY (City University of New York). She is the author of a number of influential books in political sociology, including the landmark study, *Regulating the Poor* (1972) and *The New Class War* (1982) both co-authored with Richard Cloward. Past President of the Society for the Study of Social Problems and Vice-President of the American Political Science Association, her many accomplishments in the academic and political reform arenas have earned her numerous awards including, most recently, the American Sociological Association's Distinguished Career Award for the practice of sociology in 2000.

Elmar Rieger is Associate Professor at the Centre for Social Policy, University of Bremen, Germany. He has written widely (in German and English) on policy-making in the European Union, specifically on migration and integration, agricultural and social policy-making in the EU. He is the co-author (with Stephan Leibfried) of the much cited *Limits to Globalization: Welfare States and the World Economy* (2003). His articles can be found in journals such as *Political and Society*, and Global *Social Policy.*

Nikolas Rose is Professor of Sociology at the London School of Economics. He has published widely in a variety of areas, including the genealogy of subjectivity, the changing rationalities and techniques of political power, and on cities and citizenship. His published work includes the pathbreaking, *Governing the Soul: The Shaping of the Private Self* (1990, 1999), *Powers of Freedom: Reframing Political Thought* (1999), and *Inventing Ourselves: Psychology, Power, and Personhood* (1996). His articles have appeared in journals such as *British Journal of Sociology, Environment and Planning D: Society and Space*, and *Economy and Society.*

Sanford Schram teaches social theory and social policy in the Graduate School of Social Work and Social Research at Bryn Mawr College, USA. He has published widely on the question of social protection and justice and is most well known for his award winning *Words of Welfare: The Poverty of Social Science and the Social Science of Poverty* (1995). His more recent publication include *Welfare Discipline: Discourse, Governance, and Globalization*

(2006), and *Making Political Science Matter: Debating Knowledge, Research and Method* (2006).

Lynne Segal is Anniversary Professor of Psychology and Gender Studies at Birkbeck College, University of London. The author of several books in the interdisciplinary domain of gender studies, including, *Why Feminism? Gender, Psychology, Politics* (1999, 2000), *Straight Sex: The Politics of Pleasure* (1994). Professor Segal's work is widely known in Australia (her birthplace), the USA and Europe. She is currently at work on a project that examines what remains of feminist attachments in the 21st century: *Afterwards: Identifications and Belongings.*

Bryan Turner was Professor of Sociology at the University of Cambridge (1998–2005) and is currently Professor of Sociology in the Asian Research Institute, National University of Singapore. He is also a Professorial Research Associate at School of Oriental and African Studies, University of London, and an Honorary Professor of Deakin University, Australia. Professor Turner is the founding editor of three journals: *Citizenship Studies, Body & Society* (with Mike Featherstone), and *Journal of Classical Sociology* (with John O'Neill). His many publication include *Orientalism, Post-modernism, and Globalism* (1994), *Weber and Islam* (1998), and articles in journals such as *The British Journal of Sociology* and *European Journal of Social Theory.*

Ritu Vij joined the Department of Politics and International Relations at the University of Aberdeen, UK in 2006 after completing a two-year fellowship at Keio University, Japan, under the joint auspices of the Social Science Research Council (USA) and the Japan Society for the Promotion of Science. She previously taught international and comparative politics at American University, Washington, D.C., and Ritsumeikan University in Kyoto, Japan. Her research interests include political economy, civil society and subjectivity, and the comparative study of social policy in a global age. She is the author of *Japanese Modernity and Welfare: State, Self and Civil Society in Modern Japan* (2007), and is currently at work on a related project on the social and political reconstitution of citizenship in late capitalism.

Nicola Yeates is Senior Lecturer in Social Policy at the Open University, UK. She has published widely on social policy, global governance, and labor migration. Her most recent publication include *Globalization and Social Policy* (2001), *Globalisation and Social Policy in a Development Context: Regional* Responses (2005) and articles in journals such as *Feminist Review, Policy and Politics, Social Policy and Society and Social Policy Review.* She is co-editor of *Global Social Policy: an Interdisciplinary Journal of Public Policy and Social Development.*

Introduction

Ritu Vij

Welfare without right is not a good. Similarly, right without welfare is not the good.

G.W.F. Hegel's *Philosophy of Right* 1952: 87

The ubiquitous currency of 'globalization' as the predominant nomenclature of our times, and the subsumption of all social objects to its panoptican logic, has brought to the critical enterprise an urgency unparalleled in recent history and with it, the task of uncovering its political conditions of possibility and the social antagonisms constitutive of it. Unlike, 'security,' or the 'the war on terror,' though, the main stays of high politics and media discourse and frontrunners in representations of globality as a generative scalar condition, the dangers inherent in the 'necessitarian neoliberalism'[1] unleashed by globalization's economic compulsions may have far wider implications for lives currently being subject to active restructuration in accordance with its putative logic.

The modalities of a neoliberal economic growth strategy (de-regulation, privatization, labor-market flexibilization, fiscal austerity) mandated by international lending agencies (the World Bank, International Monetary Fund (IMF), World Trade Organization (WTO)), and its effects, increased polarities of wealth and want, abundance for some and pauperization for many, have been long familiar to populations in the South. In the North, however, current hegemonic articulation of a neoliberal global economic agenda, has brought into spectral view the underside of economic growth and progress, temporarily tamed but no less imbricated, in welfare state capitalism. In the post-war period, idyllically framed as the 'golden age of capitalism,' the Keynesian welfare state appeared to have achieved a permanent stabilization, resolving enduring tensions between the principles of democratic political equality and capitalist economic inequality on the one hand, and the contradiction between individual consumption and socialized production on the other. Central to the socio-political imaginary of advanced capitalist democracies for at least five decades, the normativity of

1

the state provision of goods and services, as both social protection and risk-sharing, figured prominently in shaping public institutions, democratic praxis, and macroeconomic policy. Although societal contestation over its precise location in state and/or market never remained entirely off the political agenda, a broad consensus around the legitimacy and need for the state provision of 'basic needs,' in some instances more generous than others, served to regulate the politics of redistribution in advanced industrialized democracies.

Since the 1990s, however, crystallizing the turn to the market initiated by the supply side economic policies of Reagan and Thatcher, and the end of 'embedded liberalism' (Ruggie 1983), the strategy of globalizing market liberalization first advanced by the 'Washington consensus,'[2] and the ensuing effort to 'end welfare as a way of life' have resulted in massive cuts in unemployment, disability, childcare and health benefits and the imposition of punitive term-limits on recipients of welfare, forging a new consensus on moving people off welfare to work. These changes are occurring within a wide panoply of efforts, privatization of social security and pensions, de-regulation of labor markets, and concerted attempts to shift tax burdens from corporations to individuals,[3] in accord with a neoliberal economic growth strategy deemed unavoidable under the present condition of 'globalization.'

In the dominant narrative, globalization signifies 'the increasing extent, intensity, velocity and impact of world-wide interconnectedness,' (Held and McGrew 2002: 1) propelled by developments of new technologies of communication that have undermined the significance of space to economic and cultural production and circulation processes, resulting in an effective annihilation of space by time. In the idiom and grammar of a global register, this spatio-temporal transformation necessitates the erasure of a politics of territory, inaugurating a trans-border space of globality, supra-territorial forms of governance, and the subsumption of labor to capital on a world scale. Specifically, the state's diminished capacity to tax and spend, given the now all too real threat of capital flight, results in the 'hollowing out of the state,' it's transformation into a 'competition state' oriented now to the vicissitudes of global capital flows, bringing to an end citizen/rights-based claims and entitlements and the politics of re-distribution of an earlier era of Keynesian welfare state capitalism. Thus Ulrich Beck writes, '...the premises of the welfare state and pension system, of income support, local government and infrastructural policies.....all this melts under the withering sun of globalization and becomes susceptible to political moulding.' (Beck 2000: 1)

On an alternative critical view, however, 'globalization' portends not rupture, discontinuity, or dissemblance, but rather the universalization of the globalizing dynamic inherent to the logic of capitalism. The social and economic dislocations attendant on the deepening and extension of capitalist social relations in the contemporary period are seen in the context of the *longue durée* of capitalism's development since the 16th century, it's propensity to 'annihilate space by time' not contingent on technological innovation *per se* but a necessary feature of the self-expanding logic of capitalist development.[4] On this view, the provision of welfare, like capitalism itself, must be seen in developmental terms, its scope and provision subject to change in accordance with the dynamic of continued deterritorialization and reterritorialization that capitalist industrialization entails. Globalization, in other words, does not necessitate the retreat of welfare, but rather its rescaling, in accordance with the emergent modalities of social regulation.

From the vantage point of understanding welfare state retrenchment, is globalization a 'category error' (Rosenberg 2000: 165), 'a myth suitable for a world without illusions....one that robs us of hope,' (Hirst and Thompson 1996a: 6)? Or is it 'unavoidable,' its inevitability demanding submission to the hegemonic sway of unregulated 'free' markets? How are the 'truth effects' of neoliberal globalization best contested? From a critical standpoint, is globalization best conceived as process or project, ideology or discourse? Or does it's 'topicality' (in Derrida's sense, its putative content determined by its frame), warrant a qualitatively different register of thought? One that approaches the discourse of welfare state restructuration not as representative but constitutive, itself a strategy of demarcating forms of social visibility and invisibility? The theoretical and political implications of these alternative conceptualizations of globalization and its impact on welfare provision are considerable. Neoliberal orthodoxy on globalization *qua* condition not only legitimates current attempts to restructure welfare, naturalizing the conditions that are exacting an enormous toll on those from whom social provision has been withdrawn, but more problematically, forecloses any inquiry into the conditions of its own production. The alternative view, emphasizing processual and ideological understandings of globalization as a project, entailing new modes of regulation of social structures and subjectivities, on the other hand, leaves open the possibility of theoretical and political intervention *via* a critique of political economy, historical sociology, or the micropolitics of social recognition and redistribution.

And what about welfare? Is the fundamental question, in theory and practice, about preserving, ending, or rescaling welfare 'as we know it,' the axis on which much public and scholarly debate turns, or do we need rather to radically rethink the notion of welfare itself, calling into question the presumed equation of welfare with social right, as has been long understood, thereby making explicit the antinomies of conceptualization latent in its historical materialization? And how best does one proceed? Does one remain detached from the implications of a radical thoughtfulness towards questions of welfare, bracketing presentist concerns with questions of 'policy change' and therefore susceptible to the charge of normative lack in theory's alleged imperviousness to the immediacy of effects on the subjects of welfare restructuration? Or are we better served by Edward Said's injunction about the 'worldliness' of thought, fostering attentiveness to how thought is never wholly or only abstract but always already implicated in specific shapings of the world? Can we, that is, reach for a critique that has as its object not only the already materialized asymmetries of power, but also those immanent in the forms of critique deployed against them?

In an effort to facilitate a reflexive engagement with some of the key conceptual/theoretical questions at stake in thinking about welfare in the context of global capitalism, this reader brings together a collection of inter-disciplinary essays that rebuke the 'inevitability thesis' on welfare state restructuration. A few interrogate the hyper-liberal claims about globalization's negative effects on welfare on empirical grounds, remaining firmly within the categorical and epistemological confines of 'normal science.' The large majority of essays, however, predominantly theoretical, reject what Robert Cox has described as the 'problem-solving approach'[5] to social inquiry. They are more properly deemed critical, in that they take as their starting point a critique of disciplinary knowledge, its ontological, conceptual/theoretical and epistemological armory, in their respective efforts to make sense of ongoing contestations about the nature and provision of welfare in advanced industrialized democracies.

The objective, as I see it, is twofold: (1) to assemble for the critically engaged reader perspectives that draw on alternative theoretical resources to encourage non-economistic modes of thinking about the troubled (and troubling) question of welfare; and (2) to encourage reflexive readings of these alternatives so as to identify the social limits of the idea of welfare and its relation to states and markets. To the extent that a close engagement with these texts may help foster in its student-readers an appreciation of the pleasures and rewards of abstract thought, through the cultivation of the practice of what Zizek calls analytical 'denegation,' the Reader's designation as 'critical' may be more richly deserved.

A final note. The problem of social protection is one all societies face. The Keynesian 'welfare state,' however, as a socio-historical and discursively produced phenomenon is primarily associated with the advanced capitalist democracies of the North; the question of welfare in the South continues to be embedded within the larger problematic of 'development.' While no doubt itself open to question, this distinction, and the question of social provisioning in the South, is not explored in this Reader.

The rest of this chapter is organized as follows. Bypassing the narrative conventions that typically structure introductions to a collection such as this, and in an effort to push the limits of critique along the lines suggested above, I devote the next section to exploring some of the antinomies that result in critical scholarship's efforts to rebuke claims about the 'retreat of the state' mandated by neoliberal globalization, within the context of the larger philosophical discourse of anti-statism that underpins much of this scholarship itself. As such, this section advances a specific argument about the future development of critical scholarship on globalization and welfare, while serving as but one of many possible foils against which the reader can develop her own understanding of key issues. The second half of this chapter provides a summary of the essays included in this volume, locating them in the three dominant thematics, regulation, power, and subjectivity, that structure scholarship critical of the globalization thesis on welfare.

Contrary to the perception, common in populist and academic circles alike, that the claim that globalization necessitates 'a logic of no alternative' is the product of a specifically neoliberal frame of thought, the truth effects of naming 'globalization,' 'assembling singularities out of heterogeneous and diverse phenomena' (Larner and Walters 2004: 499), and its consequent effects on welfare (of which the neoliberal inevitability thesis offers an extreme case) may be more accurately described as multi-citational, dependent for its legitimation on seemingly opposed registers of thought and practice. Although difficult to pin down precisely, the earliest articulations of globalization orthodoxy on welfare emerged in the context of bold pronouncements about the creation of a 'borderless world.' (Ohmae 1990), 'footloose capital', and the ensuing subsumption of state power to transnational corporations (Strange 1996), and the transformation of the state into a 'competition state' (Cerny 1997) that accompanied the despatialization of knowledge, production and finance ushered in by new technologies of communication and transport.[6] The supply-side thinking that had begun in the 1980s in response to the collapse of the Bretton Woods System, coalesced in the 'Washington Consensus,' a tacit agreement between the IMF, the World Bank and the US Treasury to push for global market liberalization in a bid to prevent future economic crises. As support for a new regime of global financial discipline gathered political force on both sides of the Atlantic, a global business elite whose vision of a borderless, globalized world, while no doubt a product of their subjective experience of the world (Falk 1997), advanced an agenda that was echoed in the decision-making corridors of international economic institutions like the World Bank,[7] IMF, and OECD. A popular Labor government in the UK and a Democratic Presidency in the USA, arguably frontrunners in efforts to 'end welfare as we know it,' contributed in no small measure to elaborating a hegemonic articulation of the globalization thesis in the 1990s, its progressivist 'Third Way' encasing notwithstanding. Neoliberals advanced claims about the necessity for welfare state retrenchment based on the principles of Chicago school free-marketeers,[8] (individual freedom and market-efficiency, associated with conservative thinkers like Milton Friedman, Friedrich Hayek, and more contemporarily, Charles Murray). The intellectual and political legitimations for 'Third Way' arguments about the need for welfare reform were rooted in claims about ending dependency as a way of life, enabling individual autonomy, well-being, and the restoration of community. A pragmatic 'vehicular idea' that promised to reconcile social democratic ideals of full employment with the demands of global markets *via* a responsible capitalism, 'Third Way' thinking offered a softer landing to those whose abilities to secure a livelihood in the market was temporarily or chronically impaired.

Unlike the neoliberal solution which paradoxically advanced the revitalization of institutions of direct sociality, the family, religious charities, and private philanthropic social networks as the appropriate containers of extra-market dependency, while advocating a return to the pre-Keynesian a-social domain of the 'free' (unregulated) market, 'Third Way' thinking offered a more compassionate alternative to those whose successful reintegration into the circuits of market exchange would justify, in the last instance, the necessary retreat of the state in the face of the inevitability of globalization. Thus Robert Reich in a much cited piece entitled, 'We are All Third Wayers Now'[9] spoke both of the inevitability of globalization, its effects on the hollowing out of the state, and the urgency of integrating vast numbers of jobless and under-employed into the social domain of autonomous, civilized life. For 'Third Way' critics, the imperatives of globalization rationalized the dismantling of debilitating welfare state structures while at the same time necessitating new public programs (healthcare, education, childcare for instance) in support of efforts to move individuals from welfare to work.

Marxist scholars and activists, on the other hand, echoing a long-standing ambivalence about the precise location of welfare in class-based capitalist social order (as embodiment both of the achievement and subsequent pacification of class struggle), viewed the attack on Keynesian welfare state structures as simultaneously theoretically explicable (as the resurgence of the capitalist class against the proletariat) and as occasion for reregulation of social and economic order structurally necessitated by the self-expanding global reach of capital. Calling attention to the structural logic of the universalization of global capitalism, the renewed focus on deregulation and privatization was seen as indicative of a crisis of national economic capital formation. While some saw the resurgence of neoliberalism as the ideological scaffolding of a post-Fordist regime of accumulation, in keeping with the regulative imperatives of global capital, others focused on the apparent dissipation of working class energies in the face of a reinvigorated global capitalist class, the 'inevitability' of the reversal of earlier hard won claims to a larger share of the social product, consistent with the considerably enhanced power of global capital.

In the popular media influential voices, Thomas Friedman of the *New York Times* for instance, pronounced the inevitability of globalization, speaking in alarmist terms about the consequences of refusing to don the 'Golden Straightjacket' referring to the necessity of submission to the *dictat* of economic liberalization, deregulation, lowered taxes, balanced budgets, which would, in turn, assure the return of the Golden Calf to developed countries who would not have to endure the high costs of social protection, and prevent developing countries from the certainty of economic triage that the continuation of protectionist policies would bring.

Attempts to critically interrogate the central tenets of the globalization thesis on welfare have focused on its core claims about the effects of global economic integration on the openness of national economies, the depoliticization of economic processes, and the retreat of the state. Challenging claims about deregulating global economic flows and its underlying assumptions about the end of politics in macroeconomic managements, the 'second wave literature' has attempted to elaborate three predominant lines of critique taking as its point of departure a fundamental understanding of the economy as 'instituted process' (Polanyi 1957). Deploying a variety of conceptual/theoretic tools, the attempt to examine ongoing transformations of economic and political structures has yielded a focus on questions of the strategies of global economic reregulation, and a specification of the political conditions under which attempts at reregulation are being undertaken and contested. Accordingly, critical scholarship has directed its efforts to elaborating three counter-claims to the 'inevitability thesis' (1) the regulation of global capital (2) repoliticizing the 'retreat of the state,' and (3) the constitution of the active subject of a neoliberal global imaginary. Of these, the first two have been, for the most part, rooted within the conventions of one of the 'three pillars of welfare state theory,' liberal-pluralism, social-democratic corporatism, and Marxism, dominant in the body of literature on welfare state formation. The third, however, has emerged as a central focus of a Foucauldian inspired post-structural inquiry into the practice of government and the role of distinct strategies of power in the constitution of subjects. While liberal-pluralist and social-democratic theory has attempted to repudiate strong globalization theory's claims about the 'end of politics' by drawing attention to the continued relevance of interest groups, political parties, and electoral politics *within* nation-states in mediating and contesting efforts to roll back state-based welfare provisioning, Marxian and post-structural approaches have tended to treat neoliberalism as a politico-ideological strategy that is constitutive of the very structures and subjectivities ascribed to globalization. Although mapped through different optics in Marxian and post-structural critiques (class in one, biopower in the other), for both, neoliberalism as a globally generative matrix cannot be understood apart from its location in the post-war project of American empire. We might then say, that the thematics of regulation, power, and subjectivity emerge as central to critiques of the neoliberal orthodoxy on welfare states, and provide, for that reason, the basis of selection, and the logico-narrative order of presentation, of the essays included in this volume.

A more pressing issue, however, that must detain any mapping of the theoretical terrain of critical scholarship on the globalization/welfare problematic, one that has generally not been foregrounded in critical scholarship has to do with the deeper philosophical underpinnings of claims about the retreat of the state upon which the globalization/welfare debate turns. Although empirical claims about the 'retreat of the state' necessitated by the requirements of a neoliberal growth strategy have been effectively countered on empirical grounds in second wave literature, it is striking to note that most progressive alternatives to the retreat of the welfare state delineate supra (global) or sub-state (local) modes of rescaling welfare provision. The multicitationality of necessitarian globalization sketched above, in both its affirmative (neoliberal) and negative (critical) aspects, albeit marshaled in critical scholarship against the neoliberal variant of globalization, provides an important clue about the deeper sources of this pivotal claim. Whether conceptions of globalization demand the dismantling of the welfare state, as neoliberals and 'Third Way' thinking suggests, or its opposite, the extension of welfare benefits (now at the local or global levels) in order to insure against the increased risk a global economy begets (as many critics, including a few represented in this volume argue), the claim that economic globalization entails either the removal of regulatory mechanisms (as in the neoliberal version) or a radical revision of social, political, and economic modes of regulation (as in critical approaches), depends pivotally on a recuperation of an anti-statist discourse that structures not only neoliberal thought but also shadows approaches committed to subverting neoliberal orthodoxy on welfare provision.

In what follows below, I attempt to show how the three thematics identified in scholarship critical of the globalization thesis on welfare, regulation, power, and subjectivity are, to one degree or another, theoretically committed to an *analytical* retreat of the state that impedes in important ways their respective attempts to subvert claims about the empirical retreat of the welfare state advocated by neoliberal orthodoxy on globalization and welfare. My argument here is not to 'bring the state back in' (along the lines suggested in an earlier decade by scholars like J.P. Nettl, Theda Skocpol, and more recently Peter Evans[10]), whose uncritical approach to the state as a positivized 'thing in itself,' encounters precisely some of the difficulties outlined below, but rather an argument that takes seriously deontological claims about the state as a structure that Durkhein described as 'thinking together,' and the possibilities of the development of particularized realizations of this 'thinking together' such that the denial of alterity (and welfare or individual well-being) upon which existent states are fashioned can be rethought, and potentially transformed. That is, the attempt to develop a critique of neoliberal orthodoxy on the retreat of the state, and the related political project of sustaining and extending social protection to those inevitably left out of the system of exchange, given the vicissitudes of the working of global capitalism, can profit from an approach that I term 'critical statism,' that does not entail the affirmation of existent states and markets (as in normal science), but rather seeks to delineate the conditions of possibility for the transformation of *both* states and markets in accordance with a notion of individual well-being such that the welfare of some need not impede the welfare of many. (I develop this idea more fully below).

The effort to recover the anti-statism built into claims about the 'retreat of the state' can be accessed at multiple levels. At its most polemical, several critics have viewed the universal claim about the retreat of states in the face of a global economy as a thinly veiled displacement of the particular claim of the extension of the imperial state as the political condition of possibility for the retreat of all other states. In speaking of the 'weakening of the nation-state,' the Marxian cultural theorist Frederic Jameson asks, 'are we not actually describing the subordination of other nation states to American power,' the 'propagation of the free market across the globe,' being a crucial strategy of the pursuit of American empire. (Jameson 2000: 51). Echoing a similar sentiment Robert Cox, the noted Gramscian social theorist, writes about the making of American hegemony as 'economic systems of the combined territories of "empire" are restructured into one vast market for capital, goods and services,' (Cox 2004: 309). From a different vantage point, commenting on the simultaneous narrowing of the discourse on democracy in Anglophone democracies and the spread of liberal democracy as 'part of the larger agenda of global homogenization' Ashis Nandy and D.L. Sheth draw attention to its justification no longer in normative terms (as a superior form of governance) but 'in terms of its utility for expanding the global market and for hastening a country's economic development,' (Sheth and Nandy 1996: 15). Claims about the retreat of state(s), in other words (from domestic economic management) can be sustained only in the context of a prior claim about the advance of the imperial state. In an ironic reversal of the universal-particular debate that has periodically occupied the social sciences (particularity, European culture for instance, marked as universal culture), the retreat of the state is offered as paradigmatic to globalization, conditioning social life within not only particular (lesser states) but equally, and perhaps with greatest force, within the imperial (American) state itself. The benefits of this narration, critics repeatedly point out, are directed to groups in metropolitan centers of the North as well as the South pointing to a theory and praxis that takes metropolitan constellations of socio-economic-cultural power as its proper object of resistance. The question of resuscitating welfare 'in the North,' then, is conjoined with critical considerations of American power and nationalism and its global agenda.

While this line of reasoning can take us some distance in understanding the resonance that claims about the retreat of the state appear to have among those who frame globalization and the question of the state as inherently incompatible, the seemingly intractable appeal of the stateless economy, paradigmatic in neoliberal orthodoxy to be sure, but also in perspectives critical of the globalization thesis on welfare, liberal-pluralist, Marxian, and post-structural demands further illumination. For conservative critics, the minimalist night watchman state, interred briefly during the Keynesian interregnum, remains paradigmatic; for orthodox Marxian teleological thought, the withering of the capitalist state offers the possibility and hope for a brave new world; for contemporary theorists who see the economy as instituted process, i.e., requiring some mode of regulation, the question of rescaling the provision of welfare necessarily entails a supra-state (global) and sub-state (local) level. For anti-foundational poststructural theorists on the other hand, the enabling condition for a politics of inclusiveness depends on uncovering the exclusionary social practices constitutive of states and the identities contained therein; statelessness both marks a normative horizon of possibility, a constant state of openness to the other, as well as names a praxis of resistance to the techniques of government deployed to regulate and produce specific subjectivities.

This common ground, puzzling given the wide abyss that separates competing perspectives, can be understood in terms of a fundamental lack that structures conceptions of the state in democratic and radical perspectives on politics in general and the welfare state in particular. Briefly put, this can be seen as the *absence of a notion of the political* in conceptions of the state. In democratic theory, especially in its liberal-pluralist articulation, the state appears either as the vector of competing interest groups in society, or as an actor engaged in its own aggrandizement. As such, it constitutes simply another terrain of market behavior; as a provider of goods, the source of want satisfaction.[11] For Marxian theory, the state's function *qua* capitalist state, i.e. essentially of civil society, renders it non-separable from civil society or, at best, following Poulantzas, 'relatively autonomous.' For post-structural theorists, on the other hand, a state-centered politics marks not only the foreclosure of alternative political imaginings, but also, and perhaps, more significantly, masks the practices of inclusion/exclusion through which capillary forms of power discipline and govern individuals and populations.

This profound reluctance within contemporary social theory to conceive of the state as a separate domain of *political* activity marks, I will argue here, the limits of critiques of the globalization thesis on welfare. The (empirical) retreat of the state from economic life mandated by proponents of welfare state retrenchment, recuperates a long history of anti-statism within the social sciences which rests in uneasy tension with the forms of critique deployed against the retreat of the welfare state summoned by neoliberal globalization. The radically critical gesture then entails examining the implications of this inveterate unwillingness to view the state as analytically distinct and the accompanying tendency to treat the state as an inherently depoliticized domain of social life. The fantasy of a stateless economy that structures neoliberal imaginings then, is but an extreme articulation of the notion of a depoliticized state, reducible to either economy or society, whose retreat from both (as exemplified in the politics of welfare state retrenchment) is resisted in critical scholarship, even as the logico-narratives of dominant theorizations of the political remain committed to a prior abnegation of the state as the properly political site of politics.

The analytical retreat of the state is, in this sense, of course most easily discernible in the case of neoclassical economic theory, whose commitments to the Smithian notion of a self-regulating market demarcates a minimalist night-watchman role for the state (protection of property and contract), envisioning the market economy as an a-social domain governed by the voluntary transactions of unitary individuals driven by self-interest, a conception resurgent now in the *laissez-faire* politics of neoliberal globalization. The critiques of this position are well known and do not bear repeating here. However, two crucial elements are worth recalling, insofar as they provide one of the three central thematics (regulation) that structure critiques of the globalization thesis on welfare. By far the most widely known is Karl Polanyi's influential claim about the economy as instituted process (i.e. secured by a system of rights, of property and contract that requires extra-market regulation and administration), and that inasmuch *laissez-faire* is simply one way of channeling economic distribution, it too must be seen as a 'form of State "regulation", introduced and maintained by legislative and coercive means.' (Gramsci 1971: 160). Second, and related to the first, the focus on single transactions between juridically equal parties to market exchange in the neoclassical model, elides the system-level features of the economy considered as a whole whose functioning cannot be apprehended simply as the sum of its parts. Rather than simply enabling the redistribution of commodities between and among 'independent' individuals, markets are also dependent on system level factors rooted in structures of mutual dependence which require regulation by a public authority. The necessity of a regulatory apparatus that provides the back-stop to the workings of the 'invisible hand' of the self-regulating market, is crucial, its repudiation in neoclassical and neoliberal theory over determined to considerable degree by the very anxiety the Hobbesian world of anarchic competition in the market provokes, which colonizes not only the market, but as we see below, conceptions of the state itself.

The disavowal of this authority, as 'government' or the state in neoclassical theory, in what Antonio Gramsci referred to as 'theoretical *laissez-faire*' (quoted in Ashley 1983: 486), however, is not only limited to treatments of the economy, but fundamentally shapes liberal-pluralist approaches to the state and politics in which both are conceived simply as the market writ large. Insofar as the interest-group model of politics extends the market metaphor to an account of political life (utility-maximizing behavior of individuals mirrored by interest optimizing groups), it adopts an economistic approach to the study of politics that in itself depoliticizes political life. In this regard, approaches critical of the inevitability thesis on welfare, that seek to bring 'politics back in' reinscribe a-political notions of politics that structure liberal-pluralist approaches, and may be seen as economistic in their own regard, their rebuttal of the globalization thesis on welfare notwithstanding. To put it differently, the theoretical ground upon which claims about the 'retreat of the welfare state' are elaborated in public choice theory in which a 'stakeholder conception of state'[12] prevails, are themselves conditioned by a prior retreat from a non-economistic conception of politics that severely limits the possibility of reclaiming politics as the site for contestations about the nature and scope of social provisioning under conditions of global capitalism. This extension of the market-model into an account of political life, explained by some as an instance of logical and historical economism is, for other, indicative of the impoverished conception of politics that limits the horizon of shared meanings to a recognition of sameness (within groups that compete for dominance of power in the state). Bringing 'politics back in' then entails substantially more than an extension of what remains a fundamentally economistic logic to the terrain of the government or 'state.'

For Marxian theorists, no less, arguing against 'the fallacy of the homogenous state,'[13] the state *qua* capitalist state, represents either the interests of the capitalist class, or capital *per se*, mirroring to different degrees and in historically specific ways, the class-driven nature of civil society. While this is not the occasion to revisit fully the faultlines in the Marxian theory of the state (through which it can be shown that the creation of the welfare state can be seen as simultaneously anachronistic and necessary, given the logic of capitalist development), it is worth pointing out that given the telos of social individuation that the Marxian tradition shares in significant ways with its Hegelian forbears, *a theory of the development of the state* consistent with a Marxian critique of political economy would not be inconsistent with the fundamental Marxian insight about the structure of freedom *and* unfreedom that is intrinsic to civil society. Although Marx (and his followers), as we well know, emphasized its polarity of unfreedom, leaving the potential for freedom as a distinctly Hegelian domain of 'idealism,' Marx's central concern with the realization of individual well-being for all does not vitiate the notion of a collective agency responsible for securing conditions enabling of precisely such a materialization. Insofar as Marxians too consider the state in terms of the market writ large, they foreclose the possibility of refashioning social institutions and practices that will not simply 'humanize capitalism' while leaving its structural logic that generates hierarchies of wealth and want intact, but rather but one that will better enable both the potential for freedom that markets contain, while imposing significant limits on the market such that its equally powerful capacity for impingement on individual well-being may be curtailed. Neo-Marxian theory's paradoxical support for capitalist welfare states that provision, as we see below, basic needs, on the grounds that it supports, at the very least, 'natural life,' from within a theory committed to a revolutionary universalization of the bourgeois individual, obscures the extent to which the process of development entails not simply the 'problem of the market,' but equally, the state.

A similar problem, interestingly, confronts democratic theorists of community in their accounts of political life. Decrying the residual notion of politics that flows from the liberal-pluralist conception of politics, democratic theorists view the state as derivative of the 'will of the people,' welfare marking the achievement of social right and materialization of the obligations and entitlements that flow from the status of individuals as juridically equal citizens of a common state. The emphasis on the equality of citizenship instantiated in the democratic state's recognition of members as juridical equals, irrespective of wealth, religion, or ethnicity, is seen as a distinctive achievement, the limits of politics marked by the struggle to translate juridical equality into substantive community. Politics, in this formulation, is thus substantially more than simply the outcome of interest group competition, driven as it is by notions of the 'greater good' of community, in which solidarity of belonging as equal members of a political community within the nation-state is seen as primary. Two problems emerge in this formulation. To the extent that the state and politics are made derivative of the will of the people, the *differentia specifica* of political life is obscured,[14] rendering politics hostage once again to distinct conceptions of communities and contestations between and among them, or worse, as some critics have pointed out, to a dangerous politics of inclusion/exclusion that realizes democratic community *inside* the nation-state at the expense of others (states and communities) *outside*. From the present standpoint, however, a far deeper problem emerges. The conception of the utility-maximizing individual of neoclassical economic thought and the interest-group politics of liberal-pluralism repudiated by democratic communitarians for whom welfare marks the achievement of social right and political community, emerges not as antagonistic, an 'external opposition,' each reflecting two diametrically opposed conceptions and thereby negating the other; or alternatively as complementary, one pole balancing the 'excess of its opposite' (Zizek 1994: 3) (state social provision compensating for the lack generated by excessive atomism in the market), but rather, in the genuinely Hegelian sense 'each pole of the antagonism inherent to its opposite, so that we stumble upon it at the very moment when we endeavor to grasp the opposite pole for itself, to posit it "as such,"' (Zizek 1994: 3), where one that is necessarily encounters the other at the limits. That is, we discover the notion of the utility maximizing individual at the very moment we encounter the limits of the conception of social right pivotal to democratic thought.

In the Marshallian framework of welfare as the social 'right to a modicum of economic welfare and security' (Marshall 1963: 74), the individual's entitlement to a share of the social product stems from her status as a citizen of a specific political community, by virtue, of her being-in-common with other citizens of the same community. Indeed, for Marshall, the provision of welfare was significant to the extent that it could serve as an instrument of building civil solidarity among citizens who were otherwise strangers to each other. The quality of this being-in-common, however, is derivative of the individual's standing as a member of a group (the nation-state),[15] the sociality of provision determined by the mechanism of provision, public not private, rather than intrinsic to the individual's sociality by virtue of her quality of being-in-common with others outside substantialized (concrete) communities.[16] Sociality, in other words, is not an attribute added as it were to the atomistic self of the market by virtue of membership in the concretized political community of nation-states but intrinsic to the being-in-common that is part of unsubstantialized community. To the extent however, that politics is about a being-in-common that repudiates substantial foreclosure (belongingness in a specific community), as Jean-Luc Nancy[17] has so persuasively argued, the sociality of individual being stems primarily from this open ended quality of being-in-common, one that is repudiated by the conception of welfare as a social right rooted in specific communities. This derivation of a conception of the 'the social' from the mechanism of provision (private or public), and welfare as the materialization of the social, undermines rather than enables a recognition of sociality as a quality intrinsic to a conception of the individual, may then be seen as co-extensive, rather than contradictory to the notion of the unitary self that underpins the edifice of neoclassical economic theory. Taken to its logical end, the notion of welfare as manifested in Keynesian welfare state capitalism, rather than the achievement of an authentically social right (contra Marshall) is itself premised on an economistic conception of the individual.[18] The properly critical gesture in the globalization/welfare debate then, resides not in resisting welfare state retrenchment *per se*, the shared object of critique in much critical scholarship, but rather, delineating non-economic conceptions of welfare and individual well-being that can better realize the ideal of welfare as social right. It is to a fuller explication of this point that I now briefly turn.

In the voluminous body of work that exists on welfare state formation, and now on its retrenchment, it is striking that relatively little attention has been paid to the conception of welfare that grounds contestations about its provision and effects. Gosta Esping-Anderson's field-defining formulation on welfare state regime types locates specific welfare states on a quantitative continuum that moves from the most generous (social-democratic) to the minimalist (liberal) welfare states. At core, judgments about the levels of spending associated with different regime types rests on a notion of welfare as the provision of basic needs, food, clothing, health, shelter, social security, upon which physiological survival turns. Unlike notions of subsistence within classical political economy however, that treated subsistence not merely as the requirements of physiological survival but rather as historically and culturally specific customary need, the notion of basic needs, widely seen as the minimal ground upon which an ethics of distributive justice, development, or human rights and welfare can be elaborated remains the unexamined bedrock of welfare discourse. This equation of welfare with basic needs, however, is far from self-evident, containing as it does not only the problem of interpretation (how much food, clothing, shelter, education can be deemed basic as opposed to non-basic, and how does one adjudicate between different quantities of provision that satisfy differences in understandings of basic need across societies), but also the more vexed problem of rendering recipients of welfare into non-individuated members of species being, or group members, in contrast to others whose participation in the system of exchange relations offers opportunities for the pursuit of self-chosen ends, and the potential to satisfy non-basic individuated needs. To the extent that the emphasis on the material elements of basic need provision ignores what is most deeply human about human (as opposed to species) need, the need for self and social recognition as particular beings, welfare rather than being an achievement of social right, repudiates the sociality of being intrinsic to individuals under conditions of modernity. The loss of a means of livelihood, in other words, threatens more than simply subsistence; it threatens a way of life associated with individual identity. The economism underlying conceptions of welfare as the provision of basic needs, in other words, although appealing from a pragmatic policy-making standpoint[19] (as seen in the development and human rights discourse within international organizations like the United Nations and World Bank), mirrors, rather than repudiates the naturalized conception of the a-social atomistic self that structures neoclassical conceptions of the market. Insofar as scholarship critical of the globalization thesis on welfare fails to foreground the problems associated with this narrow, fundamentally economistic conception of welfare, its efforts to resuscitate a politics of advocacy of welfare state provisioning must be seen as inherently limited, its potential success vulnerable to the self-same contradictory logic evident in the workings of the Keynesian welfare state. On these terms then, the properly critical gesture entails first a reconception of welfare based on a full recognition of social individuation, as opposed to subsistence or basic needs, as the basis of welfare provision and a genuinely democratic retrieval

of political life. Efforts along these lines would entail neither the resuscita-
tion of the Keynesian welfare state, or even the provision of basic needs at
the supra state (global) or local levels, as currently suggested in the literature
on global governance and the re-scaling of welfare, which once again
focuses on the mechanism of provision rather than its content. Rather, it
would entail a reconceptualization of the social ends of both state and
market such each would be limited in accordance with the criteria of social
individuation so that the debilitating distinctions that have historically
marked the provision of welfare, between the deserving and undeserving
poor, or as suggested here, between deindividuated welfare and a-social
choice theoretic individuation in the market may be overcome. State *and*
civil society, in other words, would be limited in accordance with the principle of social individuation.

The anti-statism underpinning critiques of the retreat of the welfare state
is accessed somewhat differently by those whose focus on questions of sub-
jectivity/subjectification provides the last of the three thematics identified
here as central to scholarship critical of the globalization thesis on welfare.
Grounded in a Foucauldian inspired post-structural critique of sovereign
power, and more recently on the work of Carl Schmit, the preeminent theorist of sovereignty, scholars invested in critiquing sovereign power (law
and the state as the structural origin and center power), have sought to illu-
minate the workings of 'biopower' the entanglements of knowledge and
power that constitute disciplinary regimes of truth which in turn provide
the axes of self-formation for subjects variously located in the multiple constellations of capillary forms of power. Calling attention to the 'facile oppo-
sitions posed by framings of globalization and the question of the state as
inherently incompatible, or as 'long-standing complementarities,' on the
grounds that both operate on a shared register of meaning in which the
only form a modern politics can take rests on the notion of sovereignty
embodied in states and individuals, the influential theorist, R.B.J. Walker
directs attention to the hegemony of the principle of sovereignty in
modern social life that both forecloses alternative imaginings of political
life and marks the limits of politics both within and between states. On this
critical reading, the retreat of the state (as regulatory apparatuses) by no
means implies the enervation of the principle of sovereignty that structures
modern social life. Rather, the retreat of the regulatory state brings into
sharper view the systemic violence that underpins sovereignty as the
governing principle of modernity, now more sharply delineated in
the hierarchies of wealth and want within which sovereign subjects in the
hyper-liberal domain of unregulated 'free-market' patterns must fashion
themselves. The retreat of the state is thus illusory, Walker contends, since
the principle it embodies, that of sovereignty, remains alive, rendering any
claims about an immanent materialization of a post-statist (post-sovereign)
political discourse tenuous.

Walker's claim that the state constitutes a pre-political naturalized site of politics is a compelling one, reinforcing the argument advanced here about the depoliticization of the state. To the extent that the constitution of a *nation*-state necessitates a politics of exclusion, the rejection of a state-based politics can be seen as essentially a rejection of the idea of a politics based on membership in a group. A reconception of state and civil society on the lines suggested here, however, (the state as analytically distinct from economy and society such that it secures the conditions of an unsubstantiated being-in-common) uncouples the idea of the state from conceptions that equate states with group membership, rendering the antinomies of sovereignty Walker so persuasively delineates historically specific to actually existing states, but not a logically necessary feature of the state *qua* state. The search for alternatives to the foreclosure of politics crystallized in existent state-forms, in other words, need not necessarily lead in the direction of a post-sovereign anti-statism, but can also suggest its opposite, the effort (what I have described as 'critical statism'), to reclaim (and transform) the state as a properly politicized site of social life, limited by an ideal of politics which entails a commitment to securing what Jean Luc-Nancy has termed a 'being-in-common' that is *not* coterminous with substantialized community. Rather than signal a regressive move to a history that does not bear repeating, a history associated with the violence of state formation, and the politics of exclusion and inclusion that have been fundamental to the shaping of nation-states, the fact that actually existing states have failed to secure the well-being of a vast majority of their populations does not foreclose the possibility of a critical project, that takes as its focus the *development of the state as properly political* and the possibility of delimiting and transforming both states and markets such that they may enable rather than impede the welfare of many. Here the sentiment expressed in Partha Chatterjee's injunction that in order to move 'beyond the state' (the practices of violent exclusion historically associated with it), may first require a 'move through the state' (for Chatterjee, the democratization of state and society) is consistent with Jean Luc Nancy's articulation of politics not as substantive foreclosure on the notion of community but rather as a permanent opening, a community formed in the making of community.

Against this larger backdrop of anti-statism in which the state is seen as the locus of oppression and power, critical scholars' attempts to resist the 'retreat of the state' may profit from efforts directed at reclaiming the state as a properly politicized site of social life. Insofar as critical approaches to globalization and welfare collectively point to the necessity of foregrounding the *material existence* of regulation, power, and subjectivity, in social practices and institutions that are seen as constitutive (i.e. generative mechanisms), the task of imagining political alternatives (including the institutionalized provision of social protection) entails a recovery of a 'critical statism' potentially generative of a being-in-common along the lines suggested above. In lieu of the wholly negative gesture then, the task of critical theory at this juncture then may be well served not only by repudiating depoliticized notions of the state that currently dominate social thought as well as conceptions that continue to link the idea of the state with group domination in a double sense (subject to domination by private interests of particular groups in society, and itself a group agent with the potential for dominating others, states and individuals, deemed outside the group), but also by elaborating a critical recovery of the state as properly political, generative of regulatory social practices and institutions that impede rather than necessitate asymmetries of power and the impairment of subjectivities and well-being. The attempt to rescue social protection schemes from the neoliberal wrecking ball appears thus to warrant a recuperation of a genuinely statist politics, hostage neither to the demands of substantive community in society, or the self-aggrandizement of interest groups or political parties, and a rethinking of welfare other than the provision of basic needs as argued above.

The Reader is organized in four sections, Citizenship and Global Governance, Regulating Global Capital, Repoliticizing the Retreat of the State, and Governmentality and the Micropolitics of Welfare Reform. Each explores one of the three thematics identified above, regulation, power, and subjectivity.

The essays contained in the first section explore emergent modes of political regulation and governance as the locus of understanding ongoing transformations in welfare provisioning. T.H. Marshall's treatment of welfare as the concretization of citizen rights provides the point of departure for contemporary discussions of a post-national form of citizenship based on the securing of rights on a global rather than a national level. Thus there is considerable discussion of an emergent 'global welfare regime' necessitated by the crisis of legitimacy global capitalism is likely to face given sustained pressure on welfare states and the prospects for social unrest given the erosion of mass loyalty secured by the Keynesian welfare state. Increasing attention to labor rights, for instance by transnational corporations, newly fashioned commitments to social liberalism and poverty reduction within the World Bank and IMF (what some have referred to as the 'socialization of global politics'),[20] in contrast to the 'unrepentant liberalism' of the WTO which continues to resist inclusions of a social clause into its trade agreements, has helped engender a climate in which the inevitability thesis on the demise of the welfare state is interrogated *via* the conjunction of an emergent post-national form of citizenship and a global welfare regime.[21]

Bryan Turner offers a reworking of the Marshallian paradigm of social citizenship to provide a post-positivist account of the erosion of the

Keynesian welfare state and the contours of a post-nationalist account of citizenship. Conceptualizing citizenship in processual terms, as a modality for delineating boundaries of exclusion/inclusion, Turner highlights the role of warfare, work, and family in the gendered production of the soldier-citizen as the normative subject of social rights and entitlements. The end of mass warfare, the emergence of professional soldiers as the personnel of modern wars, increased levels of economic participation, especially by women, and the flexibilization of the labor force, Turner suggests, has brought about dramatic changes in the means through which individual entitlement claims can be legitimated. Where once entitlement was contingent on the normativity of status, of masculinity, nation, citizenship, transformations in status equalities renders the provision of welfare as a marker of thick convivial citizenship, moot. Thick citizenship based on communal identities, Turner suggests, is better replaced by thin citizenship better suited to the needs of securing alterity. Offering instead a framework that advocates the implementation of human rights cognizant of difference, securing environmental, aboriginal and cultural rights, Turner's intervention, one of the earliest attempts to develop a post-nationalist account of citizenship, to the extent that it draws attention to the loss of social capital entailed in the breaking up of thick identities, sounds a cautionary note, uncoupling nation from state. While many will draw from this a supra-territorial reading of citizenship, it is by no means self-evident that a commitment to these rights cannot be sustained by a plurality of states, albeit unmoored from their thick enmeshments in communal/national identities. Uncoupling nation from state may be one progressive lesson that can be drawn from this reading.

Gosta Esping-Andersen offers a synoptic diagnosis of the ongoing transformation of welfare states. Building on his earlier, *The Three Worlds of Welfare Capitalism*, Esping-Andersen examines both the reasons for the so-called crisis of the welfare state, and divergent responses to it. Contrary to the inevitability thesis, and in concurrence with the second wave literature, Esping-Andersen suggests that financial globalization does not, *per se* affect welfare state viability but that much depends on whether its finances are in order. In this he echoes the sentiment of others who have drawn attention to the fact that the inability to tax is not an economic 'fact' dictated by the logic of capital, but rather, a political choice exercised by state managers and therefore subject to contestation. The main challenge for the welfare state, he argues is 'the need to keep public finances sound and to lower structural unemployment,' (2000: 2). Distinguishing between responses to pressures among the different welfare state regime types, based on the 'logic of institutional path dependency and median voter allegiance to accustomed benefits' (2000: 2), Andersen echoes a sentiment widespread among scholars who focus on the politics of welfare state retrenchment, that the downward pressure on welfare state provisioning is neither uniform nor inevitable, but mediated by institutional and political factors that, to various degrees, impede 'the race to the bottom' in terms of welfare state devolution. Eschewing both privatization and familialization (the conservative response) as strategies of securing welfare in a post-industrial period characterized by high wage inequality and mass unemployment (and it should be added, a condition in which full employment necessitates increased wage inequality due to the growth in low-end, low-productivity service jobs), Andersen identifies a 'win-win' policy that can maximize fertility and women's employment, and enhance life chances through education and skills. A comprehensive welfare state, in other words, one that reallocates resources from old to young families, is deemed central to coping with the social and economic dislocations brought on by population aging, family instability, and the labor market consequences of technological change.

This emphasis on a renewed welfare state, albeit one more attuned to the changes wrought within the social order of global capitalism is further highlighted by Nicola Yeates, albeit *via* an embrace of a global social policy fashioned not only by international institutions (as the pioneering work of Deacon *et al.* (1997) suggest) but also, by the social dialogues taking place between social movements (such as the Other Economy Summit), direct action by non-governmental organizations, consumer groups, and 'local counter-struggles' by trade unions, women's groups, etc. Attempting to move the debate further, Yeates shows how the 'second wave' literature shares some of the flaws of strong globalization theory, insofar as it exaggerates the 'strength and degree of unity of capital interests,' underestimates the powers of the state and those of oppositional forces marshaled against economic globalization. Instead, she points to the continued relevance of 'local' factors – institutions, cultures, and politics, in shaping the different levels of governance (local, national, transnational, supranational and global) and the range of actors (state and non-state) involved in the social policy process. Yeates' critique of global governance literature's primary focus on the social policies of international institutions and their effects on regulating globalization, in sum, offers an early and useful corrective to an emergent, potentially influential discourse in which welfare, contra neoliberal orthodoxy's attempt to place it in the dustbin of history, is on the top of a global social agenda.

The next section, 'Regulating Global Capital' provides a multi-theoretic elaboration of the central Polanyian insight that markets are never 'free' but always, and as the authors here show, in different ways, shaped and sustained by extra-market agents, variously seen to be governments, public authority, or states. It is worth recalling that this recognition of the economy as governed or regulated process[22] has its origin in classical political economy, in which the notion of a 'political economy' (for James Steuart an economy governed by statesmen) replaces a household economy. Within contemporary political economy, the notion of a governed economy, in opposition to the notion of a 'self-regulating economy,' (and its presumed tendency to equilibrium) however, takes on an institutionalist perspective, in development of the classical tradition as found in the work of scholars like Karl Polanyi, Thorstein Veblen and Joseph Schumpeter. However, unlike what has come to be called a new institutionalist economics (NIE) in which institutions are simply seen as 'constraints on the behaviors of the pre-formed and unchanging individuals,' (Chang 2002: 551), classically oriented institutionalist perspectives on political economy focus on the constitutive role of institutions in shaping individual motivations, in contrast to the pre-formed motivations that ground preferences in the neoliberal imaginary. This emphasis on social institutions and structures as constitutive takes on greater specificity in work of French regulation theorists for whom the homology between social, economic, cultural and political modes of regulation enables an analytic of 'regimes of accumulation' which avoids the pitfalls of reductionism associated with the base-superstructure renditions of Marxian social theory. Claus Offe's essay on the 'Contradictions of the Welfare State' that opens this section, offers an incisive critique not only of the neoliberal orthodoxy on the demise of the welfare state, but also, more provocatively, injects a cautionary note into overly optimistic arguments about the rescaling of welfare on a global level, especially within the global governance literature. For Offe, states in capitalist democracies are, by virtue of being capitalist states, compelled to secure the system of exchange relations upon which capitalist reproduction depends. They are also, however, by virtue of being democratic states, equally compelled to seek legitimation, not only *via* procedures of electoral democracy through which they garner mass loyalty, but by seeking legitimation of the underlying principle of exchange upon which capitalist functioning depends. To this end, states are driven to pursue mutually antithetical policies: in order to secure legitimation, the state is compelled to develop strategies of recommodification directed at those thrown out of market-exchange relations to enable reentry. In so doing, however, the state's recommodifying strategies, by securing a source of livelihood outside market exchange *via* the welfare state, inadvertently have 'decommodifying' outcomes that threaten both the legitimacy of the principle of exchange and its stable functioning. The welfare state, in Offe's view, is thus a mechanism of 'crisis management' that is itself inherently (i.e. structurally) prone to crisis. It is for this reason, he suggests, capital can 'neither live with or live without the welfare state.' The significance of Offe's argument is manifold. First, his analysis cautions against any attempt to revoke the welfare state altogether on the grounds that it would invoke the very problems (delegitimation, social unrest, loss of demand) that its unraveling is meant to solve. To the extent that the welfare state as a source of increasing societal demands generates problems of 'governability' for the state, its undoing would not solve but most likely exacerbate problems of ungovernability. More to the point, however, Offe's central insight that regulating capital is both necessary and innately crisis prone, renders both the neoliberal advocacy of the 'free-market' as well as alternative provisioning strategies at the supra- or sub-state levels vulnerable to the problems he identifies as necessitating the welfare state in the first place. The alternative, to seek solutions to the problems welfare states were created to solve, *within* not outside of civil society (which, as argued above would entail placing limits on the market as opposed to leaving it untrammeled (the neoliberal image) or annihilating it altogether (the socialist vision), can profit immensely from Offe's analysis of the contradictions of the welfare state.

Drawing on French regulation theory and neo-Marxian state theory, Bob Jessop next analyses the demise of the Keynesian welfare state and the emergence of a 'Schumpeterian workfare state' in the context of a transition to a post-Fordist regime of accumulation. As a mode of social regulation, the institutions and norms and social networks that stabilized economic activity during the Fordist accumulation regime, Jessop contends, depended on the 'contingently necessary' character of the capitalist state as a Fordist state and its role in securing the social cohesion and institutional integration of a social formation consistent with Fordist mode of economic regulation, specifically the goals of full employment and mass consumption. The transition to flexible production, enabled by innovations in technologies of communications and production and the new organizational forms associated with it, occasions new forms of flexibilized labor, segmented markets and differentiated forms of consumption, all of which comprise a distinctive social mode of economic regulation. This, Jessop suggests, necessitates 'ending the exceptional crisis-oriented' Keynesian welfare state, and the creation of a state geared to the promotion of competitiveness in a global economy. The Schumpeterian workfare state then subordinates social policy to the needs of labor-market flexibility and the constraints of international competition. The emergence of the post-Fordist state form 'appropriate to the reregulation of an emerging accumulation regime,' is thus deemed central to understanding welfare state restructuration.

The essay by Rieger and Leibfried, on the other hand, makes the case that not only are national markets instituted processes, but so too is the global market. Reversing the linear causality of neoliberal orthodoxy that sees globalization as necessitating the demise of the welfare state, Rieger and Leibfried demonstrate in attentive detail how the liberalization and deregulation of foreign trade and investment in the post-70s period, and the 'complex interdependency' it inaugurated 'was itself predicated on the existence of the welfare state in the first place.' National deregulation, in other words, could not have been legitimated without the support and confidence of voters whose security had been guaranteed, to considerable degree, by citizen rights that the welfare state had helped secure. The demise of the welfare state, in other words, rather than the inevitable effect of economic globalization threatens its continued growth. That 'trade protectionism' continues to operate as a proxy for welfare policy in the United States where the neoliberal voice is at its most shrill, the authors contend, is indicative of the tight links between the continued necessity for welfare provision and the creation of a global economy.[23] Rieger and Leibfried confirm what some in the global governance literature optimistically see as an increasing, if reluctant, acknowledgment on the part of international organizations of the relation between social provisioning and economic development. While seeing domestic political coalitions as central to social policy formation, their conclusion that continued globalization will depend crucially on some manner of active social provisioning offers an effective antidote to the ideological underpinnings of the neoliberal economic manifesto.

Colin Hay's incisive account that follows, examines the institutionalization of 'necessitarian neoliberalism' as the governing economic agenda of the times and offers a close mapping of the depoliticizing and dedemocratizing effects on economic policy making (including welfare) that accompany the normalization of the neoliberal economic agenda. In a provocative argument that sees the resurgence of neoliberalism in the 1990s as the direct heir to the normative neoliberalism of the 1970s in the UK, rooted in a specific (public choice driven) narration of the crisis of the state that was itself dependent on internally inconsistent rationalist assumptions, Hay makes a compelling case for construing 'Third Way' thinking as neoliberal, thereby explaining in part the convergence in policy choices between political 'conservatives' and progressive 'Third Wayers.' In the absence of questionable assumptions about narrow instrumental rationality, indeed outside 'algebraic modeling(s) of a stylized open economy' there is little 'evidence for the predictions these assumptions support' (Hay 2004c: 520). Thus, widespread purported anxiety about the risk of capital flight in the face of heightened competition and open economies (a conclusion necessitated by the rationalist assumptions that underpin open-economy mathematical models) is, Hay points out highly questionable when one appreciates fully the realistic scenario that foreign direct investors 'are attracted to locations like Northern European economies neither for the flexibility of their labour markets nor for the cheapness of the wage [...] but for the access they provide to a highly skilled, reliable, and innovative labour force' (Hay 2004c: 521). Neoliberal discourse posits its policy preferences as the naturalized outcome of 'objective' economic globalization. In contrast, Hay helps us see the context in which what Peter Burnham (2001) describes as a condition in which 'politics as the management of depoliticization' has developed, in this instance, in the case of Britain.

From a different vantage point, Teresa Brennan offers an analogous critique of the economic rationalities underpinning 'Third Way' thinking. Eschewing notions of economic globalization as the spatial extension of capitalist organization of the economy to all corners of the globe, Brennan locates the emergence of 'Third Way' policy, specifically its restrictions on welfare and other social provisions, in the changed temporal structure of capitalist production. In a provocative reworking of Marx's labor theory of value in which nature and labor are viewed as sources of surplus-value she highlights the increasing tension between the rapidly accelerated speed of production that has come about with revolutions in the technologies of production, and 'the way that the reproduction of natural resources, including labour-power, cannot keep pace with that speed.' Unlike natural resources which can be obtained far afield, the costs of human reproduction 'become a drag on the system....both at the day-to-day level of reproduction where subsistence needs are met, and the generational level' (Brennan 2001: 42). The secular trend in the movement from welfare-to-work, Brennan surmises, is the result of this dissonance between the needs of 'the central speedy dynamic of capital' and human reproduction. The significance of her argument here has more to do with how it flags questions about the functionality of regulatory strategies to the hypothesized 'needs' of capital.

If the scholarship critical of the inevitability thesis on welfare has reached agreement on any one claim, it may be simply that 'politics matters.' As all four essays contained in the third section demonstrate, the effect of economic globalization on welfare states is neither inexorable nor homogenous, but rather, always mediated by politics. As such, they take seriously the continued relevance of politics even in at a time that Peter Burnham describes as one in which 'politics is about the management of depoliticization.' It is, thus, hardly coincidental that among the voices claiming 'politics matters,' those contained within the conceptual scaffolding of political pluralism, interest group or party competition, and path dependency, the disciplinary domain of normal political science, have garnered the most attention. Among these, the work of Paul Pierson and Geoffrey Garrett, the authors of the first two essays in this section have been especially influential in efforts to re-politicizing the 'retreat of the welfare state.' In light of the discussion in section one, however, it is important to bear in mind the very real limits that each encounters in developing a critical alternative to the *status quo*.

Pierson suggests, contra neoliberal orthodoxy that attempts to roll back welfare programs have been successfully thwarted, concerted efforts by governments notwithstanding, due to the deeply enmeshed societal networks of support that typically coalesce around specific policies. The path-dependencies generated by these extensive client-based policy interest groups, Pierson suggests, render cutbacks politically and electorally risky, resulting in a politics of retrenchment that is a distinctive enterprise, one no longer amenable to the conceptual mappings of an earlier politics of welfare expansion. Pierson's contribution was especially well received, not the least because it was among the first to offer an antidote to the neoliberal claim, but also perhaps because it sought to reclaim the theoretical terrain of political science for interest-group political pluralism from the challenges posed by structuralist and class-based accounts.

Repudiating both neoliberal orthodoxy on the logic of no alternative and Pierson's claim that the politics of welfare state retrenchment is an enterprise distinctive to the politics of welfare state expansion, Geoffrey Garrett takes one of the three pillars of welfare state theory – the scope and influence of social democratic politics – to advance the persuasive claim that there is more than one way to pursue economic growth under conditions of global economic integration. Higher rates of return on investment (arguably propelling capital's compulsion to seek out deregulated labor markets) can be assuaged not only by neoliberal strategies (privatization, deregulation, fiscal austerity, lowered taxation) but also by social democratic states that set limits on labor market institutions (by setting limits on wage bargaining, thereby restraining wage growth), in exchange for extending social protection to workers. This is an intuitively compelling claim that parallels arguments about the relation between work and productivity. The productivity of labor subject to a purely market enforced discipline (the prospect of unemployment and job loss) is of a qualitatively different order than that associated with the intrinsic (non-pecuniary) worth of work. To the extent that social democratic policies that pursue human capital investment can produce a healthy, skilled, educated workforce (*via* social protection programs) *and* maintain labor market flexibility by stabilizing and restraining real wage growth (through predictable patterns of wage setting) in exchange for continued socialized provision of some goods, social democratic policies can offer conditions equally attractive to mobile capital as the deregulated labor markets associated with capital's subsumption to a putatively neoliberal logic. For Garrett then, neoliberal economic strategic objectives can be rationally pursued either *via* de-regulating/privatization strategies, or alternatively, by continued social democratic corporatist investment in human capital formation.

Framed within the categories of normal science, Pierson and Garrett's work offers a useful and influential corrective to the economistic overtones of strong globalization theory, but leaves in place the economizing logic that underpins liberal-pluralist democratic theory. Insofar as liberal-pluralist notions of democracy simply extend market logic (competition and interest maximization) to the terrain of politics, they subsume politics to the market. For Pierson, the problem of deploying a market-based notion of politics reinscribes notions of the state as an arena of private want satisfaction, providing neither 'exit' or 'voice' to those left outside market- and state-based means of gratification. Garrett's argument, on the other hand, as Colin Hay points out, rather than revive social democratic optimism by repudiating neoliberal claims of inevitability, simply bifurcates it; rather than globalization's 'logic of no alternative' singular path to neoliberalism, there are now two.[24] To the extent, however, that both go some distance in rebuking neoliberal orthodoxy from within their disciplinary confines, both offer engagements with the question of welfare state retrenchment that merit serious consideration.

Neo-Marxian scholarship on the globalization/welfare problematic is marked by a deep ambivalence towards the welfare state. Heralded, as the hard-won outcome of class struggle, and for its role in significantly ameliorating the conditions of those subject to the vicissitudes of the working of capitalist economy, but also subject to critique for its role in mystifying the real structures of exploitation still at work beneath 'humanized capitalism,' critiques of neoliberal orthodoxy on welfare are split between those who tend to see it simply as the unfolding logic of capital, and those who see in the present juncture, class defeat. For most Marxists, however, the viability of the state *qua* capitalist state is enhanced, not circumscribed by the universalization of capitalism on a global scale.[25] Reflecting the deep divisions that structure debates within neo-Marxian understandings of the present constellation of social forces, Francis Fox-Piven and Richard Cloward in the essay that follows suggest that the demise of the Keynesian welfare state marks the end of one era of power, and signals, perhaps, the dawn of another. Firmly rooted in the Marxian notion of class struggle as the social agency of change, they view historically specific power constellations in terms of the capacities of the working class to actualize its power *vis-à-vis* the capitalist class. The Keynesian welfare state thus embodies, for them, a historical 'social compact' between the proletariat and capital, and the materialization of working-class power as seen in the growth in rates of unionization, the capacity for labor strikes to shut down manufacturing industries and the development of a self-conscious working-class culture in the industrial era. Globalization, the authors contend, has unleashed processes of economic change that have weakened old forms of working-class power due to the new forms of labor regulation economic changes have wrought. With increased limits imposed on the right to strike, the growth of union oligarchy and the flexibilization of labor, coupled with the threat of capital flight and job relocation, capital's enhanced power *vis-à-vis* the working class in the era of '*laissez-faire* capitalism' has enervated the capacities of the working class to resist capital's onslaught on the hard-won victories of an earlier power era.

In the essay that concludes this section, Lynne Segal explores the antinomies of a feminist approach to the politics of welfare reform. Although feminists, like their Marxian counterparts have shared a common skepticism about the Keynesian welfare state's ability to secure 'social citizenship' for women, and have been historically ambivalent about their orientations to the state, the recent post-structural turn in feminist theorizing has tended to complicate feminist efforts to secure economic and political rights even as their theoretical proclivities have tended elsewhere. Recalling Carole Pateman's influential defense of the state as a resource for women against dependence on patriarchal familial relations, Lynne Segal makes a persuasive case against the anti-statism she perceives has gripped feminist discourse in Britain. In a refreshingly direct and lucid account, Segal juxta-poses the perceived virtues of anti-statist feminism against the virtues, albeit limited, that dependence on the state provides. Reinforcing critiques of 'Third Way' thinking, Segal draws attention to the inevitable resurgence of traditional patriarchal family ideology that accompanies the retreat of the welfare state, and the normativity of heterosexuality it helps engender. In an argument similar in some ways to that advanced in the earlier part of this chapter, Segal warns against the perils of abandoning struggles within (and against the state). Her point is well taken: the 'effort to create a better world for women' must embrace oppositional politics that not only resist the bureaucratizing and alienating features of old welfare state structures, but equally the 'characteristic paternalism' and 'new managerialism' of a 'Third Way' policy agenda, as well as misplaced celebrations of consumer sovereignty that has come to replace critiques of 'dependency' on the welfare state. In deploying a critical statism, Segal suggests, feminist efforts to reconcile their struggles for economic autonomy and gender justice may be well served.

Drawing on Michel Foucault's analytic of governmentality as the 'conduct of conduct,' the essays contained in the last section of this volume advance a distinctive understanding of globalization, welfare and workfare, not as effects of economic imperatives bur rather as political rationalities constitutive of new subjectivities and identities. Foucault's rejection of the polarity between subjectivity and power based on the insight that 'government' is better grasped as a continuum that entails not only the regulation of the social body but also the direction of the self constitutes the center-piece of a growing body of literature devoted to exploring the analytic of 'governmentality' as especially fruitful to under-standing the modalities of neoliberal rule. Unlike pastoral or disciplinary modes of regulation that were constitutive of docile bodies (social and individual), 'governmentality' as the political rationality of neoliberal rule seeks to render the social domain economic, and the 'active' entre-preneurial self now not only the subject of market exchange relations but the governable self constituted in relation to neoliberal direction of conduct. As such, neoliberal globalization and the retreat of the state it mandates as 'inevitable' is neither an ideological ruse nor an economic reality, but a political project constitutive of the very conditions it purports to exist. Neoliberal globalization, in other words, is itself understood as a 'governmental rationality,' (Larner & Walters 2004), whose associated practices may be better grasped as constitutive rather than as contingent effects.

In his influential essay on 'The Death of the Social?,' Nikolas Rose shows how the rearticulation of identities and subjectivities (from citizens to individuals, clients to consumers) rather than marking the retreat of politics, as the globalization thesis claims, is itself politically constituted by the new tactics and social practices of government that replace older, archaic forms of power, with new modalities, better understood not as the loss of governing capacity by the state but rather the reorganization of technologies of government. Developing the Foucauldian thematic of subjectification (the production of subjectivities through specific 'mentalities of rule'), Rose suggests that the welfare state, rather than simply a mechanism of politico-administrative rule of society was itself productive of the 'social' as the territorialized plane of government. The emergence of 'community' as the new space of government, evidenced in the multifarious groups (drug abusers, gay men, youth at risk etc.) that form the discrete objects of administration signals, Rose suggests, the emergence of a post-social technology of the government of conduct in which the 'social' as the territorialized space of rule is giving way to new forms of regulation of community in which the 'active' individual rather than society is made responsible for his or her own well-being. As such the extension of the 'enterprising self' of the economy to the social domain requires the fragmentation of the social such that 'economic government is to be desocialized in the name of maximizing the entrepreneurial comportment of the individual,' (Rose 1996c: 340). Where previously government regulated the unemployed in the name of 'society,' the fragmentation of marginalized populations into newly classified 'micro-sectors' of abjected communities both naturalizes their condition and subjects them to new forms of management by a variety of specialists whose expertise in particular knowledge systems act to locate individuals as members of specific marginalized communities and contributes to the process of the fragmentation of the 'social.' The 'reinvention of the social,' through mobilization of an affirmative community in which many critical of the 'retreat of the state' invest their political energies, Rose cautions, may prove equally illusory, given the new relations of power underpinning discourses of community, as opposed to society.

In the essay that follows, Mitchell Dean takes on the challenge of clarifying the vital analytic of 'self-formation' that stands at the center of contemporary studies of governmentality *via* an elaboration of the 'active citizen' that provides the new axis of subjectification in welfare reform. Distinguishing between the governmental self 'in which authorities and agencies shape conduct, aspirations, needs, desires and capacities' of social and political categories, and processes of ethical self-formation which entails the care of the self by the self, which engages clients in their own government, Dean draws attention to the ways in which social security can be seen as a governmental-ethical practice which not only attempts to realize specific administrative goals (income redistribution, poverty alleviation) but also, and perhaps more significantly, shapes the conduct of individuals as it involves specific forms of self-formation and, in the case of the unemployed self, reformation. Illustrating his argument *via* a close engagement with the Social Security reforms advocated in Australia in the last decade or so, Dean shows how the replacement of the 'work-test' (central to Keynesian strategies of management) by the 'activity-test' in Australia (indeed in most advanced industrialized democracies) replaced the notion of welfare as the citizen-based right of 'unemployed self' with the notion of the enterprising self, the 'job-seeker,' whose status as a client and receipt of an allowance is made contingent on proof of active retooling, skill acquisition and retraining. The 'active subject' is responsible now not only for developing capacities for reentry into the labor market, but for the full range of 'goods' (social provision, education, health) that he or she may need in the course of a life. The 'trainee' thus comes to replace the welfare client as the 'governable self' as the object of governmental-ethical practices. The self-organization of self in an active society thus encompasses a neoliberal 'mentality of rule,' which is reducible neither to ideology, economic imperative, or policy framework as conventional scholarship would have it, but is rather conceived as constitutive of both the social practices, agencies, 'techniques and discourses that provide the means and conditions of administration and rule,' as well as the subjectivities wrought in and through these practices. Dean's central point, which is (indeed Foucault's about the nexus between power and knowledge), that the practical arts of government are never simply or only technical or routine, but 'contain a dimension of thought,' different policies thereby constitutive of different forms of being (citizen/client, passive/active self etc.) although pivotal to the analytic of governmentality, it is worth noting briefly, not necessarily restricted to a negative uptake alone. The realization of modes of being consistent with unsubstantialized 'being-in-common' would depend on alternative governmental practices hospitable to precisely such dimensions of thought. Rather than marking the limits of politics then the 'governmentality' optic can be productive of alternative political imaginings of the modalities of welfare or well-being.

Eschewing critiques that view workfare simply as the product of neoliberal economic rationality, marked by the retreat of the state and the imposition of labor discipline, Sanford Schram suggests that welfare and its current reform may be better viewed as a mode of social regulation that has historically had at its objective the stabilization of a cultural and economic social order centered on the family and work. Like the family-wage system that the Keynesian welfare system supported, even as its disciplinary stigmatizing practices served to reinforce the symbolic order of capitalism, workfare programs in advanced industrialized democracies, especially the US, Schram suggests, can be seen as a 'behavior modification regime' an 'elaboration of surrogate means of social control to promote adherence to family as well as work values' (Schram 2002: 201) at a time when the social institutions of family and work are being radically undermined by processes of globalization. As heightened economic insecurity, the expansion of low-wage labor markets and economic marginalization for greater numbers of people places greater burdens on families, the status of work and family is rendered increasingly fragile. To the extent that workfare imposes work and family standards on recipients in ways that are particularly demeaning, punishing recipients from deviating from family and work values, as a new 'technology of the self,' it is generative of new forms of power and domination in which this new mode of social regulation and control provides a substitute for the social institutions that globalization undermines. As such, the renewed emphasis on family and work and the self-disciplining practices associated with its enactment *via* self-reliance in the market, produces the 'compliant subjects' of what Michael Hardt and Antonio Negri (2000) have theorized as the networks of 'cooperative production' in a new world order. The microprocesses of the behavior modification regime of welfare reform, is thus seen as part of a 'larger discipline' of self-governance in the production of subjectivities consistent with a globalizing economy.

In the final essay, Jamie Peck offers a critical engagement with the currently influential debates on the theoretical status of scales and rescaling in rethinking welfare. Although not committed to the tenets of post-structuralism himself, the inclusion of Peck's essay in this segment (rather than section two on the regulation of global capital), draws attention to the significance notions of rescaling in studies of governmentality and welfare. Moreover, insofar as Peck critically interrogates the propensity within critical political-economic geography to deploy notions of scale and rescaling in binary and oppositional terms (global/national/local) by making a persuasive case for inter-scalar notions of reterritorialization, his attention to the continued relevance of the national scale in mediating the global and local offers a useful corrective to the propensity within critical (including post-structural) scholarship to embrace what I have earlier referred to as the analytical retreat of the state.

Working within and against the theoretical vocabulary of critical political-economic geography, Peck, in the last essay of this volume, makes a persuasive case for an 'explicitly politicized and transcalar conception of the processes of regulatory restructuring.' Against the naturalizing proclivities of current discourse that posits the global as the economically optimal space of markets, and 'the local as the politically optimal scale of coping and adaptation' Peck draws attention to what he describes as the 'decisive influence of inter-scalar rule regimes' including nation-states, in rescaling governance at the local level. The overdetermination of the local, either as a site for progressive resistance (belied by the relative paucity of successful workfare programs and trans-local anti-workfare political resistance), or its conservative version, as key to enhancing market competitiveness must be replaced, Peck suggests, by analytical adherence to the 'essential interconnectedness of scalar relationships' such that the nation-state's role in what he calls 'scale management and coordination at the local and international levels' (in Bob Jessop terms 'metagovernance') can be both theoretically and politically contested. In a provocative elaboration of his thesis, Peck goes on to identify the conditions of the production of workfare as a 'universal policy fix,' a technocratically stylized reform signifier itself derivative of 'fast-policy' formation that engenders a ceaseless search for transportable 'models' of successful workfare programs, imbuing some (like Wisconsin's W-2 program) as inherently rationalistic (and therefore transportable) despite overwhelming evidence to the contrary. The search for 'ideas that work' results in the thinning out of local reform models, a delocalization of strategies in service of transferable policy lessons drawn up by the armies of consultants and experts. That states continue to serve as 'arm's length managers of the workfarist policy process,' is, contra contemporary 'theoretical correctness,' Peck concludes, reason enough to reconstitute 'the national scale as the principal site of resistance' in the new politics of workfarism.

Notes

1. This description is borrowed from Hay (2000): 507.
2. The Washington consensus refers to a tacit political agreement between the IMF, the World Bank, and the US Treasury to rationalize global markets.
3. Vito Tanzi cites a survey of corporate tax rates in 14 major industrialized countries that shows a dramatic decline from an average of 46 percent in 1985 to 33 percent in 1999. Tanzi (2001): 78–9.
4. Thus, for instance, Paul Hirst points out that levels of openness today (in terms of merchandise trade and capital mobility) hardly equal those of the economy of the *belle époque* (1870–1914); in terms of migration, the 19th century witnessed proportionally far greater numbers than those recorded today.
5. Cox (1987).
6. Ohmae (1991).
7. Gregor Mclennan (2004) explains the notion of a 'vehicular idea' as a way of problem-solving and 'moving things on' that is 'resistant to theorization,' a rhetoric that is open to multiple interpretations, hospitable to including perspectives that may indeed oppose rather than complement each other, such that what Derrida terms a 'truth effect' can be created by its 'interpretative and rhetorical indeterminacy' (488). Thus, the remarkable idea that dismantling the welfare state inaugurates a democratic politics of compassion that has as its object a revival of social convivability and individual well-being is a 'truth effect' created by 'Third Way' rhetoric, even as the policies it helps legitimate (punitive term limits on welfare, moving people off welfare to work) repudiate its claims of being a pragmatic and ethical alternative to a draconian neoliberalism.

8. Defining the free market and what counts as state intervention is, as Ha Joon Chang points out, a highly complicated exercise. 'What constitutes state intervention is, in large measure, determined by the legitimate subject of policy debates....where the rights of children not to be sold is regarded as procedure, producer's rights to employ child labor can be legitimately blocked by the state.' The institutional context and the legitimacy of the underlying rights-obligations structure for the participants in the relevant market' is pivotal to understanding what counts as state intervention or not in specific markets.

9. Reich (1999): 46–51.

10. Peter Evans' recent attempt to respond to the claim that globalization has eclipsed the state in global affairs is instructive. Distinguishing between levels of 'stateness' based on conventional notions of state capacity and the effectiveness of a powerful bureaucracy, Evans draws attention to the East Asian model in which small countries like Singapore, singularly reliant on trade and foreign direct investment, have historically had a 'strong state,' authoritarian at times toward domestic populations but also remarkably effective in orienting national economic development in accordance with international economic trends. Rather than view the eclipse of stateness as inevitable, the prospects of a leaner, meaner state or 'more promising forms of stateness' depend 'not on the economic logic of globalization alone [but] also [...] on how people think of stateness.' Evans (1997): 13.

11. David P. Levine (2001) explores the psycho-analytical roots of what I call the analytical retreat of the state. See especially chapter 5.

12. The phrase is taken from Levine (2001).

13. Marcuse (2000): 24.

14. See Levine (2001) for a discussion of the implications of the separateness of the state.

15. In the recent effort to elaborate a post-national theory of citizenship, several scholars have looked to Marshall's theory of social citizenship as a crucial theoretical resource for this endeavor on the grounds that the striking absence of any explicit discussion of the national dimension of citizenship in his work renders it potentially fruitful to innovative theorizing about denationalizing citizenship. But, as John Crowley has persuasively shown, the 'national dimension is absent from his discussion not because it is irrelevant but because it is taken for granted.' See Crowley (1998): 168. Any attempt to fashion a post-national citizenship then must wrestle first with the problem of specifying institutions and social practices that can produce common membership that are not themselves contingent on substantialized group membership.

16. Sylvia Walby (2001) in a recent engagement with Nancy Fraser's thesis on reconciling the politics of distribution with the politics of recognition, points to a 'weak conceptualization of the social, especially the use of the concept of community as it signified the social, but which is actually too narrow and specific an operationalization of the concept of the social,' (2001): 114. Although directed towards an argument other than the one developed here, Marshall's equation of social right with that of a specific (what I have called substantialized) political community, betrays a similar weakness.

17. Nancy (1991).

18. Neoclassical economic theory and the neoliberal ideology that currently prevails are not identical, as is often assumed, if one recalls Hayek's scathing critique of neoclassical economics. To the extent, however, that both celebrate, albeit in

different ways, the unitary self of market exchange, the conflation of the two in normative critiques of this conception may be more readily understood.

19. As Levine (2001) points out, pragmatism in itself cannot be sufficient to the ends of development.
20. Bob Deacon's work on this is especially relevant. See Deacon and Hulse (1996).
21. See, for instance Tadzio Mueller (2001): 259–65.
22. The two are not the same, although the slippage from one to the other in contemporary discussions obscures the distinct theoretical and historical lineage of both.
23. Consider, for instance, the United States' insistence that Bolivia eradicate its cocaine fields, which it successfully did, at a punitively high cost in terms of loss of income from the sale of drugs. In return, however, the United States has continued to maintain tariffs against Bolivian exports, restricting the sale of Bolivian sugar, in direct contravention of the free trade policies it imposes on developing countries.
24. See Hay (2000): 138–52.
25. Thus Peter Marcuse, in a succinct summary of the Marxian position, suggests that the 'myth of the powerless state' is based on the non-recognition of enhanced, rather than diminished capacity as the capitalist system spreads international. 'If states do not control the movement of capital or goods, it is not because they cannot but because they will not – it is an abdication of state power, not a lack of power,' Marcuse (2000): 25.

Part I

Citizenship and Global Governance

1
The Erosion of Citizenship*

Bryan S. Turner

Marshall and the theory of citizenship

The Marshallian theory of citizenship has been extensively discussed for half a century. It will suffice here merely to summarize its principal components and to outline the major criticisms raised against it [...]. Marshall (1950) divided citizenship into three parts. The civil component was necessary for the achievement of individual freedoms and included such elements as freedom of speech, the right to own property and the right to justice. The political element was constituted by the rights to participate in the exercise of political power, in particular the rights to free elections and a secret ballot. Finally, Marshall defined the social component as the right to 'a modicum of economic welfare and security to the right to share to the full in the social heritage and to live the life of a civilized being' (Marshall 1950 [1964]: 69). These three components had evolved from the 17th to the 20th century and had become established through a process of institutional differentiation by which special agencies had evolved to express these rights. Alongside these three components, there existed a set of institutions that gave these rights social expression, namely the courts of justice, parliament and councils of local government, and the educational system and the social services.

[...] Marshall's paradigm has come under attack from [a] variety of sources – liberal, Marxist and conservative (Beiner 1995). First, the theory failed to provide an effective analysis of the causal mechanisms that produced an expansion of citizenship. The most obvious candidate to explain the growth of social rights in the nineteenth and twentieth centuries was the impact of working-class conflicts over economic rights relating to employment, sickness benefit and retirement (Montgomery 1993; Parker 1998). [...] The other major causal feature in the development of citizenship in both America and

---

* From *British Journal of Sociology* 52(2) (2000): 189–209.

Britain has been the unintended consequence of modern warfare. The idea of a comprehensive health system gained widespread acceptance during the war years and Attlee's Labour Government brought in a national health service that offered free treatment to all citizens. The welfare state in Britain after the Second World War and the civil rights movement in America after the Vietnam War were both responses to the mobilization of society and to its self-critical reflection. [...]

The second criticism is that Marshall treated citizenship as a uniform concept and did not attempt to differentiate types of citizenship, or to suggest a comparative study of different forms of citizenship in terms of distinct historical trajectories. It appears to be relatively obvious that citizenship has assumed very different forms in Europe in relation to different patterns of capitalist development. Marshall's account makes no distinction between active and passive citizenship (Turner 1990). What are the historical and social conditions that promote effective and active patterns of social participation rather than merely passive membership? In the past, revolutionary struggles and the destructive consequences of warfare produced active involvement, but, as Titmuss recognized, we may need to devise new means of national critical inquiry and citizenship formation in a period when the possibility of nuclear and biological warfare have removed the conditions that made possible the satisfaction of the demands of returning servicemen.

Thirdly, Marshall assumed a heterogeneous society in which regional, cultural and ethnic divisions were not important when compared to social class divisions. Marshall worked in a political context where the unity of the UK was not an issue and the cultural and constitutional problem of 'Englishness' within the devolution of government in modern Britain was hardly imaginable in Marshall's time. The principal weakness of Marshall was the absence of any understanding of ethnic and racial divisions in relation to national citizenship (Crowley 1998).

Finally, Marshall's theory was primarily a theory of entitlement, but had little to say about duties and obligations. As such the theory envisaged a passive citizenry in which the state protected the individual from the uncertainty of the market through a system of universal rights. Political economists have criticized Marshallian citizenship as liberal reformism that offered formal rights rather than substantive benefits. Critics have claimed the enactment of citizenship [...]. How do citizenship rights become effective forms of entitlement? My argument is that citizenship as a status position is not in itself sufficient to guarantee an effective entitlement; effective citizenship has depended on three foundations or routes of entitlement: work, war and reproduction.

Three routes of effective entitlement

Rather than define citizenship within a static framework of rights and obligations, it is valuable to [...] [conceptualize] citizenship as process

(Turner 1997). Citizenship is both an inclusionary process involving some re-allocation of resources and an exclusionary process of building identities on the basis of a common or imagined solidarity. Citizenship entitlement provides criteria for the allocation of scarce resources and at the same time creates strong identities that are not only juridical, but typically involve assumptions about ethnicity, religion and sexuality (Isin and Wood 1999). Nineteenth-century national citizenship was constituted around racial divisions, because it excluded outsiders from access to resources on the basis of an (ascribed) ethnic or national identity. Because citizenship is a set of processes for the allocation of entitlements, obligations and immunities within a political community, these entitlements are themselves based [on] a number of principles, that describe and evaluate the specific contributions that individuals have made to society, for example through war service, or reproduction, or work.

In historical terms, social citizenship has been closely associated with the involvement of individuals (typically men) in the formal labor market. Work was fundamental to the conception of citizenship in the British welfare state (Beveridge 1944 and 1948). Individuals could achieve effective entitlements through the production of goods and services, namely through gainful employment which was essential for the provision of adequate pensions and superannuation. These entitlements also typically included work care, insurance cover, retirement benefits and healthcare. Citizenship for male workers characteristically evolved out of class conflicts over conditions of employment, remuneration and retirement. [...]

Secondly, service to the state through warfare generates a range of entitlements for the soldier-citizen. Wartime service typically leads to special pension rights, health provisions, housing and education for returning servicemen and their families. War service has been important, as we have seen, in the development of the evolution of social security entitlements (Titmuss 1962). Thirdly, people achieve entitlements through the formation of households and families that become the mechanisms for the reproduction of society through the birth, maintenance and socialization of children. These services increasingly include care for the aging and elderly as generational obligations continue to be satisfied through the private sphere (Finch 1989). These services to the state through the family provide entitlements to both men and women as parents, that is as reproducers of the nation. These familial entitlements become the basis of family security systems, various forms of support for mothers, and health and educational provision for children. Although the sexual activity of adults in wedlock is regarded in law as a private activity, the state and church have clearly taken a profound interest in the conditions for and consequences of lawful (and more particularly unlawful) sexual activity. Heterosexual reproduction has been a principal feature of the regulatory activity of the modern state. [...]

These conditions of effective entitlement also established a pattern of active participation in society, that in turn contributed to civil society through what is known technically as 'social capital' (Dasgupta and Serageldin 2000). Active citizenship supported work-related associations (such as working men's clubs, trade union organizations and guilds, and political organizations such as the traditional Labour Party). These associations correspond to what Durkheim called 'intermediary associations' (Durkheim 1992), that is forms of association that mediate between the state and the individual, and provide moral regulation of society (Turner 1999). [...] While in general mass warfare in the 20th century has been destructive of traditional society, one unintended consequence of these conflicts was to produce a multitude of (male) associations that provided support and services to ex-soldiers. Ceremonials of male solidarity (ANZAC parades and other rituals of remembrance) kept alive the comradeship of war, and in Britain, the Dunkirk-spirit continued to be a norm of civilian service and sacrifice. Finally, parenthood has traditional[ly] provided solidaristic linkages to the wider community through women's groups, childcare associations, school-related groups, neighborhood groups, and church-based groups such as the Mother's Union). The growth of post-war active citizenship was also associated with activities that contributed to social solidarity.

This pattern of citizenship has been eroded because the three foundations of effective entitlement have been transformed by economic, military and social changes. [...] [W]hile increasing rates of economic activity has been a positive aspect of economic liberalization, much of this increase in economic participation has involved the casualization of the labor force. The number of men in part-time employment doubled between 1984 and 1999. Radical changes in the labor market (job sharing, casualization, flexibility, downsizing, and new management strategies) have disrupted work as a career. While for employers functional and numerical flexibility has broken down rigidities in the work place, these strategies have compromised job security (Abercrombie and Warde 2000: 81). These changes in work and career structures constitute a significant 'corrosion of character.' With the obsolescence of the social relevance of the concept of career (even among the professional classes), there is also an erosion of commitment to the company. Workers can no longer depend on a stable life course or life cycle. In addition, there has been a major decline in trade-union membership and work in a life-long career no longer so clearly defines personal identity. Union density (or the proportion of people eligible for membership who actually join) has declined steadily since 1979, and by 1996 union membership was lower than at any time since the end of the Second World War. Class-based identities are disappearing along with class-based communities. [...]

Sociological studies of social class suggest that, while levels of unemployment have been falling in association with the long American economic boom of the 1990s, the contemporary class structure has new components

– an 'underclass' of the permanently unemployable (typically lone-parent welfare claimants), a declining middle class associated with the decline of middle management, and the 'working poor' whose skill levels do not permit upward mobility. There is some academic consensus that features of the class structure do not encourage active citizenship through economic entitlement, but these changes in the nature of employment are perhaps insignificant when compared to the greying of the population and the social problem of retirement. [...]

In addition to changes in the economic foundations of Marshallian citizenship, the Titmuss-mechanism of war-related claims to entitlement has largely disappeared with the end of mass warfare. The Cold War and nuclear disarmament meant that the traditional role of the citizen-soldier gave way to a new pattern of warfare involving both professional soldiers and mercenaries as the personnel of modern wars. [...] [G]iven the technological character of modern warfare, the experience of western states in Korea, Vietnam, Afghanistan, and Kosovo suggests that modern wars corrupt and corrode democracies rather than cementing them together. [...] [T]he modern media have made it more rather than less difficult for a democracy to conduct large-scale military interventions in which there is a significant risk of casualties. [...] The result is the erosion of the citizen-soldier as a social role, the decline of servicemen's clubs as part of civil society and the diminution of military ritualism as part of the secular rituals of civil society and the state. In the age of smart bombs and stealth aircraft, involvement of the masses in military activity can no longer fortunately function as a significant feature of citizenship.

Reproductive citizenship

The third important change in the foundation of citizenship is the transformation of reproduction in relation to social rights. Recent writing in the field of citizenship studies (Richardson 2000; Yuval-Davis 1998; Voet 1998) has underlined the neglect of gender in the analysis of the national development of citizen entitlements and obligations in the nation-state. We need to extend the discussion of citizenship, nationalism and gender by examining the relationship between parenthood and entitlement. [...] Because the majority of western societies in demographic terms enjoy only modest rates of successful reproduction, the state promotes the desirability of fertility and reproductivity as a foundation of social participation. [...]

The liberal regime of modern citizenship privileges parenthood in 'normal' families, rather than heterosexuality as such, as the defining characteristic of the normal citizen and as the basis of social entitlement. [...] The introduction of technologies of artificial human reproduction in the late 1970s served to underline the manner in which reproduction plays a foundational role in citizenship, because they provide the potential for reproduction without heterosexual sexual intercourse. Despite their wide-spread acceptance as a treatment for infertility, new reproductive techno-logies remain controversial medical procedures that continue to receive extraordinary attention from the media. Since their inception in the late 1970s, methods of human artificial reproduction have prompted consider-able debate, offering new means of human fertilization and unanticipated options for family formation. The larger issues which the technologies raise explicitly concern mothering, fatherhood and conception, and implicitly the creation of the social self. The forms in which a government responds to this demographic potential reveals the assumptions of the state for fami-lies and the presence of eugenics, namely the system of reproductive values prevalent in society. The concept of 'sexual citizenship' which has been promoted by some sociologists in Britain does not adequately describe the relationship between sexuality, reproduction and citizenship. In fact, the state's interest in sexuality and sexual identity is secondary and subordinate to its demographic objective of securing and sustaining the connection between reproduction and citizenship.

The creation of institutions of citizenship in legal, political and social terms was an important feature in the construction of a national frame-work of membership within the nation-state – a process that dominated domestic politics in Europe and North America through much of the late 18th and 19th centuries (Nelson 1998). The production of an institutional framework of national citizenship required the creation of national identi-ties. Citizenship identities during the rise of the European cities had been local and urban, but with the rise of nationalism they became increasingly connected with strong nationalistic cultures that sought greater domestic coherence and simultaneously organized negative images of outsiders. The national mythologies of a society cement individual biographies and col-lective biographies of generations with the history of a nation-state and its people. It is for this reason that theories of citizenship typically connect the enhancement of citizenship entitlement through involvement in warfare, especially in defense of the nation.

It does not follow that women are excluded from nation-building. On the contrary, they are crucial for family formation and sexual reproduction; these 'domestic arrangements' in turn reproduce political society (Yuval-Davis 1998). However, women's voices in the grand narratives of nationalism tend to be muted and marginalized by a warrior ethos. [...]

Voluntary associationalism: a fourth way to entitlement?

The erosion of citizenship through the transformations of work, war and parenthood also corrodes the possibilities of participatory or associative democracy. Modern society is no longer constituted by a dense network of associations, clubs, fraternities, chapels and communal associations. The decline of social capital is a major index of the erosion of citizenship (Putnam 1993 and 1995). The late 20th century has been marked by a major decline in all forms of social participation, at least partly as a consequence of the impact of television on leisure activities. Religious membership, confirmations, baptism and marriages in the mainstream Christian churches have declined considerably since 1970, although there has been an increase in evangelical sects and in non-Christian religions. Membership of political parties and newspaper readership have also declined. [Although] 76 percent of men and 68 percent of women claimed to read a newspaper in 1981, newspaper readership had fallen to 60 and 51 percent respectively by 1998–9. These changes raise questions about the possibilities of participation in contemporary society, and specifically about the level of third-sector institutions such as voluntary associations in providing opportunities for social service and participation. It is generally recognized that individual giving to charities and voluntary associations has steadily declined in the post-war period. The conventional assumption is that participation in the voluntary sector has, like other forms of social involvement declined through the 20th century, but this pessimistic interpretation appears to underestimate the importance of charities, voluntary associations and philanthropy. [...] For example, although the membership of the Mothers' Union fell from 308,000 to 177,000 between 1971 and 1990, membership of the National Trust increased from 278,000 to just over two million in the same period (Abercrombie and Warde 2000: 330). Membership of voluntary associations increased from 0.73 memberships per capita in 1959 to 1.12 memberships in 1990. Individual involvement in voluntary associations, clubs and leisure groups is probably more robust than the Putnam thesis about the decline of social capital would suggest. If however we simply count the number of voluntary associations and chart their growth, it is evident that voluntary associations, especially in the welfare sector, have expanded significantly in the last 20 years, and in part this growth can be attributed to the decline of state activity in welfare. The John Hopkins Comparative Nonprofit Sector Project discovered that in the seven countries studied one in every 20 jobs and one in every eight service jobs are accounted for by the voluntary sector. The rolling back of the state appears to have created a social vacuum in which the third sector has expanded to satisfy communal needs.

Recent comparative research on the role of voluntary associations in welfare provision in societies that have adopted innovative market approaches to welfare, illustrate the importance of partnerships between the market, the state and the voluntary sector (Brown, Kenny and Turner 2000). The data from these studies are both comprehensive and complex, but they do begin to provide some useful insight into the functions of the third sector in a democratic but economically competitive environment. The Australian survey provides a national estimate of 93,448 non-government welfare organizations, almost three-quarters of which had a primary focus on health. The Australian sector has enjoyed a growth rate of just under 12 percent per annum between 1981 and 1994. Although the sector is large and expanding, it is heavily dependent on government sources of funding; for 39 percent of such organizations, the state government was the principal source of funding, while another 13 percent were dependent on federal funding. This funding dependency is particularly prevalent in social support agencies dealing with refugees, childcare and neighborhood houses. Government support was least common among mutual support and aid organizations, self-help groups and rights advocacy groups. This structure of funding relations between government and voluntary associations raises questions about the independence of these associations and their capacity for critical intervention in civil society. In general, this research suggests that we should, for good sociological reasons, be cautious about the optimistic claims of Third-Way strategies to resolve the dilemmas of modern democracies.

[...] The third sector, and more specifically voluntary associations, can provide opportunities for social participation, for democratic involvement at the local level, and thus for active citizenship. They are essential to the survival of the public sphere, and in terms of service delivery, they can provide welfare programs that are sensitive to local client needs. This positive view of the voluntary sector and active citizenship is often shared by both politicians and academics (Hirst 1994). Voluntary associations have the potential to be the principal organizing force in society providing public welfare and the primary means of democratic governance. Indeed, if government really is part of the problem, then Hirst's proposal should be all the more attractive since its primary aim is to reduce the scale and scope of the affairs administered by the state. Subsidiarity would be achieved through a process of devolution of state functions, authority and funding to a network of voluntary associations. Such a system would support a process where citizen choice is combined with public welfare and, because voluntary associations have the capacity for a high level of communicative democracy, this devolved political structure would allow for widespread consultation, cooperation, and collaboration. Voluntary associations are characterized by organizational autonomy from the state and where their internal organizational structures support client involvement, they are better suited to promoting welfare that is targeted to local communities than state bureaucracies. Voluntary associations have four democratic enhancing functions: they provide information to policymakers; they redress political inequalities that exist when politics is materially based; they can act as schools of democracy; they provide alternative governance to markets and public hierarchies that permits society to realize the important benefits of cooperation among citizens (Cohen and Rogers 1995). Nonprofit organizations are a crucial condition of political participation; they are more efficient than government provision and can be more sensitive and responsive to the needs of client groups; they are crucial for the reproduction of social capital that underpins effective democratic political systems and strong economies; they provide for a strong civil society that [counterweighs] the tendencies towards domination of the state and market forces.

These broad claims for the democratic functions of the voluntary sector have to be modified to take into account the extreme variation with the sector. We must in any case start with a definition of voluntary associations. The point of this definitional digression is to suggest that large voluntary associations working closely with government may share characteristics with large profit-making corporations. There is considerable criticism of the notion that voluntary associations can be entrepreneurial, democratic and responsive to client interests. Research in Australia and Britain suggests that the interests of associative democracy and social inclusion are probably better served by small community groups on the margins of the social order than by large associations that are like corporations apart from the fact a share of the profits are not distributed to the board of managers (Brown, Kenny and Turner 2000). Despite the extent of the debate about voluntary associations, there has in fact been little agreement about how they might be precisely defined (Giner and Sarasa 1996; [...]). Voluntary associations can be said to have five characteristics: they are organized, private, non-profit-distributing, self-governing and voluntary [...].

[...] There is also considerable ambiguity in the relationship of voluntary associations to the economy. Traditionally voluntary associations were not expected to function like business organizations and their funding came from philanthropy, bequests and other gifts. Although voluntary associations are still either non-profit and not-for-profit organizations, they are increasingly under pressure from marketization and commodification. In order to raise funding, they have to compete for government grants and so there is pressure for these associations to become more professional. They need to hire staff that are highly qualified, not only to run large and complex organizations, but who are knowledgeable about government strategy, costing and managing projects. These developments tend to create a gap between the board of managers and the rank and file. There appears to be an inherent tension in how voluntary associations are organized, because the growth of professional values may conflict with traditional notions of philanthropy. The rise of generic management illustrates a common professionalization of the sector. The functions and composition of the boards of voluntary associations have been critically discussed in the social policy literature, because they are sensitive sites of public debate and concern. It is also assumed that voluntary associations will be self-governing. The pressure to professionalize in order to increase financial resources also therefore creates new problems about responsibility, access and participation. These management issues are somewhat ironic, given the fact that the voluntary sector is regarded as the spearhead of grassroots democratization. If voluntary associations become large and bureaucratic, they cannot remain sensitive to local or client interests, and they reproduce the worst features of traditional, top-down, welfare bureaucracies.

We can summarize these issues by saying that, especially for large voluntary associations, the voluntary sector is now under the same financial and management pressures that shape the capitalist corporations. In particular, voluntary associations are driven by a logic of resource maximization and enhancement (Galaskiewicz and Bielefeld 1998: 35), they are forced to employ and promote managerial rationality (and thus to recruit from a pool of generic management), they are also compelled to professionalize their processes of recruitment and training, and they are dependent on rational and professional systems of fund raising. In Britain and Australia, they are very dependent on their ability to tender successfully for government grants. There is some force to the conventional criticisms of the voluntary sector: it cannot provide a universalistic service, it does not have clear performance criteria, and it may not be cost effective. Worse still, voluntary associations may often function more like social clubs than service agencies, and they may form a social hierarchy of agencies that is a mirror image of the status hierarchy of society as a whole. Some charities and voluntary associations simply serve the 'expressive needs' of the middle classes and provide social outlets for unpaid work from the middle classes (Pearce 1993). Critical research literature in the 1970s suggested that voluntary associations functioned to restrain wage increases in social services as a result of competition between paid and unpaid workers (Gold 1971).

Conclusion: new patterns of citizenship

[...]
[...] An alternative view, that forms the basis of my conclusion, is that, while Marshall's world has disappeared, a new regime of rights has emerged that reflects these changed social conditions. In brief, the social rights of nation-states are being slowly replaced or, better still, augmented by human rights. First, these new forms of citizenship are not specifically located within the nation-state, and are typically connected with human rights legislation rather than with civic rights. The communities that support these rights are global, virtual and thin, rather than local and thick. Secondly, they arise because of social issues related to global changes and pressures, and in this sense are post-national, and finally they are conceptually interconnected, because they are driven by a common problem of modern society, namely the relationship between the human body and the environment (Turner 1993). The old causal mechanisms of Marshallian

citizenship – class conflict and mobilization for warfare – have been replaced by new causal processes that are more closely connected with social movements, status contradictions and identity. This set of human rights has evolved for two basic reasons. The problems of the global order, such as the global spread of AIDS or the pollution of the environment, cannot be solved by the unilateral action of individual governments, and secondly because the social risks of modern society that are created by new technologies (such as cloning or genetically modified food) do not fit easily into the existing politico-legal framework. Although Marshall's paradigm is now sociologically obsolete, I conclude by identifying three types of post-national citizenship that parallel the three components of citizenship in his original argument.

Global concern for the negative consequences of industrial capitalism on the natural environment has become a dominant issue of contemporary politics. Individual governments have, at various levels of intervention, attempted to protect their national populations from the effects of the industrialization of agricultural production, carbon dioxide emissions from motor vehicles, contamination from civil nuclear power or oil spillage from shipping disasters. Writing about the development of environmentalism in Britain, Howard Newby (1996) identified four stages in the emergence of 'environmental citizenship'. First, from the 1880s to the turn of the century, there was a concern for preservation as epitomized by the National Trust. Secondly, in the inter-war years there was growing criticism of *laissez-faire* economics among the middle class and an emphasis on regulation and the provision of amenities. Between the early 1960s and 1970s, environmental concerns were expressed in a third stage through the debate over post-materialism and the limits to growth through organizations such as Friends of the Earth and the Ecology Party. We might note in passing that, while membership of the Mothers' Union slumped between 1971 and 1990, membership of the Royal Society for the Protection of Birds increased from 98,000 to 890,000 and for the World Wildlife Fund for Nature, membership expanded from 12,000 to 219,000. Finally, in the late 1990s the British debate, that had been decidedly parochial, was challenged by the universal dimensions of global warming and, with a new emphasis on sustainability, the traditional language of amenity was replaced by a discourse of global catastrophe.

The widespread interest in the concept of 'risk society', that was made popular in the 1990s by the German sociologist Ulrich Beck (1992), captures the critical dimension of the ecological consciousness as a lack of confidence in expert opinion and lack of trust in government policy. The recent British debate about genetically modified food is a perfect example of green politics in which ecological citizenship is expressed as a right to a safe 'natural' environment. [Although] social rights were often the consequence of class-based activity, contemporary human rights are frequently the result of social or environmental movements that have diverse social memberships. Global and national social movements, rather than social class conflicts, appear to be relatively successful in bringing about the expansion of rights. It has been argued for example that in the case of Taiwan the causal connection between awareness of rights and the growth of participatory democracy is illustrated by the anti-nuclear power movement in the 1980s. Against a background of economic growth and political reform, the movement's leadership sought more than the establishments of liberal rights, they also promoted a new right: the right to a clean environment [...] (Huag 1999: 313). [...]

While the environmental lobby and the emergence of environmental or ecological citizenship were shaped by a sociological concern over the impact of industrial capitalism on the environment, the second dimension of this debate involved anthropological concern with the impact of capitalism and colonial powers, not only on the environment, but on human communities as such. The notion that unrestrained industrial capitalism had a negative impact on the natural environment was followed by obvious conclusion that the spread of capitalist agriculture had had devastating consequences for pre-modern tribal society. The destruction of 'primitive society' was not simply a consequence of military encounters or the ravages of European disease; it also involved the removal of aboriginal society from the land in order to create a global market in beef, sheep and cereals. [...] Aboriginal society has suffered from a lack of effective political leadership, mainly because internal language and cultural divisions have precluded a coherent response to white society. Perhaps the principal historical exception has been the Maori people of New Zealand who have been able, unlike Australian aboriginals, to unite behind a constitutional framework such as the Treaty of Waitangi. The political problem in essence is whether aboriginal people can or should be treated as citizens of the nation-state, or whether their political aspirations are better served by other legal means and political structures. After some 200 years of assimilation, it is not self-evident that the Australian aboriginals have achieved even second class citizenship in terms of health, education and political participation. Assimilation can also have another less desirable dimension, namely assimilation to alcohol, prostitution, tobacco and other drugs. In these circumstances, the social rights of citizenship will need to be augmented by international intervention and human rights legislation. An alternative view, therefore, might be that aboriginals are yet to receive any effective rights or to realize their claims.

[...] These emerging rights (to a safe environment, to aboriginal culture and land, and to ethnic identity) point to and are underpinned by a generic right, namely a right to ontological security. Human beings are characterized by their vulnerability and by the precarious character of their social and political arrangements (Turner 1993). Where life is nasty, brutish and short, citizenship functions to make this Hobbesian world more secure and civilized, but the irony of globalization is that in many respects our world is becoming more risky and precariousness, because the dangers of modern technology often outweigh its advantages. This generic right of ontological security is closely connected to questions of human embodiment, and thus this right of security is a right to human existence as such. It goes beyond the rights of reproductive citizenship to include the right to be respected. This right to ontological security underpins the other environmental, cultural and identity claims that have been characteristic of modern social movements (Heidegger 1977). Central to this analysis of technology is the vulnerability of human beings and the precariousness of their social world. The argument of this lecture is that our ontological security can only be safeguarded by a new set of values that embrace stewardship of the environment, care for the precariousness of human communities, respect for cultural differences and a regard for human dignity. In short, we need a set of obligations that correspond to the demand for human rights. [...]

Note: This article was originally given as an inaugural lecture at the University of Cambridge, 11 May 2000.

2
The Sustainability of Welfare States into the 21st Century*

Gosta Esping-Andersen

It is almost universally claimed that the welfare state has become unsustainable, a fetter on the economy, and concomitantly incapable of satisfying expressed social needs. Some see the solution in scaling back, possibly privatizing the welfare state; others advocate some form of citizen's income in place of the existing structure; still others see the solution in decentralization, community, or the 'third' sector. I will attempt to show that none of these scenarios promise, on their own, a 'win-win' solution, if by this we mean optimizing welfare and efficiency at the same time. A more effective – if politically difficult – adaptation to 'post-industrial society' calls for a substantial reordering of the priorities of the welfare *state* itself. This article addresses, in highly synoptic form, four issues: (a) a diagnosis of what causes unsustainability; (b) the identification of changing social needs; (c) an overview of welfare state adaptation in the past decade(s); and (d) an examination of competing win-win reform strategies.

Diagnosis of the ills of the welfare state

The welfare state has been declared to be in crisis since its very inception. What is novel today is that the roots of the crisis are three exogenous shocks that emanate from economic and societal transformation. The first, and possibly most widely cited, is the impact of accelerated economic internationalization. This includes three components, each of which has different effects. Financial globalization does not, *per se*, affect welfare state viability or its redistributive aims – if, that is, its finances are in order and a reasonable level of savings can be assured. Capital mobility may undercut employment in uncompetitive industries and may put pressure on governments to reduce taxation so as to avoid social dumping. The evidence for this, however, is rather mixed. Global trade (but especially technological

* From *International Journal of Health Services* 30(1) (2000): 1–12.

change) weakens the position of low-skilled workers who, with young people, are the main constituents of contemporary mass unemployment. For the welfare state, then, the main challenge that emanates from globalization is the need to keep public finances sound and to lower structural unemployment. The view that ambitious welfare aims are incompatible with the new global order is hardly persuasive. Indeed, the most advanced welfare states (such as the Nordic states) evolved in the most open economies of Europe. In fact, the chain of causality probably runs in the opposite direction: small, open economies adopted strong welfare states with a 'productivist' edge as a means to enhance their capacity to compete and adjust rapidly to global forces beyond their control.

The second shock comes from population aging. Most prognoses suggest that the cost of retirement as a percentage of GDP will double by 2040. The ratio of contributors to pension beneficiaries is rapidly deteriorating. The number of contribution years has shrunk and the number of beneficiary years has expanded.[1] Italy is the first country to arrive at parity, 1:1. Equally alarming is the growth of the highly care-intensive, ultra-aged (80+) population, which is doubling every 20 years. The aging problem is, however, frequently misdiagnosed. The real problem lies not in the number of old people, but in low fertility, early retirement, delayed first job entry, and low overall employment rates. Whether fertility rates are low, 1.2 or 1.4 (as in Italy, Spain, Germany, or Japan), or about 1.8 to 2.0 (as in Scandinavia, Ireland, and North America) makes a huge difference for welfare states' financial prospects. It also makes a difference whether typical retirement age is at 55 to 58 (as in continental Europe) or 60 to 65 (as in Scandinavia). What really counts is the activity rate. In the Nordic countries the ratio of contributors to pension recipients is around 2.5:1, even if the proportion of the aged is roughly similar to that in Italy, chiefly because employment population rates are high (70 to 75 percent): 10 to 20 percentage points above countries such as France, Germany, or Italy. The real problem, then, is how to stimulate fertility and maximize employment (or alternatively, finance future pension burdens through productivity growth). The aging problem in continental Europe is especially acute because of the preference for labor reduction as a strategy to manage industrial decline.

The third shock comes from family change and women's new economic role. Families are much less stable, and women often face severe trade-offs between employment and family obligations. Given that women's educational attainment today matches (and surpasses) men's, the opportunity cost of having children becomes very high (if care services are unavailable). The new 'atypical' family forms (especially single-parent) are often highly vulnerable to poverty; a high cost of children means low fertility. There is little doubt that almost all Scandinavian women work (the rate is 80 percent among mothers with small children) because of ample day care provision. Where two-earner households have become the norm, not only are activity and fertility rates higher, but the risk of child poverty is drastically reduced.[2]

The emerging 'post-industrial' needs structure

All post-war welfare states were premised on a set of basic assumptions about social risks and needs. Families could be assumed to be stable and able to live well on the earnings of the one male breadwinner. The family remained the chief welfare provider for children, the aged, and the infirm. This, in turn, was a realistic assumption because most men, including the less-skilled, could find well-paid and stable employment. Because of productivity gains, real earnings (and hence social contributions) rose steadily. To the post-war welfare state architects, therefore, the dominant social risks bundled on two fronts: healthcare and old age. By and large, the post-war model concentrated on one tail-end of the lifecourse because it was realistically assumed that labor markets and the family were problem-free.

The paradox today is that this aged-bias has strengthened considerably in many welfare states while family instability and mass unemployment have shifted the incidence of risk toward the young. The aged-bias is especially extreme in countries such as Japan, the United States, and most of continental Europe.[3] A shift in priorities toward young families is, in contrast, limited to a few welfare states, mainly the Nordic and the Antipodean.

In parallel fashion, the tension between careers and family responsibilities, the rise of single-parent households, and longer life expectancy all contribute to an intensive demand for social and caring services. Nonetheless, most welfare states (with the exception of Scandinavia and, partially, France and Belgium) are service-adverse and very transfer-biased. The private market can be a substitute, but only if costs are moderate. For a median-income family, markets for childcare and other social services are a realistic option in the United States but not in Europe.[4]

In brief, with few exceptions we witness a growing disjuncture between the emerging need structure and welfare state organization; to use contemporary jargon, we have a 'Fordist' welfare state in a 'post-industrial' society.

Divergent models of welfare state adaptation

The shifting needs structure and the exogenous shock-effects on the welfare state have been increasing in intensity over the past two decades. The ways in which welfare states have responded, so far, reflect mainly a logic of institutional path-dependency and median voter allegiance to accustomed benefits: traditional programs have been utilized to manage acute emerging problems (such as early retirement); the existing edifice is being sustained by going on the least unpleasant diet possible.

We can distinguish welfare state models or, better, 'welfare regimes' by how they allocate social responsibilities between state, market, and family (and, as a residual, non-profit 'third sector' institutions). In one group, basically the liberal, Anglo-Saxon nations, the accent is on a residual, minimal state and 'as much market as is possible.' Despite some (in practice modest) privatization of the welfare state, the most notable trend is to increase targeting. A common feature among the liberal welfare states is to introduce some form of negative income tax as a way to provide a minimum floor for the poor and low-wage workers, while strengthening incentives among the better-off to purchase private welfare. Yet, it is not clear whether the market has responded adequately. Apart from the huge gap in US healthcare coverage (40 million), there is a more ominous long-term erosion of what has, traditionally, been the mainstay of private social protection: employer occupation plans.[5] These are declining in part because of employer cost-containment strategies, in part because of union decline, and also for structural reasons (most new employment is in services and smaller firms). Hence, we see a clear drift from collective risk-pooling toward individual market solutions in pensions, health, and services.[6]

The second group includes the prototypical Scandinavian, universalistic welfare states whose stated aim has always been to marginalize the market in the provision of welfare. Since the 1960s there has also been a deliberate attempt to 'nationalize' the family, as Assar Lindbeck puts it; that is, to collectivize families' traditional caring burdens. The Nordic welfare states have become very service heavy: 30 to 35 percent of total social outlays go to servicing, as opposed to 5 to 15 percent on the European continent. The servicing emphasis is doubly important for labor market functioning: it allows for record high female employment (with fertility) and it creates – until recently – an expanding labor market, mainly for these very same women. Since around 1970, public services have accounted for 80 percent of total net job growth. The Nordic welfare states have also been more ready to adapt to the changing needs profile by redirecting resources and expanding public programs for young families: parental leave and active labor market policies in particular. While the liberal welfare regimes have undergone an individualization of welfare, the Nordic have clearly expanded the realm of collective provision. The little comparative evidence we have does show that the informal, non-profit sector plays a very small role in Scandinavia; so does family-provided welfare services. (Note, however, that governments (especially in Sweden, but now also in Denmark) have begun to actively encourage 'competition' from (regulated) non-governmental service providers in general, and cooperatives in particular.) One way to estimate this is to look at time-budget data. The average weekly 'unpaid domestic worktime' of a woman in Denmark is 25 hours, in contrast to about 35 hours in Germany and the United Kingdom, 45 hours in Italy, and a whopping 50 pours in Spain. Yet, Danish women have more children than women in any of the other nations! Scandinavia has clearly been most capable of adapting and redesigning its welfare states to address the emerging new needs structure. It is, however, increasingly difficult to sustain them financially. Paying equal wages for low-productivity services means a creeping cost-disease; subsidizing women's permanence in the labor market and their high fertility is extremely expensive. In a highly controversial study, Summer Rosen estimates that the total cost of maintaining working mothers with small children in Sweden is 50 percent higher than the value they produce. Even if we doubt this estimate, there is little doubt that the costs of securing adequate fertility rates in today's societies can be steep indeed.

In the third group, composed of most continental European countries, the welfare regime is characterized by its employment-linked (and therefore heavily male) social insurance and its reliance on familial care (the Catholic subsidiary principle). Private welfare plans are usually very marginal and so, strangely enough, is 'third sector' welfare (with the notable exception of Germany, where a significant share of healthcare is run by non-profit associations). Despite the active attempts of the Church to assert its dominance in the field of care and social assistance, Italy scores the lowest in available international rankings of third-sector size.[7] A unique continental European model of welfare state adaptation combines two basic elements. One utilizes pension plans (and other labor reduction policies) as the main instrument of managing industrial reconversion. The underlying strategy has been to safeguard the wages and job security of the core (male) workforce and to finance the cost of pensioning off the excess through the anticipated productivity dividend of a high-quality production strategy, to use Soskice's term. The second element is not so much adaptation as continuing to delegate emerging new social problems to families. One manifestation of this 'familialism' is the sustenance of the unemployed: in Italy, 95 percent of unemployed under age 35 continue to live with their parents (my estimates based on the 1993 Italian Household Expenditure Survey). The net consequences of this combined adaptation model can be summarized as follows: an overloaded and unsustainable social insurance system; a 'low-fertility equilibrium'; and a reinforcement of the insider-outsider split in the labor market. The high labor costs and pervasive job protection for the insiders (adult males) cause unemployment among their children and wives. Relying on the sole male breadwinner's income, families (and thus unions and the median voter) are logically reluctant to accept either labor market deregulation, more wage flexibility, or an erosion of social insurance benefits. Familializing welfare responsibilities can be as costly as collectivizing them.

The search for a sustainable win-win strategy

From this very cursory overview it is evident that all welfare states have responded to the new economic and social challenges mainly by muddling through, by building on traditional premises rather than radically redesigning their welfare architecture.[8] Most welfare states, therefore, have moved from a positive-sum to a negative-sum trade-off; they not only are increasingly unsustainable but are arguably hindering an optimal welfare-efficiency combination. Although clearly the most adaptable to the new political economy, the Nordic model has become fiscally unsustainable because it was premised on universal full employment and cannot cope with mass unemployment, and also because of the inbuilt 'Baumol cost-disease' effect that, in the long run, afflicts the cost of providing an immense network of social services. The liberal model, despite its low social expenditures but because of deregulation, is increasingly hard put to address growing inequalities and poverty (a monumental increase of non-aged post-transfer poverty has occurred in all the liberal welfare states since the early 1980s, especially in families with children in the United States and Britain). Rising poverty is concentrated in two (growing) strata: single-parent households and the less-skilled. Public benefits may be modest, but so are expected earnings. The liberal model is therefore vulnerable to poverty entrapment and tends to reproduce both poverty and a low-skilled 'post-industrial proletariat.' In the absence of proactive family and labor market policies, deregulation policies risk producing what Soskice calls a low-skill equilibrium. And, as we have noted, continental Europe faces probably a worst-scenario negative-sum relation between welfare, employment, and fertility.

Not surprisingly, then, most believe that a radical overhaul, an entirely new welfare principle, is urgently needed. If we follow the diagnosis of ills presented in the beginning of this article, any realistic win-win strategy must satisfy three aims: create employment (especially for youth, women, and the less-skilled), raise fertility, and protect families with young children. Here I argue that the prevailing, purportedly win-win strategies that are currently entertained (and often even followed) are not capable of simultaneously optimizing these three aims.

Let us first examine the single most popular strategy: privatizing welfare and deregulating labor markets. [...] [I]t is still arguable that less job protection and more flexible wages is positive for employment, at least for youth and the low-skilled. This is not, however, a win-win model because of the heavy social costs of poverty and wage inequality. Moreover, Europeans may be trapped in long-term unemployment, but Americans tend to become trapped in poor jobs and poverty, and this has powerful intergenerational effects in terms of life chances. Hence, the system is not superior in equity and equal opportunity. Privatizing welfare, moreover, does not necessarily result in more allocative efficiency. This becomes clear when we contrast two welfare state extremes: Sweden and the United States. [...] [T]here is convergence in terms of total resource use at both the macro- and micro-accounting level. The US model is, however, less Pareto-efficient when we consider the huge gaps in coverage and that healthcare absorbs almost twice as much of the GDP as in Sweden. (US household budget data show that an average-income household spends about 5 to 6 percent of its income on health insurance. This jumps to more than 15 percent for households in the bottom deciles.) A final and fundamental reason why privatization is problematic is that all but individual insurance is decreasingly realistic in the emerging economic structure. Collective welfare plans could thrive in an environment of large firms and powerful unions; in a service-dominated, down-scaled economic structure they are much more difficult to establish.

A second, increasingly popular, strategy involves some form of guaranteed citizen's income. For fiscal reasons, and to avoid negative work incentives, this almost invariably takes the form of a negative income tax (such as the family credit). In reality, a basic citizen's minimum is the favored solution among two very dissimilar groups. One, mainly on the European left, sees it as the answer to the emerging 'workless society.' Its underlying 'lump-sum of labor' assumption is blatantly erroneous. The liberal version, now becoming institutionalized in many nations, follows a very different philosophy – namely, giving income support and work incentives simultaneously to low-income families. It is a means of subsidizing low-wage workers, but also low-wage employers. It should therefore slow down productivity growth, and may even reinforce the low-skill equilibrium problem.

In the past decade, growing interest has evolved in the third sector as an alternative to public sector welfare provision. This has several potential advantages: unloading burdensome government finances, decentralizing welfare delivery, and introducing an element of competition. The third sector is an amalgam of many different forms of welfare production, such as voluntary associations, cooperatives, and various non-profit organizations. Only one part of the third sector is, in reality, devoted to social welfare production. Where the sector is large (as in Germany and the United States), this is mainly due to a large network of established non-profit corporations (such as Blue Cross-Blue Shield) or cooperative movements. Otherwise, third-sector welfare is typically concentrated on the 'margins' where the welfare state often fails – aid to drug users or clandestine immigrants, for example. The role of voluntary workers can be significant, but really viable third-sector providers count on paid personnel and this implies reliance on user fees and public financial support. Hence, as a viable strategy of shifting responsibilities, it is unlikely to bring about substantial savings. The gains will mainly come from more decentralization and perhaps a stronger element of competition, but a third-sector strategy does not help resolve the basic dilemmas outlined in this article.

How, then, can we envisage a win-win strategy? How can we combine 'equality' with employment growth and high fertility? At first glance, a Scandinavian welfare model would appear positive-sum in this respect: it has universalized the dual-earner household (which sharply reduces poverty while raising families' consumption of services, thus generating jobs) and provides the services and financial incentives for working women to have children. This is of course very costly, but whether this is covered through the public budget or household expenses is essentially a problem of cost-shifting and how to pool social risks in society most effectively. The more we individualize the cost of children, the more likely we will find ourselves in a low-fertility equilibrium.

At second glance, however, the Nordic formula has an inbuilt Achilles' heel: a long-term barrier to job growth that stems from labor market regulation in general and egalitarian wages in particular. If more earnings inequality is a precondition for the growth of labor-intensive private services, we are back to the fundamental trade-off between equality and jobs. But are we?

One way to think of a win-win strategy is to recall Schumpeter's famous analogy of the autobus: always full of people, but always different people. Low wages, unpleasant work, and even poverty are not necessarily diswelfare if there is a guarantee against entrapment. If people are mobile and exit at the next bus stop, low-end jobs will have no consequences for overall life chances. The welfare state as we know assumed that the labor market would provide well-paid (but not necessarily enjoyable) jobs for all. It put its faith in simple human capital theory and delegated the responsibility of life chances to basic education and to the labor market. This assumption is anachronistic in a post-industrial labor market that is subject to very rapid technological change and can promise full employment only if we accept a mass of low-end (and low-productivity) service jobs. Income maintenance policies may help dampen income inequalities by subsidizing low-wage workers, but they do not help these workers to get off at the next bus stop. As we all know, mobility today requires the possession of skills and the capacity to be trained. And, as we also know, there is a basic problem of market failure regarding skill formation.[9] If, as the OECD shows, about 15 to 20 percent of the US adult labor force is functionally illiterate, even among high school graduates, we clearly also have a problem of public sector failure.

A Pareto-optimal strategy for recasting the welfare state does suggest itself. First, neither privatization nor familialization are Pareto-optimal. This implies that a comprehensive welfare state (with or without an extensive third sector) is unavoidable. Second, such a strategy must optimize both fertility and employment and minimize poverty risks. And it must do so in an economic environment that cannot guarantee well-paid jobs for all. Full employment implies more wage inequality. As we have seen, the maximization of employment and fertility is possible, albeit very costly. To a degree this can be offset by the enlarged tax base, to a degree by cost-shifting strategies. On the one hand, as we have seen, two earner households enjoy dramatically lower poverty risks (implying savings in both a static and dynamic sense). On the other hand, contemporary pension systems often represent a massive misallocation of resources. The average Italian pensioner receives a retirement income that is 30 percentage points above average consumption outlays. This is, of course, a source of savings, but it is also a perverse mechanism of income redistribution (and savings can be induced elsewhere). A reallocation of resources from old to young families is potentially Pareto-optimal because it satisfies the goal of fertility, maximum employment, and lessened poverty risks – if, that is, these resources are used to help families with children reconcile work and fertility. The key missing link in this strategy is the jobs-equality trade-off, a trade-off that will remain as long as we are wedded to an 'equality for all, here and now' notion of egalitarianism. As hinted above, this trade-off can be surmounted by a redefinition of what equality means, namely some kind of guarantee against entrapment in low-paid employment. We know that this necessitates a massive investment in education and skills, in making people 'trainable' in the first place.

We can all outline blueprints for reform. The bottom-line issue is essentially political: how can political majorities be mobilized for a reform that may be *societally* Pareto-optimal, but not necessarily so at the individual or group level? Trade unions and political parties aggregate the interests of a median voter who is rapidly getting older and older, a median voter whose definition of welfare and social justice reflects the kind of welfare state that was built in the post-war decades. As we have witnessed in recent years in Italy, France, Germany, and Spain, the make-up of the median voter and the interest representation system favors a politics of going on the least unpleasant diet possible.

This article is adapted from a paper published by the Fundacio Rafael Campalans, Barcelona, 1999

Notes

1. A simple comparison of the standard male life course in the 1950s and today is illuminating. When modern pension systems were designed in the post-war years, the average male was typically employed from age 16 to 65, followed by about 7 to 8 years of retirement. Given education and youth unemployment, today's workers start their 'real' careers around 20 to 25; early retirement means that they retire at age 55 to 58. And male longevity has risen by 8 years. All in all, we have cut contribution years by 15 or 20 years and have extended pension years by about the same.

2. In most countries for which we have comparable and reliable data, child poverty tends to be three or four times higher in one-earner families (my calculations from LIS data bases). There is also substantial evidence from the United States that the heightened earnings polarization and the rise of low-paid employment have been offset by a growth in spouses' labor supply.

3. A case can be made for acute misallocation of national resources. According to my analyses of Italian Household Expenditure data, the average pensioner receives an income that is over 30 percent higher than what he or she consumes. A similar case of overshooting the target has been identified for Finland and Spain. The consequence may be a perverse system of secondary income distribution, whereby the young depend on transfers from their parents and grandparents. The relative welfare of the young will, of course, come to mirror the economic success of their forebears; in other words, the welfare state may be reinforcing class inheritance.

4. The problem here is akin to the Baumol (1967) cost-disease effect in services. If long-run productivity gains in services lag behind manufacturing while real wage growth is parallel, labor-intensive services will gradually price themselves out of the market. This is precisely the situation in contemporary Europe (except for the Nordic countries, where welfare services are furnished by the public sector).

5. US occupational welfare coverage was, in the 1970s, about 70 percent for health and 50 percent for pensions. Today, the former has dropped to about 50 percent, the latter to 30 percent (excluding individual plans).

6. For lack of adequate state, market, and family social provision, one might assume that the non-profit sector acts as a substitute. True, comparative data show that voluntary, non-profit social protection is considerably larger in the United States than in most European countries. Much of it is of the not-for-profit Blue Cross-Blue Shield type. Yet, even if relatively large and abundantly tax-favored, non-profit associations are not even remotely capable of filling the welfare void.

7. Moreover, voluntary associations in Italy are invariably concentrated in the North (where need is lower) and very marginal in the South. This, as I shall argue below, reflects an inherent weakness of a third-sector welfare strategy: voluntary and cooperative welfare organizations rely on ample public funding and support and also on a strong social capital infrastructure – something that tends to be lacking exactly where most needed.

8. Some partial exceptions are New Zealand, Australia, and the United Kingdom, which have attempted to redesign their social contract, mainly by privatizing and by heavier targeting of social benefits. As Pierson has shown, the practical results pale next to the intended aims.

9. Recent data suggest that employer-provided training is much lower in the United States than in either Europe or Japan.

3

Social Politics and Policy in an Era of Globalization: Critical Reflections*

Nicola Yeates

This paper critically examines the debate on the relationship between 'globalization', social politics and social policy.

[...] I argue that the emerging debate on globalization and welfare states shares many of the flaws that can be found in globalization theory, notably with respect to the exaggeration of the strength and degree of unity of capital interests, the underestimation of the powers of the state and of both countervailing changes and oppositional political forces to globalization more generally [...]. I suggest that the enduring power of 'local' factors to impact on and mediate globalization suggests that national institutional, cultural and political differences are likely to prevail rather than be eliminated under the weight of global, 'external' forces necessitating a particular course of action.

The discussion then moves on to propose an alternative way of approaching the relationship between globalization and social policy. I argue that a global governance perspective better captures the implications of globalization for social policy because, first, it permits recognition of the multiple levels and spheres (local, national, transnational, supranational and global) and the range of actors (state and non-state) in the social policy process, and second, it captures the dialectical relationship between global and local political forces in shaping globalization as a project and as a process. This global governance framework is applied to illustrate the relationship between social politics, social policy and globalization, and I show that a number of social dialogues and political strategies, of quite different types, are taking place with global capital. Overall, the paper emphasizes a nuanced account of the dynamics of the relationship between globalization and social policy which recognizes the role of ideology and politics, the dialectical relationship between global and local, and the enduring resilience of local political forces.

---

* From *Social Policy & Administration* 33(4) (1999): 372–93

Globalization: global capital against national states

[...]

At the heart of what may be termed 'globalization studies' lies the problematic nature, status and powers of the national state in the contemporary world political and economic order. A number of related questions stand out. One set of questions has focused on whether, and the extent to which, the balance of power between states and capital has shifted to the benefit of capital – and global capital in particular. Another set has focused on how significant the national state is as a sphere of social activity and how effective governments can be in economic management. States are locked into an unprecedented scale and depth of both interdependence and competitiveness, but their capacity to effectively manage both the global, 'borderless' economy and their own 'national' economies is said to be diminished. A third set of questions has focused on whether the state is being hollowed out, is withering away, or is 'in retreat'. Few predict the actual demise of the state, and the debate has focused more on the retreat of the state *relative* to other forms of authority in the global political economy and the extent that this will cause it to undergo transformation and adaptation.

One's position on the issue of the consequences of globalization for the state and for the welfare state is likely to hinge on the acceptance of a qualitative shift from the 'old' international order based on inter-national relations primarily between nation states, to a 'new', globalized order characterized by 'global relations between organized capitals' under which relations between national states are subsumed (Teeple 1995). At its crudest, globalization theory views the world economy as dominated by uncontrollable global economic forces where the principal actors are transnational corporations which owe no allegiance to any state and (re)locate wherever market advantage exists (i.e. where profits can be maximized). [...]

[...] Overall, 'strong' globalization theories stress the primacy of global forces over national or 'local' ones, and the primacy of economic forces over political ones. National states are deemed to have become instruments of global capital: international trade and investment bear a disproportionate amount of influence over the direction and content of national policy, so much so that governments are as sensitive or 'accountable' to the requirements of international capital as to their electorates. It is important to note that those who advance claims of 'strong' globalization come from both the right and left, politically; the former celebrate what the latter condemn.

A number of welcome counter-arguments have been made against 'strong' globalization theory which cast doubt on predictions about the diminished capacities of the state as a 'logical', inevitable outcome of the globalization process. 'Strong' globalization theory is deemed to be wildly overstated, speculative and ahistorical, which is problematic in terms of its validity, accuracy and the degree of generalization from short-term, cyclical or local changes involved. A principal criticism has focused on the way in which 'globalization' is depicted as something 'new' and uncontrollable [...] Hirst and Thompson (1996a) show that current levels of trade and investment are actually little higher than at the beginning of the 20th century, that much of what is passed off as 'globalization' amounts to no more than the intensification of existing exchanges between distinct national entities, and that capital flows have firmly remained within the Triad of Western Europe, North America and East Asia.

A further failing of 'strong' globalization theory is its assumption of a predetermined economic 'logic'. This renders it vulnerable to accusations of being a totalizing theory and a crude form of economic determinism, particularly the representation of globalization as a homogeneous and unitary process (Hirst and Thompson 1996a; Patel and Pavitt 1991; Green 1997). 'Strong' globalization portrays capital as a unified force, whereas capital is as fragmented and fractured as the forces it faces globally. For example, foreign direct investment in a productive plant in a peripheral country has very different interests than speculative capital that flows into real estate and currency speculation. Domestic and global capital also have different interests; domestic capital has often been at the forefront of arguments for greater, not less, protectionism.

Furthermore, the economic determinism of strong globalization underestimates the continued importance of politics in the globalization process. The depiction of the huge resources of capital and its ability to leave the 'bargaining table' and set up elsewhere has been exaggerated. Most 'global' corporations are still decidedly national in their location and make-up (Ruigrok and Van Tulder 1995; De Angelis 1997). [...] Capital is dependent on states to perform a range of functions that secure the conditions in which it can operate: the enforcement of property rights and the provision of infrastructure, education, training and the maintenance of social stability. Anyone who is in doubt of the powers of states need only look to their role in the downfall of the Multilateral Agreement on Investment (MAI). The MAI, if successful, would have significantly strengthened the powers of capital over states by allowing 'investment rights' even where it was against national or broader social interests (Sanger 1998).

A related point about the importance of the state in shaping globalization, rather than merely 'receiving' it, is the idea that much of the literature on globalization has focused on unifying economic and technological processes as evidence of greater global interdependence. In so doing, it has neglected the more fragmented political and social spheres which point to more moderate claims about the nature of 'globalization' as well as offering important evidence of resistance to it. Although recent economic trends may be correctly identified, it is not clear how these relate to long-term structural changes, or how they are moderated by counterchanges or opposing forces. On this point, Green argues that 'the dialectic of history is missing... globalization theory has a strong tendency towards economism, reading the political off unproblematically from what it takes to be inevitable economic trends.' (1997: 157). [...]

Global economic forces, then, should not automatically be elevated above, or assumed to steamroll over, 'local' factors and forces which are internal to states and which can restrict both the state's and capital's margin of operation. These 'local' forces include the nature and strength of ideologies, social movements and traditions within countries which may resist or oppose 'investment' by global capital and the implementation of the policies of international institutions. Neither have been unopposed, and inhabitants of affected countries have responded with civil and political unrest, with the result that 'the new uprisings of the world's poor have altered the international political economy' (Walton 1987: 384). [...]

The impact of globalization on the welfare state

[...] International economic forces are said to have eroded the 'domestic' economic (and political) basis and conditions that have historically underpinned the welfare state. The relocation of corporations from 'high-cost' to 'low-cost' countries impacts on the employment structure in the exited country, leaving behind unemployment and a fiscal deficit, while the transnational nature of economic activity makes its control and taxation much more difficult (Perraton *et al.* 1997). Stryker (1998) identifies a number of ways in which the structure and operation of the global economy may shape national social policy. First, financial globalization exacerbates the structural dependence of the state on all forms of capital (domestic and foreign). Second, globalized financial and productive capital increase the perceived risk, or the credibility of the threat, of capital flight. Third, financial integration reduces the possibilities for national states to pursue expansionary economic policies to cushion unemployment and encourages them to pursue fiscal austerity. Fourth, the global economy has severed the link between domestic economic growth and full employment in First World countries – the concerns for private profit do not sit easily alongside national economic and employment health (witness record profits alongside redundancies). The fifth factor that Stryker identifies is an ideological one, and is possibly the most important of all – the transnational diffusion of neoliberalism. This stresses the 'complete impotence or perversity of national level economic and social policy making', and encourages governments to believe they cannot change the structure, operation or outcomes of the global economy and must therefore conform with the requirements of international competitiveness (reduce or remove barriers to trade, reduce the size and cost of the state, taxation and welfare) (Stryker 1998: 8–9).

Contemporary globalization, it is argued, alters the internal dynamics of welfare state development and heralds the decline of social democratic reformist politics and projects upon which the welfare state was built (Teeple 1995; Rhodes 1996). The balance of 'external', global influences to 'internal', national ones (e.g. demography, labour markets, the balance of political forces) is held to have altered in favour of the former. As Ash Amin argues, 'state policy *is* becoming more and more driven by external forces' (1996: 129, original italics). The range of 'structurally viable' policy options has not only been narrowed by economic forces but state policy will be primarily oriented to supporting market forces and promoting economic competitiveness. Governments will increasingly stay clear of radical programmes of redistribution, renationalization or other forms of intervention that capital does not 'approve' of. The outcome will be 'the retrenchment of national state intervention in spheres of social reproduction' (Teeple 1995: 5). Those that stray too far from these parameters will be punished electorally and economically due to loss of investment and employment and will leave themselves vulnerable to lower credit ratings, higher interest rates on borrowing, as well as currency speculation by international financial markets (Andrews 1994; Goodman and Pauly 1993; Stewart 1984).

[...] A major problem with these predictions about the power of the global economic forces, in particular global capital, to force a particular course of action is that they share many of the assumptions of 'strong' globalization theories insofar as they regard globalization as an 'external', naturalistic phenomenon; assume that capital interests are unified; assign a determinant degree of power to (global) economic forces over the course of (national) political action; and assume that globalization is a force primarily of unification. The criticisms levied against 'strong' globalization theories [...] suggest that the political and economic resources of global capital to directly determine individual states' public policies have been exaggerated and that globalization is not homogeneous or unitary in process or effect, either within or across states. Indeed, the issue is far more complex than one of simple causality for the reasons I have just described, as well as for the reasons outlined below.

Of prime importance, first of all, is ideology. [...] Neoliberal ideology emphasizes the limited influence and effect that governments can exert over national economic performance or in subverting the 'natural' outcomes of global markets, while stressing the costs of certain courses of political action: economic success (and prosperity) or failure (and hardship) in an interdependent and competitive global economy is seen as depending on maintaining a competitive advantage. From here it is but a short step to making explicit links between the extent and nature of state provision and delivery of welfare and national economic competitiveness. Stryker (1998: 11) argues that the impact of globalization on welfare states occurs *primarily* through ideological shifts which in turn cause national expenditure reductions, privatization and marketization in some social welfare programs. However, even here, he asserts that the evidence over the past 20 years of left governments slowing welfare expansion and/or embarking on austerity programs 'does not prove the idea that financial globalization and global diffusion of market-oriented cultural ideals facilitate welfare state retrenchment. But it is consistent with these ideas' (1998: 11). On a similar line, Jordan (1998) also notes the consistency between the 'new politics of welfare' of the British and American governments which put the wage-relation at the center of welfare reform, and globalization which also hinges on the wage-relation. Ultimately, it seems, at best we may be able to demonstrate consistency rather than causality.

Ideology, rather than crude economic determinism, is important, therefore, in any explanation of the impact of globalization on welfare states. Policymakers' beliefs, values and assumptions about the global economy are shaped by ideology: they may believe that particular interventions will prompt speculation on the national currency, mass capital flight abroad, or a downturn in investment by foreign firms. Moran and Wood (1996) refer to this framing of social policy by ideas and beliefs about national competitiveness in the global economy as 'contextual internationalization'. The contemporary welfare state 'dilemma' can be attributed to the political power of economic ideas, in particular neoliberal ideas, which have shaped perceptions of global economic 'logics' and foreclosed 'the parameters of the politically possible' (Hay 1998: 529). Jordan similarly argues that 'the idea of a global market is probably even more powerful than global forces themselves; governments believe that they are competing for prizes in budgetary rectitude before a panel of international financial institutions, and this affects their actions' (1998: 9).

The second reason why it is not possible to establish causality is that states have other functions than economic ones and governments have to respond to a wider range of constituencies than just the international business community. These 'local' factors are decisive rather than incidental in determining the content of public and social policy and how sweeping any reforms may be. These 'local' factors include the political and institutional constellation of national welfare states, historical and cultural traditions, social structures, electoral politics, the partisan nature of government, the presence of strong 'veto players', and the internal structure of the state (Esping-Andersen 1996; Rhodes 1996; Hallerberg and Basinger 1998; Garrett 1998). Other 'local' factors mediating the way in which globalization is 'received' also include the degree of integration of the national economy into the international economy and the particular species of capitalism that has developed nationally.

The emphasis on welfare retrenchment, residualization and marketization as an *inevitable* and *direct* outcome of globalization may also be somewhat misplaced for the reason that the attention to unifying forces of economic change masks counterchanges. Cerny (1997) argues that although states may indeed become oriented towards maintaining economic competitiveness – indeed, he predicts the rise of 'competition states' – they may become more, not less, interventionist in certain spheres. They may become more authoritarian in policing the consequences of economic globalization – poverty, marginalization and crime. In fact, far from overriding pressures for the state to reduce its welfare effort, a range of pressures to expand the scope of public policy intervention may be placed on governments to counteract marginalization and promote social integration, equality and justice. Public (social) expenditure may increase as a direct consequence of policies that pursue economic competitiveness (Garrett and Mitchell 1996, cited in Wilding 1997), while social protection programs may be extended to cushion individuals, households and communities against increased economic risk. It is not evident that the predominant theme, or the only way forward, is marketization, as the recent nationalization of care insurance in Germany has illustrated.

Global governance and social policy

[...] Global governance is predominantly associated with 'the development of international organizations and global institutions which attempt to address such issues' (Bretherton 1996: 8). Governments collaborate with each other through cooperative arrangements in conjunction with, and through, international governmental organizations; they operate within a complex legal and political framework of international agreements, treaties, regulations and accords regulating economic exchange and accumulation between countries (Townsend and Donkor 1996). [...]

International economic and trade institutions – notably the International Monetary Fund, the World Bank and GATT/WTO – have exerted a more tangible influence on states and national policies than has global capital. Government policies are legally bound to comply with the principles and regulations of international governmental organizations, international and supranational organizations (World Bank, IMF, UN system, EU, WTO). These institutions possess substantial financial and legal powers to regulate the international economy; they underwrite the conditions and patterns of international economic investment, production and exchange, set the parameters of national macroeconomic policy and, through this, largely determine the terms and conditions of social development (Townsend and Donkor 1996). They may override nation states' juridical sovereignty by, for example, legally obliging legislation of signatory states to conform with international principles. The economic and foreign-trade policies of states signed up to multilateral trade agreements are subject to enforceable WTO rules on 'free trade'. WTO rules restrict the range of policies that can be pursued nationally, even forbidding certain policies and courses of action if they present a barrier to the 'free' trade of foreign capital locally (e.g. subsidies, social and environmental legislation) (Nader and Wallach 1996).

There is, of course, nothing new about international governmental institutions, which have been in existence for over a century and have coexisted with major periods of welfare-state-building in the advanced industrialized countries. What appears to differ now is that one species of capitalism – global 'free trade' – is being sponsored by international institutions to compete with other species of capitalism (e.g. socially-regulated capitalism) that have historically developed at national level (Gray 1998). One notable example of this is the conditions attached to the receipt of economic aid from the World Bank and IMF. These include the implementation of economic and social reform ('structural adjustment'), common elements of which are the reduction of public sector debt, expenditure and subsidies, deregulation, and the reduction of public service provision. The policy autonomy of governments in such countries has been undermined by the imposition of a particular model of social and economic development which prohibits them from acting to protect the social cohesion of their societies.

Although global governance is predominantly associated with the institutional framework of national states and international bureaucracies, a far wider range of actors participate in global governance. In its broadest sense, global governance refers to all non-state sources of 'authority' which have the power to allocate values and influence the distribution of resources: outlaw business organizations (such as drug cartels, the mafia); professional associations; transnational authorities in sports, art, music; transnational social, political and religious movements (Strange 1996). The Commission on Global Governance (1995: 3) also includes as actors in global governance non-governmental organizations, citizens' movements, multinational organizations, the global capital market and even the global mass media. Non-governmental organizations, for example, are increasingly seeking legitimacy, and justification for their rights claims, from the global as well as the national arena. They have helped raise the profile of social issues on international agendas (notably, social development, the environment, equality, poverty and population), and generally shape international responses to global problems. They also have formal channels of influence, working through bodies such as the UN Commission on Human Rights and the Commission on the Status of Women (Holton 1998; Gordenker and Weiss 1996). Whether or not NGOs' participation in global governance can be considered evidence of the existence of a 'global civil society', it is certainly evidence of the globalization of political and social action.

[...] The European Union is another example of the ways that the changing institutional and political processes affect social policy. The European Union has been characterized as a system of multitiered governance (Pierson and Leibfried 1995). Although its institutional architecture is predominantly intergovernmental, states are only one, if an important, player amongst other non-state authorities, such as the EU administrative, political and legal institutions, business organizations, trades unions and non-governmental organizations. Political action is 'now having to be carried out through a web of common institutions, states, regional and local authorities and voluntary associations on the domestic front and simultaneously, in national and/or transnational alliances at the common level' (Meehan 1992: 159). Such alliances may consist of domestic interests, that may be antagonistic at times, against another state, or they may be bound by a 'shared interest among civil associations in promoting a common policy against the wishes of their respective governments' (1992: 159; Streeck 1995). The consequences of European political integration are that social policy (agenda-setting, consultation, policy-making, policy implementation and delivery) is no longer confined and controlled within the national sphere. Transnational alliances and formalized channels of influence over the content and direction of supranational social policy have introduced new dynamics into social policy development nationally (Streeck 1995). 'Sovereign' welfare states have been transformed into 'semi-sovereign' welfare states, or parts of multitiered systems of social policy (Leibfried and Pierson 1995, 1996) through: 'positive' social policy initiatives to construct areas of competence for uniform social standards at EU level (e.g. gender equality, health and safety); 'negative' social policy reform *via* the imposition of market compatibility requirements (labour mobility and coordination, freedom of services, regional and sectoral subsidies); and indirect (*de facto*) pressures of integration that force adaptation of national welfare states (social dumping, tax harmonization, stages of EMU) (1996: 187).

Global social dialogues and the social regulation of globalization

[...]

Global social policy has emerged as a consequence of two interrelated processes: global politics have become 'socialized' – 'the major agenda issues at intergovernmental meetings are now in essence social (and environmental) questions' (Deacon *et al.* 1997: 3); social policy has become 'globalized' – international institutions are essentially preoccupied with issues such as poverty, employment, health and welfare, and with 'the best way to regulate capitalism in the interests of social welfare East and West, North and South' (1997: 195). As in the EU where the social policy debate has focused on the choice to be made between Anglo-American-style welfare capitalism and continental Western European-style welfare capitalism, so the global political arena has also become a battleground over which contemporary ideological struggles about the role and the future of welfare states are fought out.

Deacon, Stubbs and Hulse argue that national social policy and social development are increasingly decided by international institutions: 'the social policy of a country or locality... is increasingly shaped... by the implicit and explicit social policies of numerous supranational agencies, ranging from global institutions like the World Bank and the International Monetary Fund, through supranational bodies such as the OECD and the European Commission, to supranational non-government agencies like OXFAM' (1997: 10). However, even here, they acknowledge that much is still contingent on local factors. In the countries of Central and Eastern Europe, for example, international institutions have been instrumental in restructuring post-communist social policy, but the social policy prescriptions of the IMF have been accepted and implemented because they are consistent with the interests of national bureaucratic and political elites. In short, the national sphere is still a decisive site of struggle, and 'external' forces – be they capital or international institutions – are dependent on the 'ideological integration' of local political elites into the international economy.

Deacon's work on the social dialogue at the global level has been extremely useful in mapping the dominant political and ideological positions of different international institutions in the debate on how globalization should be socially regulated. [...] However, of notable importance in the context of the present discussion is that their work has showed that the 'socialization of global politics' in no way signals the emergence of a unitary view about the role of welfare states or about their future development. [...] Competing discourses emerge from within the same institution, while institutional prescriptions vary according to the world-region in which they are embedded. Thus the prescriptions of the EU and ILO reflect their continental European origins, while those of the IMF reflect its US origins (Deacon *et al.* 1997). This very diversity warns us against apocalyptic interpretations of globalization as 'the end of politics', or as a unifying, hegemonic force. However, Deacon *et al.*'s research also confirms that the range of welfare alternatives backed by these institutions is confined to variants of social liberalism, and there is a marked absence of any institution arguing a social democratic or redistributive welfare agenda.

The work of Deacon and his colleagues on the social policies of international institutions has been pioneering. Their focus can be explained by the fact that it is at this level that the most obvious attempt is being made to formulate global social policy; but it is also a result of the institutionalist tendency in social policy analysis itself. However, this approach must be supplemented to explain the complexity of levels at which global social policy occurs and operates as well as the dialectical relationship between these levels. The focus on social politics and policy at the level of international institutions draws attention to the more visible actors, but in its emphasis on the forces and initiatives to modify 'globalization from above' the forces against 'globalization from below' are neglected (Falk 1997). It confines our view only to the social dialogue that takes place at international level and excludes other 'social dialogues' taking place at different levels and in various locations outside the boardrooms and bureaux of international institutions. A similar type of 'global social dialogue' has been going on between social movements in the shadow congresses that now accompany meetings of the G8, such as the Other Economy summit. Nor is this dialogue purely reactive; the International Encounter against Neoliberalism, for example, was brought together in response to calls from Zapatistas and social and political activists from a wide variety of countries. Another type of global social dialogue has been facilitated by the development of the internet; this technological factor makes global dialogue easier for highly disparate and isolated groups, many of whom cannot afford international travel.

In fact, a range of strategies and initiatives to regulate globalization can be identified, [—]. Some of these seek not to oppose globalization but instead seek negotiated reform, working with and through international institutions and/or corporations. The Trades Union Advisory Committee to the OECD has argued for more effective global social governance by strengthening the 'social dimension' of globalization (Evans n.d.). Social clauses have been central to these attempts to strengthen the social regulation of global capital. [...]

Other strategies which engage in a 'social dialogue' with global capital take the form of direct action, often through the market mechanism. Market-based strategies include international campaigns by consumer groups and NGOs to bring about improved standards for groups of workers in particular industries by mobilizing consumers to redirect their spending power away from offending companies' products. [...]

Global social politics also includes strategies of outright opposition and disruptive action at the local level, for example against local branches of transnational corporations. Numerous examples of such action can be cited, for example, of various tribal and indigenous groups and NGOs which have taken their concerns to the AGMs of transnational companies such as RTZ (Rio Tinto Zinc), Shell, BP and Monsanto. With genetic engineering, for example, which can be expected to have far-reaching social, economic and environmental effects, the introduction of new technology by capital on a global scale, often aided by permissive state regulation of this technology, has encountered a range of popular opposition strategies. Just as globalization prompts a variety of national responses, so a variety of national opposition strategies have arisen in relation to genetically modified foods. Here, the types of resistance vary geographically: in England, consumer boycotts and activist attacks on test crops have been the principal forms of resistance; in Asia and Europe, opposition has developed on an ideological level, often with a religious basis; in India resistance has taken the form of attacks on companies by mass farmers' organizations.

[...] Demands and movements for local economic autonomy, self-sufficiency and economic nationalism may also be regarded as forms of resistance and opposition to globalization. At the local level, self-help and community groups, cooperative movements have mobilized to fill in the gaps left by the failure of capitalism to provide employment. In both the First and Third Worlds alike new forms of local economic organization and cooperation have emerged amongst the poor (Rowbotham and Miller 1994; Norberg-Hodge 1996). Local exchange trading systems (LETS) and local currency schemes which strive to relocalize the economy can be regarded as a symbolic and practical response to the local social and economic consequences of globalization.' [—] (Paccione 1997: 1179–80; Meeker-Lowry 1996).

[...]

Acknowledgment

I would like to thank Tomas Mac Sheoin for his helpful comments and suggestions on early drafts of this paper.

Part II
Regulating Global Capital

4
Some Contradictions of the Modern Welfare State*

Claus Offe

The welfare state has served as the major peace formula of advanced capitalist democracies for the period following the Second World War. This peace formula basically consists, first, in the explicit obligation of the state apparatus to provide assistance and support (either in money or in kind) to those citizens who suffer from specific needs and risks which are characteristic of the market society; such assistance is provided as a matter of legal claims granted to the citizens. Second, the welfare state is based on the recognition of the formal role of labor unions both in collective bargaining and the formation of public policy. Both of these structural components of the welfare state are considered to limit and mitigate class conflict, to balance the asymmetrical power relation of labor and capital, and thus to overcome the condition of disruptive struggle and contradictions that was the most prominent feature of pre-welfare state, or liberal, capitalism. In sum, the welfare state has been celebrated throughout the post-war period as the political solution to societal contradictions.

Until quite recently, this seemed to be the converging view of political elites both in countries in which the welfare state is fully developed (for example, Great Britain, Sweden), and in those where it is still an incompletely realized model. Political conflict in these latter societies, such as the USA, was not centered on the basic desirability and functional indispensability, but on the pace and modalities of the implementation of the welfare state model.

This was true, with very minor exceptions, until the mid-1970s. From that point on we see that in many capitalist societies this established peace formula itself becomes the object of doubts, fundamental critique, and political conflict. It appears that the most widely accepted device of political problem-solving has itself become problematic, and that, at any

* From Claus Offe, *Contradictions of the Welfare State*, ed. John Keane. Boston: MIT (1984): 147–61.

rate, the unquestioning confidence in the welfare state and its future expansion has rapidly vanished. It is to these doubts and criticisms that I will direct our attention. The point to start with is the observation that the almost universally accepted model of creating a measure of social peace and harmony in European post-war societies has itself become the source of new contradictions and political divisions in the 1970s.

Historically, the welfare state has been the combined outcome of a variety of factors which change in composition from country to country. Social democratic reformism, Christian socialism, enlightened conservative political and economic elites, and large industrial unions were the most important forces which fought for and conceded more and more comprehensive compulsory insurance schemes, labor protection legislation, minimum wages, the expansion of health and education facilities and state-subsidized housing, as well as the recognition of unions as legitimate economic and political representatives of labor. These continuous developments in Western societies were often dramatically accelerated in a context of intense social conflict and crisis, particularly under war and post-war conditions. The accomplishments which were won under conditions of war and in post-war periods were regularly maintained and added to them were the innovations that could be introduced in periods of prosperity and growth. In the light of the Keynesian doctrine of economic policy, the welfare state came to be seen not so much as a burden imposed upon the economy, but as a built-in economic and political stabilizer which could help to regenerate the forces of economic growth and prevent the economy from spiralling downward into deep recessions. Thus, a variety of quite heterogeneous ends (ranging from reactionary pre-emptive strikes against the working-class movement in the case of Bismarck to socialist reformism in the case of the Weimar social democrats; from the social-political consolidation of war and defense economies to the stabilization of the business cycle, etc.) converged on the adoption of identical institutional means which today make up the welfare state. It is exactly its multifunctional character, its ability to serve many conflicting ends and strategies simultaneously, which made the political arrangement of the welfare state so attractive to a broad alliance of heterogeneous forces. But it is equally true that the very diversity of the forces that inaugurated and supported the welfare state could not be accommodated forever within the institutional framework which today appears to come increasingly under attack. The machinery of class compromise has itself become the object of class conflict.

The attack from the Right

The sharp economic recession of the mid-1970s has given rise to an intellectually and politically powerful renaissance of neo-*laissez-faire* and monetarist economic doctrines. These doctrines amount to a fundamental critique of the welfare state that is seen to be the illness of what it pretends to be the cure: rather than effectively harmonizing the conflicts of a market society, it exacerbates them and prevents the forces of social peace and progress (namely, the forces of the market-place) from functioning properly and beneficially. This is said to be so for two major reasons. First, the welfare state apparatus imposes a burden of taxation and regulation upon capital which amounts to a *disincentive to investment*. Second, at the same time, the welfare state grants claims, entitlements and collective power positions to workers and unions which amount to a *disincentive to work*, or at least to work as hard and productively as they would be forced to under the reign of unfettered market forces. Taken together, these two effects lead into a dynamic of declining growth and increased expectations, of economic 'demand overload' (known as inflation) as well as political demand overload ('ungovernability'), which can be satisfied less and less by the available output.

As obvious as the reactionary political uses are that this analysis is usually meant to support or suggest, it may well be that the truth of the analysis itself is greater than the desirability of its practical conclusions. Although the democratic Left has often measured the former by the latter, the two deserve at least a separate evaluation. In my view the above analysis is not so much false in what it says but in what it remains silent about.

For instance, to take up the first point of the conservative analysis: is it not true that, under conditions of declining growth rates and vehement competition on domestic and international markets, individual capitalists, at least those firms which do not enjoy the privileges of the monopolistic sector, have many good reasons to consider the prospects for investment and profits bleak, and to blame the welfare state, which imposes social security taxes and a great variety of regulations on them, for reducing profitability even further? Is it not true that the power position of unions, which, in turn, is based on rights they have won through industrial relations, collective bargaining, and other laws, is great enough to make an increasing number of industrial producers unprofitable or to force them to seek investment opportunities abroad? And is it not also true that capitalist firms will make investment (and hence employment) decisions according to criteria of expected profitability, and that they consequently will fail to invest as soon as long-term profitability is considered unattractive by them, thus causing an aggregate relative decline in the production output of the economy?

To be sure, no one would deny that there are causes of declining growth rates and capitalists' failure to invest which have nothing to do with the impact of the welfare state upon business, but which are rather to be looked for in inherent crisis tendencies of the capitalist economy such as overaccumulation, the business cycle, or uncontrolled technical change. But even if so, it still might make sense to alleviate the hardship imposed upon capital – and therefore, by definition, upon the rest of society, within the confines of a capitalist society – by dropping some of the burdens and constraints of the welfare state. This, of course, is exactly what most proponents of this argument are suggesting as a practical consequence. But after all, so the fairly compelling logic of the argument continues, who benefits from the operation of a welfare state that undermines and eventually destroys the production system upon which it has to rely in order to make its own promises become true? Does not a kind of 'welfare' become merely nominal and worthless anyway that punishes capital by a high burden of costs and hence everyone else by inflation, unemployment, or both? In my view, the valuable insight to be gained from the type of analysis I have just described is this: the welfare state, rather than being a separate and autonomous source of well-being which provides incomes and services as a citizen right, is itself highly dependent upon the prosperity and continued profitability of the economy. While being designed to be a cure to some ills of capitalist accumulation, the nature of the illness is such that it may force the patient to refrain from using the cure.

A conceivable objection to the above argument would be that capitalists and conservative political elites 'exaggerate' the harm imposed upon them by welfare state arrangements. To be sure, in the political game they have good tactical reasons to make the welfare state burden appear more intolerable than it 'really' is. The question boils down then to what we mean by – and how we measure – 'reality' in this context. In answering this question, we will have to keep in mind that the power position of private investors includes the power to *define* reality. That is to say, whatever they *consider* an intolerable burden in fact *is* an intolerable burden which will *in fact* lead to a declining propensity to invest, at least as long as they can expect to effectively reduce welfare-state-related costs by applying such economic sanctions. The debate about whether or not the welfare state is 'really' squeezing profits is thus purely academic because investors are in a position to *create the reality – and the effects – of 'profit squeeze'*.

The second major argument of the conservative analysis postulates that the effect of the welfare state is a disincentive to work. 'Labour does not work!' was one of the slogans in the campaign that brought Margaret Thatcher into the office of the British Prime Minister. But, again, the analytical content of the argument must be carefully separated from the political uses to which it is put. And, again, this analytical argument can, often contrary to the intentions of its proponents, be read in a way that does make a lot of empirical sense. For instance, there is little doubt that elaborate labor protection legislation puts workers in a position to resist practices of exploitation that would be applied, as a rule, in the absence of such regulations. Powerful and recognized unions can in fact obtain wage increases in excess of productivity increases. And extensive social security provisions make it easier – at least for some workers, for some of the time – to avoid undesirable jobs. Large-scale unemployment insurance covering most of the working population makes unemployment less undesirable for many workers and thus partially obstructs the reserve army mechanism. Thus, the welfare state has made the exploitation of labor more complicated and less predictable. On the other side, as the welfare state imposes regulations and rights upon the labor-capital exchange that goes on in production, while leaving the authority structure and the property relations of production itself untouched, it is hardly surprising to see that the workers are not, as a rule, so intrinsically motivated to work that they would work as productively as they possibly could. In other words, the welfare state maintains the control of capital over production, and thus the basic source of industrial and class conflict between labor and capital; by no means does it establish anything resembling 'workers control'. At the same time, it strengthens workers' potential for resistance against capital's control – the net effect being that an unchanged conflict is fought out with means that have changed in favor of labor. Exploitative production relations coexist with expanded possibilities to resist, escape and mitigate exploitation. While the *reason* for struggle remained unchanged, the *means* of struggle increased for the workers. It is not surprising to see that this condition undermines the 'work ethic', or at least requires more costly and less reliable strategies to enforce such an ethic.[1]

My point, so far, is that the two key arguments of the liberal-conservative analysis are valid to a large extent, contrary to what critics from the Left have often argued. The basic fault I see in this analysis has less to do with what it explicitly states than with what it leaves out of its consideration. Every political theory worth its name has to answer two questions. First, what is the desirable form of the organization of society and state and how can we demonstrate that it is at all 'workable', i.e., consistent with our basic normative and factual assumptions about social life? This is the problem of defining a consistent *model* or goal of transformation. Second, how do we get there? This is the problem of identifying the dynamic forces and *strategies* that could bring about the transformation.

The conservative analysis of the welfare state fails on both counts. To start with the latter problem, it is extremely hard today in Western Europe to conceive of a promising political strategy that would aim at even partially eliminating the established institutional components of the welfare state, to say nothing about its wholesale abolition. That is to say, the welfare state has, in a certain sense, become an irreversible structure, the abolition of which would require nothing less than the abolition of political democracy and the unions, as well as fundamental changes in the party system. A political force that could bring about such dramatic changes is nowhere visible as a significant factor, Right-wing middle-class populist movements that occasionally spring up in some countries notwithstanding. Moreover, it is a well-known fact from political opinion research that the fiercest advocates of *laissez-faire* capitalism and economic individualism show marked differences between their *general* ideological outlook and their willingness to have *special* transfers, subsidies, and social security schemes abandoned from which they *personally* derive benefits. Thus, in the absence of a powerful ideological and organizational undercurrent in Western politics (such as a neo-fascist or authoritarian one), the vision of overcoming the welfare state and resurrecting a 'healthy' market economy is not much more than the politically impotent day-dream of some ideologues of the old middle class. This class is nowhere strong enough to effect, as the examples of Margaret Thatcher and – hypothetically – Ronald Reagan demonstrate, more than marginal alterations of an institutional scheme that such figures, too, have to accept as given when taking office.

Even more significant, however, is the second failure of the conservative analysis; its failure to demonstrate that 'advanced-capitalism-*minus*-the-welfare-state' would actually be a workable model. The reasons why it is not, and consequently why the neo-*laissez-faire* ideology would be a very dangerous cure even *if* it could be administered, are fairly obvious. In the absence of large-scale state-subsidized housing, public education and health services, as well as extensive compulsory social security schemes, the working of an industrial economy would be simply inconceivable. Given the conditions and requirements of urbanization, large-scale concentration of labor power in industrial production plants, rapid technical, economic and regional change, the reduced ability of the family to cope with the difficulties of life in industrial society, the secularization of the moral order, the quantitative reduction and growing dependence of the propertied middle classes – all of which are well-known characteristics of capitalist social structures – the sudden disappearance of the welfare state would leave the system in a state of exploding conflict and anarchy. The embarrassing secret of the welfare state is that, while its impact upon capitalist accumulation may well become destructive (as the conservative analysis so emphatically demonstrates), its abolition would be plainly disruptive (a fact that is systematically ignored by the conservative critics). The contradiction is that while capitalism cannot coexist *with*, neither can it exist *without*, the welfare state. This is exactly the condition to which we refer when using the concept 'contradiction'. The flaw in the conservative analysis is in the one-sided emphasis it puts on the first side of this contradiction, and its silence about the second one. This basic contradiction of the capitalist welfare state could, of course, be thought to be a mere 'dilemma' which then would be 'solved' or 'managed' by a circumspect balancing of the two components. This, however, would presuppose two things, both of which are at least highly uncertain: first, that there is something like an 'optimum point' at which the order-maintaining functions of the welfare state are preserved while its disruptive effects are avoided; and, second, if so, that political procedures and administrative practices will be sufficiently 'rational' to accomplish this precarious balance. Before I consider the prospects for this solution, let me first summarize some elements of the contending socialist critique of the welfare state.

The critique from the socialist Left

Although it would be nonsensical to deny the fact that the struggle for labor protection legislation, expanded social services, social security and the recognition of unions led by the working-class movement for over a century now has brought substantial improvements of the living conditions of most wage earners, the socialist critique of the welfare state is, nevertheless, a fundamental one. It can be summarized in three points which we will consider in turn. The welfare state is said to be:

1 ineffective and inefficient;
2 repressive;
3 conditioning a false ('ideological') understanding of social and political reality within the working class.

   In sum, it is a device to stabilize, rather than a step in the transformation of, capitalist society.
   In spite of the undeniable gains in the living conditions of wage earners, the institutional structure of the welfare state has done little or nothing to alter the income distribution between the two principal classes of labor and capital. The huge machinery of redistribution does not work in the vertical, but in the horizontal direction, namely, *within* the class of wage earners. A further aspect of its ineffectiveness is that the welfare state does not *eliminate the causes* of individual contingencies and needs (such as work-related diseases, the disorganization of cities by the capitalist real estate market, the obsolescence of skills, unemployment, etc.), but *compensates for* (parts of) the *consequences* of such events (by the provision of health services and health insurance, housing subsidies, training and retraining facilities, unemployment benefits and the like). Generally speaking, the kind of social intervention most typical of the welfare state is always 'too late', and hence its *ex post facto* measures are more costly and less effective than a more 'causal' type of intervention would allow them to be. This is a generally recognized dilemma of social policy-making, the standard answer to which is the recommendation to adopt more 'preventive' strategies. Equally generally, however, it is also recognized that effective prevention would almost everywhere mean interfering with the prerogatives of investors and management, that is, the sphere of the market and private

property which the welfare state has only very limited legal and *de facto* powers to regulate.

A further argument pointing at the ineffectiveness of the welfare state emphasizes the constant threat to which social policies and social services are exposed due to the fiscal crisis of the state, which, in turn, is a reflection of both cyclical and structural discontinuities of the process of accumulation. All West European countries experienced a sharp economic recession in the mid-1970s, and we know of many examples of cutting social policy expenditures in response to the fiscal consequences of this recession. But even if and when the absolute and relative rise of social policy expenditures as a percentage of GNP continues uninterrupted, it is by no means certain, as Ian Gough and others before him have argued, that increases in the expenditures are paralleled by increases in real 'welfare'. The dual fallacy, known in the technical literature as the 'spending-serving-cliché', is this: first, a marginal increase in expenditures must not necessarily correspond to a marginal increment in the 'outputs' of the welfare state apparatus; it may well be used up in feeding the bureaucratic machinery itself. But, second, even if the output (say of health services) is increased, a still larger increase in the level of risks and needs (or a qualitative change of these) may occur on the part of the clients or recipients of such services, so as to make the net effect negative.

The bureaucratic and professional form through which the welfare state dispenses its services is increasingly seen to be a source of its own inefficiency. Bureaucracies absorb more resources and provide less services than other democratic and decentralized structures of social policy could. The reason why the bureaucratic form of administering social services is maintained in spite of its inefficiency and ineffectiveness, which becomes increasingly obvious to more and more observers, must, therefore, be connected with the social control function exercised by centralized welfare bureaucracies. This analysis leads to the critique of the *repressiveness* of the welfare state, its social control aspect. Such repressiveness is, in the view of the critics, indicated by the fact that, in order to qualify for the benefits and services of the welfare state, the client must not only prove his or her 'need', but must also be a *deserving* client – a client, that is, who complies with the dominant economic, political, and cultural standards and norms of the society. The heavier the needs, the stricter these requirements tend to be defined. Only if, for instance, the unemployed are willing to keep themselves available for any alternative employment (often considerably inferior to the job they have lost) that eventually may be made available to them by employment agencies are they entitled to unemployment benefits; and the claim for welfare payments to the poor is everywhere made conditional upon their conformity to standards of behavior which the better-to-do strata of the population are perfectly free to violate. In these and many other cases, the welfare state can be looked upon as an exchange transaction in which material benefits for the needy are traded for their submissive recognition of the 'moral order' of the society which generates such need. One important pre-condition for obtaining the services of the welfare state is the ability of the individual to comply with the routines and requirements of welfare bureaucracies and service organizations, an ability which, needless to say, often is inversely correlated to need itself.

A third major aspect of the socialist critique of the welfare state is to demonstrate its *political-ideological* control function. The welfare state is seen not only as the source of benefits and services, but, at the same time, as the source of false conceptions about historical reality which have damaging effects for working-class consciousness, organization and struggle. First of all, the welfare state creates the false image of two separated spheres of working-class life. On the one side, the sphere of work, the economy, production and 'primary' income distribution; on the other, the sphere of citizenship, the state, reproduction and 'secondary' distribution. This division of the socio-political world obscures the causal and functional links and ties that exist between the two, and thus prevents the formation of a political understanding which views society as a coherent totality-to-be-changed. That is to say, the structural arrangements of the welfare state tend to make people ignore or forget that the needs and contingencies which the welfare state responds to are themselves constituted, directly or indirectly, in the sphere of work and production, that the welfare state itself is materially and institutionally constrained by the dynamics of the sphere of production, and that a reliable conception of social security does, therefore, presuppose not only the expansion of 'citizen rights', but of 'workers rights' in the process of production. Contrary to such insights, which are part of the analytical starting points of any conceivable socialist strategy of societal transformation, the inherent symbolic indoctrination of the welfare state suggests the ideas of class cooperation, the disjunction of economic and political struggles, and the evidently more and more ill-based confidence in an ever-continuing cycle of economic growth and social security.

The welfare state and political change

What emerges from our sketchy comparative discussion of the 'Right' and the 'Left' analyses of the welfare state are three points on which the liberal-conservative and the socialist critics exhibit somewhat surprising parallels.

First, contrary to the ideological consensus that flourished in some of the most advanced welfare states throughout the 1950s and 1960s, nowhere is the welfare state believed any longer to be the promising and permanently valid answer to the problems of the socio-political order of advanced capitalist economies. Critics in both camps have become more vociferous and fundamental in their negative appraisal of welfare state arrangements.

Second, neither of the two approaches to the welfare state could and would be prepared, in the best interest of its respective clientele, to abandon the welfare state, as it performs essential and indispensable functions both for the accumulation process as well as for the social and economic well-being of the working class.

Third, while there is, on the conservative side, neither a consistent theory nor a realistic strategy about the social order of a non-welfare state (as I have argued before), it is not perfectly evident that the situation is much better on the Left where one could possibly speak of a consistent theory of socialism, but certainly not of an agreed-upon and realistic strategy for its construction. In the absence of the latter, the welfare state remains a theoretically contested, though in reality firmly entrenched, fact of the social order of advanced capitalist societies. In short, it appears that the welfare state, while being contested both from the Right and the Left, will not be easily replaced by a conservative or progressive alternative.

To be sure, there are a number of normative models of the social and economic order which are, however, advocated by intellectuals and other minorities rather than being supported by any broad political current. One is the neo-*laissez-faire* model according to which the welfare state can and should be abolished so that the resurrection of the free and harmonious market society can take place. This solution is typically supported by political forces from the old middle class, such as farmers and shopkeepers, who also often favor tax-resistance movements. The political problem with this solution is that the further and more evenly capitalist modernization has taken place within one country, the smaller the social base of this backward-looking alternative will be. Its polar opposite is a model favored by elements of the new middle class, combining 'post-material' values with certain ideas inherited from the anarchist and syndicalist tradition of political thought. This model would imply that the functions of the welfare state could be taken over by libertarian, egalitarian and largely self-reliant communities working within a highly decentralized and debureaucratized setting.

Typically, both of these alternative models have no more than a very marginal role to play as long as they fail to form alliances with one of the principal classes, respectively, and the political forces representing them. But such alliances, either between the old middle class and the centers of capital or the new middle class and the established working-class organizations, are immensely difficult to form and sustain. Nevertheless, it would probably not be too speculative an assumption to expect such struggles for new alliances to occupy the stage of social policy and welfare state reform in the years to come. In my view, three potential alternative outcomes of these political efforts can be envisaged.

First, under conditions of heightened economic crisis and international tension, a relative success of the neo-*laissez-faire* coalition, based on an alliance of big capital and the old middle class, is not entirely to be excluded as a possibility. Second, in countries with a strong social democratic (and possibly also in those with a strong Euro-communist) element, it is more likely that new forms of interest intermediation and relatively peaceful accommodation will emerge which are designed to determine the 'right dose' of welfare state expansion, that is, one that is compatible both with the requirements of accumulation as well as with the key demands of working-class organizations. This model would involve the extensive reliance on 'neo-corporatist' or 'tripartite' modes of decision-making, carried out by representatives of highly centralized employers' organizations and unions under the supervision of specialized agencies of the state. This second conceivable configuration, however, will operate, especially under economic crisis conditions, at the expense not only of the old middle class, but also of those sectors of the working class which are less well-organized and represented within such highly exclusive frameworks of inter-group negotiation and decision-making. Not entirely inconceivable is, third, a type of alliance that combines working-class organizations and elements from the new middle class on the basis of a non-bureaucratic, decentralized, and egalitarian model of a self-reliant 'welfare society'. Proponents of this solution are to be found within the new social movements who find some resonance in the theoretical ideas of authors like Illich, Gorz, Touraine, Cooley and others.

Rather than speculating about the likely outcome of this configuration of forces and ideas, which would require a much more detailed analysis than is possible within the confines of this essay, I want to turn in my concluding remarks to the nature of the political process which will eventually decide one or the other of these outcomes. This process can best be conceived of as consisting of three tiers, or three cumulative arenas of conflict. The first and most obvious is the arena of political *decision-making within the state apparatus*. Its actors are political elites competing with each other for electoral victories and scarce resources. They decide on social policy programs, legislations and budgets. This is the most superficial and most visible level of politics, the one publicized by the media and involved whenever the citizen is called upon to act in his or her political role, for example, as voter.

But this is by no means the only level at which political power is generated, distributed and utilized. For the space of possible decisions of political elites is determined by societal forces that, on a far less visible level, shape and change the politicians' view and perception of reality, that is, of the alternatives open to decision-making and the consequences to be expected from each of the alternatives. This is the level at which the agenda of politics and the relative priority of issues and solutions is determined, and the durability of alliances and compromises is conditioned. On this level, it is more difficult to identify specific actors; the forces operating here are most often the aggregate outcome of a multitude of anonymous actors and actions which nevertheless shape the politicians' view of reality and space of action. Examples of such conditioning forces are events in the international environment (such as wars or revolutions), macroeconomic indicators (terms of trade, growth rates, changes in the level of unemployment and inflation, etc.), and changes in the cultural parameters of social life (ranging from the rates of secondary school attendance to divorce rates). The experience of these indicators shapes the elites' image of reality, their view of what they can and must do, what they have to expect as consequences of their actions, and what they must refrain from doing. The important point here is this: although the power to structure the politicians' reality, agenda and attention cannot be as easily traced back to personal actors as is the case on the first level of political conflict, there is, nevertheless, a *matrix of social power* according to which social classes, collective actors and other social categories have a greater chance of shaping and reshaping political reality, opening or closing the political agenda, than others. Access to and control over the means of production, the means of organization and the means of communication are highly unevenly distributed within the social structure, and each of them can be utilized, to a different degree of effectiveness, to shape and to challenge what politicians perceive as their *environment of decision-making*. The relative weight of these different resources which, partly, may balance each other, but which also can be concentrated in the hands of one and the same class or group, depends also on cyclical and conjunctural variations which may allow a group to exploit its specific social power to a larger or smaller extent at different points in time.

Underlying this second level of politics (the social power matrix), however, is a third level at which changes within the matrix itself occur, that is, changes in the relative 'weight' collective actors enjoy in shaping the agenda of politics. If, as we have argued before, the second level consists in the process of shaping the space of political action by the exercise of veto power, blackmail, threat, mobilization and social discourse about political issues, or merely the silent force of 'anticipated reaction', this does not mean that the amount and effectiveness of political resources that each social class and social category controls must remain fixed. That is to say, social power is never great enough to reproduce itself eternally. Power positions are, almost by definition, contested and hence subject to change and redistribution. The struggle for the *redistribution of social power* is what takes place on the third, and most fundamental, level of politics. For instance, the market power, or political legitimacy, or the organizational strength that one group or class has enjoyed so far may be restricted (with the effect of making the political agenda less vulnerable *vis-à-vis* this group), or another group may open up new channels of influence, may form new alliances, or win a hegemonic position through the appeal to new values, ideals and visions. Both relative losses of power and relative gains in power can be promoted, facilitated or triggered off (if only through the unequivocal demonstration of failures) on the level of formal politics. The veto power attached to certain groups can be limited and constrained, and the institutional underpinnings of social power can be abolished. It therefore appears that the three levels are interrelated, not in a strictly hierarchical but in a cyclical manner: although the action space of level one ('formal politics') is largely determined by the matrix of social power ('level two'), it may itself facilitate and promote a revision of the distribution of social power ('level three'). And the state of democratic politics would thus have to be looked upon as both determined by, and a potential determinant of, social power.

I trust that I can leave it to the reader to apply this analytical model of the political process to the contemporary controversy about the welfare state that I have reviewed and discussed, and, thereby, to explore the extent of its usefulness. The question with which I wish to conclude is as much of academic as it is of political significance: will the agenda of the welfare state, its space of action and future development, be shaped and limited by the matrix of social power of advanced capitalist social structures? Or will it conversely, itself open up possibilities of reshaping this matrix, either through its own accomplishments or failures?

(This essay was first presented as a paper to the Facoltà de Scienze Politiche, Università di Perugia, Italy, February 1980. It is here reprinted, with minor alterations, from the version published in Praxis International, 1 no. 3 (October 1981), pp. 219–29.)

Note

1 A corollary argument often used in the conservative analysis is this: not only does the welfare state undermine the *quality* of working behavior by inducing workers to be more 'demanding' and, at the same time, less willing to spend strong efforts on their work, etc., but also it cuts the *quantity* of available productive labor. This is said to be so because the welfare state ideology puts strong emphasis on public sector services, bureaucratic careers, and especially education and training, all of which drain the labor market of 'productive' labor in a variety of ways.

5

The Normalizing Role of Rationalist Assumptions in the Institutional Embedding of Neoliberalism*

Colin Hay

The 'disaffection' of previously engaged citizens from the democratic process is a key theme in much contemporary political discourse. Extrapolating, often wildly, from low and declining levels of political participation and identification in the Anglophone democracies, a growing chorus of conservative commentators has pointed with consternation to a lack of social capital, civic engagement and respect for the obligations and duties of citizenship in a democratic polity (see, for instance, Putnam 1993, 1995, 2000, 2002; Pharr and Putnam 2000). Yet, however influential and convenient such a diagnosis may be, especially for governing elites, this is to look at the problem exclusively from the demand-side. It is certainly no less plausible to view the problem of disaffection and disengagement from the supply-side (see also Hay 2003a).

[...] An altogether different set of reflections is prompted if we take as our starting premise the assumption that *democratic polities get the levels of political participation they deserve*. If we take this view then, where there is a choice in apportioning responsibility for low levels of participation, we should look first to the purveyors of political goods and the goods they purvey, not the consumers of those wares. The problem may more plausibly lie on the supply-side; it is, in other words, as much a question of the character of the choice the electorate is presented with at the ballot box as it is one of the (lack of) character of those presented with that choice.

In keeping with this supply-side corrective to the prevailing demand-side orthodoxy, the principal aim of this paper is to assess the extent to which the normalization and institutionalization of a governing neoliberal economic paradigm might be seen to have contributed to this contemporary condition of disaffection and disengagement. The argument, though potentially generalizable, is here developed for the British case.

---

* From *Economy and Society* 33(4) (2004): 500–27

A number of general and preliminary observations might serve to contextualize what follows. First, the relationship between neoliberalism as a governing economic paradigm and political disenchantment and disengagement is not a simple one. Arguably, by significantly raising the stakes of electoral competition in the late 1970s and throughout the 1980s, the normative neoliberalism of the New Right may have served to promote political identification and participation. From the 1990s onwards, however, the normalization and institutionalization of neoliberalism and its depiction as a largely technical set of devices for managing an open economy has served to depoliticize and dedemocratize economic policy-making. This, I suggest, has contributed to a process of disengagement and disenfranchisement. At the same time, however, the cycle of political reengagement-disengagement that this points to is by no means peculiar to the neoliberal economic paradigm and may relate, as discussed in some detail in the next section, to the evolution and contestation of economic paradigms more generally.

Second, in internalizing neoliberal economic assumptions, governing political parties in the Anglophone democracies have increasingly translated the political power conferred upon them at the ballot box into a self-denying ordinance. In Britain, as elsewhere, political parties vying for office now couch their political rhetoric to a considerable extent in terms of: (1) the non-negotiable character of external (principally economic) imperatives; (2) the powerlessness of domestic political actors in the face of such (ostensibly self-evident) constraints; and (3) the need, in such a context, to displace responsibility to quasi-independent and supra-democratic authorities such as independent central banks.[1] Elections, it seems, are increasingly about appointing officers to be trusted to take the necessary technical decisions dictated by shifting external circumstances; they are not public plebiscites on manifesto policy commitments. As Peter Burnham (2001) has observed, politics today is about the management of depoliticization. The decision by the Blair administration, only days after its election in 1997, to grant operational independence to the Bank of England despite the absence of any supporting manifesto commitment is a case in point.

It is in this context that a third factor, the marketization of political competition, acquires particular significance. It, too, has arguably contributed to declining political engagement, participation and turnout (Levi 1996: 49). If the competition between parties for votes is assumed analogous to that between businesses for market-share, then parties will behave in a quasi-Downsian manner. In a first-past-the-post two-party electoral system, such as Britain's, they will tend to scrabble over the centre ground in a race towards the median voter (for a detailed elaboration of this logic, see Hay 1999a: 76–104; also Downs 1957). The result, *ceteris paribus*, is bipartisan convergence.

Yet there is, in fact, something of a tension here. For the quasi-Downsian logic of political marketing tends to rest on the assumption that parties continue to compete in terms of clearly articulated policy preferences which are presented to the electorate. In so far as this is the case, parties animated by the marketing analogy will seek to adapt their expressed preferences to those of the median voter, internalizing the terms of a new consensus in so doing. Yet, as noted above, it is by no means clear that parties today do compete principally over clearly expressed manifesto policy commitments. Rather more plausible, perhaps, is that parties compete for the electorate's trust. They present themselves as credible and competent administrators, not, for the most part, as principled advocates of a set of policy preferences. Policy (economic policy in particular) is increasingly presented as the product of a process – the pragmatic accommodation to potentially rapidly changing external circumstances and pressures. It is the competence of candidates for high office to respond appropriately to external stimuli and not the resulting policy content that is presented and legitimated to the electorate. Policy itself is seen as contingent upon circumstance and is not, consequently, something which can be presented for approval in advance of its execution.[2]

Yet, in a rather circular double-bind, what is seen to make policymakers – and the policies they make – credible is predictability in response to any given external stimulus, shock or set of circumstances. Policy must be rules-bounded rather than discretionary. In other words, competence rests on technical proficiency which is, in turn, conditional upon the internalization of the guiding assumptions of the prevailing economic paradigm. It is perhaps not then surprising that the higher-order assumptions of the dominant (neoliberal) economic paradigm seem to be accepted by all serious contenders for high office in contemporary Britain – for this is now taken as a token of their electoral competence and credibility.

[...]

Towards a 'normal science' of neoliberalism

Analysts of economic policy-making in the Anglophone democracies have been attracted for some time by the logic of exposition of Thomas Kuhn's celebrated *The Structure of Scientific Revolutions* (1962; see, for instance, Blyth 2002; Hall 1993; Hay 2001; Oliver 1997). In this seminal work Kuhn argues that scientific progression can be understood in terms of the emergence and institutionalization of a succession of more or less enduring paradigms. The development of such paradigms is punctuated by periodic 'revolutions' in which prevailing scientific assumptions are challenged and overturned. During phases of 'normal science', a single paradigm is ascendant and remains largely unchallenged. It provides an interpretative framework delineating a legitimate range of problems (and indeed non-problems), techniques and criteria of scientific adequacy. In phases of 'exceptional' science, by contrast, an accumulation of anomalies within the old paradigm (principally experimental outcomes which do not conform to the predictions of current theories) lead some scientists to break from the paradigm and the constraints it imposes. Such entrepreneurs search for alternative theoretical approaches that might account for (and hence resolve) the anomalies of the old paradigm, thereby opening a space for a renewed phase of normal science under the dominance of a new paradigm (internalized by the scientific community).

A range of authors, most notably perhaps Peter A. Hall (1993), have sought to explore the extent to which ostensibly similar dynamics might be observed within the policy-making process. Within such a schema policy paradigms are internalized by politicians, state managers and policy experts alike and may become institutionally embedded in norms, conventions and standard operating procedures. In this way, paradigms come to define legitimate and appropriate action. Accordingly, they serve to delimit the range of feasible policy options in any given context providing cognitive template through which policymakers come to understand the environment in which they find themselves. As Hall himself suggests,

> policymakers customarily work within a framework of ideas and standards that specifies not only the goals of policy and the kind of instruments that can be used to attain them, but also the very nature of the problems they are meant to be addressing ... [T]his framework is embedded in the very terminology through which policymakers communicate about their work, and it is influential precisely because so much of it is taken for granted and unamenable to scrutiny as a whole.
> (Hall 1993: 279)

'Keynesianism' and 'neoliberalism' might be seen as examples of such policy paradigms in the economic sphere.[3] Extending the Kuhnian analogy, we can differentiate between (1) periods of 'normal' policy-making (and change), in which the paradigm remains largely unchallenged (at least within the confines of the policy-making arena) and in which change is largely incremental and evolutionary; and (2) periods of 'exceptional' policy-making (and change), in which the very parameters that previously circumscribed policy options are cast asunder and replaced, and in which the realm of the politically possible, feasible and desirable is correspondingly reconfigured.

[...] The narration of the crisis and of the conditions appropriate for its resolution are here especially significant if a new paradigm is to emerge and to be consolidated.

Paradigms, within this framework, are sticky. Policymakers are reluctant to concede the need to revise their most cherished and habitual assumptions, even in the face of significant policy failure and, *ceteris paribus*, they strive to resolve any such contradictions within the confines of the existing (and evolving) paradigm. Policy-making in such a context tends to be normalized (if not necessarily necessitarian). Consequently, paradigm shifts are relatively rare and tend to be associated with the spectacular and invariably highly normative politics of crisis and contestation [...].

This perspective, adapted, revised and extended from the work of Peter A. Hall and others (again, see Hay 2001 for a fuller exposition), provides the theoretical basis of the present contribution. Neoliberalism, I suggest, can usefully be seen as a governing economic paradigm, arising in Britain in the late 1970s in the context of a widely perceived crisis of the state that came to be narrated in neoliberal terms. This process was highly normative and, whatever one might think of its consequences, engaging politically. Yet it is with the subsequent normalization and institutionalization of neoliberalism, and in particular with the role of ideas in this process, that this paper is principally concerned.[4] I argue that, from the early 1990s onwards, we see evidence of a significant shift from a *normative neoliberalism* unleashed in the exceptional politics of crisis in the late 1970s to the *normalized* and *necessitarian neoliberalism* which now characterizes British political discourse. I argue that rationalist assumptions (whether in the form of public choice theory, the rational expectations revolution or the hyperglobalization and structural dependence theses) have played a crucial role in this normalization and institutionalization of neoliberalism as a policy paradigm. [...].

Neoliberalism defined

If we are to chart the development of neoliberalism as an economic policy paradigm in Britain it is important at the outset to provide a working definition of the term – against which the suggested neoliberalism of Thatcherite and 'Third Way' political economy might be gauged. Yet this immediately raises a problem. Definitions are static; paradigms evolve. Tempting though it is to fashion a generic and trans-historical definition of neoliberalism as a set of policy preferences, this will not do. For, arguably, in suggesting that 'Third Way' political economy is neoliberal it is less important to demonstrate some natural affinity with such a trans-historical definitional standard than it is to show how 'Third Way' political economy can credibly be presented as part of an evolving neoliberal paradigm. Yet there is an equal danger of a definition rendered vague and imprecise by virtue of the aim to recognize the temporal variability in the content of neoliberalism.

What is required, then, is a definition of neoliberalism capable of identifying a set of core precepts and principles that might be said to capture the identity of neoliberalism, but which is sufficiently general to allow for quite significant variations over time in the policy content designed to further such principles. Economic neoliberalism, I suggest, can be defined in terms of the following traits:

1. A confidence in the market as an efficient mechanism for the allocation of scarce resources.
2. A belief in the desirability of a global regime of free trade and free capital mobility.
3. A belief in the desirability, all things being equal, of a limited and non-interventionist role for the state and of the state as a facilitator and custodian rather than a substitute for market mechanisms.
4. A rejection of Keynesian demand-management techniques in favor of monetarism, neo-monetarism and supply-side economics.
5. A commitment to the removal of those welfare benefits which might be seen to act as disincentives to market participation (in short, a subordination of the principles of social justice to those of perceived economic imperatives).
6. A defense of labor-market flexibility and the promotion and nurturing of cost competitiveness.
7. A confidence in the use of private finance in public projects and, more generally, in the allocative efficiency of market and quasi-market mechanisms in the provision of public goods.

Understood in this way, New Labour's broad policy agenda might be judged neoliberal in each of the following respects (for a more thorough-going defense of this characterization, see Hay (2004a):

1. Its commitment to the maintenance and consolidation of the inherited public/private mix and to a variety of internal market mechanisms and new public management incentivizing techniques (such as league tables and the competitive allocation of resources).
2. Its commitment to a global regime of free trade and free capital mobility.
3. The new monetarism of its rules- (rather than discretion-) based macroeconomic policy regime.
4. Its fiscal prudence and passivity, its antipathy both to deficit financing and to the use of fiscal policy as an instrument in the fight against inflation, and its commitment not to raise top rates of direct taxation.
5. Its identification of unemployment as an exclusively supply-side phenomenon, its effective acceptance of a 'natural' or 'equilibrium' rate of unemployment, its rejection of any notion of a long-term trade-off between inflation and unemployment, and its acceptance that there is no longer a role in macroeconomic policy for adjustments in aggregate or effective demand.
6. Its agenda of labor-market flexibilization, designed to enhance cost competitiveness through the removal of labor-market rigidities.

At this point it is important to clear up a potential misinterpretation of the argument here presented. In suggesting that there is a case to be made for labeling important features of the 'Third Way' neoliberal, I am not seeking to suggest that all aspects of its policy agenda can be labeled similarly, nor that its distinctive character is in any sense reducible to its neoliberalism.[5] What I am suggesting, however, is that much of its political economy can be seen as an evolution of the neoliberal economic paradigm, such as it has developed in Britain since the late 1970s. Moreover, this neoliberalism has a series of spill-over effects and consequences for other areas of policy. Indeed, one might well suggest that those elements of its policy agenda that are defended in more normative terms, such as its occasionally redistributivist interventions and its broader emphasis upon social justice and inclusion, have been thwarted somewhat by their articulation within an economic paradigm which is broadly neoliberal.

[...]

Neoliberalism as 'exceptional' politics

The neoliberal offensive in Britain was unleashed in the context of a developing 'crisis' of the state from the mid-1970s. The problem was one of 'stagflation' – a condition of high and rising inflation combined with high and rising unemployment in a welfare state society whose citizenship contract was premised upon the commitment to full employment. In the context of widely perceived crisis (associated in the public's imagination with a succession of public dramas and debacles from the 'Three Day Week', *via* the negotiation of the IMF loan in 1976, to the long 'Winter of Discontent' of 1978–9), dominant economic understandings changed as the intellectual pendulum swung from left to right, from Keynesianism to neoliberalism.[6] We enter the phase of neoliberalism as 'exceptional' politics.

The new right's diagnosis was elegant in its simplicity and in its simplicity lay its persuasive capacity. It was premised upon the crudest variants of public choice theory and, in turn, upon the assumed narrow instrumental rationality of bureaucrats (in maximizing agency and bureau budgets), politicians (in maximizing votes irrespective of the economic consequences of so doing) and electors (whose soul motivation for voting was assumed to be the blind pursuit of material self-interest). Given these parsimonious if unrealistic assumptions, the rest was merely a matter of logical deduction. Accept the assumptions, and neoliberalism was rationalized.

Thinking merely of narrow electoral advantage, politicians would seek to accommodate themselves to the (rational, i.e. instrumental) preferences of the electorate for immediate material gain by sanctioning ever spiralling and ever more costly expectations. Consequently, in the run up to a general election the parties (rationally maximizing their electoral prospects) would seek to outbid one another in terms of the promises they made to the electorate and sectional interests therein. This served to establish a political competition for votes, yet one lacking the disciplining price mechanism of a genuine market – in which consumers are forced to bear the costs of their choices. Since the cost of each vote could effectively be discounted by politicians motivated only by short-term electoral advantage, and voters themselves would discount the long-term cumulative consequences of the parties' budgetary indiscipline that their greed encouraged, the effective price of a vote would spiral from one election to the next. Eventually demand would increase to the point of political 'overload'. The result was a fiscal crisis of the state born of political irresponsibility or rationality (depending on one's audience). This, according to the new right, was the point that had now been reached.

The image was a simple one – a vicious political whirlpool from whose watery clutches parties could escape only at considerable cost to their electoral prospects. The solution, however politically unpalatable to an electorate that had come to conceive of government as a simple relay for it preferences and however incompatible with the diagnosis of the affliction (a point to which we return), was simple: a severe bout of fiscal austerity, tight monetary control and a programmatic withdrawal of an overloaded, overburdened yet beleaguered state. Yet it is important to note that the substantive content of that response was not in any direct way deducible from the overload thesis itself (or, really for that matter, from public choice theory). In effect, the overload thesis provided a populist narration of the crisis capable of attributing responsibility to the then-ascendant Keynesian paradigm and the parties that had internalized it. It opened the discursive terrain for both monetarism and supply-side economics, which were to provide an alternative economic paradigm, but which were perhaps less capable in and of themselves of providing a spectacular and populist narration of the crisis of Keynesianism. In short, it constituted the crisis as a crisis of an overextended state, encouraged to over-reach itself by both Keynesianism and corporatism. To this narration of the crisis, monetarism and supply-side economics provided a ready solution.[7]

Before turning to the details of that solution, and to monetarism and supply-side economics more directly, it is first important to establish the inconsistencies and obvious distortions of the overload thesis. For here two key themes of this paper emerge for the first time – (1) the reliance of public legitimations of neoliberalism upon simple, rationalist premises for which no substantiating evidence was presented or sought and (2) the sensitivity of such legitimations to variations in these undefended assumptions. The former is an empirical/evidential claim, the latter an analytical observation. Stated more boldly, *the overload thesis (like other rationalist legitimations of neoliberalism) rests on unrealistic assumptions; render the assumptions more realistic and the 'rationalization' of neoliberalism that it- offers evaporates.*

Though in many respects a simple, indeed simplistic, account – a simplicity it might be suggested, making it all the more politically attractive – the overload thesis contains a number of profound internal contradiction tensions.[8]

First, its proponents conjure the impression of a cynical and self-serving electorate looking to the state to satisfy its every whim and desire. Yet this depiction of the electorate as greedy, unprincipled and simply too stupid to consider the consequences of its actions stands in some tension with the rest of the analysis. It is also, of course, a product of the theory's most fundamental-analytical assumption – for which no evidence is presented. The tension is well expressed by Anthony King in his influential essay on 'overload' published in *Political Studies* in 1975.

> It was once thought that governments would be extremely difficult to remove from office, given their ability to manage the economy. Now we are inclined to assume the opposite: that the tenure of governments is precarious and that for the foreseeable future it will be a lucky government that survives for more than a term.
>
> (King 1975: 282)

This implies – and the evidence clearly supports such a claim – that a (possibly *the*) principal factor determining success at the polls at the time was the perceived state of the economy and not the ability of parties to outbid one another in making irresponsible budgetary commitments to sectional interests (for instance, Pissarides 1980; Price and Sanders 1993). Ironically, Thatcher would rely on this very fact for her election in 1979.

Second, in its call for a decisive break with the practices responsible for overload, the thesis's proponents appeal to precisely the good sense of the electorate that the assumption of instrumental rationality denies. Either the electorate is motivated solely by instrumental material self-interest or it is not. The argument would then appear at best somewhat disingenuous. Ironically, the election of an administration designed to break the cycle of overload would appear to provide a compelling refutation of the overload thesis.

[...] Yet, as noted above, while capable of providing a public rationale and legitimation of neoliberalism, the overload thesis and indeed public choice theory more broadly, was not capable of animating a neoliberal 'project' or of providing an alternative economic paradigm to Keynesianism. That role was performed by monetarism and supply-side economics. It is to them that we must now turn.

The neoliberal paradigm: monetarist macroeconomics, supply-side microeconomics

Much has been written on the extent to which Thatcherism was predicated upon monetarism and supply-side economics. It is certainly the case that the first Thatcher administration was monetarist in its general inclinations – and, perhaps more importantly; it was seen to be monetarist where Labour and previous administrations were seen to be Keynesian. This generic monetarism was expressed in its public subordination of fiscal to monetary policy, its resolute commitment to price stability (or, at least, the control of inflation) as the principal objective of macroeconomic policy, its rhetorical (if not always substantive) commitment to inflation as an exclusively monetary phenomenon and its (nominal) targeting of both the money supply (albeit in a variety of different forms) and the public sector borrowing requirement in its (eventually abortive) medium-term financial strategy. Moreover, monetarism was certainly presented as the paradigmatic successor to a failed Keynesianism and policy was couched in terms of the theory and its supporting assumptions (predominantly those of rational expectations). Nonetheless, despite the open advocacy of monetarism and the presentation of macroeconomic policy in monetarist terms, some caution is required here.

[...] In fact, despite the emphasis placed upon monetarism by the Thatcherites, it was supply-side economics which was arguably more central to the agenda pursued in the first and subsequent terms. In contrast to the Reagan administration, only passing reference was made to the maverick Californian economist Arthur Laffer who had famously predicted that a lowering of personal taxation would result in such a significant boost to economic activity that it would increase revenue (Laffer 1981; Wanniski 1978). Yet, this notwithstanding, much of the Thatcher government's microeconomic agenda was driven by the concern to eliminate a variety of supply-side and labor-market rigidities and to restore the incentivizing and disciplining role of market mechanisms. The program of denationalization and welfare reform, the prioritization of the cost competitiveness of British industry, the barrage of anti-union legislation, the introduction of internal markets within a residual public sector and the broader agenda of labor-market flexibilization might all be seen as expressions of the new supply-side economics [...].

[...] Having, albeit briefly, examined the initial rationalization of *normative* neoliberalism, we can now turn to its subsequent *normalization*. My argument here is simple. Though each has evolved significantly since the 1980s, the 'open economy macroeconomics' of New Labour is a recognizable descendant of the monetarism of the first Thatcher term, just as New Labour's labor-market and welfare reform agenda is a recognizable descendant of Thatcher's supply-side economics. In this way New Labour's 'Third Way' political economy is decidedly neoliberal (see also Arestis and Sawyer 2001; Thain 2000). Yet, whereas the neoliberalism of the first Thatcher term was normative and spectacular, that of the 'Third Way' is normalized, necessitarian and vernacular. Nonetheless, just as rationalist assumptions and stylized models proved crucial to the popular articulation of normative neoliberalism, so rationalist assumptions – in the form of the rational expectations literature on the time-inconsistent inflationary preferences of governments and the stylized open economy macroeconomic assumptions of the business school hyperglobalization thesis – have proved crucial in normalizing neoliberalism in recent years. It is to the role of rational expectations and the hyperglobalization thesis in the normalization of neoliberal macroeconomics and microeconomics, respectively, that we now turn.

Rationalizing neoliberal macroeconomics: rational expectations and the time-inconsistency problem

The new monetarism of New Labour's self-styled 'open economy macroeconomics', though not openly declared, is not very well-hidden either (Balls 1998; Balls and O'Donnell 2002). It is perhaps clearest in the public rationale for the ceding of operational independence to the Bank of England. This is couched, in now highly orthodox fashion in terms of assumptions as to the time-inconsistent inflationary preferences of public authorities and the rational expectations of market actors.[9] Labour's theoretical route to operational independence is, as Ed Balls (1998) makes very clear, *via* public choice theory, Friedmanite monetarism and the rational expectations revolution. The rationale, given the assumption of rational expectations, is very simple. Given (the perception of) a short-term trade-off between inflation and unemployment, rational politicians will seek to orchestrate a political business cycle, trading inflation in the immediate aftermath of their anticipated re-election for growth and employment in the run up to that election. This can only serve to dampen the aggregate long-term growth potential of the economy while, at the same time, driving up the natural or equilibrium rate of unemployment. It is, in short, rational for politicians to set for themselves inflation targets that they have no intention of keeping.

In a world of rational (or, indeed, adaptive) expectations, market actors will anticipate such defection (rationally) adapting their investment behavior accordingly. In such a world, the consequences of *anticipated* inflation for the investment behavior of market actors are just as severe as if that inflation were real. Accordingly, as long as control of monetary policy rests in the hands of public officials, unemployment, the aggregate rate of inflation and interest rates will all be higher than they need otherwise be (the literature is extensive, but see, especially Alesina 1989; Alesina and Gatti 1995; Kydland and Prescott 1977).

If anti-inflationary credibility is to be restored, the public authorities need to be able to make a credible pre-commitment to a given inflation target (just as in the earlier monetarist account governments need to make strong and firm commitments to a money supply target). This entails an institutionally guaranteed depoliticization of monetary policy – in other words, an independent central bank mandated constitutionally to deliver a specific inflation target (typically in low to mid-single digits). In such a scenario (rational) inflationary expectations are diminished, with consequent beneficial effects upon both the cost of borrowing and the equilibrium rate of unemployment.

The pedigree of New Labour's new monetarist macroeconomics could scarcely be clearer. Though, in the strictest terms, post-monetarist (no emphasis is placed upon control of the money supply), New Labour's open macroeconomics is a clear and direct descendant of the monetarism of successive British governments since 1979. It is, moreover, a product of the internalization of (now conventional) rational expectations assumptions. The time-inconsistency problem is presented as a non-negotiable bind on elected officials, necessitating the institutionalization of an independently accountable new monetarist macroeconomic regime which guarantees the privileged status of price stability as macroeconomic objective number one. That status is seen to be inviolable and beyond political contestation – indeed, it is only because it is inviolable and beyond political contestation that any credible commitment to its delivery can be made [...].

In other words, New Labour's open economy (neoliberal) macroeconomics is justified, not principally in its own terms, but as the only possible (and hence purely technical) solution to the time-inconsistency problem in a world of rational expectations. In this way rationalist assumptions normalize and institutionalize neoliberal policy such that no alternative is conceivable. Macroeconomic policy (certainly monetary policy) is thus relegated to a purely technical and entirely apolitical matter beyond the sphere of effective democratic scrutiny or accountability. The perpetuation of neoliberal macroeconomics is guaranteed.

This is an interesting point which immediately raises the question of New Labour's motivation for presenting its 'open economy macroeconomics' in such terms.[10] Three answers to that question almost naturally present themselves: (1) that New Labour policymakers are believers in the time-inconsistency thesis and have simply internalized its policy implications; (2) that an expressed belief in the time-inconsistency thesis is seen as an appropriate signal to the markets and market analysts of New Labour's moderation and competence; and (3) that invoking the time-inconsistency thesis and internalizing its policy implications is a means to an end – the insulation, from critique, of neo-monetarist economics.[11] Of these, the first is the easiest to discount. For, were it the case that New Labour policymakers were genuine converts to the non-negotiable bind implied by the time-inconsistency thesis, they would surely not be able to contemplate British membership of the single European currency. As argued elsewhere, were Britain to join the Eurozone, the likely disparity in interest rates between that set by the European Central Bank and that which would have been set by the Bank of England would effectively restore responsibility for anti-inflationary policy to the Treasury. This clearly violates the most basic policy prescriptions of the time-inconsistency thesis (Hay 2003b).

In all likelihood, then, New Labour's adoption of a time-inconsistency rationale for its open economy macroeconomics arises from a combination of the second and third factors. It is both a marker of credibility and competence and, at the same time, an effective guarantor of the kind of monetary policy discretion the New Labour Treasury clearly wishes to deny itself. As such it is part of a strategy of depoliticization (see also Burnham 2001).
[...]

Rationalizing neoliberal microeconomics: the globalization thesis

If New Labour's neoliberal macroeconomics has been rationalized (and thereby normalized) through rational expectations assumptions, then a similar role in the rationalization of its supply-side microeconomics has been performed by the stylized open economy macroeconomic assumptions of the business school globalization literature [...].

As has been widely noted, much of the distinctiveness of New Labour's political economy rests on the sustained and systematic appeal to globalization as an external economic constraint. Here, again, economic imperatives claim precedence over political discretion as, it is argued, heightened capital mobility serves to tilt the balance of power from immobile government and comparatively immobile labor to fluid capital. In such an inauspicious context for economic policy autonomy, the state (as fiscal authority) must adapt and accommodate itself to the perceived interest of capital (for labor market flexibility, a 'competitive' taxation environment and so forth) if it is not to precipitate a haemorrhaging of invested funds. The judgment of mobile assets (whether of invested or still liquid funds) is assumed to be both harsh and immediate, selecting for fiscal responsibility, prudence, a rules-bounded economic policy (as guarantor of credibility and competence) and both flexible labor markets and low levels of corporate and personal taxation. The appeal to globalization thus conjures a logic of economic necessity and, indeed, compulsion, driving a non-negotiable agenda for welfare retrenchment and labor-market reform – while further shoring up its open economy macroeconomics.

[...] The policy implications of such an account are painfully clear. As globalization serves to establish competitive selection mechanisms within the international economy, there is little choice but to cast all regulatory impediments to the efficient operation of the market on the bonfire of welfare institutions, regulatory controls and labor-market rigidities.

[...]

[...] While it may seem entirely appropriate to attribute to capital the sole motive of seeking the greatest return on its investment, the political and economic history of capital provides little or no support for the notion that capital is blessed either with complete information or even with a relatively clear and consistent conception of what its own best interest is. Moreover, as the political economy of the advanced capitalist democracies demonstrates well, capital has a history of resisting social and economic reforms which it has later come both to rely upon and actively to defend (see, for instance, Swenson 2000).

The second assumption is, again, a convenient fiction, used in neoclassical macroeconomics to make possible the modeling of an open economy. Few if any economists would defend the claim that markets for goods or services are fully integrated or clear instantly.

If the first two assumptions are problematic, then the third is demonstrably false, at least with respect to certain types of capital. For, while portfolio capital may indeed exhibit almost perfect mobility in a digital economy, the same is simply not the case for capital invested in infrastructure, machinery and personnel. Once attracted to a particular locality, foreign direct investors acquire a range of non-recuperable or 'sunk' costs – such as their investment in physical infrastructure, plant and machinery. Consequently, their exit options become seriously depleted.

No less problematic are assumptions four and five – that capital can compete in a more intensely competitive environment only on the basis of productivity gains secured through tax reductions and cost-shedding and that the welfare state is, for business, merely a drain on profits. This is to extrapolate wildly and inappropriately from labor-intensive sectors of the international economy in which competitiveness is conventionally enhanced in this way to the global economy more generally. It fails to appreciate that foreign direct investors in capital-intensive sectors of the international economy are attracted to locations like the Northern European economies neither for the flexibility of their labor markets nor for the cheapness of the wage and non-wage labor costs that they impose, but for the access they provide to a highly skilled, reliable and innovative labor force (Cooke and Noble 1998). High wages and high non-wage labor costs (in the form of payroll taxes) would seem to be a price many multinational corporations regard as worth paying for a dynamic and highly skilled workforce.

As the above paragraphs suggest once again, *stylized rationalist and open economy assumptions deliver a spurious necessity to economic policy choices.* Overly parsimonious rationalist assumptions have played a crucial role in consolidating, normalizing and, above all, depoliticizing a neoliberal economic paradigm which is disingenuously presented as a simple and necessary accommodation to global economic realities.

This again raises the question of New Labour's motivation for invoking globalization as a non-negotiable external economic imperative. What is clear is that this serves to insulate from potential critique the supply-side reform agenda (of labor-market flexibilization and the marketization of public-sector incentive structures) that it has inherited, and arguably enervated, from its Conservative predecessors. Once again, three options immediately present themselves: (1) that New Labour policymakers are believers in the globalization thesis and have simply internalized its policy implications; (2) that an expressed belief in the globalization thesis is seen as an appropriate signal to the markets and market analysts of New Labour's moderation and competence; and (3) that invoking the globalization thesis and internalizing its policy implications is a means to an end – the insulation, from critique, of its supply-side reform agenda. Here it is the second of these that is probably the easiest to discount – as it is by no means clear that market analysts pay great attention to the extent to which elected officials publicly endorse the constraints they attribute to globalization. It would seem that the first and third, in combination, provide a more plausible sense of New Labour's motivations here. Invoking globalization as the source of a series of non-negotiable imperatives that must be internalized almost certainly reflects the prevailing and genuinely held assumptions of many policymakers. Moreover, insofar as it is acknowledged that there is a choice here, there are clear strategic advantages to the pubic legitimation of a reform trajectory that may be unpalatable to many in terms of imperatives that are (ostensibly) transparent and non-contestable.

Conclusions

[...]

First, our ability to offer alternatives to neoliberalism rests now on our ability to identify that there is a choice in such matters and, in so doing, to demystify and deconstruct the rationalist premises upon which its public legitimation has been predicated. This, it would seem, is a condition of the return of a more normative and engaging form of politics in which more is at stake than the personnel to administer a largely agreed and ostensibly technical neoliberal reform agenda.

Second, the present custodians of neoliberalism are, in many cases, reluctant converts, whose accommodation to neoliberalism is essentially borne of perceived pragmatism and necessity rather than out of any deep normative commitment to the sanctity of the market. Thus, rather than defend neoliberalism publicly and in its own terms, they have sought instead to appeal to the absence of a choice which might be defended in such terms. Consequently, political discourse is technocratic rather than political.

Furthermore, as Peter Burnham has recently noted, neoliberalism is itself a deeply depoliticizing paradigm (2001), whose effect is to subordinate social and political priorities, such as might arise from a more dialogic, responsive and democratic politics, to perceived economic imperatives and to the ruthless efficiency of the market. As I have sought to demonstrate, this antipathy to 'politics' is a direct correlate of public choice theory's projection of its most cherished assumption of instrumental rationality onto public officials. This is an important point, for it suggests the crucial role played by stylized rationalist assumptions, particularly (as in the overload thesis, public choice theory more generally and even the time-inconsistency thesis) those which relate to the rational conduct of public officials, in contributing to the depoliticizing dynamics now reflected in political disaffection and disengagement.

As this perhaps serves to indicate, seemingly innocent assumptions may have alarmingly cumulative consequences. Indeed, the internalization of a neoliberalism predicated on rationalist assumptions may well serve to render the so-called 'rational voter paradox' something of a self-fulfilling prophecy.[12] The rational voter paradox – that in a democratic polity in which parties behave in a 'rational' manner, it is irrational for citizens to vote (since the chances of the vote they cast proving decisive are negligible) – has always been seen as the central weakness of rational choice theory as a set of analytical techniques for exploring electoral competition. Yet, as the above analysis suggests, in a world constructed in the image of rationalist assumptions, it may become depressingly accurate. Political parties behaving in a narrowly 'rational' manner, assuming others (electors and market participants) to behave in a similarly 'rational' fashion will contribute to a dynamic which sees real electors (rational or otherwise) disengage in increasing numbers from the facade of electoral competition.

That this is so is only reinforced by a final factor. The institutionalization and normalization of neoliberalism in many advanced liberal democracies in recent years have been defended in largely technical and rationalist terms and in a manner almost entirely inaccessible to public political scrutiny, contestation and debate. The electorate, in recent years, has not been invited to choose between competing programmatic mandates to be delivered in office, but to pass a judgment on the credibility and competence of the respective candidates for high office to behave in the appropriate (technical) manner in response to contingent external stimuli. Is it any wonder that they have chosen, in increasing numbers, not to exercise any such judgment at all at the ballot box?

As this final point suggests, the rejection of the neoliberal paradigm, the demystification of its presumed inevitability and the rejection of the technical and rationalist terms in which that defence has been constructed are intimately connected. They are, moreover, likely to be a condition not only of the return of normative politics but also of the re-animation of a worryingly disaffected and disengaged democratic culture.

Acknowledgments

Earlier versions of this paper were presented to the Interdisciplinary Symposium on 'The Dynamics of Ideas', University of Bristol, 7–8 November 2003, and to the International Workshop on 'Critical Political Economy', Institute for Advanced Studies, Lancaster University, 3–4 June 2004. I should like to thank participants on both occasions and two anonymous referees for *Economy and Society* for their perceptive and encouraging comments.

Notes

1. Such bodies are 'supra-democratic' in the sense that, although they receive their constitutional mandate from democratically accountable entities, the content of their (ostensibly technical) deliberations and decisions are subject only in a retrospective fashion to any kind of democratic audit. As such, they are above and beyond effective democratic scrutiny. In the case of independent central banks, it is precisely this supra-democratic character that is seen to hold the key to their (relative) technical competence and efficacy (see, for instance, Kydland and Prescott 1977).
2. Such a message is reinforced, as we shall see presently by the appropriation of rational expectations assumptions in the dominant (neoliberal) economic paradigm. For, within rational expectations economics, governments and indeed political parties cannot credibly commit themselves, for instance, to a given inflation target – for it is rational, given their 'time-inconsistent' inflation preferences, for them to renege on any such commitment they might make.
3. The quote marks are important. For there is no guarantee that what passes for, say, Keynesianism as an institutionalized economic paradigm in any given national context will bear any striking resemblance to textbook Keynesianism – nor, as a consequence, that national 'Keynesianisms' will necessarily bear any close family resemblance.
4. There is something of a tendency in the existing literature to assume that it is only really in moments of crisis for – Mark Blyth (2002), moments of 'Knightian uncertainty' in which actors struggle to identify their genuine interests – that 'ideas matter'. While it may well be that the causal and/or constitutive role of ideas in such moments is of particular interest to political analysts, it is problematic (and ontologically uneven) to see the effect of ideas as being temporally limited in such a way. The aim of the present contribution, as much as anything, is to establish the crucial role of ideas between moments of punctuation – in the institutionalization and normalization of economic paradigms.
5. In fact, its character derives less from its neoliberalism than the manner in which it comes to accommodate itself to neoliberalism. For whereas the neoliberalism of successive Conservative administrations in Britain has been defended in normative terms, that of New Labour and the 'Third Way' is far more necessitarian in character.

6. As I have elsewhere argued, the crisis was constituted as a crisis through a series of influential and populist neoliberal and neoconservative narratives. In particular, 'stagflation' was seen as indicative of a crisis of an overextended state increasingly held to ransom by the sectional interests of the trade unions.
7. At this point it is perhaps important to introduce one further observation. Proponents of Thatcherite neoliberalism were certainly animated by a normative conviction as to the moral/ethical superiority of the reform agenda they espoused. What is far less clear is how deeply wedded they were to the rationalist terms in which the public rationale for neoliberalism was presented. Indeed, it seems quite plausible to suggest that the overload thesis was regarded by proponents of a normative neoliberalism as a convenient, even disingenuous, means to an ethically defensible and principled end.
8. As hinted at above, these were, in all likelihood, clearly visible to its proponents at the time. Yet such logical inconsistency was, of course, no impediment to constructing a series of powerful resonances with the electorate's experiences of the 'crisis'. In a situation of a high and rising public deficit there is an obvious appeal to narratives of overload and over-reach, particularly those which identify as culpable the very same public-sector unions striking for inflationary wage deals.
9. The status of such assumptions provides a very interesting and potentially illuminating contrast to the pre-history of Thatcherism. The latter, as we have seen, was ostensibly predicated on the rationalist assumptions of the overload thesis and public choice theory more broadly. Though part of a normative neoliberalism, these assumptions were adopted, it seems, for instrumental and strategic reasons and as means to an ethically defensible end – they served effectively to legitimate the paradigm shift to neoliberalism. The status of rational expectations assumptions in New Labour's political economy is rather different. For, insofar as it is acknowledged that such assumptions are consciously adopted (and hence that there is a choice to make), these are presented as the only credible assumptions to adopt – reflective of a consensus among contemporary neoclassical economists. Rational expectations assumptions are, then, for New Labour an index of its economic literacy and competence; the equivalent rationalist assumptions for Thatcherism were adopted in a far more strategic and instrumental fashion. Arguably this has much to do with the development and institutionalization of neoliberalism as an economic paradigm. As neoliberalism has become paradigmatic, supporting assumptions which were once considered highly contentious have now become normalized, an index of competence and credibility.
10. I should like to thank one of the anonymous referees for probing me further on this important point.
11. In the sense that the adoption of such a rationale for monetary policy choices (and the institutional architecture for their delivery) translates what might otherwise be public and political disputes about appropriate policy instruments and settings into purely private and technical matters, to be adjudicated by competent professionals. Moreover, it diverts attention from the neo-monetarist content of monetary policy choices, allowing them to be presented as a simple consequence of sound economic management. As such it both institutionalizes and insulates from public scrutiny a neo-monetarist macroeconomic regime.
12. On the self-fulfilling nature of rationalist assumptions more generally, see Hay (2004b).

6

Towards a Schumpeterian Workfare State? Preliminary Remarks on Post-Fordist Political Economy*

Bob Jessop

[...] This paper is aimed at introducing some state-theoretical concerns into regulation theory rather than introducing regulationist concepts into analyses of the state. Its starting point is the insight that, since economic activity is both socially embedded and socially regulated, an adequate account of the economy must adopt an 'integral' approach. Thus the following analysis is concerned with the expanded economic and social reproduction of capitalism or, to paraphrase Gramsci, the 'economy in its inclusive sense.'[1] This can be defined in turn as comprising an 'accumulation regime + mode of social regulation.' The state is an important structural and strategic force in this regard and has major roles in securing the expanded reproduction and regulation of capitalism.[2] Two general functions are particularly important here: first, helping to secure the conditions for the valorization of capital; and, second, helping to secure the conditions for the reproduction of labor-power. Indeed these two broad functions arc incorporated into the very definitions of the Keynesian welfare and Schumpeterian workfare states. Thus, while the terms 'Keynesian' and 'Schumpeterian' in each concept refer to the distinctive form of state economic intervention characteristic of a given mode of social regulation, the terms 'welfare' and 'workfare' refer to the distinctive form of social intervention favored by the state. From the sort of integral economic viewpoint adumbrated here, the Keynesian welfare state (or KWS) and Schumpeterian workfare state (or SWS) are likely to correspond to different accumulation regimes.

Thus I hope to show that, whereas the former was an 'integral' element in the expanded reproduction of Fordism, the latter could become just as 'integral' to its still emerging successor regime.[3]

---

* From *Studies in Political Economy* 40 (1993): 7–39.

The Schumpeterian workfare state

[...] [A]s the crisis of the KWS unfolded and efforts to restore the conditions for post-war growth through economic austerity and social retrenchment failed, the emphasis shifted to attempts to restructure and reorient the state in the light of significantly changed perceptions of the conditions making for economic expansion. What is emerging, hesitantly and unevenly, from these attempts is a new regime which could be termed, albeit rather inelegantly,[4] the Schumpeterian workfare state (SWS). Its distinctive economic and social objectives can be summarized in abstract terms as: the promotion of product, process, organizational, and market innovation; the enhancement of the structural competitiveness of open economies mainly through supply-side intervention; and the subordination of social policy to the demands of labor market flexibility and structural competitiveness. Although the distinctive features of the SWS emerge most clearly in contrast with the KWS, it is important to note that the appearance of the SWS is not dependent on the presence of any more or less crisis-prone KWS. While this development may be typical in European cases for instance, there are important East Asian examples which do not fit such a pattern. Indeed these latter examples are often taken nowadays as models for crisis resolution in the West.

The 'hollowing out' of the national state

In each of the core triad regions, in North America, the European Community, and East Asia, the national state is subject to various changes leading to its 'hollowing out.' This does not mean that the national state has lost all importance: far from it. Indeed it remains crucial as an institutional site and discursive framework for political struggles; and it even keeps much of its sovereignty – albeit primarily as a juridical fiction reproduced through mutual recognition in the international political community. At the same time its capacities to project power even within its own national borders are becoming ever more limited due to a complex triple displacement of powers upward, downward, and, to some extent, outward. Thus, some state capacities are transferred to pan-regional, plurinational, or international bodies; others are devolved to the regional or local level inside the national state; and yet others are assumed by emerging horizontal networks of power – regional and/or local – which bypass central states and link regions or localities in several societies. These shifts are also associated with the blurring of the state's boundaries and its growing involvement in decentralized societal guidance strategies rather than centralized imperative coordination. Moreover, while such shifts sometimes emerge as conjunctural products of short-term crisis management or displacement strategies, they also correspond to long-term structural changes in the global economy. At stake here is not just a series of formal or tactical shifts but also the practical rearticulation of political capacities. For the national state's tendential loss of autonomy creates both the need for supranational coordination and the space for sub-national resurgence. The precise mix of the three main forms of 'hollowing out' will clearly vary with the existing economic and political regime, the structural constraints it confronts, and the changing balance of forces.

From Fordism to post-Fordism

The general consistency of these shifts across a wide range of economic and political regimes suggests that more than mere happenstance or local economic and political conditions are at work. Hence the third claim is that these two shifts are closely related and grounded in a set of processes which is often, if somewhat misleadingly, characterized as the transition from Fordism to post-Fordism. However, while this characterization has certainly helped to contextualize and shape the responses to the crisis of the KWS, it also obscures the real complexity of the changes grouped there under, as well as the problems faced in finding anything like a comprehensive solution. [...] [A]ttention should also be paid to such factors as the rise of new technologies, the accelerated pace of internationalization, and basic shifts in the regional forms of global and national economies. All four trends are closely connected. Together they undermine the KWS's effectiveness as a force in economic and political regulation and set the parameters within which solutions for the crisis of the postwar economic order must be sought.

The best possible political shell?

This leads to the fourth, and most audacious, claim: namely, that the 'hollowed out' SWS could be regarded as the best possible political shell for post-Fordism. There is an obvious risk with this metaphor. For it might encourage the mistaken idea that the state is merely a protective political shell inside which an economic kernel might germinate securely. An integral economic viewpoint, with its explicit focus on the structural coupling and contingent co-evolution[5] of accumulation regimes and modes of social regulation, excludes any such interpretation. It does suggest the possibility, however, of attempting to justify this claim in at least three ways: by showing that KWS regimes were structurally coupled in major respects to the growth dynamic of Atlantic Fordism[6] and that the transition to the SWS helps resolve the principal crisis tendencies of Atlantic Fordism and/or its associated KWS regimes so that a new wave of accumulation becomes possible; that the distinctive aspects of the evolving SWS correspond in crucial respects to the emerging growth dynamic of the new global economy and contribute significantly to the overall shaping of this dynamic considered from an integral viewpoint; and that the most competitive economic spaces in this emerging order have actually pioneered this form of state and have thereby gained a paradigmatic, exemplary status for restructuring efforts elsewhere. All three lines of analysis could lend credence to the (now redefined, less metaphorical) claim that the 'hollowed out' SWS is peculiarly well-suited to promote and consolidate (and not merely to encapsulate) the still evolving post-Fordist, 'integral' economic order – with all that this implies for the losers as well as those who benefit from the process. Just such an experimental threefold demonstration is attempted below.

Once more on the Schumpeterian workfare state

[...]
The distinctive features of the Schumpeterian workfare state are: a concern to promote innovation and structural competitiveness in the field of economic policy; and a concern to promote flexibility and competitiveness in the field of social policy. Naturally the SWS will also express other concerns and perform many other functions typical of capitalist states but it is the combination of these twin concerns, together with their implications for the overall functioning of the state which differentiate it from other capitalist regimes. Together they become an integral part of its accumulation strategy and are also reflected in the state and hegemonic projects with which it is associated. Thus, while most advanced capitalist states have some form of innovation policy, the SWS is distinctive for its explicit, strategically self-conscious concern with promoting innovation and for its broad interpretation of the factors bearing on successful innovation. Likewise, while most advanced capitalist states have some form of competition policy, the SWS is distinctive for its explicit, strategically self-conscious concern with the many and varied conditions which make for structural competitiveness in open economies. Similarly, turning to SWS social policy, while concern with training and labor market functioning has long been a feature of state involvement in the social reproduction of labor power, flexibility has been accorded greater weight and acquired new connotations in both fields. Complementing these various new strategic concerns in economic and social policy has been the demotion or even rejection of other, earlier policy objectives. Thus, while the KWS was committed to securing full employment, the SWS demotes this goal in favor of promoting structural competitiveness. Similarly, while the KWS tried to extend the social rights of its citizens, the SWS is concerned to provide welfare services that benefit business with the result that individual needs take second place.

Implicit in the preceding analysis is the crucial working assumption that the rise of the SWS is reflected in, and reinforced by, changes in economic discourse, modes of calculation, and strategic concepts. Such changes are an important correlate of the restructuring and reorientation of the national state in the current period. They provide an important mediating link between the structural changes in the global economy and the transformation of the state by providing an interpretative framework within which to make sense of these changes, the crises that often accompany them, and the responses which might be appropriate to them. One particularly telling discursive-strategic shift in the transition from the KWS to the SWS is the demotion of concern with 'productivity' and 'planning' and the emphasis now put on the need for 'flexibility' and 'entrepreneurialism.' It is the articulation of these and related discursive-strategic shifts into new accumulation strategies, state projects, and hegemonic projects and their capacity to mobilize support and deliver effective state policies that helps to shape the restructuring and reorientation of the contemporary state and to produce different regulatory regimes. And it is precisely the need for such mediation (as well as, for example, variability in state capacities) which ensure that successful consolidation of a Schumpeterian workfare state is far from automatic.

Let us now consider how the respective economic and social functions of the KWS and SWS are reflected in two major structural (as opposed to discursive-strategic) features of the two regimes. These concern the articulation of the money, wage, and state forms. The money and wage forms both embody the structural contradictions of capital as a social relation and thereby give rise to strategic dilemmas. One expression of this in the money form is the fact that it can circulate both as a national money and as an international currency. In the case of the wage form, there is a contradiction between its function as a cost to capital and a source of demand. These contradictions are reflected in quite different ways in Keynesian welfare and Schumpeterian workfare regimes.

Firstly, whereas money functions primarily as a national money in the KWS and its circulation within the national economy is controlled by the national state, in the SWS this position is threatened by increasing cross-border flows of financial capital and their adverse implications for monetary control by national states.[7] Indeed the crisis of national money is a major contributory factor to the crisis of the Keynesian welfare state. Recognition of national economic vulnerability to massive and volatile currency movements is central to the SWS. For, if the strength of the national money increasingly depends on the competitive strength of the national economy in an increasingly open world economy, then economic intervention must increasingly take the form of guiding supply-side developments rather than trying in vain to manage the demand side. In turn this reinforces the need for spending to serve productive and competitive needs even in the erstwhile welfare state.

Secondly, while the wage functioned primarily as a source of demand within the KWS, it is seen primarily as a production cost in the SWS. In the former, growth in wages served capital's interests in attaining full capacity utilization in a closed economy in which mass production was dominant. Provided that wages and productivity in the consumer goods sector moved in a similar range, this would offset any tendencies towards a crisis of underconsumption due to insufficient demand or a wage-induced profits squeeze.[8] The KWS contributed to this result by legitimating collective bargaining, generalizing norms of mass consumption, and engaging in contracyclical demand management. But the growing internationalization accompanying the final stages of Fordism transforms this situation: wages are increasingly seen as a cost of production. Where this is seen as a fixed cost (e.g., core workforces in Japan or Germany), this can encourage innovation and reskilling in order to retain a high-wage, high-growth accumulation strategy. Conversely, where it is seen as a variable cost (as in the differently organized British and American cases), 'short-termism' and 'hire-and-fire' may result in the hope that neoliberal flexibility may help to sustain competitiveness. Since such remarks highlight the need to discuss variant forms of the SWS, however, further discussion will be deferred to the appropriate section.

Let me end with two more substantive caveats.[9] First, in identifying the SWS with supply-side intervention, I am not implying that it can safely ignore the demand side. It is quite clear that the continuing crisis of Fordism and the current transition to post-Fordism are both linked to problems on the demand side. Excessive budgetary deficits, overly restrictive monetary policies, and frequent and large international current account imbalances have all created serious impediments to the creation of a new long wave of economic expansion. But these problems are exacerbated by the global trends noted above and so demand international as well as national solutions: this is reflected in calls for international Keynesianism as well as national efforts to manage these demand-side problems by restructuring social policy in accordance with workfare principles. It is the increasingly international character of these demand-side problems which reinforces the 'hollowing out' process noted above. And this in turn creates space for increasing supply-side intervention by the national and regional state. Secondly, and conversely, designating the post-war state form as just 'Keynesian' would seem to downplay its contributions to the supply of technological innovation through increased support for science, massive funding of higher education, and often vast support for military research and development. But here too it is important to emphasize how the four global trends noted above fundamentally transform the relationship between such demand- and supply-side policies. KWS supply-side policies were shaped by the Fordist paradigm with its emphasis on economies of scale, big science, and productivity growth, SWS supply-side policies are oriented to permanent innovation, economies of scope, and structural competitiveness. This puts a far greater premium on the self-reflexive management of the national innovation system and the capacity for institutional learning than would have been typical of the Fordist KWS.

'Hollowing out' and the development of the SWS

A further key aspect of the development of the SWS is the national state's subjection to a complex series of changes which result in its 'hollowing out.' This term is intentionally reminiscent of 'hollow corporations,' i.e., transnationals headquartered in one country whose operations are mostly pursued elsewhere. By analogy, the 'hollow state' metaphor is intended to indicate two trends: first, that the national state retains many of its head-quarters functions – including the trappings of central executive authority and national sovereignty as well as the discourses that sustain them; and, second, that its capacities to translate this authority and sovereignty into effective control are becoming limited by a complex displacement of powers. The resulting changes in the formal articulation and operational autonomy of national states have major repercussions on forms of repre-sentation, intervention, internal hierarchies, social bases, and state projects across all levels of state organization.

First, the role of supranational state systems is expanding. Such interna-tional, transnational, and pan-regional bodies are not new in themselves: they have a long history. What is significant today is the sheer increase in their numbers, the growth in their territorial scope, and their acquisition of important new functions. This reflects the steady emergence of a world society rooted in a growing number of global functional systems (eco-nomic, scientific, legal, political, military, and so on) and in wider recogni-tion of the global reach of old and new risks. This functional expansion is notably evident in the interest that supranational bodies display in foster-ing structural competitiveness within the territories that they manage. This goes well beyond concern with managing international monetary relations, foreign investment, or trade to encompass a wide range of supply-side factors, both economic and extra-economic in nature.

[...] Second, in tandem with the rise of international state apparatuses, we find a stronger role for the local state. This reflects growing interna-tionalization as well as the economic retreat of the nation-state. For global-ization means that 'the local economy can only be seen as a node within a global economic network (with) no meaningful existence outside this context.'[10] During the Fordist era, local states operated as extensions of the central Keynesian welfare state and regional policy was mainly oriented to the (re-)location of industry in the interests of spreading full employment and reducing inflationary pressures due to localized overheating. Such states provided local infrastructure to support Fordist mass production, promoted collective consumption and local welfare state policies, and, in some cases (especially as the crisis of Fordism unfolded), offered subsidies in an effort to compete with each other to attract new jobs or prevent the loss of established jobs. In the wake of Fordist crisis, however, local economic activities involve greater emphasis on economic regeneration and competitiveness. The central concern is 'how state institutions can shape regional economies to make them more competitive in the new world economy.'[11] There is growing interest in regional labor market policies, education and training, technology transfer, local venture capital, innovation centers, science parks, and so on. This led van Hoogstraten to suggest that the state, 'although badly challenged at the national level because of its Fordist involvement with crisis management, seems to have risen from the ashes at the regional and local level.'[12]

In turn this is linked to the reorganization of the local state as new forms of local partnership emerge to guide and promote the development of local resources. Economic regeneration involves more than a technical fix and calls for coordinated action in areas such as education policy, training, infrastructural provision, the availability of venture capital, cultural policy, and so on. In turn this leads to the involvement of local unions, local chambers of commerce, local venture capital, local education bodies, local research centers as well as local states. This trend is reinforced by the inability of the central state to pursue sufficiently differentiated and sensitive programs to tackle the specific problems of particular localities. It therefore devolves such tasks to local states and provides the latter with general support and resources.[13] More optimistic accounts of this trend see it leading to a confederation of job-creating, risk-sharing local states rooted in strong regional economies which provide reciprocal support in the ongoing struggle to retain a competitive edge.[14] But more pessimistic scenarios anticipate growing polarization in localities as well as increased regional inequalities.

Third, there are growing links among local states, a phenomenon closely linked to the first two changes. Indeed Dyson writes that 'one of the most interesting political developments since the 1970s has been the erratic but gradual shift of ever more local authorities from an identification of their role in purely national terms towards a new interest in transnational relationships.'[15] In Europe this involves both vertical links with EC institutions, especially the European Commission, and direct links among local and regional authorities in member states. The search for cross-border support is strengthened to the extent that the central state pursues a more neoliberal strategy, but it can be found in other countries too.[16] Similar trends are discernible in East Asia (notably in links between Hong Kong, Macao, and Guangdong and in the so-called 'growth triangle' formed by Singapore, Johor, and Riau). As yet this third trend is less marked in North America (even though the entrepreneurial city and local state have seen remarkable expansion). But striking examples can be found in the expansion of transborder cooperation of linked cities along the US-Mexican boundary. And, even in the USA itself, the growth of subnational links across nations has led Duchacek to talk of the spread of 'perforated sovereignty'[17] as nations become more open to trans-sovereign contacts at both the local and regional level.

Post-Fordism and the SWS

The concept of post-Fordism can be applied meaningfully only if there are both continuities and discontinuities in the development of the accumulation regime and its mode of social regulation: without continuities, the new system could not be said to be post-*Fordist*; without discontinuities, it could not be *post*-Fordist. In this context one could regard the continuities as mediated through the crises of Fordism and the discontinuities as introduced by structural and/or strategic changes which might resolve for a significant time the crises in Fordist modes of growth and regulation and/or create the conditions for non-Fordist accumulation and regulation to succeed. Thus we can regard the SWS as post-Fordist to the extent that: it directly or indirectly resolves (or is held to do so) the crisis tendencies of Fordist accumulation and/or of the KWS as one of its main regulatory forms; its emergence (for whatever reason) helps to shape and consolidate the dynamic of the emerging global economy and thereby encourages the renewal and reregulation of capitalism after its Fordist period; and its alleged contribution to competitiveness in some economies (even if they themselves were never really Fordist) leads to its acquiring paradigmatic status elsewhere as the key to the regeneration and/or reregulation of a capitalist growth dynamic [...].

[...] Before considering possible grounds for describing the SWS as post-Fordist, let us consider some relevant crisis tendencies in the Fordist mode of growth. These include: the gradual (and always relative) exhaustion of the growth potential which came from extending mass production into new branches; the relative saturation of markets for mass consumer durables; the disruption of the virtuous circle of Fordist accumulation through internationalization; the growing incoherence and ineffectiveness of national economic management as national economies become more open; the stagflationary impact of the KWS on the Fordist growth dynamic (especially where state economic intervention is too concerned with sustaining employment in sunset sectors); a growing fiscal crisis due to the ratchet-like expansion of social consumption expenditure; and an emerging crisis of social security due to the expansion of part-time, temporary, and discontinuous employment at the expense of a full-time Fordist norm. An emerging post-Fordist accumulation regime could be said to respond to these crisis tendencies in various ways. It transforms mass production and goes beyond it, segments old markets and opens new ones, is less constrained by national demand conditions but makes new demands upon regional and national innovation systems, replaces macroeconomic planning in autocentric economies with supply-side flexibility in response to international turbulence, offers new ways of regenerating old industries as well as replacing them, promises new ways of organizing social consumption to reduce costs and make it more functional for business, and is able to further exploit the fragmentation and polarization of the labor force consequent upon the crisis in Fordism.

This account raises the question whether the distinctive aspects of the SWS match the dynamic of post-Fordist accumulation regimes. An affirmative answer seems to be justified if only on definitional grounds. For, given the evident crisis in the KWS that accompanies the crisis of Fordism, a consolidated SWS as defined here would clearly perform better. It engages in supply-side intervention to promote permanent innovation and enhance structural competitiveness; and it also goes beyond the mere retrenchment of social welfare to restructure and subordinate it to market forces. A less tautological answer must await specification of variant forms of the SWS and empirical assessment of the viability of these different forms in specific conjunctures.

A second approach to the correspondence between the SWS and the new global economic order relates to the four economic trends noted above. The strategic orientation of the SWS to innovation takes account of the enormous ramifications of new technologies; its concern with structural competitiveness recognizes the changing terms and conditions of international competition as well as its increased significance; its restructuring and reorientation of social reproduction towards flexibility and retrenchment signifies its awareness of the post-Fordist paradigm shift as well as the impact of internationalization on the primary functions of money and wages; and its complex 'hollowing out' reflects the complex dialectic between globalization and regionalization. In short, for all four trends, a 'hollowed out' SWS could help both to shape and consolidate key features of the new regime of accumulation on a world scale. This approach must also rely largely on assertion for its persuasive effect until the effectiveness of specific SWS regimes (and alternative modes of social regulation of the emerging global order) have been properly examined.

A third approach is more promising for present purposes, however, since its persuasive force depends on past performance rather than possible post-Fordist futures. It would involve demonstrating that those economies which have grown most rapidly during the global crisis of Fordism and which have become models for those in crisis are especially advanced in developing Schumpeterian workfare state regimes. Among the most prominent examples might be Japan, Germany, South Korea, Taiwan, Brazil, the Third Italy, and some of the most successful regional economies

in otherwise crisis-prone economies. Even if it would be wrong to catego-
rize all these national and/or regional economies as literally post-Fordist
(because they were never truly Fordist), their increasing role as exemplars of
alternative (and apparently successful) trajectories for Fordist regimes in
crisis does mean that they have a paradigmatic post-Fordist status.

Alternative SWS strategies

[...] For heuristic purposes, however, one can posit three ideal-typical
forms: neoliberal, neocorporatist, and neostatist. In using the prefix 'neo'
to identify them, I want to emphasize that all three would embody important discontinuities with the liberal, corporatist, and statist KWS regimes
linked to Fordism. And, in identifying them here as ideal-types, I want to
emphasize that it is unlikely they will be found in pure form. The particular
strategy mixes to be found in individual cases will depend on institutional
legacies, the balance of political forces, and the changing economic and
political conjunctures in which different strategies are pursued.

Neoliberalism is concerned to promote a market-led transition towards
the new economic regime. For the public sector, it involves privatization,
liberalization, and imposition of commercial criteria in the residual state
sector; for the private sector, it involves deregulation and a new legal and
political framework to provide passive support for market solutions. This is
reflected in government promotion of hire-and-fire, flexi-time, and flexi-
wage labor markets; growth of tax expenditures steered by private initiatives based on fiscal subsidies for favored economic activities; measures to
transform the welfare state into a means of supporting and subsidizing low
wages as well as to enhance the disciplinary force of social security measures and programs; and the more general reorientation of economic and
social policy to the perceived needs of the private sector. Coupled with
such measures is disavowal of social partnership in favor of managerial prerogatives, market forces, and a strong state. Neoliberalism also involves a
cosmopolitan approach that welcomes internationalization of domestic
economic space in the form of both outward and inward investment and
also calls for the liberalization of international trade and investment within
regional blocs and more generally. Innovation is expected to follow spontaneously from the liberation of the animal spirits of individual entrepreneurs as they take advantage of incentives in the new market-led climate
and from the more general government promotion of an enterprise culture.
In turn national competitiveness is understood as the aggregate effect of
the microeconomic competitiveness of individual firms. Hence there is
little state concern to maintain a sufficiently deep and coherent set of core
economic competencies in the home economy, and/or adequate national
or regional innovation systems, to provide the basis for structural competitiveness. In this context, local and international state apparatuses are

expected to act as relays for the market-led approach to innovation and workfare. [...]

Neocorporatism relies on the institutionalization of a continuing, negotiated, concerted approach to the economic strategies, decisions and conduct of economic agents. Based on a self-reflexive understanding of the linkages between their own private economic interests and the importance of collective agreements to the stability of a socially embedded, socially regulated economy, the economic forces involved in neocorporatism strive to balance competition and cooperation. Influenced by the four global trends noted above, however, this system differs from a Fordist corporatism based on the dominance of mass production and mass unions and on the primacy of full employment and stagflation as economic concerns. Thus, the scope of neocorporatist arrangements reflects the diversity of policy communities and networks relevant to an innovation-driven mode of growth as well as the increasing heterogeneity of labor forces and labor markets. Neocorporatist arrangements in an emerging SWS are also more directly and explicitly oriented to the crucial importance of innovation and structural competitiveness. They will extend beyond business associations and labor unions to include policy communities representing distinct functional systems (e.g., science, health, education); and policy implementation will become more flexible through the extension of 'regulated self-regulation' and private interest government, so that there is less direct state involvement in managing the 'supply side' and more emphasis on private industrial policies. Corporatist arrangements may also become more selective (e.g., excluding some previously entrenched industrial interests and peripheral or marginal workers, integrating some sunrise sectors and giving more weight to core workers); and, reflecting the greater flexibility and decentralization of key features of the post-Fordist economy, the centers of neocorporatist gravity will move toward the microlevel of firms and localities at the expense of centralized macroeconomic concentration. [...]

Neostatism involves a market-conforming but state-sponsored approach to economic reorganization in which the state intervenes to guide the development of market forces. It does so through deploying its own powers of imperative coordination, its own economic resources and activities, and its own knowledge bases and organizational intelligence. In deploying these various resources in support of a national accumulation strategy, however, it is well aware of the changing nature of international competition. It involves a mixture of decommodification, state-sponsored flexibility, and other state activities aimed at securing the dynamic efficiency of a productive core. This is reflected in an active structural policy in which the state sets strategic targets relating to new technologies, technology transfer, innovation systems, infrastructure, and other factors affecting the overall structural competitiveness of the economy. It favors an active labor market policy to reskill the labor force and to encourage a flexi-skill rather than flexi-price labor market; it intervenes directly and openly with its own political and economic resources to restructure declining industries and to promote sunrise sectors; and it engages in a range of societal guidance strategies, based on its own strategic intelligence and economic resources, to promote specific objectives through concerted action with varied policy communities, which embrace public, mixed, and private interests. These activities aim to move the domestic economy up the technological hierarchy by creating and maintaining a coherent and competitive productive base, and pursuing a strategy of flexible specialization in specific high technology sectors. While the central state retains a key strategic role in these areas, it also allows and encourages parallel and complementary activities at regional and/or local levels. But its desire to protect the core technological and economic competencies of its productive base is often associated with neomercantilism at the supranational level.

[...]

Acknowledgments

This is a revised and shortened version of a paper first presented at the Eighth Conference of Europeanists, Chicago, 26–28 March 1992; it has benefited greatly from the comments of Bill Carroll, Des King, Colin Hay, Jane Jenson. Rianne Mahon, Klaus Nielsen, Leo Panitch, Sum Ngai-Ling, and David Wolfe. An unfortunate effect of the paper's abbreviation has been the excision of many references and supporting examples.

Notes

1. The reference is to Gramsci's analysis of '*lo stato integrale*' (the state in its inclusive sense) in terms of 'political society + civil society.' See Gramsci (1971). Gramsci's state theory is compared with the 'integral economic' approach implicit in regulation theory in B. Jessop 'Regulation und Politik: "Integral Economy" and "Integral State",' in A. Demirovic, *et al.* (eds), *Akkumulation, Hegemonie und Staat* (Muenster: Westfaelisches Dampfboot Verlag, in press).

2. The forms, functions, and activities of the state cannot be reduced to its role in regulating the economy in its inclusive sense. In approaching it from an integral economic viewpoint one necessarily produces a partial account of the state; just as an integral political approach to the economy would produce a partial account of the latter – limited in Gramsci's case, for example, to its role in securing the decisive economic nucleus of an historic bloc. For further comments, see Jessop (1992a).

3. I am well aware of the many difficulties involved in deploying terms such as Fordism and, even more seriously, post-Fordism; nonetheless for some purposes they can do real theoretical work and/or have real empirical relevance. See Jessop (1992b): 43–5.

4. At least in the view of Cochrane (1992): 5. In an earlier paper, I simply referred to it as the post-Fordist welfare state but this term lacks both formal and functional specificity: see Jessop (1991): 82–l04.

5. Structural coupling occurs when two or more operationally autonomous but otherwise interdependent systems coexist in the same environment and react both to changes in that environment and to each others' reactions; intertwined in this way, they also co-evolve in a partly contingent, partly path-dependent manner. For more information on these concepts, see Jessop (1992a): 327–9.

6. In this context I follow analysts such as van der Pijl in viewing Fordism as an accumulation regime whose growth dynamic was rooted in the diffusion of the US-American industrial paradigm to north-western Europe. See K. van der Pijl (1984). I would add that a number of non-Fordist economies whose growth dynamic proved complementary to that of the dominant Fordist regime were also able to expand significantly during the long post-war boom (these included Canada and several European economies). In both contexts there was a tendential emergence of the Keynesian welfare state mode of social regulation. Cf. Esping-Andersen (1985).

7. There is a countertendency to this: the formation of currency blocs in each of the triad growth poles. Monetary union in the EC is the most obvious example with the DM becoming the *de facto* monetary standard; the US dollar is crucial in the North American Free Trade Area; and the yen plays a key role (together with the dollar) in East Asia.

8. See Lipietz (1982): 33–47. Lipietz also notes the need for another proportionality to be satisfied if the virtuous circle of Fordist accumulation is to continue: that increased productivity in the capital goods sector should offset the rising technical composition of capital if the capital/output ratio is not to grow and so depress profits.

9. I am grateful to David Wolfe for pointing out the dangers of one-sided approaches to the KWS and SWS regarding the focus of state intervention.

10. Amin and Robins (1990): 7–34. Cf. Morales and Quandt (1992): 462–75.

11. Cf. Fosler (ed.) (1988): 5.

12. P. Van Hoogstraten (1983): 17. Cf. Moulaert, Swyngedouw and Wilson (1988): 11–23.

13. Dyson (ed.) (1989): 118.

14. Sabel (1989): 17–70.

15. Cf. Dyson (1989).

16. *Ibid.*

17. Duchacek, Latouch, and Stevenson (eds) (1988).

7
Welfare State Limits to Globalization*
Elmar Rieger and Stephan Leibfried

[...]

The political conflicts over globalization and the welfare state are myopic in at least two ways. First, the general notion of an inexorable globalization pressure to shrink welfare states is untenable. In fact, at least in Western Europe in general and in Germany in particular, economic globalization has not led to any radical dismantling of welfare states. On the contrary, the stronger the pressure of globalization and the more open a country's economy is, the more difficult it becomes to touch the *status quo* of the welfare state. Social policies have proven highly resistant to change. On balance, globalization presently tends to function as a *blocking mechanism vis-à-vis* policy reforms deemed necessary from an 'internal,' domestic perspective; it has *not* become a forcing mechanism for such reforms.[1] A comparison of the most recent social policy developments in the United States and Germany illustrates not only symmetric relationships between social policy and foreign economic policy, but also how radical interventions in the institutional structure of social policy are more likely under conditions in which international linkage and national dependency on world markets is less pronounced. It has to be recognized that the need for reforms of the social policies of developed welfare states is not a direct result of globalization; it has merely become more clearly and urgently visible. The prime example of this is the combination of declining fertility rates and the burden of increasing proportions of aged people and the consequences for financing the system of social transfer payments.

Second, today's globalization conflicts are characterized by short-term considerations only. The functions of institutions of the welfare states in achieving and ensuring economic openness are overlooked. The way globalization and the welfare state are discussed makes it seem as if there were a completely new constellation and challenge. But movements toward the

* From *Politics and Society* 26 (3) (1998), pp. 391–422.

internationalization of the economy and national countertrends are recurrent phenomena. The decisive novelty of the current constellation is the existence of the welfare state and its internal transformation. It was the institutionalization of income maintenance programs after World War II that enabled governments to switch to free trade policies. Welfare state systems, however, create their own inequalities and rigidities. Moreover, the privileged strata they produce became powerful defendants of the distributional *status quo*. With this transformation, perception of the results of economic globalization on internal conditions in developed societies has changed along with the institutions regulating the economy on an international level.

That growth rates in international trade exceeded production growth rates was already characteristic for the world economy of the late 19th century.[2] The same is true for the level of integration and interdependence of financial markets.[3] From a historical perspective, it is most striking that all earlier movements toward globalization or internationalization lasted only for a short time and were soon followed by long periods of economic closure.[4] In the current situation, this raises two questions. First, what is the welfare state's contribution to the most recent wave of globalization as it reaches the end of the 20th century? Second, what role does the internal transformation of developed welfare states play in the internationalization of trade, production, and investment?

[...] This article attempts to describe *one* of the preconditions for economic globalization and the national integration in the world market of developed Western industrial societies of the OECD type. Our general thesis is that the movement toward and the trends in a globalized economy have been triggered, contained, differentiated or modified, weakened or strengthened, and slowed down or speeded up through *national structures of social policy and their developments*, to the degree that these could replace protectionism. The crucial variables are the institutional characteristics of social policy. They are the starting and focusing points for new social groups, varying political mobilization, and structural change in interest mediation in the welfare state. The conditions for action and the capacity to exert power, to veto, and to implement policy have all been changed substantially by the welfare state transformation of the post-war societies. The new social groups – 'claimant classes' and 'provider classes' – try to monopolize their new income sources and to build up strong lobbying positions. Depending on their institutional and political clout, they embody different potentials for the paralysis or for the adaptability of welfare states; therefore, when these groups are challenged by welfare state reforms and, at the same time, economic insecurity increases due to economic change induced by globalization, we can expect the emergence of new interest coalitions urging protectionism and resisting domestic deregulation that would enhance competitiveness. How

salient such developments will be depends mainly on social policy's
capacity for reform and adaptation.

Here, 'free trade' is an approach to 'globalization'. This article reviews the
arguments expressed in various historical periods for and against free trade.
We are primarily concerned not with their theoretical value but with their
ties to period, location, and interest. We believe that these arguments are
reactions to specific connections between intrasocietal and foreign-trade
conditions and developments. They provide indications of barriers to the
introduction of free trade policies.[5]

[...]

The social dimensions of an open international economy

For the classical theory on the foundations and the development of foreign
trade, the key variable for interdependence is the cost of transborder economic transactions. If these costs fall, international transactions become
cheaper than national transactions, markets become transnational, and
the division of labor spreads geographically and deepens in terms of
production technology.[6] [...]

Taken to its archetypical extreme, free trade is an international economic regime in which cross-border trade encounters no barriers whatso-
ever; thus, once transport and other transaction costs are accounted for,
there are no systematic differences between internal ('domestic') and
external ('international') prices. Prices denote relative scarcity or relative
surplus of goods. They thus reflect the decision-relevant opportunity
costs of national enterprises and budgets, since world markets allow
transactions at these price levels at any time.[7] Actual conditions seldom
approached this ideal model, but free trade theory was still able to dominate economic theory. A survey of economists in 1984 revealed that
95 percent of US economists and 88 percent of an aggregate of US,
German, French, Austrian, and Swiss economists agreed fully or condi-
tionally with the statement that 'tariffs and import quotas decrease
the level of general economic welfare'.[8]

[...] Three arguments have been made repeatedly against free trade as the
leading principle of foreign economic policy. These arguments address the
most important sources of difficulties confronting any policy of opening
national economies (and societies) and of deepening and dynamizing the
world division of labor.

The first difficulty lies in the temporal dimension of realizing higher
levels of national welfare and in the social insecurities stemming from permanently revolutionizing economic structures, structures that are themselves an outcome of the movements of world markets for national
communities. The costs of economic change after ever new waves of import
competition and export expansion – loss of income and jobs, falling wages,

devaluation of occupational qualifications, and corrosion of industrial relations regimes – are easy to grasp, materialize in the short run for the groups and sectors concerned, are concentrated in certain sectors, and thus continuously create new imbalances between regions and between social groups. The benefits of these changes, however, like falling prices for consumer goods, new chances for profits and jobs, productivity increases, and a higher valuation of certain qualifications and jobs are rather diffuse, are slow in taking effect, and seem to be beyond the horizons of public and private calculability and intervention. The autonomous dynamics of world market developments appear to preclude any forecast as to which sectors of the economy will produce which jobs and what their qualifications and earnings profile will be. Therefore, the comparative advantage in internationalization will become visible only when new profits and jobs seem highly and permanently secured. Risk and the political – as well as associated social – problems also exist in the ideal free trade world. The inherent difficulties in promising later beneficial effects for all social groups in an open economy were early fielded as an argument against free trade doctrine. Protectionism lives from the illusion that certain groups' losses in employment and income can be prevented without having other groups or the community foot the bill in the form of higher prices and slower economic growth. [...]

A second standard argument against international economic openness is the risk incurred when national welfare becomes politically dependent on external conditions beyond the nation-state's control. Aside from autonomous developments in world markets, political groups can also inhibit, direct, or stop the international flow of goods and moneys. [...]

Of special importance is the repeated temptation of national governments to instrumentalize foreign economic policy for their goals in international politics. The institutional weakness of the international order provides a fertile ground for playing with national economic closure and for attempting to gain international economic advantages with political means. This interaction of domestic and foreign economic policy-making fuels the fragmentation and anarchy of the international system, repeatedly leading social groups to renew efforts to secure and monopolize their advantages by political means. Under such constraints, national actors see international economic policy as a zero-sum game, even if this attitude makes no economic sense.[9]

A third argument against free trade focuses on the huge differences in the level of economic and social development among countries. Falling transport and transaction costs bring together economies whose level of development is radically different. Under free trade, national achievements like high wages, high standards of living, occupational and state benefits, job guarantees, and the like may turn into disadvantages in site competition with less developed economies. [...]

[...] The effects of competition among unequally developed societies have always been held against free trade, though this argument did not gain political prominence until the end of the 19th century. The conflicts and discussion of that period reveal the same constellation of forces that still characterizes the present struggle about the effects of globalization on national welfare and wage levels. In David Hume's and Adam Smith's times, the individual causes of the success of import competition were not considered a legitimate argument against free trade. The decisive consideration was seen in savings due to cheap imports and in the competitive pressure to rationalize enterprises, to increase productivity, and to increase efforts to achieve new profits. [...]

International wage competition became the central *political* argument against free trade after the industrial revolution and after developed national labor markets became the primary source of life opportunities for large segments of the population.[10] This argument was based on the wage dependency of increasing portions of the population that had no property. Policy, especially democratic parliamentarian policy, could not ignore the economic situation of such social groups. Thus, the political salience of economic change due to autonomous world market developments greatly increased. Unemployment, regional economic shifts, and stagnating or falling wages could no longer be dealt with simply by pointing out that in the long run all members of society would benefit.[11] This was especially true when these negative experiences could be attributed to competition with countries whose level of development was much lower. In 1894, Max Weber wrote about the increased competition German farm products were exposed to from the new South American settler nations. He noted that the magnitude of the discrepancies in development prohibited any 'true' competition between such countries.

[...]

The primacy of national welfare levels became more and more pronounced as state activity and social rights expanded in the 20th century. The expansion of the public sector; the nationalization of many sectors of production; the more intense and continuous macroeconomic management and general economic planning; the proliferation of finely meshed state regulation, control, and supervision of private employers; the growing importance of the state for professional qualifications, research, and development; and the various forms of welfare state intervention all became motors and accompaniments of growing economic nationalism. These developments were driven by the expansion of the right to vote and by the democratization and parliamentarization of politics. In the eyes of quite a few political scientists and economists, the social results of democratization and parliamentarization became the major cause of the fragmentation of the world economy into closed national spaces.[12]

Democracy and foreign economic policy in the nation-state

Parliamentarization and the extension of the right to vote generalized and increased the capacity to use political means to secure jobs and life chances. This not only changed the microeconomic prerequisites for a domestic and international liberal system but also transformed the context in which national policies were formulated. This structural change of the national economy and its politics was seen as an unsurmountable limit to the development of global free trade and of the attendant deepening of the division of labor. The extension of the right to vote to the wage-earning classes had become the foundation of a new primacy of politics over the economy. Societies between the world wars were fields of experimentation toward new political constructions of relationships between the domestic and the external.[13] The new domestic political system reduced the private economy's degree of freedom. In particular, this change in the political system was seen as undermining the dynamic, self-regulating economic order. [...]

Political intervention also constrained the process of setting wages. This already removed one major pillar of self-regulating economic development. A major mechanism for economic growth and progress is that ages move in line with relative changes in productivity. But in the modern mass democracies between the wars, politics slowly suspended the downward movement of wages in non-competitive industries that economic dynamics requires. [...]

In addition to the flexibility of wages, a second condition must be met if free trade is to fulfill the promise of increasing the general welfare: There has to be a sufficiently great demand in other sectors for workers who have lost their employment as a result of global economic change. Keynes saw no political chance for a policy of economic openness if this condition was not met [....].

Keynes saw a basic condition for free trade suspended in times of mass unemployment and in the actual situation in Great Britain during the Depression: [T]hat if you throw men out of work in one direction you reemploy them in another. As soon as that link in the chain is broken the whole of the free trade argument breaks down.[14]

[...]

Another constitutive element of the social consolidation of the nation-state was its closure against immigration, fencing in the national labor market. Two factors were responsible. First, this stopped the 'race to the bottom' in wage levels that successive waves of immigration had exposed natives to. The closure of the national labor market was an inescapable consequence of the political emancipation of wage labor.[15] A second factor also contributed to social closure: Only closure seemed to protect the massive investments in national human capital – the welfare state's move toward the education, health, and social state – and to increase the efficiency of political rule. For the classical theoreticians of free trade, it had still seemed natural that free trade also meant unhindered international mobility of labor quite in contrast to the developments after World War I. [...]

The welfare state foundations of an open international economy

Contrary to the expectations of leading political scientists and economists, the transformation of industrial societies to welfare states did not put an end to economic openness. On the contrary, this transformation became a foundation and guarantee of openness and made feasible a level of international division of labor and integration formerly unimaginable.[16] Decisive were changes in the calculus of interests and security strategies by those groups that had been most exposed to the risks of world market integration. A look at the welfare state's changes in the perception and evaluation of economic risks shows the degree to which economic openness depends on certain domestic social and political preconditions of societies interested in free trade. These preconditions and their functional equivalence to protectionism are hard to fulfill and even harder to sustain. Relevant here are three effects of welfare state-building: the stabilization of expectations, the organization of non-market sources of life chances, and the possibility of compensating those unable to adapt.

Even under ideal conditions, the realization of the national welfare gains of a free trade regime is bound to a time factor doubly dependent on subjective estimations: It involves the comparison of a present state with a future level of welfare, and also, the attainment of the future level is itself dependent on expectations.[17] The stability of these expectations is all the more precarious, the less it is determined solely by economic development. The more comprehensively and the more exclusively individual subsistence depends on the market, and the more the market is determined by external, international developments, the more expectations for the future will shrink and the more risk-averse individual decision making is likely to be. Protectionism is a promise to work successfully against this constellation, but it becomes superfluous if social policy ensures income in times of sickness, invalidity, unemployment, and so on in order to steady and secure life 'courses.'[18] Returns on investments in a person's social capital will be easier for him to calculate, and they will be higher, and will thus grow.[19]

[...]

[...]The government budget is not independent of domestic or international cycles, but it institutionalizes a counterweight to autonomous market developments. As they expand the welfare state, governments can use social policy 'to supersede, supplement, or modify operations of the economic system in order to achieve results that the economic system would not achieve on its own, and ... in doing so it is guided by values other than those determined by open market forces'.[20] Social policy can thus stabilize the market economy.

[...]

But it took until the welfare state had developed completely before this mechanism for abandoning protectionism revealed its decisive effectiveness. Social policy after World War II, in the 1950s and 1960s, changed structurally from a subsidiary security against emergencies to a comprehensive securing of achieved standards of living. This change in the structure and function of social policy also massively affected national integration into the world market. Social policy changes were augmented by a more extensive and intensive policy of occupational qualification, of upgrading human capital.[21] For the first time, social and educational policy could be used as a general compensation (transfers, qualification) of globalization losers. These policies provided a general, transsectoral, and transbranch mechanism for redistributive adaptation. The expansion of the welfare state to the middle classes, in particular to some of the self-employed, also increased their tolerance for accelerated economic developments and for the higher risks implied in the economic changes brought about by deeper integration into the world market and the increase of competitive pressure from imports.

Welfare state limits to globalization

Developed welfare states can require reforms as a result of domestic transformations. The organization of groups to politically defend life chances originating with the welfare state – such as pensions, jobs in social services, and entitlements – the juridification and bureaucratization of redistributive systems, and the institutionalization of 'spiraling entitlements' are highly probable consequences of welfare state expansion. Myrdal's description of internal flexibility and external closure is not necessarily true for the developed welfare state, but then the relationship between domestic integration and economic globalization also can change. Instead of guaranteeing dynamic labor markets, compensating the losers of globalization on short notice, and assuring social and geographic mobility in the long term, the welfare state may turn into a platform for defensive coalitions of the *status quo*. The deeper social policy structures are embedded in interest groups, and the more political parties have internalized the welfare state ambitions of the claimant and provider classes, the higher are the hurdles for efficient welfare state reform. The internal challenges to reform the welfare state stemming from demographic change and changes in the labor market, in gender relationships, and in the organization of family life[22] turn into additional, autonomous adaptive problems for national systems *vis-à-vis* the economy. The domestic formation of distributive coalitions then becomes an independent source of hurdles for economic internationalization and of economic closure: the tax and contribution burdens of the welfare state are not reduced, and the economic and social regulation of the labor markets, jobs, products, and trade remain untouched. This increases the danger that investment capital will move abroad as the domestic market loses its attractiveness for foreign investors.

In addition to the external shocks of globalization, internal blockades of institutional policy in the welfare state have become the second great challenge for national government at the turn of the millennium. This domestic policy produces winners and losers in its own way. As when opening the economy for free trade, the costs of institutional change immediately and concentratedly affect specific social groups, while the benefits of reforms are diffuse and relegated to an uncertain future.[23] The result is political advantages for reform losers. The crucial point is, therefore, that social policy reform can produce its own insecurities and, above all, can provoke resistance against further internationalization of the economy, if those affected directly connect the probable, reform-induced worsening of their position with site policy and international competition.

That the positive relationship between the expansion of the welfare state and the internationalization of trade, production, and investment may have changed due to the autonomous dynamics of social policy can be attributed mainly to two consequences of the institutionalization of the welfare state itself: the development and consolidation of 'claimant' as well as provider classes and the social policy induced immobilization and increased cost of labor. The rise of manifest and latent claimant and provider classes – primarily pensioners, long-term benefit recipients, and public sector employees – has decisively shrunk the social base for an open economy and at the same time sharpened political parties' attention to these new interests at the cost of the free market system. The numerical growth of these classes *via* broader access to a prolonged education and the institutionalization of the pension age, but also through welfare and unemployment insurance transfers, which can to a great extent replace market income, and finally through fiscal welfare's vastly complex structures of benefits and systems of equalizing burdens has shifted the lines of social conflict, highly socialized the structures of mediating interests, and thus altered the functional laws of the political market in favor of the welfare state clientele.[24] The portion of the population receiving market income, for whom the market provides the most important avenue for resources and mobility, and which is thus actively interested in the 'anonymous social policy of a free market economy (Hans Rosenberg), shrank while the portion primarily interested in public regulation and redistribution grew'.[25]

For the fate of free trade as the guiding principle of foreign economic policy, this development is ambivalent at best. On one hand, it reduces the social risks of increasing integration in the world market, because the living conditions of large parts of the population are less dependent on the movements of the world market. More important, perhaps, early retirement programs and other means of exiting labor markets help companies to restructure and reorganize internally by removing those people who, because of seniority rules, not only are the most expensive but also have the most incentives to resist change.[26] On the other hand, the social political situation of groups depending on the welfare state is threatened by the constraints of adaptation that globalization dictates to national budget and finance policy; this expresses itself as resistance to the open economy. As the general increase in the public debt in the welfare states shows, it has been some time since social policy has been able to be financed through current tax and contribution revenues.[27] Over the long term, what may be decisive is that the combination of welfare-state transformation and demographic aging has greatly reduced the social basis for open foreign trade. This development could become the basis for the formation of new redistributive coalitions that find a common interest in resisting the feared redistributive effects of globalization and attendant changes in welfare state policies.

Social policy norms overlying labor contracts, the creation of habits, and the welfare state's modeling of a normal biography create their own barriers to flexibility that block the structural economic change that would otherwise characterize world market integration and its autonomous developments. The welfare state institutionalizes, regulates, and shapes life courses.[28] It intervenes in life courses, in William Beveridge's words, 'from cradle to grave' or even seems to constitute life courses in the first place – and thus narrows the dynamics of economic development, channels and hinders necessary adaptation at the market level through 'creative destruction,' and deforms or prevents the rationalization of company operations toward greater productivity. The specific incentive structures of the social policy institutions of developed welfare states are regularly at odds with or preclude those of the market. When certain types of employment are privileged by social policy because they produce additional returns in the form of insurance and pensions other types become less attractive. The more labor contracts are overlaid with welfare norms, making them the basis and reference point for claims unrelated to the market, the more difficult it will be for the labor market to orient itself to the economic rationality of those changes in the productivity of workplaces that result from the dynamics of import competition and export expansion.

The presently increasing valuation of the political *vis-à-vis* the economic results from a process in which the putative or real losers of economic change and social policy reforms try to increase their power by shifting these interest and redistributive conflicts into the political arena and to defend the *status quo* by grasping the strategic opportunities offered by the

competition between political parties. The more politicians point to international competitive pressures, the European Monetary Union (EMU), and
so on to legitimate and push through changes in structures of social policy,
the more they run the risk that potential, putative, and real losers of such
policies will turn against globalization, European integration, and other
such processes, and demand more control over foreign economic policy in
short, protectionism.

If we shelve the question of how rational and efficient present social
policy structures are, we can make a strong argument for the following
thesis: With increasing economic openness and international interdependence, social policy orients itself increasingly to the *status quo*. A comparative look at the United States and West European countries seems to
indicate that, with growing external pressures from globalization, the
capacity to adapt national social policy shrinks. The radical change in US
welfare policy in 1996, the discontinuation of a federal guarantee of a right
to welfare, the introduction of time limits for income transfers, the devolution of welfare to the states indicates how a relatively low level of globalization pressure goes hand in hand with a broad capacity for massive change,
while in Western Europe and Germany a high level of external pressure
seems almost to prohibit any change in the social policy *status quo*.[29] In
Germany the stickiness of social policy structures at least up to now assists
in sustaining a high level of economic international integration, the United
States currently experiences a political backlash against free trade policies.
In the framework of our argument it is the fragmentation and downgrading
of safety nets which decreases the chances for the instalment of free trade
policies. The recent failure of the fast track bill is a case in point. Despite
the attempt to bolster the bid for fast track negotiation authority with
the promise of programs to aid workers and communities hurt by future
trade agreements, concern about the negative consequences of further
international economic integration prevailed.[30] [...]

Notes

1. Obviously, this assessment is based mainly on the (Western) European experience. In this context one can also note that the predicament of the European
   Monetary Union seems quite similar: EMU is linked to domestic reforms in fiscal
   and budgetary affairs, which resulted in mutual hostage-taking and gridlock,
   rather than functioning as a means of external enforcement of internal reforms,
   as the heads of state had hoped at Maastricht. See Eichengreen (1997).
2. See Deutsch and Eckstein (1960/61): 267–99; and James (1996): 1–26.
3. The sheer volume of globalized financial transactions is often advanced as
   evidence of an unparalleled qualitative change. This is untenable in the historical context – not to mention the equally routine assertion of associated negative
   consequences for the autonomy of nation-states:

   > Some measurements of the degree of financial integration in the world
   > economy indicate that at the beginning of the twentieth century the world

was more interconnected than at any subsequent time (including the 1990s, despite the trillions of dollars of daily currency movements). These measurements examine the behavior of saving and investment levels. Investment and savings were coordinated on a global level, with the result that a surplus of investment in one area or state (that is, a balance of payments current account deficit) could be smoothly financed by the export of surplus savings from another area. Even in the highly integrated 1980s and 1990s, such transfers were much more difficult and raised many more political eyebrows than in the golden era that preceded the First World War.

(James 1996: 12).

4. See Bairoch (1993); Bhagwati (1989); Kindleberger (1996); and Rogowski (1989).
5. This approach, however, cannot replace the analysis of actual structures and processes of the internationalization of trade, production, and investment. Here we try to argue for a particular view on possible interactions between welfare state structures on one hand and systems of foreign economic policy on the other.
6. See Frieden and Rogowski (1996): 25–47.
7. See Irwin (1996): 5.
8. Frey, Pommerehne, Schneider, and Gilbert (1984): 986–94.
9. See Gilpin (1987): 31–4, 46–50.
10. This is especially true for the United States. See Irwin (1996): 160; and Eckes (1995).
11. For a return of this argument see Greider (1997): 9. He argues that those people are right who no longer believe in the beneficial logic of comparative advantage and who now think that economic globalization is a zero-sum game producing losses and insecurity [...].
12. Joseph Schumpeter expressed this best in a speech given in 1949. See Schumpeter (1950): 418.
13. For a comparative analysis see Somary (1929).
14. See Irwin (1996): 196.
15. See Carr (1965): 22; and Dowty (1987). The political history of US immigration shows that early democratization and parliamentarization led to an early foreign economic policy focused on regulating labor markets by means of immigration control. See Jones (1982) 2nd edn.
16. We do not claim that the politics leading to the expansion of the welfare state after World War II can be explained in terms of conscious decisions to provide for an institutional foundation for a closer integration of world markets. We believe that the relationship between social policies and foreign economic policies is much more fruitfully analysed in terms of unintended consequences.
17. See Hirschman (1980) [1945]: 51.
18. The same argument of a positive function of institutionally differentiated social policies for a turn toward free trade was advanced by Warner M. Corden in his analysis of the social origins of protectionism [...] (1974): 4.
19. See Hans-Werner Sinn (1986): 557–71; and (1996).
20. Marshall (1975): 15.
21. On the economic-historical context of this 'Golden Age' and on the labor and social policy components of the social compact formulated in the 1950s, see Eichengreen, (1996): 38–72.
22. For a comprehensive account of the internal challenges see Kaufmann (1997).

23. For a corresponding study of UK and US social policy developments in the 1980s, see Pierson (1994). For an extension of this analysis to additional countries see *idem*. (1996): 147–79.

24. Alber (1989); Janowitz (1976); and Lepsius (1979): 166–209.

25. For empirical evidence see Flora (1989): 149–62.

26. See Schmid (1997): 302–37; and Wolff (1997).

27. Between 1981 and 1996, the average quotient of government outlays on all levels to the nominal domestic product rose from 47 to 49 percent, while state debt – the quotient of gross obligations of all levels of government to gross domestic product climbed from 44 to 76 percent. See Spahn and Föttinger (1997): 140–59.

28. Allmendinger and Hinz (1998): 61–82; Mayer and Müller (1986): 217–45; *idem*. (1989): 41–60; Lindbeck (1988): 19–37; and *idem*. (1995): 477–94.

29. On the United States see Gebhardt (1997); Seeleib-Kaiser (1996): 239–68; and Wiseman (1996): 1–54. On the contrasting German case, see Jacobs (1997). In Germany, a 'leaning' of the welfare state is discernible with means- and income-tested benefits. Germany's 1996 introduction of old-age nursing-care insurance, however, indicates how well entrenched the welfare state is, since this policy did not consider the imperatives of integration in the global market for German industry. On the failure of the United States's 1995 health insurance reform, proposed as a strategy to expand the welfare state, see Hacker (1997).

30. See Broder (1997): 3; Pfaff (1997): 8; Abramson and Greenhouse (1997): 3; and Friedman (1997): 8.

8
Which Third Way?*

Teresa Brennan

[...]

To some, the Third Way is no more than the First Way with cosmopolitan, liberal adjectives. It is about appearing radical while 'standing still and emoting fuzzily' (Judt 1998: 15). But let us credit some of the less opportunistic of its proponents with a genuine desire to go beyond the present world in which the First Way rules and the Second failed. Let us rather assume that the confused mixture of rhetoric and rationalization in Third Way speak is symptomatic of any attempt to move beyond the present impasse without really understanding its economic dynamics and the ideology surrounding them.

Unless those economic trends are grasped one can easily advocate and interpret as 'radical' the very moves that leave capital unrestrained. This is what the Third Way is doing for the main part. While various items on the initial US Third Way agenda have fallen through, items which might have led to a real alternative, those items which directly reflect the present needs of capital have done much better. This is apparent if we consider, as the main part of this article will consider, the recent attempts to establish a multilateral charter for multinationals giving them rights over governments, and the recent welfare reform on both sides of the Atlantic.

It began when, amid much cant about family values. Clinton and the 1996 US Congress introduced what is now known as the Workfare bill. Basically, Workfare means getting single mothers off welfare: in essence, it does this by placing a time limit.

Shortly before the Workfare bill was enacted, the OECD inaugurated a proposed Multilateral Agreement on Investment (MAI).[1] The prime mover behind the MAI in the OECD was the US (*Financial Times* 1998: 21). [...] When the MAI failed after the French left the negotiating table in October 1998, plans were launched immediately for a similar agreement in the WTO.

---

* From *Thesis Eleven* 64 (2001): 39–64.

The agreement which the OECD hoped for, and which the WTO now has in mind, will be the most far-reaching in a series of trade and anti-regulatory agreements extending the global reach of corporations. Under MAI-type legislation, corporations may be able to indict national governments that mandate labor conditions and environmental safeguards, among other things, on the grounds that such regulations are anti-competitive (Ad Hoc Working Group on the MAI, n.d.). Such legislation is now in place with the NAFTA, and a series of over 1600 bilateral agreements which made it easy for labour and environmental standards to be bypassed. The pressure for more such agreements, with an extended international range, is mounting, and Third Way advocates are right behind it.[2]

[...] The explanation of why Workfare and multilateral agreements are pushed for now is based on my reworking of value theory (Brennan 1993: 156ff.; 2000: 81ff.). In this reworking, value theory becomes a theory of time, space and speed: I retain the idea that profit is realized through the disjunction between what is added in production, and the cost of reproduction: but I argue that nature, as well as labour, is a source of surplus-value. Time and speed matter because of an ongoing tension between the speed of production, and the way that the reproduction of natural resources, including labour-power, cannot keep pace with that speed. In the case of other natural resources apart from labour-power, this tension may be resolved by going further afield. Rather than waiting for the natural sources and resources at issue to regenerate on the local scale, one finds them somewhere else, 'over there', using distance to substitute for linear or generational reproduction or regeneration, and trade investment and manufacturing agreements to facilitate this substitution across space. But this procedure does not work easily for the reproduction of labour-power, which means that human reproduction becomes a drag on the system. Welfare is devoted to human reproduction, both the day-to-day level of reproduction where subsistence needs are met and the generational level: the reproduction of the next generation of labour. If welfare is a drag, if the idea that human reproduction is out of time with the central speedy dynamic of capital is correct, then we can predict that more welfare-to-work legislation will eventuate; we can predict too that more multilateral agreements will be made, unless moves to this end are actively resisted at the level of social policy, rather than valorized a so-called Third Way. That said, we do not need to think of Workfare as a plot. It is just that those with more entitlement, determined by class confidence and position, have more ability to contest their fates. They have a more uncritical identification with the values that the Third Way seeks to enshrine. What I am at pains to show here is the economic undesirability of welfare to the present course of capital, an unwantedness that weakens the capacity of those affected by its demise to resist, or to further their own cause. What I hope to show in concluding is how the Third Way, as presently conceived, serves the ends of multinational capital rather nicely. A real alternative to late capitalism would have to address the realities of time and space very differently.

Clinton's legislation

Clinton's bill HR3734 is titled 'The Personal Responsibility and Work Opportunity Reconciliation Act of 1996.' [...]

The effects of Clinton's legislation on those who now lack any visible means of support were largely overlooked, obscured by a series of wars and scandals. But so far (August 1996–January 2000), 4.3 million people have been taken off the welfare rolls. One state has decreased its welfare case-loads by a staggering 91 percent (USDHHS 1999; DeParle 1999: 1, 20). These figures can only grow. [...] [T]he first studies showed that only a little over half of those leaving welfare since the reforms have found jobs, and those they have found are mainly in the service and retail industries, at wages of about $6 an hour.[3] This figure has varied, but not significantly. This is specially noteworthy given that unemployment in the US this year (2000) is at its lowest for 29 years. There is no sense in which Workfare has been subjected to serious test.

In addition to hunger and homelessness, Workfare's consequences include a remarkable shifting of the burden of childcare onto the pension generation. The number of children in their grandparents' care has increased by 50 percent in the last decade. Half of these grandparents are single women, over half are black, over half are below the poverty line. The grandmothers are paid $215 a month, which, they suggest, is not worth the exhaustion of full-time childcare (DeParle 1999: 1, 20).[4]

Blair's government in its initial stipulations about welfare reform insisted that those who really needed a safety net would have it (Blair/Field 1998: 1). This was basic to the Green Paper on welfare reform, co-authored by Frank Field, then a Minister in Blair's cabinet. The stress on a safety net may have been tacit recognition of the negative effects of Clinton's enact-ment. But the reality of the final Welfare Reform and Pensions bill is other-wise: it introduces a means test (one of the factors that led to Frank Field's resignation) and other cuts for those who do not respond to 'the message of work' (Field 1998).

Both Clinton's and Blair's bills assume public-private partnerships.[5] This applies not only to pension proposals. It also means giving subsidies to employers for taking on former welfare recipients. At least Blair recognizes, unlike the US Republican Congress, that the 'male breadwinner model' is no longer apposite (Blair/Field 1998: 7). In the British case, the rhetorical emphasis was on 'a woman's right to choose'. British women were hitherto unable to work, it was claimed, because the financial incentive was not there in real terms: paid childcare cost them more than staying on benefits.

Furthermore, they would if they wished (and if they had mothers or other kin available) be able to keep childcare in the family. Blair, like Clinton, made a place for grandmothers to take over childcare – for a fee. This looks good, but if the US experience is any indication, it underestimates what it means for granny to do childcare 10 hours a day, five days a week.

[...]

[...] Regardless of whether the rhetoric is manipulative or moralistic, my argument here is that it conceals a tension inherent in the dynamics of latter-day capital. And it seems reasonable to ask whether the Third Way itself is not the product of the same tension, the same dynamics. These dynamics demand unimpeded access to labour and natural resources, access across national borders without tariffs or other restrictions. To keep pace with this fast-moving production, these dynamics demand mobile individuals, and the speedier reproduction of the next generation of workers, or at the least, minimal expenditure in the overall social cost of human reproduction. [...] As we shall see, a reduced social cost of reproduction will compensate to some degree for the loss of speed. But before turning to this issue, let us examine the latest developments in a series of trade and anti-regulatory agreements which foster the speedy unimpeded access to global resources.

The most famous of these agreements are the 1947 General Agreement on Tariffs and Trade (GATT) and the 1994 North American Free Trade Agreement (NAFTA). The GATT was designed to encourage free trade among its member states, which now number at least 111 countries, by regulating and reducing tariffs. It does not have the power to override national sovereignty on labour standards. In this it is more innocuous than the NAFTA. The NAFTA has benefited multinational companies, but has led to reduced real wages in the United States and Canada and a marked decline in Mexican labour standards. [...]

The OECD's MAI, which was intended to secure a global extension of these conditions, was in fact far more than a pure investment agreement as it is mooted as the prototype for a WTO agreement. We will begin with the MAI's self-definition. The basic premise of the MAI Negotiating Text was that every investor in a contracting country should be treated in the same way. This concern with equal rights is reflected in provisions concerning National Treatment (NT), Most Favoured Nation status (MFN), and Performance Requirements. [...]

While there were gestures to labour and the environment and even to local manufacturing standards in the MAI text, these were not meaningful, because its goal was more than investment in enterprises which may or may not adhere to labour and environmental standards. Its object encompassed the direct expropriation of labour and resources. The MAI defined investment very broadly, and a note records that further work is required to determine the 'appropriate treatment in the MAI [of] indirect investment, intellectual property, concessions, public debt and real estate' (OECD

1988a, s. II, 2, viii, p. 11 and n). Indeed the envisioned scope of the MAI's operations can be gauged by the fact that one lone delegation suggested a clause protecting linguistic and cultural diversity, because of the MAI's potentially homogenizing effects on the 'audio-visual and press sectors' (OECD 1988a, annex 1: 128). It was this concern that brought the OECD agreement to its knees, when the French delegation walked out because of the agreement's failure to protect countries, especially France, from the impact of the American movie industry.

[...] France rethought its approach both because of cultural concerns, and because of 'mounting organized opposition by labour and ecology groups' (Agence France-Presse 1998). As I indicated, the MAI would have allowed investors to sue national governments or governmental agencies for restrictive 'performance requirements': that is to say, if local labour or environmental safeguards meant that the conditions for investment in a particular country were 'restricted' (Ad Hoc Working Group on the MAI, n.d.).

Unless a country was protected by a prior exception clause in the GATT, the MAI would have permitted direct, unimpeded access by external 'investors' to a contracting party's energy and natural resources, with no requirement that the 'investor' contribute to the regeneration of those resources, including the reproduction of labour-power.

There is every indication that the WTO will take the MAI as its blueprint. Six weeks after the OECD negotiations ended, a leaked discussion paper for the EU Council outlined an initial strategy for including a multilateral investment agreement 'as one of the new issues' in the WTO's Millennial Round of negotiations called for by the EU commission's vice president Leon Brittan. These negotiations were scheduled for December 1999 in Seattle. Their fate is now history. But as far as the WTO is concerned, they have been postponed, which is not to underestimate the victory for labour and the environment signaled by that postponement.

[...]

Reworking Marx's value theory

Contemporary sociologists and other critics have argued that the organization of time/space should be fundamental in any social explanation (Giddens 1984; Harvey 1989). The difficulty lies in taking a spatiotemporal account beyond a Weberian formal description, in making space and time integral in a dynamic and hence genuinely explanatory theory that accounts for disparities and change within a social formation. Traditionally, if ultimately inaccurately, the dynamic and explanatory level has been the province of Marxist sociology. What I want to argue is that time and space can be made central to the dynamic level, hence to the generation of hypotheses concerning class and economy, by reworking the fundamental premises at root of Marx's value theory. [...]

What precisely does reworking Marx's fundamental premises entail? [...]

[...]

The essence of my revision of this theory lies in the definition of constant capital. At the risk of a scholastic dispute, I would and have argued that labour-power in the last analysis is energy, even for Marx (Brennan 2000: 81ff.). But there are other natural sources of energy aside from labour-power, and other things that share the living quality of labour in that they are able to reproduce. In short, I argued that just as surplus-value is realized through the disjunction between the cost of reproducing labour-power and what labour adds in production, so also is surplus-value realized through the disjunction between the reproduction cost of other natural sources capable of adding energy, and what these sources add in production. The difference is that capital does not pay for the reproduction cost of other natural sources of energy unless it has to, which means that the reproduction time of these energy sources is not allowed for: as a rule, they are consumed more rapidly than they can reproduce or be reproduced. As we have seen, capital more or less pays for labour-power, although it succeeds more rather than less in forcing down its costs.[6] That it strives not to pay for human reproduction unless it has to is evident in the history of slave economies. Where slave labour could be imported cheaply and was readily available, plantation owners worked their labour to death; the average life expectancy of a young African was seven years from the date of his or her enslavement (Blackburn 1997: 339–40). When the labour ceased to be readily available, breeding by slaves was mandated and sometimes even rewarded (Blackburn 1997: 429). [...]

[...]

To put this another way, in my theory there are two axes of production: the spatial axis of acquisition, which puts on pressure to speed up all things; and the temporal, reproduction axis, where surplus-value is measured as it has always been, in terms of the cost of reproduction. In other words, goods can be acquired by being either temporally reproduced (their reproduction time is allowed for) or by being acquired across space (reproduction time is discounted). From this perspective, I argued that exchange-value is set by the intersection of the speed of acquisition and the materialization of energy in production. I argued further that the speed of acquisition is reflected directly in the price of a commodity. The speed of acquisition is the measure of short-term profit. Long-term profit, on the other hand, is set by the disjunction between the energy added in production and the cost of reproduction. This gives us the real measure of the cost of these natural resources, as it does the cost of labour-power. But, while the cost of the energy added should be determined in this way, this measure will be disregarded wherever the speed of acquisition can substitute for reproduction time. Exchange-value is produced regardless of whether its origin is temporal or spatial; this is why I see the speed of acquisition as a measure of exchange-value. Given that capital's interest is always in short-term profit, its technologies are geared to the speed of acquisition. However, when capital cannot speed up production by acquiring its raw materials elsewhere, it will not rest easy and allow their natural reproduction time to be. Capital will attempt to speed up that natural time of reproduction. Here lies the incentive underlying genetic engineering and genetic modification for agriculture, for fertilizers increasing soil yield without regard to their long-term environmental consequences, and so forth.

It follows from this argument that a social organization that restricts the scope of production, so that reproduction time must be allowed for, will be fundamentally at odds with short-term profit based on the speed of acquisition. Short-term profit substitutes substances and energies acquired through the economic and physical conquest of space for equivalent energies reproduced over time. This means, among other things, that the notion that capitalism as we know it 'grew' out of 17th century petty commodity production obscures one central fact: these systems of production (the temporal and regionally based on the one hand; the expansionist on the other) are actually in competition. Not that this is clear to small businesses, who usually hope to become big ones. Just as the myth of the upward mobility of the working class is stressed, and stories told of the 'man who makes it from nowhere against the odds', so are the success stories told of the occasional small business. If this obfuscation of class interest is taken into account, then the notorious vacillating nature of the 'petty bourgeoisie', first on the side of labour, now on the side of capital, can be explained by the fact that their interests are rarely articulated as interests opposed to large-scale capitalization. Nor were their interests addressed by state socialism. I will return to this in my concluding comments.

[...] By my argument, the rate of profit will only fall where constant capital is really 'fixed' in relation to labour-power, fixed in that no other natural force – disguised as constant capital – figures in production. One consequence of this is that labour-power can benefit: it can be the aristocracy of energy sources, in an economy rich in other forms of natural energy. When oil, trees, etc. are the menials, even the most exploited forms of labour-power can do somewhat better. Hence we are in a position to account for the rise of a new and vast middle class in the very heartlands of advanced capital, and the explanation goes beyond, although it is consistent with, imperialism in general.

Next, that favourite theme of modern critics,[7] the elimination of time in favour of space, is revealed as the inevitable consequence of the speed of acquisition, manifest in an ever-expanding reach through conquest or trade agreements – anything that facilitates the more rapid acquisition of energies and the substitution of one energy source for another. Capital is not only seeking cheap labour-power through imperialism (although it is certainly doing that); it is also seeking to exploit other natural sources of value. In that capital's continued profit must be based more and more on the speed of acquisition, it must expand more, command more unregulated distance, and in this respect space must take the place of generational time. This is the core contradiction, or inherent dynamic, in capitalism today: you must go further in space to obtain your raw materials, and in doing so, you cannot stay home to reproduce. The process of reproduction is thus 'out of time', which means that in the event that the natural process of reproduction cannot be speeded up, then the cost of natural reproduction has to be reduced to make up for its drag on exchange-value [...].

States and the Third Way

If the speed of acquisition is critical to profit, if its imperatives strive to override the day-to-day and generational reproduction of natural substances and sources of energy, and to push down the cost of labour where it cannot be speeded up, we can gauge political positions in terms of how far they abet or countermand this process. Most, but not all, Third Way thinking assists it. For instance Giddens is evidently concerned for the environment: his critique of social democracy is based not only on its language of victimization, but also on its neglect of ecological concerns. He is also committed to microinvestment and small business as a source of community renewal (Giddens 1998: 82–3), and this, as we will see, does have real Third Way potential. Problems arise for Giddens because he is also committed to globalization. The thrust of modern capital is towards deregulation in trade and investment: hence the GATT, NAFTA, the WTO agreements (existing and proposed) and numerous other bilateral and multilateral trade and investment pacts. These are the logical outcome of the demand that standards of efficiency in the speed of acquisition should be set globally. Giddens would add an economic security council in the UN (and in fact the UN organization UNCTED is already being mentioned as an alternative to the WTO). He notes that 'a global commitment to free trade depends upon effective regulation rather than dispenses with the need for it' (Giddens 1998: 148). But while Giddens makes suggestions in this respect, how the Third Way would deal with the environment is never clear, nor can it be clear, for it would conflict with the cosmopolitan policy of globalization. The most we get from Giddens is that 'It isn't really convincing to suppose that environmental protection and economic development fit together comfortably – the one is bound sometimes to come into conflict with the other' (Giddens 1998: 58). Sometimes? When do they not conflict? This unclarity is symptomatic of the ideological mix I mentioned at the outset. On the one hand, Third Way-ites recognize that the environment is at maximum risk, and even that global inequality is increasing. On the other hand, they put their faith in the idea that remedies will emerge if we let the fox into the henhouse. Only a strong global fox, they tell us, can keep these scattered hens in order. The inherent contradiction in Third Way ideology is the awareness of the needs combined with remedies that will exacerbate those needs; and it results in prescriptions that say nothing. Cautions about dangers to the environment lead nowhere if they are attached to policies which damage it, as the debate preceding the NAFTA'S passage make clear.[8] Blair and Clinton are merciless towards national capitals, which they see as relics of feudalism. Welfare 'dependency' is seen as a similar relic. But in fact abolishing or impairing both local production and welfare merely smoothes the way for the direction capital is taking anyway, a direction which requires that there are no temporal obstacles, no out-of-time moments in which the pace or cost of social reproduction lags behind that of production, distribution and consumption.

[...]

A thoroughly modern state, in short, is one that abolishes these impediments; the state that is 'out of step with modern times' maintains them. [...] In the short term, it is plain that the state that is efficient either at eliminating geographical impediments to the speed of acquisition or subsuming its own economic sovereignty in a union aimed at eliminating them will also have to reckon with the palpable inefficiency presented by any concern for natural reproduction time. The reason, as should now be abundantly evident, is that natural reproduction time constitutes a 'drag' on the speed of acquisition.

Chief among such natural reproduction 'drags' today is the reproduction of labour. This is one form of reproduction that cannot be speeded up, unless it is through the introduction of what I term a 'lateral' labour supply, a supply drawn across space through migration rather than through the linear time it takes to reproduce the next generation of labour-power. While I have emphasized migration, this lateral labour supply can also be obtained through outsourcing, which is also increasing; easy outsourcing in short can offset capital's needs for migration, just at it will influence estimates of the cost-efficiency of human reproduction.

But in general capital, from its industrial genesis onwards, has demanded mobility on the part of its labour supply. In the light of the fore-going analysis, we can see that mobility is basic. [...]

But while capital demands ever-increasing mobility on the part of its workers (and it has to demand ever more mobility to keep pace with the inevitable expansion mandated by the speed of acquisition), it must also contend with the drag represented by the natural linear reproduction of labour. This takes us to the heart of why the state which is most efficient when it comes to embracing 'progressive' economic unions and trade agreements will also be a state bent on lowering the cost of producing the next generation of labour-power.

[...]

That labour-power has to be free to sell itself in the marketplace is plain enough. [...] What went under-recognized in Marx's critique is just how much 'freedom' in fact means mobility. [...]

As I have argued elsewhere (Brennan 2000: 146ff.), those who need to migrate in search of work are far more likely to be men, moving because they have no choice if they are to secure work. [...]

Women as a rule are less able to wander. One of the additional evils of the present legislation is that, while it stigmatizes migration as desertion, it ignores the fact that it is far harder for women with sole responsibility for children to be mobile. [...]

[...]

Policy implications

[...]

As to more immediate issues: in the light of the foregoing theory, and the inherent, dynamic tensions it isolates, is there an alternative to the welfare state? Obviously, I do not think the welfare state should be abolished; any institutional tendency that countermands the gallop of acquisition across the globe is a tendency towards long-term survival. But there may be alternatives that also work against that tendency in more creative ways. We might consider paid work that is household-based (provided that it is unionized). Piecework or outsourcing has long since been discredited because it lent itself to exploitation. Supervised outwork should be a different story, provided that it is union and government supervision that is at issue, however, of itself working at home with a small child does not solve the childcare issue; it just makes it less onerous in terms of organizing time and space. Nor does it deal with the real problem of isolation. What would address both issues would be production cooperatives of parents, single or partnered.[9]

In turn, the idea of cooperatives could lead from government assistance programs to ownership. That is to say, one can envisage 'small business' grants for the ownership of certain enterprises by local households, groups and cooperatives, enterprises whose nature fits with approved guidelines geared to establishing regionally-based production. The Third Way's most interesting deviation from a checklist for globalizing capital is the Clinton/Gore stress on 'microinvestment': as I have already noted, small businesses, where their compass is limited to the region in which they operate, are opposed to globalization, although they may not perceive their self-interest for what it is.

'Regionally-based production' means that the natural raw materials needed for the enterprise are also reproduced within the same region. Regional production does not mean 'the end of all trade': it means the end of trade that does not allow for reproduction time. A region might produce and allow for the reproduction of silk, and trade it where it will. But 'Silk

Enterprises' of London could not exhaust the worms of China and then move on to those of India and Japan.

[...] Structurally, there is potential in the growth of small businesses.[10] At the same time, changing the position of women means not returning to regional and local production as it was. Under the 17th century's patriarchal contract, the woman was formally subordinate to her husband, even if she was economically better off. Without her formal subordination, the supersession of household and small-scale production by large-scale capital would have appeared as the defeat for women that it was.

I have tried to show here why capital must be governed by the speed of acquisition and expanding scale, why it has to negate reproduction time, and why, accordingly, it will not act against its own economic interests by respecting environmental measures,[11] or trade agreements that protect small-scale or even national enterprises, let alone countenance care for the reproduction time of working women and many men day-to-day, or the next generation. But in the small-scale and regional, in the residues of the welfare state and protection policies, in the efflorescence of small enterprises owned increasingly by women, enterprises which, when they exploit neither labour nor nature, are in opposition to large-scale capital's laws of motion, in these things lies more than a democratic alternative. In them lies a real Third Way.

Notes

1. The 'MAI Negotiating Group' began meeting in 1995. The OECD's Directorate for Financial, Fiscal and Enterprise Affairs drafted the document discussed here titled *The MAI Negotiating Text* (1998a): 1.
2. Clinton has consistently sought 'fast-track' negotiating authority for trade agreements. This means that Congress has to vote yes or no with no amendments. The trade agreements he wished to negotiate when he launched the fast-track campaign in September 1997 included: 'the inclusion of Chile in NAFTA; the Free Trade Agreement of the Americas (FTAA); a NAFTA-like pact encompassing the entire Western Hemisphere except Cuba; and the multilateral Agreement on Investment....' Collier (1997): 3A.
3. These figures are based on studies from nine of the 50 states, National Conference of State Legislatures (1998).
4. DeParle's figures are based on the US Census Bureau's statistics.
5. Under Clinton's legislation, states are no longer required to use government funding explicitly for cash assistance; block grants can be used to fund other state programs that could be deemed assistance to the poor, such as – and this is critical – subsidies to companies for new production projects which will employ those previously on welfare (HR 3734, section 103). The Blair/Field Green Paper, in addition to recommending more private pensions to supplement the state pensions, also promises £75 per week for six months to employers for each long-term welfare recipient they take on, and £60 per week for each young unemployed person (see Blair/Field Green Paper (1998) ch. 3: 3–4.
6. How far one energy source will be replaced by another depends on what I term the law of substitution. According to the law of substitution, capital will, all

other things being equal, take the cheapest form of energy adequate to sustaining production of a particular commodity at the prevailing socially necessary time governing its production, or prevailing level of competition. Nor, to be valuable, need these other natural energies remain untouched. These energies can be transformed many times over, removed more and more from the natural state from which they are initially extracted. See Brennan (2000): 96–8; and Benton (1989).

7. Harvey (1989), however, is acutely aware of capital's role in this process.

8. See Lang and Hines (1993) for a discussion of the concerted opposition to NAFTA in the US Congress, and how the clauses its opponents managed to insert in the name of environmental protection have been vitiated completely in the legal interpretations of the agreement.

9. There are various possibilities. For instance cooperatives might be organized on a neighborhood basis, with some members devoting themselves to childcare. There will be issues of safety and training and space, but these are soluble, and the solutions of themselves counter any trend to the 'passification' of those involved.

10. Their inherent antagonism to large-scale capitals could be made explicit if the ideological greed of their owners was challenged at the outset. One way that this could be done is to restrict holdings, so that no profit could be retained past a certain point. This suggestion may have a place in the current quest to find alternatives to a socialism based on large-scale industrialization, a dream that has most clearly failed See Buck-Morss (1994): 10–17 n.13.

11. The arguments that one can 'Go Green and Prosper' are comforting, and even plausible if read in isolation from capital's overall dynamics. But such arguments refer to a tentative link between the environmental record of large 'well-managed companies' and their performance for shareholders. It is also the case that shareholders are wary of expensive environmental investment. See *Financial Times* (1999): 13.

Part III

Repoliticizing the Retreat of the State

9
The New Politics of the Welfare State*

Paul Pierson

[...]

Why the politics of retrenchment is different

This essay's central claim is that because retrenchment is a distinctive process, it is unlikely to follow the same rules of development that operated during the long phase of welfare state expansion. There are two fundamental reasons for this. First, the political goals of policymakers are different; second, there have been dramatic changes in the political context. Each of these points requires elaboration.

There is a profound difference between extending benefits to large numbers of people and taking benefits away.[1] For the past half century, expanding social benefits was generally a process of political credit claiming. Reformers needed only to overcome diffuse concern about tax rates (often sidestepped through resort to social insurance 'contributions') and the frequently important pressures of entrenched interests. Not surprisingly, the expansion of social programs had until recently been a favored political activity, contributing greatly to both state-building projects and the popularity of reform-minded politicians.[2]

A combination of economic changes, political shifts to the right, and rising costs associated with maturing welfare states has provoked growing calls for retrenchment. At the heart of efforts to turn these demands into policy have been newly ascendant conservative politicians. Conservative governments have generally advocated major social policy reforms, often receiving significant external support in their effort, especially from the business community.[3] Yet the new policy agenda stands in sharp contrast to the credit-claiming initiatives pursued during the long period of welfare state expansion. The politics of retrenchment is typically treacherous,

* From World Politics 48(2)(1996): 143–79.

147

because it imposes tangible losses on concentrated groups of voters in return for diffuse and uncertain gains. Retrenchment entails a delicate effort either to transform programmatic change into an electorally attractive proposition or, at the least, to minimize the political costs involved. Advocates of retrenchment must persuade wavering supporters that the price of reform is manageable – a task that a substantial public outcry makes almost impossible.

Retrenchment is generally an exercise in blame avoidance rather than credit claiming, primarily because the costs of retrenchment are concentrated (and often immediate), while the benefits are not. That concentrated interests will be in a stronger political position than diffuse ones is a standard proposition in political science.[4] As interests become more concentrated, the prospect that individuals will find it worth their while to engage in collective action improves. Furthermore, concentrated interests are more likely to be linked to organizational networks that keep them informed about how policies affect their interests. These informational networks also facilitate political action.

An additional reason that politicians rarely get credit for program cutbacks concerns the well-documented asymmetry in the way that voters react to losses and gains. Extensive experiments in social psychology have demonstrated that individuals respond differently to positive and negative risks. Individuals exhibit a negativity bias: they will take more chances – seeking conflict and accepting the possibility of even greater losses – to prevent any worsening of their current position.[5] Studies of electoral behavior, at least in the United States, confirm these findings. Negative attitudes toward candidates are more strongly linked with a range of behaviors (for example, turnout, deserting the voter's normal party choice) than are positive attitudes.[6]

While the reasons for this negativity bias are unclear, the constraints that it imposes on elected officials are not. When added to the imbalance between concentrated and diffuse interests, the message for advocates of retrenchment is straightforward. A simple 'redistributive' transfer of resources from program beneficiaries to taxpayers, engineered through cuts in social programs, is generally a losing proposition. The concentrated beneficiary groups are more likely to be cognizant of the change, are easier to mobilize, and because they are experiencing losses rather than gains are more likely to incorporate the change in their voting calculations. Retrenchment advocates thus confront a clash between their policy preferences and their electoral ambitions.

If the shift in goals from expansion to cutbacks creates new political dynamics, so does the emergence of a new context: the development of the welfare state itself. Large public social programs are now a central part of the political landscape. [...] The maturation of the welfare state fundamentally transforms the nature of interest-group politics. In short, the emergence of powerful groups surrounding social programs may make the welfare state less dependent on the political parties, social movements, and labor organizations that expanded social programs in the first place. Nor is the context altered simply because welfare states create their own constituencies. The structures of social programs may also have implications for the decision rules governing policy change (for example, whether national officials need the acquiescence of local ones) and for how visible cutbacks will be. 'Policy feedback' from earlier rounds of welfare state development is likely to be a prominent feature of retrenchment politics.[7]

[...]

Retrenchment politics [...]

To what extent have welfare states undergone retrenchment? What countries and programs have been most vulnerable to retrenchment initiatives and why? In this section I address these questions by reviewing the evolution of welfare states in four affluent democracies since the late 1970s. The evidence supports a number of claims. (1) There is little evidence for broad propositions about the centrality of strong states or left power resources to retrenchment outcomes. (2) The unpopularity of retrenchment makes major cutbacks unlikely except under conditions of budgetary crisis, and radical restructuring is unlikely even then. (3) For the same reason, governments generally seek to negotiate consensus packages rather than to impose reforms unilaterally, which further diminishes the potential for radical reform. And (4) far from creating a self-reinforcing dynamic, cutbacks tend to replenish support for the welfare state.

[...] Beginning with the quantitative evidence, aggregate measures provide little evidence that any of the four welfare states have undergone dramatic cutbacks. From 1974 through 1990 the expenditure patterns across the four cases are quite similar, despite widely different starting points. [...] [S]ocial security spending and total government outlays as a percentage of GDP are relatively flat over most of the relevant period.[...] There is a slight upward trend overall, with fluctuations related to the business cycle. [...] [P]ublic employment, reveals a similar pattern (although the expansion of Swedish public employment from an already high base stands out). For none of the countries does the evidence reveal a sharp curtailment of the public sector.

[...] [V]ery few program areas – notably British housing and German pensions – experienced significant reductions. Nonetheless, similarities across countries remain more striking than differences. None of the cases show major rises or declines in overall effort, and there are few indications of dramatic change in any of the sub-categories of expenditure.

The data suggest a surprisingly high level of continuity and stability.[8] These figures must be treated with caution, however, since major changes in the spending for particular programs could be occurring within these broad categories. Policy reforms could have imposed lagged cutbacks that do not show up in spending figures. Furthermore, many other features of programs, not just spending levels, are of significance. To investigate these issues and to get a better sense of the processes that generated these aggregate outcomes, we turn to a more detailed investigation of the [...] cases.

[...]

The United States

Many have seen the United States as another likely candidate for a dismantling of the welfare state. Like Britain, the United States experienced a significant rightward shift in power resources during the 1980s. Republicans captured the presidency in 1980 (as well as the Senate until 1986). Union power – never that extensive to begin with – continued a seemingly inexorable decline. The American welfare state was already fairly modest in scope, suggesting to some observers that public support for maintaining it would be weak. Unlike Thatcher, however, retrenchment advocates in the United States operated in a context of severely fragmented political authority. The combination of weak parties, separation of powers, and federalism created an institutional environment that was in many respects the polar opposite of that in Britain.

Yet at least through 1994 the American story reads like the British one, minus most of Thatcher's sporadic successes. Reagan's first year was the exception. Riding the anti-tax wave that had helped to elect him, Reagan was able to cobble together a loose coalition of southern Democrats and Republicans in his first year to pass some cuts in social programs, especially those affecting the poor. A decade-long expansion of low-income housing programs was rapidly reversed. Significant cuts were introduced in the main program for the poor, Aid to families with Dependent Children (AFDC), and in Unemployment Insurance. The Reagan administration successfully exploited the fact that responsibility for these two programs was shared with fiscally strapped state governments. Both fared poorly in the 1980s, although many of the cutbacks occurred at the state level.[9]

This first-year record has shaped many appraisals of the Reagan revolution.[10] As in other countries, however, popular support for retrenchment dissipated rapidly. The Reagan assault petered out in 1982, when further budget cuts were overwhelmingly rejected. Reagan's single major reform initiative, the New Federalism proposal, would have transferred responsibility for AFDC and food stamps to the states (in return for the federal government's assumption of complete control over Medicaid). The proposal was so unpopular, however, that it could not find even a single congressional sponsor and died without ever being introduced.[11] By Reagan's second term, incremental expansions of various social programs for the poor were back on the agenda, and Congress passed modest increases in food stamps and Medicaid and a dramatic expansion of the earned income tax credit for poor working families.[12]

Middle-class programs also weathered the storm. Trust fund difficulties forced significant reforms of Social Security, and there was a series of efforts to trim Medicare's exploding costs (mostly through cuts in provider compensation). In all these efforts, however, Republicans fearful of the electoral consequences of retrenchment refused to move forward in the absence of bipartisan agreement. The need for consensus in turn assured that reforms would be acceptable to program defenders within the Democratic Party. This was most clearly evident in the 1983 Social Security amendments, where the reliance on a bipartisan, quasi-corporatist commission assured that radical reforms would be rejected.[13] It was also true, however, of the series of broad budget packages that sought cutbacks in the Medicare system.[14]

Although it is generally argued that the residual nature of the welfare state in the United States creates a narrow political base, the initial backlash against the welfare state was short-lived. Declining support for social programs preceded Reagan's election. From 1982 onward – that is, immediately following the first round of budget cuts – polls revealed growing support for the welfare state.[15] As is true elsewhere, support for means-tested programs was far lower than that for middle-class programs, but the same public opinion pattern of modest declines in support followed by rapid recovery is evident for both targeted and universal programs. Reagan became much more hesitant as popular enthusiasm for retrenchment faded. In any event, the fragmented nature of American political institutions assured that plans for further cutbacks met a hostile reception in Congress.

To be sure, with both the emergence of a large structural budget deficit during the 1980s and resistance to tax increases, little room was left for social policy expansion. The American welfare state moved into a zero-sum era, in which gains for some programs often came at the expense of others. This atmosphere continued when the Democrats returned to the White House in 1992, although social spending for the poor was a prime beneficiary of the 1993 budget agreement. From the late 1980s through 1994 the situation was one of reallocation within an essentially stagnant budget.[16]

The 1994 elections, which ended 40 years of Democratic predominance in Congress, precipitated the most vigorous challenge yet to the American welfare state. Republicans had learned important lessons from past defeats. Social Security was taken off the table. The issue was carefully framed as a matter of controlling the deficit and bringing government 'closer to the people.' Efforts at institutional change (the line-item veto and balanced-budget amendment) preceded (though with limited success) attacks on social programs. To diminish visibility, most of the major cuts were scheduled for the year 2000 and beyond. If fully implemented, the Republican budget proposals introduced in 1995 would represent a fundamental reform of American social policy. It will, however, be several years before the outcome of this latest battle is clear. Republican cutbacks are only now being formulated, and it will take some time for their impact to register with the electorate. While the current political environment poses a major test of the resilience of the welfare state, both American precedent and the experience elsewhere cast doubt on the proposition that Republicans will discover a deep reservoir of public tolerance for sharp cuts in social programs.

Germany

Germany, like Sweden, has a very extensive welfare state, though the German system is geared toward transfer payments rather than public services, and toward redistribution over the life cycle rather than across income groups. As in Britain and the United States, there has been a considerable swing to the right in elections during the period of austerity. A right-of-center coalition has been in office since 1982. In recent years, however, the Social Democrats, with their majority in the Bundesrat, have gained considerable influence. And although Germany's powerful unions have been under pressure, compared with unions in other countries their organizational strength has held up quite well.[17] Thus, Germany represents a case of moderately diminished left power resources and relatively fragmented political authority.

The German welfare state is based, not on maximizing employment, but on providing subsidies to the 'outsiders,' who are encouraged to leave the labor market to those who are highly productive. Esping-Andersen has speculated that the result is likely to be an 'insider-outsider' conflict in which the employed (along with employers) increasingly balk at the cost of subsidizing a large and growing 'surplus population.'[18] Indeed, within the recent wave of commentary about the contribution of high wages and extensive social protection to Europe's economic problems, Germany's huge wage costs (including steeply rising payroll taxes) have received particular attention.[19] Adding to the stress has been the cost of unification, as the West German welfare state was extended to cover the far less productive East Germany.

The fiscal pressures facing Germany are evident and are unlikely to go away. Demographic shifts will increase costs even if expenses related to unification begin to subside. There is, however, little sign that these pressures will translate into a sharp insider/outsider conflict. This line of potential cleavage is based largely on age, with by far the largest and most expensive group of outsiders consisting of former insiders: pensioners and early retirees. There are formidable barriers to the development of political cleavages along generational lines.[20] Where costs associated with aging are the main source of budgetary pressure, insiders will have to recognize that in the future they too will be outsiders. This is likely to temper any tendency toward a polarization between 'them' and 'us.'[21]

Far from revealing a sharp new political cleavage, the reform of pensions in the late 1980s fits the general cross-national pattern for retrenchment in popular social programs.[22] With projections indicating enormous long-term deficits as a result of demographic trends, the need for pension reform was widely recognized. While some critics pressed for a rethinking of the entire scheme, the Kohl government instead searched for consensus among experts and the social partners, and eagerly sought support from the opposition Social Democrats. Union and business representatives submitted joint statements on pension reform. All parties except the Greens supported the Pension Reform Act passed in November 1989.[23] The resulting plan incorporated familiar pruning techniques: slightly lower replacement rates, an increase in the retirement age, and increased contributions. Combined with earlier cutbacks, these reforms have generated substantial budgetary savings. The basic structure of Germany's generous pension system remained unaltered, however. In the case of health care reform as well, corporatist accommodation of entrenched interests and a search for cross-party consensus has been the rule.[24]

The one indication of a distinctly conservative cast to retrenchment initiatives prior to 1989 came in the pattern of benefit cuts. Most affected were welfare and unemployment insurance benefits that could be considered a hindrance to labor market flexibility. While these benefits were relatively well protected under the SPD-led coalition of the late 1970s, they experienced disproportionate reductions after 1982.[25] Still, the differences were limited and did not overturn the basic reality that social welfare policy operated within a relatively consensual framework. As Offe has argued, moderate cutbacks were carefully designed by a '*de facto* bipartisan coalition' and orchestrated to prevent a political outcry.[26]

The strains of the post-unification period raised the possibility of more dramatic reform. Germany's worsening fiscal situation, combined with concern about industrial competitiveness, generated growing criticism of the welfare state. Yet the response to unification emphasized continuity: East Germans were brought into the West German social policy regime on extremely generous terms. In response to budgetary pressures since then, a series of cuts have been introduced in major social programs, and more cuts are probably on the way.[27] Again, however, the pattern has been to trim benefit levels rather than challenge the basic structure of programs.

The recent ambitious expansion of long-term care covering in-home and nursing-home services is clear grounds for skepticism about the prospects for radical retrenchment or a generational backlash against the German welfare state.[28] The system will relieve the sickness funds and local social assistance budgets of responsibility for long-term care expenditures. While the scheme partly amounts to fiscal relief for strapped Länder (state) governments, it involves significant new benefits as well. Its introduction at a time of budgetary stress and widespread discussion of high social wage costs indicates the continuing political attractiveness of social programs, as well as the electoral clout of the elderly.[29]

[...] Demographic and budgetary pressures assure that an atmosphere of austerity will continue to surround the German welfare state. Indeed, the German government has been quite successful in holding the line on spending. Yet, as Offe aptly puts it, it has been a period of 'smooth consolidation.' A fundamental rethinking of social policy seems a remote possibility. The structure of political institutions – both constitutional rules and corporatist policy networks – puts a premium on consensus. The SPD's significant gains in the October 1994 elections, where Kohl's coalition government retained only a razor-thin majority, are unlikely to invigorate a governing coalition that has never shown much appetite for radical initiatives.

[...]

The new politics of the welfare state

Economic, political, and social pressures have fostered an image of welfare states under siege. Yet if one turns from abstract discussions of social transformation to an examination of actual policy, it becomes difficult to sustain the proposition that these strains have generated fundamental shifts. This review of four cases does indeed suggest a distinctly new environment, but not one that has provoked anything like a dismantling of the welfare state. Nor is it possible to attribute this to case selection, since the choice of two prototypical cases of neoconservatism (Britain and the United States) and two cases of severe budgetary shocks (Germany and Sweden) gave ample room for various scenarios of radical retrenchment. Even in Thatcher's Britain, where an ideologically-committed Conservative Party has controlled one of Europe's most centralized political systems for over a decade, reform has been incremental rather than revolutionary, leaving the British welfare state largely intact. In most other countries the evidence of continuity is even more apparent.[30]

[To be sure, there has been change. [...] What is striking is how hard it is to find radical changes in advanced welfare states. Retrenchment has been pursued cautiously: whenever possible, governments have sought all-party consensus for significant reforms and have chosen to trim existing structures rather than experiment with new programs or pursue privatization.

[...] I have suggested that to understand what has been happening requires looking beyond the considerable pressures on the welfare state to consider enduring sources of support. There are powerful political forces that stabilize welfare states and channel change in the direction of incremental modifications of existing policies. The first major protection for social programs stems from the generally conservative characteristics of democratic political institutions. The welfare state now represents the *status quo*, with all the political advantages that this status confers. Non-decisions generally favor the welfare state. Major policy change usually requires the acquiescence of numerous actors. Where power is shared among different institutions (for example, Germany, the United States), radical reform will be difficult.

[...] Nor does the welfare state's political position seem to have been seriously eroded – at least in the medium term – by the decline of its key traditional constituency, organized labor. Only for those benefits where unions are the sole organized constituency, such as unemployment insurance, has labor's declining power presented immediate problems, and even here the impact can be exaggerated.[31] The growth of social spending has reconfigured the terrain of welfare state politics. Maturing social programs produce new organized interests, the consumers and providers of social services, that are usually well placed to defend the welfare state.

The networks associated with mature welfare state programs constitute a barrier to radical change in another sense as well. As recent research on path dependence has demonstrated, once initiated, certain courses of development are hard to reverse.[32] Organizations and individuals adapt to particular arrangements, making commitments that may render the costs of change (even to some potentially more efficient alternative) far higher than the costs of continuity. Existing commitments lock in policymakers. Old-age pension systems provide a good example. Most countries operate pensions on a pay-as-you-go basis: current workers pay 'contributions' that finance the previous generation's] retirement. Once in place, such systems may face incremental cutbacks, but they are notoriously resistant to radical reform.[33] Shifting to private, occupationally-based arrangements would place an untenable burden on current workers, requiring them to finance the previous generation's retirement while simultaneously saving for their own.

Over time, all institutions undergo change. This is especially so for very large ones, which cannot be isolated from broad social developments. The welfare state is no exception. But there is little sign that the last two decades have been a transformative period for systems of social provision. As I have argued, expectations for greater change have rested in part on the implicit application of models from the period of welfare state expansion, which can be read to suggest that economic change, the decline in union power, or the presence of a strong state creates the preconditions for radical retrenchment. I find little evidence for these claims.

This preliminary investigation still leaves us some distance from a coherent comparative theory of retrenchment politics. It does, however, suggest some of the building blocks for such a theory. The pressures of a shifting global economy, which have long been at the center of discussions of the contemporary welfare state, continue to deserve major (if more nuanced) attention. What needs more consideration is what happens when these considerable pressures collide with popular, deeply institutionalized public policies. I have emphasized that politicians are likely to pursue strategies that will not damage their chances for reelection. The centrality of electoral considerations, combined with the general unpopularity of welfare state cutbacks, suggests some plausible hypotheses about the political preconditions for significant reform. These hypotheses are only tentative and would need to be subjected to sustained comparative scrutiny. Each, however, is compatible with the analysis of retrenchment outlined here and with the evidence presented.

First, radical retrenchment may be facilitated when there is significant electoral slack, that is, when governments believe that they are in a strong enough position to absorb the electoral consequences of unpopular decisions.[34] Thus, one reason for Thatcher's *relative* (though still limited) success may have been the division among her opponents within a first-past-the-post electoral system. This may have given her more room to pursue unpopular policies that would have been beyond the reach of a government in a precarious electoral position. However, calculating electoral slack *ex ante* is a tricky business, and most governments are likely to proceed cautiously. As I have indicated, even the Thatcher Government generally retreated when confronted with widespread opposition.

Second, moments of budgetary crisis may open opportunities for reform. Advocates of retrenchment will try to exploit such moments to present reforms as an effort to save the welfare state rather than destroy it. Framing the issue in this manner may allow governments to avoid widespread blame for program cutbacks. Making the claim of crisis credible, however, generally requires collaboration with the political opposition. In turn, the need for consensus makes it difficult to utilize crises to promote radical restructuring. Thus, while the appearance of fiscal stress encourages downward adjustments in social programs, it is far less clear that it provides a platform for a radical overhaul of social policy.

Third, the success of retrenchment advocates will vary with the chances for lowering the visibility of reforms. Those seeking retrenchment will try to avoid political outcries by diminishing the visibility of their cutbacks or by trying to hide their own responsibility for unpopular outcomes. Success in these efforts, I have argued, depends partly on the design of political institutions. Whether political authority is concentrated or not helps to structure the choices available to retrenchment advocates. Where authority is concentrated (as in Britain and Sweden), governments will be hard-pressed to avoid blame for unpopular decisions, but they will have a greater capacity to develop and implement strategies that obscure cutbacks.

Governments in more fragmented systems must fashion strategies that minimize the need to force multiple policy changes through institutional veto points. However, they may find it easier to duck accountability for unpopular policies. Federalism, for example, opened up considerable possibilities for Reagan to shift the blame for cuts in some programs, a tactic that is central to the current efforts of congressional Republicans.

Finally, the prospects for changing institutions (the rules of the game) may be of great significance. If retrenchment advocates can restructure the ways in which trade-offs between taxes, spending, and deficits are presented, evaluated, and decided, they may be able to shift the balance of political power. So far, these institutional shifts have been rare, but several instances may be of growing relevance. In Europe the increasing policy significance of the EC may alter the terrain for struggles over the welfare state. If reforms can be presented as legally required or economically imperative because of the single market or moves toward monetary union, national governments may be freed from some blame for welfare-state cutbacks.[35] In the United States the new Republican majority in Congress deferred efforts to cut programs until after a strong (but only modestly successful) push to change the rules of the game. The intent of the rule changes was to increase the salience of taxes and create a more favorable climate for attacking social spending.

If this analysis suggests some plausible sources of cross-national variation, it also highlights the need to disaggregate welfare states and consider variations across programs. Indeed, in the four cases considered outcomes often differed more across programs (for example, the contrast between council housing and the NHS in Britain) than across countries. It is commonly argued that the crucial distinction across programs will be between universal programs and those that target the poor, and that the latter will be especially vulnerable.[36] Yet the current investigation does not support this assertion. Rather, variations in outcomes across programs in the four countries do not generally track the universal/targeted divide. Among the likely reasons that targeted programs have generally not proved more vulnerable: cuts in these programs tend to yield only minimal budgetary savings, and conservative governments interested in radical reform object the most to the universal programs that require high tax rates and compete with plausible private alternatives. Instead, the current investigation suggests that a promising area of research concerns the features of programs that allow governments either to obscure the impact of retrenchment on voters or to diminish their own accountability for unpopular reforms.[37] Programs that are poorly indexed, for example, make it easier to pursue a low-visibility strategy of allowing inflation to gradually erode the value of benefits.

All of these hypotheses build on the core argument of this essay: that frontal assaults on the welfare state carry tremendous electoral risks. The contemporary politics of the welfare state is the politics of blame avoidance. Governments confronting the electoral imperatives of modern democracy will undertake retrenchment only when they discover ways to minimize the political costs involved. But as I emphasize, such techniques are hard to come by. While this analysis suggests some of the possible keys to variation in policy outcomes, the most significant finding concerns not variation but commonality. Everywhere, retrenchment is a difficult undertaking. The welfare state remains the most resilient aspect of the post-war political economy.

Understanding why this is so requires that old arguments be rethought and recast to address the exigencies of a new setting. At a time when historical institutionalism has become fashionable, this conclusion has broad implications for the study of comparative politics. The strong calls to incorporate historical analysis into the study of contemporary politics are compelling.[38] Yet we must remain cognizant of the hazards of drawing on history in the wrong way. There are significant dangers in using historical analogies to study contemporary social politics, since the goals of social policy reformers and the context in which they operate have undergone profound change. Instead, historically grounded analysis should emphasize that social policy change is a process that unfolds over time. My focus on the impact of inherited social policy structures draws on this precise point. The growth of the welfare state has transformed the politics of social policy. A historical perspective should stress that today's policymakers operate in an environment fundamentally shaped by policies inherited from the past, rather than suggesting that current politics will echo the conflicts of a previous era.

Notes

1. Weaver (1986).
2. Flora and Heidenheimer (eds) (1982).
3. As recent research has suggested, it would be wrong to treat business as always and everywhere opposed to welfare state programs. For illuminating studies of the United States see, for example, C. Gordon (1994); and Martin (1995). Nonetheless, it is clear that most business organizations in all the advanced industrial democracies have favored – often vehemently – cutbacks in the welfare state over the past fifteen years.
4. Olson (1973); Wilson (1973): 330–7.
5. Kahneman and Tversky (1979); and (1984).
6. Bloom and Price (1975); Kernell (1977); and Lau (1985).
7. Esping-Andersen (1985); Pierson (July 1993).
8. This broad conclusion is echoed for a much larger number of cases in Stephens, Huber and Ray (1995).
9. In the case of AFDC, which is not indexed, this happened largely because state governments failed to index benefits to inflation. Given this structural feature of the program, 'non-decisions' allowed quiet retrenchment. This trend predated Reagan's arrival in office. Indeed, cuts in real benefits were greater during Carter's presidency (when inflation was high) than under Reagan.

10. See, for example, two frequently cited studies, Rosenberry (1982); and Palmer and Sawhill (eds) (1982).
11. Conlan (1988): 95–238.
12. Peterson (1988): 95–238, (1990–91); Greenstein (1991).
13. Light (1985).
14. White and Wildavsky (1989).
15. Cook and Barret (1992); Shapiro and Young (1989). In line with my general argument, Shapiro and Young's research indicates similar patterns in other countries.
16. On recent spending trends, see House Ways and Means Committee (1994).
17. Thelen (1993).
18. Esping-Andersen (1992a); and (1992b).
19. Combined employer and employee social insurance contributions were 26.5 percent of gross income in 1970, 32.4 percent in 1980, and are forecast to hit 39.2 percent in 1994. *Financial Times*, July 2, 1993, p. 13.
20. Heclo (1988).
21. Esping-Andersen (1992b) rightly suggests that the development of private pension schemes could encourage such a polarization, since it would allow current workers to sever the link between their own retirement situation and that of the preceding generation. Yet the enormous institutional and political barriers to any radical change in a mature, pay-as-you-go pension system make a major development along these lines highly unlikely. See Pierson (1992).
22. Hinrichs (1993); Schmahl (1992).
23. Friedbert Rüb and Frank Nullmeier, 'Alterssicherungspolitik in der Bundesrepublik,' in Berhard Blanke and Hellmut Wollmann (eds) *Die alte Bundesrepublik: Kontinuität und Wandel* (Opladen: Westdeutscher Verlag 1991).
24. Webber (1988).
25. Alber (1988); Offe (1991).
26. *Ibid.*, 140.
27. Plaschke (1994).
28. Alber (1994); Götting, Haug and Hinrichs (1994).
29. Tyll Necker, President of the Association of German Industry (BDI), described the original proposal (which did not include the reduction of one paid holiday as an offset) as an official declaration of war against German industry. Alber (1994).
30. Schwartz (1994) argues that there has been major change in the four small states he studies: Sweden, Denmark, Australia, and New Zealand. His study focuses on the internal organization of public service provision, rather than on the level and quality of services actually provided, and it does not even discuss the transfer payments that account for the majority of welfare-state spending. Even on its own narrow terms, however, Schwartz's study provides remarkably little evidence that the changes he catalogs add up to radical reform rather than the continuous tinkering common in all modern public sectors. The evidence looks credible only for New Zealand, a tiny country on the periphery of the world economy, which clearly faced severe adjustment problems in light of its long (and unusual) tradition of protectionism. It seems far more reasonable to treat this case as an outlier than to view it as the pacesetter in a global march toward radical reform of the welfare state. See Stephens, Huber, and Ray (1994).
31. Indeed, a cross-national comparison of unemployment programs provides further support for this analysis. The OECD has measured replacement rates for UI (benefits as a percentage of previous income) over time in 20 countries, with

data through 1991. This data thus permit, for one program, a recent quantitative appraisal of program generosity rather than simply spending levels. In the majority of cases (12 out of 20), replacement rates were higher in 1991 than the average rate for either the 1970s or the 1980s, while most of the other cases experienced very marginal declines (OECD 1994).

32. See David (1985); and Arthur (1989): 116–31. For good extensions to political processes, see Krasner (1989); and North (1990).

33. Thus in Germany, Sweden, and the United States the maturity of existing schemes limited policymakers to very gradual and incremental reforms of earnings-related pension systems. More dramatic reform was possible in Britain because the unfunded earnings-related scheme was far from maturity, having been passed only in 1975. Pierson (1992).

34. For an example of this argument, see Garrett (1993).

35. For an argument about how EC institutions may allow blame-avoiding behavior on the part of member state governments, see Andrew Moravcsik's 'Why the EC Strengthens the State' (Manuscript, 1994).

36. Robert Kuttner has called this 'the most fundamental principle in the political economy of social spending.' Kuttner (1988): 113. For a critique, see Pierson (1994): 6, 170.

37. *Ibid.*, 17–26, 169–75.

38. Steinmo, Thelen, and Longstreth (eds) (1992).

10
Shrinking States? Globalization and National Autonomy in the OECD*

Geoffrey Garrett

[...]

One of the most widely held beliefs about the globalization of markets is that it has substantially decreased the autonomy of the nation-state, resulting in a 'race to the bottom' whereby governments competing for mobile economic resources race to dismantle their welfare states. For many, globalization threatens the prosperity and stability that has characterized the advanced industrial countries since World War II, if not the legitimacy of the democratic state itself. Visions of widespread social upheaval abound, and they are often accompanied by pleas for international political cooperation to regulate global capitalism. The bottom line of the conventional wisdom is that there is a fundamental mismatch between the global scope of markets and the national level at which politics are organized. Something has to give, and most commentators assume that it will be the nation-state, *de facto* if not *de jure*.

This article assesses the merits of the globalization thesis, both theoretically and empirically. I begin by articulating three discrete mechanisms which market integration might influence domestic politics – increasing exposure to trade, the multinationalization of production and the integration of financial markets – and then develop rebuttals to the notion that each of these erodes national policy autonomy. My basic claim is that the globalization of markets imposes far fewer constraints on the range of feasible economic policies than is commonly thought. Most importantly, there are many types of government interventions in the economy that are compatible with globally competitive markets. These certainly include the policies emphasized in the 'new growth' literature, such as the provision of education and training and physical infrastructure (Barro & Sala-I-Martin 1995); but they should also be conceived more broadly to encompass many aspects of the traditional welfare state, particularly when these policies are

* From *Oxford Development Studies* 26(1) (1998): 71–98.

pursued in countries with dense networks of socio-economic institutions ('corporatism').

The second half of my article is empirical and makes three basic points. First, globalization is not a uni-dimensional phenomenon. In particular, one must distinguish between exposure to trade and openness to international financial markets. Although both forms of market integration have increased rapidly in recent years, there remains a tendency for countries that are highly exposed to trade to have less open capital markets.

Second, the evidence is far from clear that even the globalization of finance has exerted systematic lowest common denominator pressures on the OECD countries. As I have shown elsewhere (Garrett 1995, 1997, 1998), capital market integration has been associated with increasing divergence in most facets of taxing and spending policy. Moreover, much of this variation continues to be explained by traditional domestic politics variables such as government partisanship and the strength of organized labor. [Although] governments in countries with strong conservative parties and weak organized labor movements have reacted to financial openness with cutbacks in the public economy, strong left-labor regimes have done precisely the opposite.

Third, although real macroeconomic performance (growth and unemployment) has deteriorated badly in most OECD countries in the past two decades (as price stability has largely been achieved), there is little evidence to suggest that these changes in performance can be attributed to globalization – even in countries where governments have reacted to market integration with more interventionist economic policies.

Needless to say, there is a marked disjuncture between my analysis and the dire predictions about the mismatch between the global economy and national policy autonomy that are so common in the rhetoric of politicians, journalists and academics. I conclude by arguing that the problems confronting interventionist government in the OECD – slower growth, higher unemployment and the aging of populations – have little to do with the globalization of markets. It is possible to reap the benefits of market integration without being forced to pay a heavy domestic price. This is the lesson of globalization that should be preached by the World Bank and the IMF, not a creed based on narrow views of market-friendly government.

Three globalization mechanisms

[...] The first and oldest argument about the domestic effects of market integration concerns trade. Attention in recent years has been focused on the question: can the welfare state compete? For many, the answer is 'no'. Modern welfare states comprise two basic elements – the public provision of social services (most importantly, education and health) and income transfers programs (pensions, unemployment benefits, family allowances and some other smaller programs). Both facets of the welfare state reduce market disciplines on labor, creating wage-push pressures. Moreover, government spending must be funded either by higher taxes or by borrowing. Taxes add to the costs of doing business. Borrowing results in higher inflation and higher interest rates, depressing investment. If borrowing also increases the real exchange rate, the competitiveness of national producers is decreased further. Over time, output and employment will stagnate. Since no government can afford these outcomes, the conventional view about trade integration is that it forces governments to roll back the public economy. But the feedback from competitiveness pressures to changes in national arrangements is likely to be quite slow. There is no reason to expect tectonic changes in deeply-rooted domestic institutions just because these adversely affect the bottom lines of firms. This is particularly true of the welfare state, which remains extremely popular among most citizens across the OECD (Pierson 1996). Only if macroeconomic performance were to deteriorate significantly as a result of outmoded policies would there be sufficient incentives for governments to act. Even then, substantial political obstacles to institutional reform are likely to remain (Garrett and Lange 1995).

The second globalization mechanism is the multinationalization of production. News stories and academic commentary these days are replete with examples of the 'exit' threats of multinational firms to move production from one country to another in search of higher returns. This was the 'giant sucking sound' of lost jobs Ross Perot predicted to result from NAFTA; it was also given considerable play in Europe when Hoover decided to move some production back to the UK after John Major's government chose to opt-out of the EU's social protocol at Maastricht. The logic behind these assertions is very similar to that for trade competitiveness. Firms want to minimize the costs of production; government interventions in the economy raise the costs of doing business. The big difference, of course, is the availability of exit as an option for firms: the multinationalization of production allows firms to evade these costs, rather than to be forced to lobby governments to change policy.

One would thus expect that the constraints imposed by the multinationalization of production on government autonomy would be felt more quickly than the effects of trade. Multinational companies (MNCs) cannot close a plant in one country and open a new one in a foreign location instantaneously, or without incurring significant startup costs. But downsizing one facility and expanding another existing one is a feasible short-term strategy for many multinationals. Thus, governments will probably respond more quickly to their exit threats than to the protests of less mobile businesses about their eroding competitive positions.

The final and most prevalent argument made about globalization concerns the domestic effects of the international integration of financial markets. Traders operating 24 hours a day instantaneously move mind-boggling amounts of money around the globe in ceaseless efforts to arbitrage profits. For many commentators, the potential for massive capital flight acts as the ultimate discipline on governments that may want to pursue autonomous economic policies. The logic that underpins all of these assertions is the same. Governments are held to ransom by mobile capital, the price is high and the punishment is swift. If the policies and institutions of which the financial markets approve are not entrenched in a country, money will hemorrhage until they are.

Of course, financial capital is widely thought to disapprove of all government policies that distort markets, from counter-cyclical demand management all the way down to programs to support single mothers. Governments that disobey the dictates of the market will be forced to pay ever-higher interest rates, retarding domestic economic activity. Unless policies are changed, rising mountains of debt will cripple countries. This is supposedly the lesson of the Latin American debt crises of the 1980s, the peso crisis of the winter of 1995, the European Monetary System (EMS) crises of the early 1990s – in fact, of all episodes of financial instability since the end of the Bretton Woods era it would seem.

How many degrees of freedom are there in the global economy?

[...] Let us begin with the multinationalization of production. There is no doubt that MNCs today have credible exit threats. But should we expect firms' production decisions to be primarily – if not solely – influenced by cost considerations, and that they will always choose to locate where market conditions most closely approximate the neo-classical ideal? The evidence hardly supports this view. Most foreign direct investment (FDI) flows inside the OECD, where wages and taxes are relatively similar, rather than to the lower-cost developing world. Furthermore, unit labor costs (that is relative to productivity) are not necessarily lower in less developed economies than in the OECD. In 1990, for example, unit labor costs in manufacturing were actually higher in India, Malaysia and the Philippines than they were in the USA (*The Economist* 1996: 12).

In fact, patterns of foreign direct investment are primarily determined by the desire for access to new technology, new distribution channels and new markets, rather than by a narrow definition of cost advantages (Cantwell 1989; Caves 1996; Dunning 1988). As Krugman (1991) has argued, there are thus good reasons to believe that market integration will not inexorably lead to the movement of production and jobs out of the OECD. Indeed, the flows may be in the opposite direction as firms take advantage of the numerous market complementarities offered by locating in advanced market economies.

This is not to claim that cost factors are irrelevant to multinational firms. Relative costs may also be a tiebreaker between otherwise equivalent locations. Consider, for example, the recent decisions by Mercedes-Benz and BMW to build automobile plants in the American south. The companies chose to locate in the USA, rather than say, Mexico, because being physically located inside the large US market for luxury cars was of paramount importance. Having chosen to build in the USA, however, the firms were in a position to seek tax concessions from the southern states that were competing for foreign investment (for more general evidence of this type, see Hines 1997). But BMW's choice of South Carolina over other southern states as a production site is a far cry from the apocalyptic visions of multinational mayhem that often characterize the globalization debate.

Turning to the domestic effects of financial integration, there is only one clear case where globalization vitiates national policy autonomy: monetary policy where there are no barriers to cross-border capital movements and where a country's exchange rate is fixed. For all countries (except the anchor in an 'n-1' system), efforts to run expansionary monetary policies will result in capital outflows until domestic interest rates rise sufficiently to hold capital at home. In recent times, this situation has been most closely approximated in the OECD by the 'hard' EMS from 1987 until 1992; it would certainly describe Europe's would-be monetary union.

Many scholars seem to believe, however, that under conditions of high capital mobility, governments – fearing wild swings in exchange rates caused by unwarranted speculative attacks in the currency markets – have little choice but to fix exchange rates, and hence to give up monetary policy autonomy; but the costs of floating under conditions of high capital mobility are often significantly overstated. The headline currency crises of the 1990s – the breakup of the EMS and the Mexican peso crisis – reflected untenable commitments to fixed exchange rates (Eichengreen *et al.* 1995). Moreover, the countries whose currencies were forced out of the EMS – notably sterling and the lira – did not suffer as a result. Indeed, the UK and Italian economies thrived under the relatively smooth and sensible depreciations of their currencies that followed their governments' very public U-turns away from fixed rates. This has led some economists to contend that reverting to a floating exchange rate regime may be the best policy option for many European countries (Goodhart 1995).

Now consider the ability of governments to run budget deficits in a world of global capital. Many assume that deficits signal fiscal recklessness that will be severely punished by the financial markets with the imposition of higher interest rates. But how much higher? Globalization has created a very large and competitive pool of lenders willing to fund government debt, easing the monetary costs of fiscal expansion (Corsetti and Roubini 1995). At some point, of course, higher debt burdens may trigger fears among the financial markets of governments' defaulting on their loans – resulting in dramatic reductions in the availability of credit. Unlike the

Latin American debt crises of the 1980s, however, this limit manifestly has not been reached by any industrial democracy (Corsetti and Roubini 1991). What about the size of government, *per se* (that is, assuming new spending is balanced by increased revenues)? The conventional view is that the threat of capital flight will lead governments to cut taxes and spending, with heavy lowest common denominator forces at work. Of course, this assumes that capital will always choose to exit in the face of a large public economy – because government spending is inefficient and because taxes are distortionary. But might not some facets of public spending be good for business? This is certainly true for the provision of services that promote the rule of law, but it might also hold for the production of other collective goods that are under-supplied by the market, such as highly skilled workers, cooperation between labor and capital and overall social stability. If this is the case, paying taxes might be a reasonable investment for firms.

In sum, the conventional view about the impact of the multinationalization of production and financial integration on national economic policy regimes is overly simplistic. Rather than viewing the managers of multinational firms and mutual funds as unsophisticated capitalists whose reaction to interventionist government is everywhere and always the same (exit!), mobile capital may well choose to invest and produce in countries that are far from the neoclassicists' idyll. As a result, governments may retain considerably more autonomy in the era of global markets than is often presumed.

Corporatism in the global economy

I do not want to suggest, however, that all governments can intervene in the economy at will. Rather, I wish to develop a notion of 'institutional comparative advantage' (Soskice 1997) in which the effects of different policy regimes are contingent upon the matrix of institutions that exist in a country. In particular, the large literature on corporatism suggests that the combination of interventionist government and highly organized labor generates macroeconomic outcomes that are at least as strong as in more free market-oriented systems (Alvarez *et al.* 1991). The potential costs of interventionist government are more than offset by the combination of generalized wage regulation (geared to the competitiveness of the exposed sector of the economy) and the upgrading of workers' skills through active labor market policies (Garrett 1998).

[...] Of course, not all government interventions in the economy can be justified under the rubric of corporatism. The literature highlights economic policies that produce economically-important goods that are under-supplied by the market – education and training, not defensive industrial policies designed to prop up declining sectors, for example. Moreover, these are layered upon deeply entrenched institutions that provide mechanisms for coordinating economic activity in ways that are very different from those envisaged by the Chicago school. These institutions do not exist in all countries, and many would suggest that they are under attack even in their historical bastions of northern Europe (Iversen 1996; Pontusson and Swenson 1996). Nonetheless, my contention is that corporatism still offers an alternative to the free market that is well suited to a world of mobile capital.

[...]

Globalization, economic policy and economic performance

The conventional wisdom about globalization generates three basic predictions about the domestic consequences of market integration. First, globalization puts downward pressures on interventionist economic policies. Second, globalization creates incentives for economic policies to converge around those that facilitate the free play of market forces. Finally, governments that seek to buck these globalization imperatives will preside over deteriorating macroeconomic performance. In contrast, I have presented counterarguments that yield very different hypotheses: market integration does not exert lowest common denominator pressures on economic policies regimes; domestic institutional variables continue to play a powerful role in economic policy choice, and it is not likely that there will be any clear deleterious effects of interventionist government on the macroeconomy in the global economy.

[...]

[...] Total government spending doubled from 1960 to 1994, constituting more than half of GDP in the early 1990s. Transfers programs grew at a slightly faster pace, whereas the rate of growth for government consumption expenditures was a little slower. By the end of the period, transfers had replaced consumption spending as the largest component of the public economy. At the same time, the average size of public sector deficits increased from under 1 percent of GDP in the 1960s to over 4 percent in the early 1980s to over 6 percent in the early 1990s.

[...] [G]lobalization and public sector expansion have moved more or less in lock step since the 1960s; but correlation is not causation. Following Wagner's (1883/1958) law, for example, few would dispute that increasing prosperity has been the primary driver behind the growth of the OECD public economies in the post-war period. Similarly, most people would not be surprised to know that deficits have tended to rise, because in modern democracies it is an iron law that citizens want both higher spending and lower taxes. As a result, it is perhaps better to look for changes in the rate of public sector expansion and growth in deficits.

Total government spending, transfers and deficits all increased most rapidly during widespread recessions in the OECD (1973–75, 1980–82 and

1989–93) because downturns in the business cycle put upward pressures on entitlement programs while simultaneously reducing tax receipts. What may be of more interest is the fact that – with the conspicuous exception of the mid-1980s – the public economy did not contract during economic recoveries. Indeed, slower growth in the public economy in the 1980s was an important stimulus for the whole notion of globalization constraints on national autonomy and prosperity. Of course, this view fails to acknowledge the rapid pace of spending growth in the 1990s. The depth of the European recession after the end of the Cold War certainly had a lot to do with this; nonetheless, the first half of the 1990s should give pause to those wishing to draw facile conclusions about the constraining effects of globalization.

[...] [G]lobalization increases the demands on governments to cushion market dislocations but that some governments are more likely to respond to these demands than others. [...] There were dramatic differences in the size of the public economy and in the financing of government spending in the past decade, and in changes from the previous decades. Sweden's public economy was fully twice as large as that of Japan's. Government spending has grown since the 1960s and 1970s more than five times as much in Spain as in the USA. With respect to budget balances, Japan, Luxembourg and Norway all ran surpluses in the period 1985–94, maintaining or improving their fiscal performance from their historic averages. On the other hand, double-digit deficits were the norm in Greece and Italy, representing significant increases from the 1960s and 1970s.

These cross-national variations in fiscal policy were clearly influenced both by market integration and by domestic political conditions. Let me begin with the latter. There is a long history of studies in political science and sociology demonstrating a positive relationship between the political power of the left and organized labor and larger public economies (Cameron 1978, 1984; Garrett and Lange 1991), with the effects of left-labor power being felt more strongly on consumption expenditures than on income transfer programs (Garrett 1998; Huber and Stephens 1996). Given the stickiness of government budgets, it is not surprising that these relationships continued to hold over 1985–94. Moreover, left-labor power was not associated with larger budget deficits – another distinctive feature of these regimes in the golden age of the mixed economy.

More interestingly perhaps, the combined power of the left and organized labor was also associated with faster public sector expansion when one moved from the 1960s–1970s to the 1980s–1990s. Moreover, [...] left-labor regimes were able to expand the public economy without generating budget deficits that were out of line with those in other countries. Deficits increased across the board in the past decade compared with the 25 preceding years, but the rate of growth in deficits was not appreciably faster in countries with strong governing left parties and large trade union movements. This suggests that the fiscal constraints on interventionist government continue to be considerably weaker than is commonly presumed.

How did cross-national variations in market integration – with respect to trade, FDI and financial openness – factor in the fiscal policy equation? Three broad trends stand out. First, market integration was positively correlated with larger public economies in the post-1985 period (and particularly with greater income transfer expenditures) and negatively correlated with the size of budget deficits. Both findings are discordant with the thrust of the globalization thesis, which would expect market integration to have put downward pressures on public spending and, even more so, on taxes (i.e. leading to bigger deficits). One could argue, however, that the levels data are misleading since the structures of public economies have been forged over many decades, and that the effects of the more recent globalization of markets should have been most apparent at the margins, with respect to changes in trends.

Second, the data on changes in the public economy from historic averages to the 1985–94 period do lend more support to the notion that market integration has constrained the pace of public sector expansion. Almost all of the change in spending – globalization correlations were negative, while the growth of public sector deficits was also slower in countries that were more integrated into global markets.

Finally, the speed with which globalization effects are transmitted inside countries had a marked impact on government spending (but not on deficits). At one end of the spectrum, total trade exposure was positively associated with higher spending levels in the past decade but bore no relation to changes in spending. In marked contrast, financial openness had little correlation with spending levels in the 1985–94 period, but was consistently and strongly negatively correlated with changes in spending.

[...] On the one hand, the correlations between left-labor power and greater government spending were strong in the 1985–94 period, stronger than they were in the preceding 25 years. It would thus be hard to argue that domestic autonomy, understood as the ability of citizens to influence economic policy, has been reduced by globalization. On the other hand, financial openness in the contemporary period was correlated with smaller growth in the public economy, indicative of the lowest common denominator pressures commonly alluded to in the globalization literature.

[...]

This analysis suggests that the compromise of 'embedded liberalism' (Ruggie, 1983) – acceptance of an open international order combined with domestic policies that cushion short-term market losers – is today increasingly dependent upon the political power of the left and organized labor. In these 'social democratic corporatist' regimes, governments wish to derive the benefits of market integration, but they also seek to shield those most vulnerable with extensive public provision of social services and income transfers. Under more 'market liberal' regimes, in contrast, the dampening effects of the public economy against market generated risk and inequality are being eroded.

Capital, labor and consumption taxes

[...]

[...] Capital tax rates have tended to increase in recent years, whereas consumption taxes have, if anything, fallen. The former is troubling because the conventional view is that mobile capital should have been able to bid down its tax rate, not only relative to other forms of taxation but also in absolute terms. The absence of a trend toward increasing consumption taxes also seems strange since one would expect these to be the preferred method of raising revenues in the global economy. The owners of capital (and neoclassical economists) favor consumption taxes because they do not distort investment decisions; they are also often thought to be the most regressive form of taxation because poor people tend to consume much of their incomes (rather than save and invest).

[...] If anything, countries have come to pursue increasingly divergent policies with respect to the taxation of labor and consumption. The taxation of capital has been very volatile over time, with spikes in cross-national divergence corresponding to the deep recessions (1974, 1981, 1990) when governments have reacted very differently to sharp reductions in corporate profits. But overall, cross-national variations in capital taxes have not diminished with increased market integration.

[...] There is considerable dispersion in these national data, often belying traditional characterizations of regime types. Sweden's effective capital tax rate was more than three times as high as that in Austria, even though both countries have long histories of interventionist and redistributive government. Capital taxes in dirigiste France were less than half as high as those in Thatcher's Britain; effective rates in the USA were considerably higher than in Germany. Turning to changes from the 1970s, Reagan-Bush America was the only country in the OECD that cut its effective capital tax rate, whereas Sweden witnessed one of the greatest increases. But capital taxes rose fastest of all in Japan, notwithstanding its small public economy and the close relationship between the Liberal Democratic Party (LDP) and business.

The basic pattern of correlations between capital taxation and globalization was similar to that for government spending, although the evidence is more supportive of the conventional wisdom about globalization. Left-labor power was only weakly positively correlated with capital tax rates after 1985 and with changes in capital taxation from the previous 15 years, whereas financial openness was strongly negatively correlated with changes in effective rates of taxation from the 1970s and early 1980s to the most recent period. The pace of growth in capital tax rates (which it should be remembered continued to rise) was significantly lower in countries with more internationally integrated capital markets.

[...] My results demonstrate that left-labor regimes have responded to the globalization of financial markets by increasing the rates at which they effectively tax capital; only countries with more conservative politics have chosen to cut back capital taxation as financial integration has increased (Garrett 1997).

How could it be that capital taxes have not been reduced by capital mobility? This relationship is at the core of the conventional wisdom about globalization. For most analysts, the only solution to this puzzle is that countries that have persisted with high capital taxes have had to endure damaging capital flight and ultimately poorer macroeconomic performance. I assess this proposition in the next subsection. But there is another possibility: the changes in capital taxation that have taken place in recent years have been more or less consistent with the interests of mobile investors and multinational firms. This seems plausible when one delves into changes in the incidence of corporate taxation. Marginal rates of corporate income taxation have been cut significantly in most countries (Cummins *et al.* 1995), but at the same time, investment incentives – long favored by social democrats – have been taken out of the tax code because they have judged to be ineffective (Swank 1997). The net effect of this restructuring has been an increase in the tax take from capital – by expanding the tax base – while the methods of taxation have become more consonant with business preferences (Auerbach and Slemrod 1997).

[...] The data on changes in labor taxation are very interesting. Taxes did not increase most in the latter 1980s and early 1990s in the big spending countries of northern Europe, but rather in Canada and Japan. At the other end of the spectrum, the *laissez-faire* revolution in New Zealand was clearly evident with respect to taxes on labor – it was the only country that actually lowered effective rates between the two periods. The Thatcher decade was not quite as successful, but nonetheless successive Conservative governments in the UK were able to stabilize labor taxes.

As these individual cases suggest, average effective rates of labor taxation were very strongly and positively correlated with government spending in the period 1985–92, although there was no correlation between the size of government and the growth in labor taxation. Big spending regimes have always levied very high taxes on labor. The data also show that big traders and strong left-labor regimes have relied heavily on labor taxes (but the growth of labor taxes was slower in left-labor regimes).

Perhaps the most interesting facet of the labor taxation data is that the financial openness was not correlated with significant increases in the rate of growth of labor taxation. This would seem to stand as a clear refutation of Rodrik's (1997) argument about globalization-induced changes in the structure of taxation (a move from capital taxes to raising revenue from less mobile actors). However, it may still have been the case that reductions in capital taxes were offset by increasing use of consumption taxes.

The data on effective rates of consumption taxation are very surprising. Four countries whose political economies are quite dissimilar in many respects (but none of them has traditionally coupled dominant left-wing parties with powerful organized labor movements) continue not to use consumption taxes to any great degree – Australia, Japan, Switzerland and, above all, the USA. In contrast, consumption tax rates in the period 1985–91 were above 30 percent in Denmark, Finland, Norway and Sweden, well above average rates for EU members (for whom consumption taxes are partially 'harmonized', with a lowest common floor). These cross-national variations in consumption taxation have been quite stable over time. There were only two cases where consumption taxes increased markedly after the mid-1980s. On the one hand, New Zealand's introduction of a generalized sales tax is yet another demonstration of the neoliberal fever that gripped the country. On the other hand, Finland dramatically increased not only consumption taxes but also capital and labor taxes to fund its rapid expansion of the public economy (particularly after 1989 with the collapse of its export markets in the former Soviet Union).

Two broad trends stand out in the consumption tax data. On the one hand, there was only one positive correlation between any facet of globalization and consumption taxes – the level of trade and the level of taxes after 1985. Financial openness was associated with both lower rates of consumption taxes and with smaller increases in them from the 1970s. This stands in marked contrast with the expectations of the conventional wisdom concerning the attractiveness of consumption taxes to mobile capital.

On the other hand, left-labor power was strongly and positively associated both with consumption tax levels in the post-1985 period and with faster increases since the 1970s. One interpretation of this relationship is that left-labor regimes could only feed their appetites for ever-higher levels of public spending by relying on the most regressive form of taxation. This interpretation is clearly consistent with the conventional wisdom about taxation in the global economy; but it should be remembered that consumption taxes are only regressive to the extent that they fall disproportionately on poor people. In practice most governments exempt numerous consumer staples – such as food, clothing and medicine – from consumption taxes (OECD 1997). Thus, one should not make too much of the reliance of corporatist northern Europe on this form of taxation.

[...] Taking the tax data as a whole, the most important developments in recent years concerning globalization have to do with the taxation of capital. While the overall effect of financial integration has been somewhat to reduce capital tax burden, this correlation masks very strong partisan effects that have if anything strengthened in recent years. With respect to broader debates about the fate of national policy autonomy in the era of global markets, people may differ on whether this glass is half full or half empty. Either way, conventional views about globalization constraints would suggest that big government regimes with high rates of capital taxation should have suffered macroeconomically under conditions of integrated markets, and particularly financial markets. The next subsection examines this contention.

[...]

The global future of national autonomy

This article has sought to paint in broad brushstrokes the impact of the globalization of markets on national autonomy among the OECD countries. My basic contention is that the relationships among globalization, domestic political conditions and economic policy regimes in the past decade belie common predictions of national autonomy in decline. I have demonstrated that although, on balance, financial openness has been recently associated with marginally less interventionist government, this masks growing differences among countries with respect to most facets of economic policy. Rather than becoming increasingly irrelevant, domestic political factors such as the partisan balance of political power and the strength of organized labor movements are at least as important today as they have ever been to the course of economic policy. Moreover, there is little evidence that countries which have chosen to expand their public economies in the era of global markets have suffered the dire macroeconomic consequences predicted by most analysts.

[...] I would think that a better explanation for the lack of globalization constraints is that 'the markets' are far more sophisticated than is often presumed. The conventional view is that the markets are allergic to all forms of interventionist government, and react in knee-jerk fashion to any such policies with capital flight. But surely the economic effects of active government vary. It is consensually believed these days that the markets demand from governments that they secure property rights and enforce contracts. But the new growth literature extends the argument about the collective goods of government to the provision of health and education; and government policies that cushion market forces more generally are likely to promote investment-friendly social stability.

This does not mean that all aspects of big government are good for the economy – few today support industrial policies that prop up declining sectors, and large public sector deficits should be avoided. Nonetheless, the scope of 'market-friendly' policies can be extended much farther than is commonly believed. Moreover, it seems that mobile asset holders under-stand this. Perhaps most importantly, there is no evidence that high rates of capital taxation – the thin end of the globalization wedge for many ana-lysts – promote capital flight. Nor do I want to suggest that the economic effects of government policies are invariant across countries. The broad thrust of the corporatism literature is that interventionist economic policies are better suited to countries where socio-economic institutions facilitate the coordination of economic activity among business, labor and govern-ment. Rather than being characterized by short-termism, opportunism and free riding, these political economies are based on the notion that coopera-tion to manage market forces will benefit all segments of society. Of course, this should be contrasted with the Anglo-American variant of capitalist democracy, where the lack of coordinating institutions in society and the promotion of individualism mean that market disciplines must be imposed in the manner envisaged by Adam Smith.

None of this is to deny that big government does not face real problems in the OECD. Deteriorating macroeconomic performance coupled with the aging of society is a very dangerous cocktail for the contemporary welfare state. Governments must take bold measures that may well displease powerful constituencies if these challenges are to be met. But it must be acknowledged that the problems facing government today in the OECD have little to do with globalization. [...]

Note

I would like to thank Dennis Quinn and Duane Swank for sharing with me unpub-lished data on financial openness, international capital flows and government parti-sanship. I received helpful comments on earlier drafts of this paper from Robert Keohane, Peter Lange and Ngaire Woods.

11
Eras of Power*

Frances Fox Piven and Richard A. Cloward

During the past few years a strong challenge has been mounted in the pages of *Monthly Review* (*MR*) to the argument prevalent on the left as well as the right – that globalization and technological change have combined to bring us into a new era. Ellen Meiksins Wood captured the gist of the emerging *MR* position in an essay entitled 'Modernity, Postmodernity, or Capitalism' in which she asserts that there has been no historic rupture, no epochal shift, to usher in globalization or post-Fordism or post-modernism. All these concepts have 'the effect of obscuring the historical specificity of capitalism' which 'by definition means constant change and development....' What we are witnessing is the diversification and extension of the old logic of the mass production economy.[1] 'This *is* capitalism.'[2]

We agree with much of the empirical basis for the *MR* challenge to the new catechisms about globalization and technological change. We agree, for example, with the arguments, made variously by Wood, Tabb, and Henwood in the pages of *MR*, and by Gordon, Zevin, Hirst, and Thompson, and others elsewhere, that the competitive pressures in domestic markets attributed to increased global trade and capital movement have been vastly overstated, especially with regard to the United States, which remains less exposed to international trade and capital flight than most other rich industrial countries.[3] And we also agree that much of this is not really new in any case, that international integration characterized earlier periods of capitalist development, particularly the years before the First World War.

But if the system is basically the same, why is so much changing? In particular, why are class power relations changing? The evidence is considerable. Unions, once the bedrock of working-class power, are on the defensive, losing members in most capitalist countries, and in Britain and the United States, losing battles as well – at least when they dare to fight them.[4] Meanwhile, historic left parties are refashioning themselves as the

---

* From *Monthly Review* 49(6) (1997): 11–23.

champions of neoliberal policies, and turning their backs on the organized working class that was once their base. Welfare state protections,
the main political achievement of the industrial working class, are being
whittled back in the interest of labor market 'flexibility;' cutbacks in
social benefits intensify worker insecurity, smoothing the way for lower
wages and less secure conditions of employment. And inequalities are
widening, especially in Britain and the Untied States, where income and
wealth inequalities are spiraling to 19th-century levels.

To be sure, it still *is* capitalism. But we think the innovation and development characteristic of capitalism is interacting with shifts in class power
to produce convulsive changes not only in patterns of production and
exchange, but in patterns of culture and politics. And, contrary to Wood, we
think these developments are usefully characterized as ruptures with the
past, the continuities of capitalist social relations notwithstanding. Indeed,
we think such ruptures have studded the history of capitalism, sometimes
affecting particular industries, but sometimes transforming entire societies.
Capitalism develops not only through gradual and incremental changes propelled by the logic of accumulation, but also through wrenching upheavals
forged by momentous class power conflicts, as when the organization of
steel production was transformed by smashing the craft workers in the
19th-century United States, or when public sector unionism was crushed in
the post-First World War period. And, again contrary to Wood, we think
such upheavals are sometimes so broad in scope and consequence that they
usefully demarcate distinctive eras or epochs. The events which culminated
in the termination of English poor relief in favor of an 'unregulated' market
in labor in the 1830s marked such an epochal change, which the intense
protests of the Chartist movement could not reverse. It may be that the
interplay of contemporary economic restructuring and power shifts in the
advanced capitalist countries, and especially in the United States, is also
epochal in its significance. In any case, it is a class power struggle which has
to be understood in power terms, a predatory mobilization by capitalists
made possible by working-class weakness and disarray, although justified in
economic terms as the result of new market imperatives.

We make our argument about power upheavals in two parts. First,
we discuss the theoretical basis for the long-standing left conviction that
labor power is rooted in capitalist production relations, and in the organization of workers for political power that production relations facilitate.
MR authors share this conviction, and so do we. Second, and this is our
more distinctive argument, we think that actualization of the power is by
no means automatic or inevitable, but is realized only over time and with
difficulty, as ordinary people penetrate dominant ideologies, build the solidarities that make the actualization of power possible, and challenge the
rules which guarantee their quiescent cooperation. The disturbances which
ensue as people discover and act on the power capacities yielded them by

specific forms of economic and political organization lead to new institutional arrangements: the creation of a social compact to conciliate popular forces, while also regulating and caging them. Economic change may shatter these achievements, not because capital no longer depends on labor in the abstract, or because state rulers no longer depend on mass publics, but because the painfully constructed forms of popular understanding and organization, which made possible the realization of some power from the bottom, weaken. The erosion of popular power capacities in turn smooths the way for new assertions of power from the top. Capital breaks the social compact which working-class power made necessary. By doing so, however, it may also unleash new possibilities for popular struggle.

Capitalist societies organize production and exchange through networks of specialized and interdependent activities. These networks of cooperation are also networks of contention. They help to shape the interests and values which give rise to conflict. More important for our argument, networks of interdependency also generate dispersed power capacities. Agricultural workers depend on landowners, but landowners also depend on agricultural workers, as industrial capitalist depend on workers, the prince depends in some measure on the urban crowd, and governing elites in the modern state depend on the acquiescence if not the approval of enfranchised publics.

Actual power relations are of course tangled and intricate, since urban, democratic, and capitalist societies generate multiple and cross-cutting forms of interdependence. We take for granted, however, that some relationships are much more important than others. The *dominant* interdependencies and the power constellations they make possible – develop within economic relationships, and within the relations which anchor state elites to the societies they rule. Thus dominant interdependencies, and dominant forms of power, reflect the cooperative activities that generate the material bases for social life, and that sustain the force and authority of the state. If workers withhold their labor, production stops; if they withhold their votes, regimes fall. And, of course, the one set of relations is deeply intertwined with the other. States define and enforce property rights, regulate money and credit, and regulate the relations between employer and employees, for example.[5] The relations between class-based interest groups and state authorities inevitably focus importantly on these economic policies. And the broadly parallel evolution of industrial capitalism and electoral-representative institutions in the 20th century means that working-class economic challenges are systematically transported into the relations between voting publics and the state.

This emphasis on power capacities shaped by the interdependent relations which constitute economy and polity is clearly consistent with the Marxist view of working-class power as rooted in the role of the proletariat as a force in capitalist production. It is, we should note, also consistent with other important theoretical traditions, including, for example, Norbert Elias' depiction of the development of European central states as propelled by the dynamics generated by the networks of interdependency which developed among the warrior rulers of these societies.[6] And it fits Schumpeter's model characterizing the capitalist state as the 'tax state' which, because it depends on economic resources it does not control, ties state authorities in close interdependence with the owners of private property who do control those resources.[7]

The left confidence in working-class power was also expressed in the belief that working-class power would grow. Marx had rooted the growth of proletarian power in the development of industrial capitalism; Bernstein saw roughly parallel possibilities for working-class power in the development of electoral representative arrangements. Social democratic perspectives later melded the power yielded workers by industrial capitalism with the power generated by electoral representative arrangements, so that working-class power resources were said to grow in tandem with both industrial capitalism and electoral democracy.[8] In the happiest variants, these power resources resulted in a welfare state compact which promoted the 'decommodification' of labor, and therefore a fundamental empowerment of labor in market relations.[9]

A broadly compatible view of the growth of working-class power is incorporated in the work of historians dedicated to recovering the history of 'protest from below' in preindustrial Europe, such as Eric J. Hobsbawm, George Rude, and Charles Tilly. Even pluralist analysts point to the interdependencies of voters and political elites generated by liberal democracy itself, arguing that periodic elections and an enfranchised mass public forces elites to defer to the popular will. One variant or another of this optimistic perspective has nourished the left for at least a century and a half.

With these points made, it is clear that the globalization thesis cuts to the core of left political conviction. The effective exercise of labor power has always been premised on the limited ability of capital to exit or threaten to exit from economic relations. Globalization, together with post-Fordist production methods, seems to open unlimited opportunities for exit, whether through the relocation of production, accelerated trade, worker replacement, or capital flight, all of which seems to radically reduce the dependence of capital on labor. Workers, for their part, tied as they are by their merely human fear of change and rupture, can never match these exit options. And while working-class voters may still be able to make regimes topple, the significance of voting power depends on the significance of state power. But, so the argument goes, states whose sovereignty is confined to fixed territories also must knuckle under to the whims of a mobile capital. Economic globalization thus presumably eviscerates both economic and political forms of working-class power. As a result, workers and voters in the mother countries of capitalism are now pitted against low-wage workers and feeble governments everywhere, and pitted against technological advances as well. So, if the globalization thesis is true, it is devastating to the left as we have known it.

No wonder the determination with which *MR* authors (and we as well) scrutinize and challenge the argument. But scrutinizing and disputing the extent of global trade or capital movement does not quite grapple with the realities of class power under new conditions. What is at issue is not simply whether it is still capitalism, or whether capital is still dependent on labor in the abstract, or whether nation-states still matter, but whether economic changes have undermined the conditions which once made at least the partial actualization of economic and political power from the bottom possible.

Over the broad sweep of Western and capitalist development, the old idea that working-class power will grow as capitalism develops may yet prove to be correct. There are some strong theoretical reasons for thinking so. If power is rotted in interdependent relations, then the increasingly elaborate division of labor that characterizes capitalist societies, as well as the continued penetration of the core into the periphery with the consequent absorption of previously marginal groups in the capitalist division of labor, would diffuse power capacities more and more widely. (Our reading of the organic solidarity is similar; a tighter grid of interdependencies means that everyone in the grid has some leverage, at least under some conditions.) This line of reasoning reverses the conventional wisdom: it is not decentralization but centralization and the integration that it implies that enlarges at least the abstract possibility of popular power. The remote village may be shielded by its remoteness from a predatory state or a predatory capital, but neither can it have influence on the state or capital until it is brought into some kind of relationship with them.

But while capitalist development increases the *potential* power of working class and previously marginal groups, it can also work to impede the actualization of that power potential. Whatever is true in principle of the advancing division of labor, the power capacity of lower strata groups has certainly not advanced smoothly. At the very least, there have been periodic sharp reversals, and we appear to be witnessing such a reversal now.

In principle, economic and political organizations yields power to all parties who make necessary contributions to economic or political processes. In principle, workers in a capitalist economy always have potential power over capitalists whether they labor as agricultural tenants, or as industrial workers, or as technicians in a post-industrial economy. In principle, they have power because their contributions are necessary to ongoing processes of production and exchange. But the actualization of those power capacities is conditional on their ability to withhold or threaten to withhold their cooperation, and this capacity depends on other features of worker-employer relationships beyond the fact of interdependency. To understand class power dynamics, and especially to understand the impact of post-industrial changes on worker economic and political power, we have to pay attention to the ways that economic change affects the ideas and capacities for organization of working-class groups, and their ability to withstand threats of capital exit or deploy threats of exit themselves.

The first condition for the assertion of power from below is that people *recognize* their contribution to economic and political life. Economic and political interdependencies are real in the sense that they have real consequences. But they are also cultural constructions. To be sure, if people do in fact have agency, which we take to mean at a minimum some ability to penetrate a dominant ideology, and some capacity to act outside the rules which strip them of power, then the very fact of participation in interdependent activities would incline them to recognize their contributions, and therefore their power capacities. Perhaps so, or at least to some extent, or at least under some conditions.[10] But such recognition must always overcome inherited and deeply imprinted interpretations which privilege the contributions of dominant groups,[11] and must also overcome the continuing ability of dominant groups to project new and obscuring interpretations.

Second, since the relevant contributions to ongoing economic and political activities typically involve numerous individuals, people must develop a sense of solidarity and some capacity for concerted action so that their collective leverage can be deployed against those who depend on them, for work, votes, or acquiescence in the rules of civic life. This is the classical problem of organizing, whether workers, or voters, or community residents. And finally, the threat of exit, including the threat that employers will turn to replacement workers or that politicians will court alternative voter blocs must be limited, or at least the prospect of exit must not be so frightening that people cannot imagine enduring it.

These conditions for the realization of class power, and the ability of groups to manipulate them, depend on very specific and concrete historical circumstances. To appreciate this, we have to forgo our tendency to speak of classes and systems. For some purposes, these abstractions are of course useful. But the interdependencies which sometimes make assertions of popular power possible don't exist in general or in the abstract. They exist for particular groups, who are in particular relationships with particular capitalists or particular state authorities, at particular places and particular times.

Economic changes can be significant not because class interdependencies evaporate, but because economic change, especially rapid and uneven change, transforms these concrete particularities. People recognize their leverage over particular employers, not over capital in general, although they are surely influenced by more general ideas about the relationship of employers to employees. They recognize commonalities and capacities for collective action among members of particular concrete groups far more readily than among the working class in general, although here too broader group identities and antagonisms may predispose them one way or the other. And people fear the loss of particular forms of employment to which they have access, and in the particular places where their lives are rooted, although once again they are surely more likely to be alert to these dangers if they think capital exit is a more widespread phenomenon. The decline of hand-loom weaving in 19th-century England is an example, for it did not mean that manufacturers no longer depended on labor. But it did mean that the hand-loom weavers and framework-knitters could be starved out as manufacturers turned to women and children to work in the new mills. And as this happened, the understandings, forms of solidarity, and strategies for controlling exit, developed in an earlier era of putting-out manufacturing, eroded.

Thus, while capital still depends on labor in general, ongoing contemporary economic changes are undermining the ideas, the solidarities, and the strategies for curbing exit threats that were developed by concrete groups under the concrete circumstances of industrial capitalism. The old occupational categories – the miners, the steelworkers, the dockers, and so on – that were at the forefront of labor struggles have been depleted. And those who remain no longer have the confidence that they can act to 'shut it down,' paralyse an industry, and even make an entire economy falter. Meanwhile, the working-class towns and neighborhoods are emptying out, the particular working-class culture they nourished is fading. The unions that drew on all of this are necessarily enfeebled. They are enfeebled even more by employer strategies that take advantage of the decline of older forms of working-class power to launch new and terrifying exit threats – by hiring contingent workers and strike replacements, by restructuring production, or by threatening to close plants or to shift production elsewhere.

Incessant talk about globalization and downsizing figures indirectly in all of this, as the rise of an ideology that asserts the necessary and inevitable autonomy of markets and therefore of capital, a resurrection of 19th-century *laissez-faire* doctrines about the unregulated market now expanded to world scale. But none of this talk would be especially forceful by itself. The ideology is frighteningly persuasive not only because it is heard on all sides, but because it appears to explain the decline of concrete and particular working-class groups. Globalization talk gains force not from abstract generalities about trade and capital movement, but when jobs are cut or restructured, when trucks labeled 'Mexico' pull up to a striking plant, or simply when a business moves across the state line.

Understandably, there is a good deal of nostalgia for the working-class formations of the industrial era. We are all social democrats now, so to speak, and we mourn the passing of the old sureties of the mass strike, of big union and of labor parties which help to produce not only welfare state protections, but the political legitimation of the industrial-era working class. All of this was won not only because the economic and political relations of the industrial era made capital dependent on workers in the abstract, but because people in specific situations could make that dependence work for them. The loss is awesome.

But there is another face to economic change. Economic change weakens old forms of working-class power, and frees capital to smash the compact that power from below made necessary. This means new hardships, especially for more vulnerable groups. But it also means a kind of liberation from the constraints which were a condition of whatever concessions the compact granted. Federal protection for the right to organize was a victory. So was union recognition by the big industrialists a victory. These victories did not come unencumbered, however. They brought with them a new regime of labor regulation which limited the right to strike, encouraged union oligarchy, and allowed employer influence to gradually increase over time. Now, as the old victories are whittled away, the curbs on popular politics imposed with them may lose force. If they do, the possibilities of new surges of disruptive politics from below will increase.

Meanwhile, economic change also creates concrete new possibilities for worker power. People work at new and different occupations, they have different skills, and in time they will see the power potential inherent in the interdependencies of a new and fabulously complex and precarious communications-driven economy that is as vulnerable to mass disruption as the manufacturing-driven economy was. In time, maybe only a little time, they will develop the awareness of commonalities and capacities for joint action which will make working-class power possible again. And they are also likely to find the imagination and the daring to break the new rules governing communications which are even now being promulgated to criminalize the exercise of power from below. It is the end of a power era. It is also the beginning of a power era.

Notes

1. Wood (1996): 34; *Ibid.*, 38.
2. *Ibid.*, 38.
3. Henwood (1996) and (1997); Tabb (1997). See also D. Gordon (1988); Hirst and Thompson (1996a); and Zevin (1992): 45 and 72. Zevin concludes after a careful examination of trends in world financial markets that 'there is no convincing evidence that the policy/political "discipline" of the capital markets is greater than it ever was.' Indeed, he sees no trend toward financial openness not only over the past century, but over the last three centuries. There are disagreements in this emerging school of skeptics, of course. For example, Tabb seems to think technological change is more important than does Henwood, and Zevin also argues persuasively that financial trends have not been influenced by communications technology.

4. Western (1995).
5. For a discussion, see Block (1994).
6. Elias (1982).
7. Schumpeter (1991).
8. See for example Korpi (1983).
9. On decommodification, see Esping-Andersen (1988) and (1990); and see also Piven and Cloward (1985). Other class analysts saw the welfare state as less the expression of working-class interests, and more the instrument for the domination of workers, although this analysis has lost salience as welfare state programs have come under attack.
10. Moore (1966), and before him de Tocqueville (1955). Both seemed to think that the recognition of interdependencies was inevitable when they argued that peasants would come to see the extractions of a predatory landed aristocracy as unjust unless those extractions were balanced by contributions to the peasant community.
11. This includes of course the interpretations produced by intellectuals which privilege the contributions of dominant groups. A curious example is in the literature on exchange theory, which advances a definition of power as rooted in the exchange of services and benefits, and is thus at the outset similar to our definition. But the drift of this literature, and particularly of the work of Peter Blau, is to define power in relationships as the result of furnishing needed contributions, a tautology that of course works to justify unequal power.

12

Subject to Suspicion: Feminism and Anti-Statism in Britain*

Lynne Segal

Only state intervention and welfare reforms can put an end to women's economic dependency, and thereby free women from men's control, that doughty feminist reformer Eleanor Rathbone argued just over 80 years ago.[1] How her old statist rhetoric betrays her. Women's economic dependency and welfare reforms are currently on everyone's minds, but in an ambience generating thoughts only of purging most of those receiving any benefits at all.

Today in Britain, in the long shadow of the United States, the political usage of the term *economic dependency* is being definitively transformed. The notion of welfare benefit no longer promises the hard-fought-for amelioration, but rather the definitive symptom, of dependency: the erstwhile utopian cure is resignified as the disease. It is some years since Nancy Fraser and Linda Gordon traced the genealogical transformation of *dependency* in the United States, noting its conjunction with a flourishing, deceptively feminist-sounding self-help literature on autonomy.[2] This is why single mothers can be demonized if they *don't* work, even while married women with young children can be demonized if they *do*. Shifting a mother from dependency on the state to reliance on a man for economic support, in this troubling slippage, supposedly removes her from the pathologies of dependency. It is a massive deception.

The continuing offensive against welfare provides perhaps the single most general threat to Western women's interests at present – at least for those many women who are not wealthy and who still take the major responsibility for caring work in the home. As feminists in the 1970s made so clear, and sought so hard to transform, women are most vulnerable to the very worst pathologies of dependency when they are most at the mercy of husbands or male partners, especially during and after pregnancy and childbirth. Indeed, midwives in Britain have recently been asked to look for

* From *Social Text* 18(1) (2000): 143–51.

signs of abuse in just such women, following alarming reports from the United States examining the bruised bodies of pregnant women and those who have recently become mothers.[3] Similar antitheses exist in relation to needy children. Carolyn Steedman has written eloquently of how the expansion of welfare in the late 1940s gave a particular confidence to working-class children like herself:

> I think I would be a different person now if orange juice and milk and dinners at school hadn't told me, in a covert way, that I had a right exist, was worth something... its central benefit being that, unlike my mother, the state asked for nothing in return. Psychic structures are shaped by these huge historical labels: 'charity', 'philanthropy,' 'state intervention.'[4]

Liz Heron echoes these sentiments, although, like Steedman herself, she was well aware of the limitations of such services: it was their paternalistic, undemocratic delivery that made them vulnerable to subsequent attack. Introducing her anthology of autobiographical writings by girls growing up in Britain in the 1950s, Heron writes: 'Along with the orange juice and the cod-liver oil, the malt supplement and the free school milk, we may also have absorbed a certain sense of our own worth and the sense of a future that would get better and better, as if history were on our side.'[5] Not any more! The shedding of public responsibility for the welfare of poorer women threatens to devastate the lives of millions of children in Britain, just as it has already done in the United States over the last two decades.[6]

Increasingly in Britain the new myth of 'dependency culture' is used to condemn those receiving any form of state service, marking them out as vulnerable to 'welfare dependency.' Yet, despite the hassles and indignities they now face, surveys of single mothers have shown that a majority would still prefer dependency on the state to their experience of dependency on a man.[7] That option is now disappearing. In alliance with Reagan and the American Right, there was no doubting Margaret Thatcher's determination to overturn all traces of the post-war Keynesian economic orthodoxy with its support for spending on welfare – while upholding and abetting warfare spending. What is somewhat less clear is the extent to which the government, like Clinton's 'New' Democratic Party, is simply a continuation of the same proscarcity neoliberal policies undermining the public realm while encouraging market forces into every institutional domain.

To date, Blair's self-declared respect for his Tory predecessors, his unlimited admiration for Clinton (despite the latter's capitulation to dismantling welfare), his government's tireless discourse of fiscal 'prudence' and obeisance toward the dynamism of unfettered market forces, and his comprehensive ardor for Britain's 'special relationship' with the United States have all impeded the production of any distinct or convincing alternative vision to the one he inherited. The legacy of neoliberalism leaves the United Kingdom, in marked contrast to the rest of the European Economic Community (EEC), tailing the United States in its soaring inequality, with poverty in the United States estimated at twice that of any other European nation, despite having the highest per capita income. (Sweden, with the longest tradition of social democratic organizations, still has the lowest incidence of poverty and inequality).[8]

Searching for a third way between the interventionist market constraints of welfare states and the turbulence of neoliberalism, Blair – like Clinton – has moved toward what has been labeled the 'new paternalism.'[9] This third way fully endorses the earlier neoliberal 'modernizing' crusade on restraining public spending while insisting that market economics must reign supreme. Its characteristic paternalism (better seen as a new managerialism, in that women are as likely as men to implement its objectives) aims to tackle the escalating poverty, inequality, crime, and social disintegration through closer supervision of the poor: rectifying what is seen as their personal inadequacies or fecklessness. Demanding an end to the 'poverty of ambition,' social deprivation and welfare are to be reduced and managed through welfare-to-work regimes, with strong encouragement of private-sector backing for training and resources in the public sector: from the teaching of parenting skills or job application techniques to finance and pension management.[10] However, there is scant evidence that workfare serves as a springboard to real jobs (initial studies of the program's success in New York reveal that only 29 percent of workfare participants forced off the welfare rolls were able to find even casual work).[11] Meanwhile, although in acute tension with its aim of creating the fullest possible employment of poor and needy people (many of whom are women caring for children or other dependents), recent attempts to roll back welfare have also strongly encouraged the promotion of traditional, patriarchal family ideology.

In stark contrast with the repeated avowal of the 'pathologies' of welfare dependency is the steadfast disavowal of knowledge of the actual casualties when women and children are most financially dependent on familial male authority. Such denial has been strenuously cultivated by the growing strength of 'family values' campaigners over the last two decades. The 'profamily' movements that arose in the 1970s were part of an explicit New Right backlash against feminism and sexual liberation, soon to be underwritten by Reagan and Thatcher. However, two decades later such rhetoric seems ubiquitous across the political spectrum. Meanwhile, the knowledge that the traditional heterosexual marriage can create a living hell of cruelty, neglect, and abuse is beaten back by what American sociologist Judith Stacy calls the 'virtual social science' of distorted data about the perils of 'fatherless,' 'divorced,' or 'lone' parent families constantly disseminated by the media.[12] This not only encourages the continuing denial of lesbian and gay rights but also dismisses the often invaluable role of friendships, community resources, and wider structures of social support, which may be all that many individuals have to rely on to keep them sane.

From Britain, looking anxiously at trends across the Atlantic, one can observe that the once explicit, but now more often disguised or denied, anti-feminist and anti-gay sentiments expressed in family values crusades are all of a piece with a sweeping anti-statist rhetoric – increasingly as prevalent on the Left as on the Right. I was dismayingly alerted to further political reversals that may lie ahead for antiquated socialist feminists such as myself by recent thoughts about the state expressed by that once enduringly hopeful and combative feminist radical (and old friend of mine) Barbara Ehrenreich. In her 'Confessions of a Recovering Statist,' she publicly renounces any hopes for progressive social reforms in the United States, whether around childcare or parental leave (or environmental reform). 'For the time being,' she declares, 'we're not going to get anywhere with a progressive agenda consisting of ... government initiatives. *Believe me. I have tried.*'[13] And she certainly has.

Ehrenreich contrasts the situation in the United States with the kinds of universal state provision she assumes is taken for granted in Western Europe. She argues that there is now no combating the Right's anti-state propaganda in the United States: that is, after two decades of radical conservative pressure, and after Clinton's welfare 'reform,' which removed federal responsibility for assisting children in poverty while at the same time authorizing millions of dollars to be spent not on sex education, contraception, or to prevent violence against women, but rather on a puritanical morality that consigns single mothers to courses in 'abstinence education' (Clinton's way of having sex perhaps). Other feminist political scientists based in the United States, such as Zillah Eisenstein and Anna Marie Smith, also express their increasing suspicions of the costs of what they call the 'insider strategy.' They believe that feminist support for Clinton facilitated his successful presentation of 'feminine' and 'feminist' signifiers, making women's votes decisive in his reelection in 1996 (with the largest gender gap in the history of US presidential voting), but ultimately helping to neutralize opposition to his welfare cuts.[14] Even some of the most sophisticated theoretical works, like Wendy Brown's *States of Injury* – which skillfully exposes both the logic of victimhood and the theoretical incoherence in feminist rhetoric like Catharine MacKinnon's demand for legal protection from 'pornographic' imagery – retain a near exclusive focus on 'the state as a negative domain for democratic political transformation,' stressing the 'perils' attending all feminist appeals to it for gender justice.[15] Without wanting to deny the oppressive role of the modern state (not only in its official policing and militaristic role but also in its protection of already dominant groups *via* normative regimes regulating access to welfare and social resources) it seems to me that those seeking a better world for all women can hardly afford to abandon struggles 'in and against' it.

Meanwhile, although terminally pessimistic about feminists having any progressive alignment with mainstream politics in the United States, Ehrenreich herself is perhaps too optimistic about Europe. Here too, welfare 'reform' is underway. Some feminists in Britain are watching the New Labor government with their initial rising hopes moving toward despairing resignation, and wondering how long Anglo-American contrasts will hold.[16] There has been some progress, with support for childcare for single mothers to encourage (or will it mean force?) them into jobs. But Blair's new Britain, as we have seen, still sanctifies the Thatcherite and old American way, with its litany for limiting public spending. As Mary McIntosh comments on the production of new terminology for the redefining of social needs: 'Typical of the new lexicon is the "Benefit Integrity Project," in which thousands of people who had previously been deemed severely disabled were deprived of their Disability Living Allowance.'[17]

Such shifts in the vernacular of needs and entitlement indicate that it is the notion of universal welfare rights (as opposed to meager provision for the poor) that is being eliminated. This serves to undermine the whole heritage and rationale of the British welfare state: one that relied on progressive taxation to deliver a comprehensive social insurance system, giving those in need of benefit a sense of entitlement. Using the defense that the 'deserving' poor – those who are absolutely unable to work for wages or have no crumb of private resources – can only be adequately assisted by removing benefits from the more 'affluent,' progressive legislation involving general entitlements to child benefits, disability, or old-age pensions is now under threat in Britain. Increasingly more people will have increasingly less reason to support a national insurance system from which they will, in principle, be excluded, feeding the destructively antisocial, anti-government feelings now so dominant in the United States: the sense that people get nothing in return for the taxes they pay, since they must take out private insurance for everything anyway. It has also been shown that welfare programs regularly deteriorate once they assist only the most disadvantaged, and once they no longer cater for more powerful, middle-class interest groups.[18] Comparing the failure of US rationing with the success of austerity measures in Britain during World War II, Harvey Levenstein concludes that the British, unlike the Americans, still had 'faith in their government.'[19] In this age of socially regulated austerity, that faith in government and the social infrastructure of the public sector is being deliberately undermined.

With incentives to work as the prime focus of welfare reform, the hardship faced by significant numbers of women looks here to stay. These are the women trapped between the Scylla of longer hours at work and the

Charybdis of increasing demands from children and other needy people at home, for which they are still held, and often feel, uniquely responsible. No amount of hollow familial ideology, contradictory workfare incentives, or redefining of equality as 'social inclusion' solves the problems faced by so many working women today. As Suzanne Franks concludes, 'It seems unlikely the new millennium will bring a new balance of working and sharing – more likely a society that exacerbates the all or nothing divisions. Work will mean either the all-consuming 60-hour week or the insecure temporary life. Caring and everything else will have to fit in between.'[20]

As I see it, feminist concerns cannot be separated from struggles for an alternative vision and politics to those now so dismissive of any progressive possibilities of state intervention. Childcare provision, expanding social services, state regulation of minimum wages and maximum working hours, recognition of household diversity, and strong incentives for the full sharing of caring in the home would all form part of that vision – not unlike the socialist feminist agenda of a recent proscribed era. Accepting its elimination, Toril Moi has commented that '"socialist feminism" is not really a meaningful term in the 1990s'; curiously, though, she does want to know 'what kind of feminist a socialist feminist could be today.' The creature is dead, but her specter survives her.[21] The decline and disparagement of feminist calls on the state are everywhere encouraged by the liberal promotion of the dubious doctrine that nation-states are today necessarily powerless in the face of market globalization.[22] Yet the market dictatorship that has fostered the crisis of public finance, allowing the wealthy worldwide to contribute less and less to the financing of public expenditure, is still dominated by Anglo-American capital and ideological convictions. There are continuing, large differences in state expenditures on welfare, with – contrary to most globalization rhetoric – no consistent effect on growth rates.[23] Moreover, the global economy always displays strong national elements. While transnational corporations currently operate in the context of volatile world financial markets, both the production and consumption of most goods and services occurs at national levels: only 15 percent of commodities derive from lower-wage countries.[24] Progressives have every reason to combat rather than accede to simplistic assertions about the disappearance of the state in some forms of globalization theory. It is this thinking that abets the collapse of democratic politics, as participation in the market substitutes for participation in politics.

Only a decade ago, feminists still hoped to transform the relations between employment and family lives. Today, Blair's new Britain installs an old and punishing 'work' ethic that, despite three decades of feminist attention to the 'labors of love,' remains incapable of questioning any of the old terms – whether that of *labor* or *love*. A decade ago, there was still a debate in the British and American media on the future of the nuclear family. Today the superiority of that family structure over all possible alternatives is once again everywhere trumpeted, even as its prevalence continues to decline. In the most technologically innovative of times, as some feminists write of women's particular affinity with the supposed freedoms of cyberspace (despite men's dominance of 90 percent of its highways),[25] many women face a future where we are leading the most comprehensively conservative of lives: less politically engaged, less utopian in vision, less time, even, for friends and family.

Writing of the unexpected decline of leisure in the United States, Juliet Schor points out that for the last three decades there has been a steady increase in the number of hours on the job put in by fully employed workers; the same alarms about expanding working hours are now sounding in the United Kingdom.[26] It is primarily women who are still somehow expected to make up for the hours lost from creating loving homes and healthy communities while simultaneously applauded for how far they have come in gaining equality with men. Given the persistent strength of this aspect of traditional gender ideology, it is, as it always has been, the daily lives of women that most directly absorb the shocks and contradictions of these mean yet widely disparate times. What women do, when they do what is most expected of them as women, is not something best organized according to the dictates of profit or capitalist market relations. Therein lies the radical potential of feminism as an oppositional politics: one that dares to fight a culture and a political system which tries to numb us into accepting that it can fulfill our needs and desires through notions of consumer sovereignty alone.

Notes

These arguments can be found developed more fully within the larger project of assessing the place of feminism at the opening of the 21st century in my forthcoming book, *Why Feminism? Gender, Psychology, Politics* (Columbia University Press).

1. Quoted in Pedersen (1989): 86.
2. Fraser and Gordon (1997).
3. 'Midwives to Look for Abuse of Women,' *Guardian* (29 December 1997): 8. 'There seems to be evidence of violence starting or being exacerbated when a woman is pregnant or postnatally, with the violence directed towards her stomach, breasts, and genitals.'
4. Steedman (1992): 36.
5. Heron (1985): 6.
6. Castells (1997): 235.
7. McIntosh (1998): 5.
8. McFate, Lawson, and Wilson (eds) (1995).
9. Mead (ed.) (1997); MacGregor (1999): 91–118.
10. Cutler and Waine (1997).
11. Finder (1998): B1, B30.
12. Stacey (1998): 1–2, and (1996) ch. 4.
13. Ehrenreich (1997): 12.
14. Smith (1997): 25–35.

15. Brown (1995): x. In this essay I do not address the influential strand of anti-pornography feminism, though I have done so frequently elsewhere, because I believe it has served primarily to reinvigorate the moral Right rather than any progressive leftist politics. See Segal (1994); and Segal and McIntosh (eds) (1992).
16. See, for example, McIntosh (1998) [n.16]: 2.
17. *Ibid.*, 3.
18. Pierson (1994).
19. Levenstein (1993): 81.
20. Franks (1999a): 7; see also Franks (1999b).
21. Moi (1994): 937.
22. See Hirst and Thompson (1996a); Bromley (1996): 2–5.
23. Hirst and Thompson (1996b): 62.
24. Moody (1997).
25. For example, Plant (1997).
26. Schor (1991); WFD/Management Today survey, London, published May 1998.

Part IV

Governmentality and the Micropolitics of Welfare Reform

13

The Death of the Social? Refiguring the Territory of Government*

Nikolas Rose

In almost all advanced industrial countries, from Sweden to New Zealand, the old certainties of 'the welfare state' are under attack, and welfare systems are undergoing transformation.[1] [...] At the level of 'governmentality' – in the sense that the term was used by Foucault: the deliberations, strategies, tactics and devices employed by authorities for making up and acting upon a population and its constituents to ensure good and avert ill – it seems as if we are seeing the emergence of a range of rationalities and techniques that seek to govern without governing *society*, to govern through regulated choices made by discrete and autonomous actors in the context of their particular commitments to families and communities (Rose 1993b, 1994a). Of course, these changes, which are not confined to nations with right-wing regimes, may prove to be ephemeral. None the less, these shifts in policy appear to be paralleled in a shift within knowledge itself. The approaches often unified under the term 'post-modernism', together with a number of more local analyses, suggest that the object 'society', in the sense that began to be accorded to it in the 19th century (the sum of the bonds and relations between individuals and events – economic, moral, political – within a more or less bounded territory governed by its own laws) has also begun to lose its self-evidence, and 'sociology', as the field of knowledge which ratified the existence of this territory, is undergoing something of a crisis of identity.

While the destabilization of social theory has often been pioneered by those who think of themselves as progressives, the relation of those on the left to the transformations in the welfare state has been almost entirely negative. This is not surprising, given the intimate relations between socialism, as a rationality for politics, and the proliferation of social devices that made up welfare: the social state, social insurance, social service, the social wage, social protection and the rest. But perhaps we need to interrogate

* From *Economy and Society* 25(3) (1996): 327–56.

this opposition, in which the forces of progress seem obliged to take the side of the social against the forces of reaction which stand for individualism, competition, the market and the like. To begin such a task, we might usefully start by interrogating the notion of 'the social' itself. Are we witnessing not just a temporary shift in political and theoretical fashions but an event: 'the death of the social'?

Government from 'the social point of view'[2]

When, over a decade ago, Jean Baudrillard diagnosed 'the end of the social' (Baudrillard 1983), he offered his readers three propositions: That *the social has never existed*, but has always been a kind of simulation of a social relation that has now undergone a dissimulation, a disintegration of what was, in any event, an imaginary space of reference and play of mirrors; that *the social has really existed and now invests everything*, has extended from a process of the rational control of residues – vagrants, lunatics, the sick – to a state in which everyone is completely excluded and taken in charge for a project of functional integration sanctified by the social sciences; that *the social has existed in the past but has ceased to do so* – the sociality of the contract, of the relation of state to civil society, of the dialectic of the social and the individual has been destroyed by the fragmentations of the media, information, computer simulation and the rise of the simulacrum. Baudrillard concludes with a tender recollection of 'the unbelievable naivety of social and socialist thinking, for thus having been able to reify as universal and to elevate as ideal of transparency such a totally ambiguous and contradictory – worse, such a residual or imaginary – worse, such an already abolished in its very simulation "reality": the social' (Baudrillard 1983: 86).

This diagnosis undoubtedly catches something significant, despite its characteristically apocalyptic tone and opaque field of reference. It reminds us, if we should need reminding, that 'the social' is invented by history and cathected by political passions: we should be wary of embracing it as an inevitable horizon for our thought or standard for our evaluations. Gilles Deleuze, in his introduction to Jacques Donzelot's *The Policing of Families*, puts the issue in rather more sober terms: 'Clearly it is not a question of the adjective that qualifies the set of phenomena which sociology deals with: *the* social refers to a *particular sector* in which quite diverse problems and special cases can be grouped together, a sector comprising specific institutions and an entire body of qualified personnel' (Deleuze 1979: ix). 'The social', that is to say, does not represent an eternal existential sphere of human sociality. Rather, within a limited geographical and temporal field, it set the terms for the way in which human intellectual, political and moral authorities, in certain places and contexts, thought about and acted upon their collective experience. This novel plane of territorialization existed within, across, in tension with other spatializations: blood and territory; race and religion; town, region and nation.

[...]

To speak of 'the death of the social' is undoubtedly misleading. Indeed 'social' policies are increasingly articulated at a supra-national level through international bodies such as the Organization of Economic Cooperation and Development, the World Health Organization, the United Nations and the European Union. But, despite the undoubted persistence of the theme of society and social cohesion in contemporary political argument, '*the* social' in the sense in which it has been understood for about a century is none the less undergoing a mutation. The conditions for this mutation, and the correlative emergence and proliferation of 'advanced liberal' programs of government under a variety of different national political regimes, are heterogeneous and dispersed. [...]

[...] Central to the ethos of the novel mentalities and strategies of government that I have termed 'advanced liberal' is a new relationship between strategies for the government of others and techniques for the government of the self, situated within new relations of mutual obligation: the community.

The birth of the community

Until recently, the apparently 'a-moral' language of the market captured most attention in debates over changes in welfare – privatization, competition, financial calculation and so forth. But contemporary political rationalities also think in terms of another language which is just as important, which is highly morally invested and which intersects with markets, contracts and consumption in complex and surprising ways: 'community'. Consider the contemporary salience of the vocabulary of community care, community homes, community workers, community safety, for example. Consider the emergence of the idea of risk communities – drug abusers, gay men, carriers of particular genes, youth at risk. Consider the prominence of the language of community in debates over multiculturalism and the problems posed for politicians, psychiatrists, police and others working in conditions of cultural, ethical and religious pluralism. All these seem to signal that 'the social' may be giving way to 'the community' as a new territory for the administration of individual and collective existence, a new plane or surface upon which micro-moral relations among persons are conceptualized and administered. [...] These new political languages are embodied in the ways in which a whole series of issues are problematized – made amenable to authoritative action *in terms of* features of communities and their strengths, cultures, pathologies. They shape the strategies and programs that address such problems by seeking to *act upon* the dynamics of communities. They configure *the imagined territory* upon which these strategies should act – such as community mental health. And they extend to the *specification of the subjects* of government as individuals who are also, actually or potentially, the subjects of allegiance to a particular set of community values, beliefs and commitments.

We should not seek any single origin or cause of this complex reconfiguration of the territory of government. The social formed as a complex plane of interconnection among diverse minor lines of force, shifts in knowledge, in devices for charting populations and their vicissitudes, in practices of regulation and the pathways of action and calculation they traced out, contingent problematizations and ethical and political reformulations. Contemporary deployments of community are similarly heterogeneous, complex and mobile resultants of revised ways of representing, problematizing and intervening in a whole number of different arenas.[3] The term community, of course, has long been salient in political thought; it becomes governmental, however, when it is made technical. By the 1960s, community was already being invoked by sociologists as a possible antidote to the loneliness and isolation of the individual generated by 'mass society'. This idea of community as lost authenticity and common belonging was initially deployed in the social field as part of the language of critique and opposition directed against remote bureaucracy. Community activists were to identify, not with a welfare system that they saw as degrading, policing and controlling, but with those who were the subjects of that system – the inhabitants of the housing estates, projects and ghettos. More or less simultaneously, the language of community was utilized by authorities such as police to comprehend the problems they encountered in dealing with difficult zones – 'the West Indian community', the criminal community. Community here is a point of penetration of a kind of ethnographic sociology into the vocabularies and classifications of authorities; reciprocally, sociology itself intensified its investigations of collective life in terms of community and its anatomizing of the bonds of culture and the ties of locality that were thought to be essential conditions for its moral order. Within a rather short period, what began as a language of resistance and critique was transformed, no doubt for the best of motives, [...], into an expert discourse and a professional vocation- [...]. Communities became zones to be investigated, mapped, classified, documented, interpreted [...].

No doubt a whole range of other local shifts in vocabulary in diverse sites contributed to the emergence of community as a valorized alternative, antidote or even cure to the ills that the social had not been able to address – or even to the ills of the social itself. But what began to take shape here was a new way of demarcating a sector for government, a sector whose vectors and forces could be mobilized, enrolled, deployed in novel programs and techniques which operated through the instrumentalization of personal allegiances and active responsibilities: *government through community*. It is this sense of community that has come to the fore in recent political arguments (e.g. Etzioni 1993; Grey 1996). Society is to be regenerated, and social justice to be maximized, through the building of responsible communities, prepared to invest in themselves (Commission on Social Justice 1994). [...]

The refiguring of the territory of government in terms of community has a number of significant features. The first is spatial: a kind of 'detotalization'. The social, overarching all its stratifications and variations, was imagined as a single space, territorialized across a nation. Correlatively, government 'from the social point of view' posited a single matrix of solidarity, a relation between organically interconnected society and all the individuals contained therein, given a politico-ethical form in the notion of social citizenship. Today, in contrast, a diversity of 'communities' is thought to, actually or potentially, command our allegiance: moral communities (religious, ecological, feminist...), lifestyle communities (defined in terms of tastes, styles of dress and modes of life), communities of commitment (to disability, problems of health, local activism) and so forth. Such communities are construed as localized, heterogeneous, overlapping and multiple. Sometimes they are defined in terms of the geographical coordinates of a micro-locale. Sometimes they are 'virtual communities' associated in neither 'real' space nor 'real' time but through a network of relays of communication, symbols, images, styles of dress and other devices of identification: the gay community, the disabled community, the Asian community (cf. Barry 1996). Such virtual communities are 'diasporic': they exist only to the extent that their constituents are linked together through identifications constructed in the non-geographic spaces of activist discourses, cultural products and media images.[4] And, while the language of community often locates discrete communities within a larger collectivity – a nation, a society, the planet itself, the nature of this superordinate allegiance is now most frequently posed as a problem. Hence arguments over 'multiculturalism', the rise of political controversies over the implications of 'pluralism' – of ethnicity, religion, of sexuality, of ability and disability – together with conflicts over the competing and mutually exclusive 'rights' and 'values' of different communities.

A second significant feature of the birth of community is its changed ethical character. The social was an order of collective being and collective responsibilities and obligations. While the policies and programs of the social accorded individuals personal responsibility for their conduct, this individual responsibility was always traversed by external determinations: the advantages or disadvantages conferred by family background, social class, life history, located within a wider array of social and economic forces such as changes in the labor market, booms, slumps, industrial cycles, the exigencies of urban environments, problems of housing supply. Of course, the extent to which such external determinants could or should mitigate personal responsibility was subject to continual dispute, as was the extent to which they could or should be compensated for in education, in the decisions of the criminal court and so forth. [...] Conduct is retrieved from a social order of determination into a new ethical perception of the individualized and autonomized actor, each of whom has unique, localized and specific ties to their particular family and to a particular moral community. [...]

A third key aspect of the birth of community concerns the role of identification. The practices that assembled the social certainly entailed 'identification projects': programs of mass schooling, of public housing, of public broadcasting, of social insurance and so forth had at their heart an image and a goal of the socially identified citizen, the person who, above all, understood themselves to be a member of a single integrated national society. The vocabulary of community also implicates a psychology of identification; indeed the very condition of possibility for a community to be imagined is its actual or potential existence as a fulcrum of personal identity. Yet these lines of identification are configured differently. Community proposes a relation that appears less 'remote', more 'direct', one which occurs not in the 'artificial' political space of society, but in matrices of affinity that appear more natural. One's communities are nothing more – or less – than those networks of allegiance with which one identifies existentially, traditionally, emotionally or spontaneously, seemingly beyond and above any calculated assessment of self-interest. [...]

'Government through community' involves a variety of strategies for inventing and instrumentalizing these dimensions of allegiance between individuals and communities in the service of projects of regulation, reform or mobilization [...]

My first example is security. Within social rationalities of government, a domain of collective security was envisaged to be maintained by the State on behalf of all citizens, through universal measures ranging from social insurance to the enforcement of the criminal law by a unified and socially funded police force. Today, this social image – and the practices to which it was linked – is displaced by a variety of different ways of imagining security, each of which mobilizes a particular sense of community. One image is of the 'gated city' preserving the security of its own residents, of the shopping mall policed by private security guards: that is to say, of a diversity of zones each circumscribing what Clifford Shearing has termed a 'contractual' community assuming – or being forced to assume – responsibility for 'its own' health, happiness, wealth and security (O'Malley 1992; Shearing 1995). Such patterns of reconfiguring urban space can be observed in cities as distant as Sydney and Istanbul. The collective logics of community are here brought into alliance with the individualized ethos of neoliberal politics: choice, personal responsibility, control over one's own fate, self-promotion and self-government. In a second image, community is promoted as an antidote to the combined depredations of market forces, remote central government, insensitive local authorities in new programs for the regeneration of delimited locales – paradigmatically areas of disadvantaged inner cities (Etzioni 1993; Atkinson 1994). Here, new modes of neighborhood participation, local empowerment and engagement of residents in decisions over their own lives will, it is thought, reactivate self-motivation, self-responsibility and self-reliance in the form of active citizenship within a self-governing community.[5] Government through the activation of individual commitments, energies and choices, through personal morality within a community setting, is counterposed to centralizing, patronizing and disabling social government. Paradoxically, given their apparent ideological differences, these opposed versions of security utilize similar images of the subject as an *active and responsible agent* in the securing of security for themselves and those to whom they are or should be affiliated. Equally, they envision the space of government in similar ways, no longer territorialized across a national space, but organized in terms of the relations of identification between the person and 'their community' – the particular collectivity to which each person is bound by kinship, religion, residence, shared plight or moral affinity. In each case, community is not simply the territory of government, but a *means* of government: its ties, bonds, forces and affiliations are to be celebrated, encouraged, nurtured, shaped and instrumentalized in the hope of producing consequences that are desirable for all and for each.

[...]

A desocialization of economic government

[...]

In the strategies of government that developed over the course of the 20th century, the domains of the economic and the social were distinguished, but governed according to a principle of joint optimization. Economic activity, in the form of wage labor was given a new set of *social* responsibilities, seen as a mechanism which would link males into the social order, and which would establish a proper relationship between the familial, the social and the economic orders (Meuret 1981; Miller and Rose 1990; Rose 1990: II; Rose and Miller 1992; Walters 1994). Simultaneously, the privacy of the wage contract was weakened, as politicians came to accept that conditions of labor and pay should be regulated in the name of social peace. The production of a labor market itself became part of the responsibilities of economic government, and a range of interventions into the social would maximize the economic efficacy of the population as a workforce, from vocational guidance and labor exchanges to various methods of maintaining the social habits of labor among the unemployed. Gradually, over the next six decades, new indexes of economic activity were invented that would render the economy amenable to management, and new techno-logies of macroeconomic regulations were brought into being. Through mechanisms of social insurance – unemployment benefit, accident insur-ance, health and safety legislation and so forth – and through an array of forms of economic government – tax regimes, interest rates and other tech-niques of 'demand management' – the state assumed responsibility for the management of a whole variety of risks – to individuals, to employers, to the state itself – in the name of society.

But the perception of 'the economy' which underpinned such endeavors is now undergoing a mutation (Hindess 1994b). 'An economy' is no longer so easily imagined as naturally coextensive with the realm of a nation-state, with different 'national economies' inhabiting a wider common field in which they traded, competed, and exploited one another. Theorists and practitioners alike now construe economic relations as 'globalized', and this new spatialization of the economy is coupled with arguments to the effect that flexible economic relations need to be established in particular localities (Reich 1992; Hirst and Thompson 1992; both cited and discussed in Hindess 1994b). Overlaying this 'dialectic of the global and the local' are other transnational spatializations of economic relations, such as the argument that there is a 'global economy' of 'world cities', in which Birmingham, Sydney, Baltimore, Budapest compete among one another for the economic benefit of company location, conferences, sporting events, tourism (Zukin 1991; Lash and Urry 1994).

Irrespective of the accuracy with which these trends are identified and portrayed, the economic problems of government are being rethought in terms of a revised image of economic space and the means by which it can be acted upon. It appears that, while national governments still have to manage a national population, the economic well-being of the nation and of its population can no longer be so easily mapped upon one another and governed according to principles of mutual maximization. Government of the social in the name of the national economy gives way to government of particular zones – regions, towns, sectors, communities – in the interests of economic circuits which flow between regions and across national boundaries. The economic fates of citizens within a national territory are uncoupled from one another, and are now understood and governed as a function of their own particular levels of enterprise, skill, inventiveness and flexibility.

This is coupled with a shift in rationalities and techniques for the gov-ernment of employment and unemployment. Unemployment is now understood as a phenomenon to be governed – both at the macroeconomic level and at the level of the conduct of the unemployed person him or herself – through enhancing the activity of the individual in search of work, and obliging the individual to engage in a constant and active search for employment and for the skills that will provide employment. On the one hand, the general problem of unemployment is reconceived in terms of the respective competitiveness of different labor forces, understood at least in part in terms of the psychological, dispositional and aspirational capacities of those that make them up. On the other, each individual is solicited as an ally of economic success through ensuring that they invest in the management, presentation, promotion and enhancement of their own economic capital as a capacity of their selves and as a lifelong project (Walters 1994; Dean 1995).

This emphasis upon the individual as an active agent in their own economic governance through the capitalization of their own existence is paralleled in a whole new set of vocabularies and devices for managing individuals within the workplace in terms of the enhancement of their own skills, capacities and entrepreneurship. These attempt an alliance between the desires of the worker or manager for self-enhancement and actualization through work and the perceived need of the enterprise to become flexible, competitive, agile, creative, etc. In labor, too, work is no longer to be construed as a social obligation, or its efficiency to be enhanced through maximizing the social benefits that the laborer finds in the workplace, or its primary role to be one of binding the individual into the collective through the socializing effects of the habit of work. Rather, the workplace itself – for laborers and for managers – is to be an area of self-promotion and the government of work is to be undertaken in terms of the enhancement of the active capacities of the entrepreneurial individual. [...]

In short, one could suggest that, within those strategies of government that I have termed 'advanced liberal', one finds the emergence of a new way of conceptualizing and acting upon the relations between the government of economic life and the self-government of the individual: the economy is no longer to be governed in the name of the social, nor is the economy to be the justification for the government of a whole range of other sectors in a social form. The social and the economic are now seen as antagonistic, and the former is to be fragmented in order to transform the moral and psychological obligations of economic citizenship in the direction of active self-advancement. Simultaneously, government of a whole range of previously social apparatuses is to be restructured according to a particular image of the economic – the market. Economic government is to be desocialized in the name of maximizing the entrepreneurial comportment of the individual.

The subjects of government

This transformation in the government of economic life links to a more general mutation in arrangements for the government of conduct. New ways are taking shape for understanding, classifying and acting upon the subjects of government, entailing new relations between the ways in which people are governed by others and the ways in which they are advised to govern themselves. Fundamental to this general field is a recoding of dividing practices, revising the distinctions between the *affiliated* and the *marginalized*. By the affiliated I mean those who are considered 'included': the individuals and families who have the financial, educational and moral means to 'pass' in their role as active citizens in responsible communities. To remain affiliated one must 'enterprise' one's life through active choice, within authoritative terms and limits that have become integrated within all the practices of everyday life, sustained by a heterogeneous array of 'civilized' images and devices for lifestyle promotion. In rearing children, in schooling, in training and employment, in ceaseless consumption, the included must calculate their actions in terms of a kind of 'investment' in themselves, in their families, and maximize this investment with reference to the codes of their own particular communities. But the marginal are those who cannot be considered affiliated to such sanctioned and civilized cultural communities. Either they are not considered as affiliated to *any* collectivity by virtue of their incapacity to manage themselves as subjects or they are considered affiliated to some kind of 'anti-community' whose morality, lifestyle or comportment is considered a threat or a reproach to public contentment and political order. On this division between the affiliated and the marginalized are articulated two rather different sets of debates, and two rather different governmental strategies, neither of which seem to be undertaken from 'the social point of view'.

The problem of risk provides us with a point of entry for an investigation of these novel 'post-social' strategies of governing conduct. [...] Most significant for present purposes have been genealogies of social insurance, that have traced the ways in which, over the course of the 20th century, *security* against risk was socialized.

In the late 19th century, the respectable working man was urged to be *prudent*, an obligation which required him to take a range of active steps to secure himself, his family and his dependants against future misfortune. [...] At the turn of the century, in most European countries, these voluntary relations of prudence – mutual or commercial – were further transformed with the implementation of national schemes of compulsory social insurance. [...]

Social insurance was acquired as a benefit of citizenship. As is well known, schemes were structured with the aim that they would not 'demoralize' those who were their members through the inculcation of dependency, but, on the contrary, produce moral effects of responsibility, regularity of habits of labor and social obligation in those who were their beneficiaries (Gilbert 1966). Of course, the injunction to personal prudence on one's own behalf and that of one's dependants did not disappear over the 20th century. But none the less, today, a strategic shift is occurring in the politics of security. Individuals are, once again, being urged by politicians and others to *take upon themselves* the responsibility for their own security and that of their families: to insure against the costs of ill health through private medical insurance, to make provisions for their future through private pensions, to take an active role in securing themselves against all that could possibly threaten the security of, their chosen style of life. This 'new prudentialism' (O'Malley 1992) uses the technologies of consumption – advertising, market research, niche marketing and so forth – to exacerbate anxieties about one's own future and that of one's loved ones, to encourage us to subdue these risks and to tame our fate by purchasing insurance designed especially for us and our individual situation. [...]

This contemporary prudentialism differs from its 19th-century forebear in a number of ways. The person who is to be made prudent is no longer mutualized but autonomized. Thrift is recast as investment in a future lifestyle of freedom. Insurantial expertise is no longer a matter of actuarial wisdom, the assurance of stability and probity, and the personal relation with the contributions collector, but works through amplifying the very anxieties against which security is to protect and promote the dreams of tranquility and a golden future which insurance can provide, through the use of all the techniques of advertising and marketing. [...] Protection against risk through an investment in security becomes part of the responsibilities of each active individual, if they are not to feel guilt at failing to protect themselves and their loved ones against future misfortunes. The ethics of lifestyle maximization, coupled with a logic in which someone must be held to blame for any event that threatens an individual's 'quality of life', generates a relentless imperative of risk management not simply in relation to contracting for insurance, but also through daily lifestyle management, choices of where to live and shop, what to eat and drink, stress management, exercise and so forth. [...]

These assemblages of risk are related in complex ways to the valorization of community which I discussed earlier. The exhortation to risk management can itself be organized on the territory of community, where it can have a range of diverse effects, from consumer campaigns against the use of pesticides in fruit production to ecological mobilizations against the dumping of nuclear waste: 'not in our back yard' becomes a cliché to describe these responses to threatened introduction of new risks. [...]

In this new configuration, 'social insurance' is no longer a key technical component for a general rationality of social solidarity: taxation for the purposes of welfare becomes, instead, the minimum price that respectable individuals and communities are prepared to pay for insuring themselves against the riskiness now seen to be concentrated within certain problematic sectors.

This discussion of risk highlights certain more general features of the new 'post-social', technologies of governing conduct which are taking shape.

Under the rationalities of welfare, social, technologies were to civilize individuals, render them as citizens with obligations to conduct themselves with prudence in exchange for certain guarantees against uncertainty. In the new prudential regimes, individuals, educated through the mechanisms of marketing and the pedagogies of consumption and lifestyle, are to gain access to previously 'social' benefits such as educational advantage, health status and contentment in old age through purchase in a competitive market. Promotion of private insurance by market mechanisms thus exemplifies the widespread mechanisms through which consumption and markets have become powerful new mechanisms for the shaping of conduct. These are not guided by a political logic, but they none the less make it possible to transform political technologies for the government of subjectivity. Affiliation to communities of lifestyle through the practices of consumption displaces older devices of habit formation that enjoined obligations upon citizens as part of their social responsibilities. [...]

Governing the margins

It is, I think, only in relation to these logics of inclusion through choice, autonomy and consumption that one can understand the new ways that are taking shape for conceptualizing and acting upon those subjects who inhabit those zones that Beveridge termed the 'five giants on the road of reconstruction': Want, Disease, Ignorance, Squalor and Idleness – the five enemies that were to be attacked by 'a comprehensive policy of social progress' based on co-operation between the State and the individual (Beveridge 1942: 6). It would certainly be misleading to interpret the contemporary redrawing of the boundaries of the political as merely a 'reduction of the role of the State in society'. On the one hand, we have seen the spread of the mechanisms which Deleuze characterized under the rubric of 'societies of control', where conduct is continually monitored and reshaped by logics immanent within all networks of practice. In such practices we are continually subject to processes of functional integration: 'life long learning', 'continual retraining', 'constant job readiness', and ceaseless consumption (Deleuze 1995). But these processes of continuous modulation of conduct have been accompanied by the intensification of direct, disciplinary, often coercive and carceral, political interventions in relation to particular zones and persons – the prison population is rising throughout Europe, for example. As civility is understood as affiliation by consumption, dividing practices are reconfigured to problematize certain 'abjected' persons, sectors and locales for specific reformatory attention: the underclass, the excluded, the marginal.

[...] Of course, even within this unified vision there were concerns with those who eluded the bonds of citizenship – one only has to consider the debate in the 1960s over the 'cycle of deprivation'. But the emergence of the notion of an 'underclass' in the United States at the end of the 1970s does seem to mark a moment in which the social vision of a continuous *quantitative* variability in levels of civility becomes recoded as a *qualitative* distinction. 'Behind the [ghetto's] crumbling walls lives a large group of people who are more intractable, more socially alien and more hostile than almost anyone had imagined... . Their bleak environment nurtures values that are often at odds with those of the majority – even the majority of the poor.

[...]

Despite their great differences in notions of economic causation and personal responsibility, these different rationalities operate with a surprisingly consonant picture of the abjected persons and groups that are their object. On the one hand, they are dispersed. They are no longer seen as part of a single group with common social characteristics, to be managed by a unified 'social service' and 'generic social workers' who can recognize the common roots of all social problems. The marginalized, the excluded, the underclass are fragmented and divided; their particular difficulties thus need to be addressed through the activities of a variety of specialists each of whom is an expert in a particular problem – training schemes for those excluded through unemployment, specialist agencies working with those with disabilities, rehabilitation of addicts undertaken by specialist drug workers, education in social skills by workers with the single homeless, specialized hostels for battered women, for alcoholics, etc. Yet, on the other hand, these abjected subjects are reunified ethically and spatially. Ethically, in that they are accorded a new active relation to their status in terms of their strategies and capacities for the management of themselves: they have either refused the bonds of civility and self-responsibility or they aspire to them but have not been given the skills, capacities and means. And spatially, in that the unified space of the social is reconfigured, and the abjected are relocated, in both imagination and strategy, in 'marginalized' spaces: in the decaying council estate, in the chaotic lone-parent family, in the shop doorway of inner-city streets. [...]

It is in this sense that it is possible to argue that new territory is emerging, after the welfare state, for the management of these micro-sectors, traced out by a plethora of quasi-autonomous agencies working within the 'savage spaces', in the 'anti-communities' on the margins, or with those abjected by virtue of their lack of competence or capacity for responsible ethical self-management: 'voluntary' endeavors (often run by users, survivors or philanthropists but funded by various grant regimes) – drug projects, disability organizations, self-help groups, concept houses and so forth (oppositional forces transformed into service providers). Private and for-profit organizations – old people's homes, hostels and so forth – make their money from private insurance or from the collection of the state benefits to their individual inmates. In the huge and murky industry of 'training' unemployment is reproblematized as a matter of the lack of individual and marketable skills among the unemployed themselves, to be countered by a multitude of training organizations that are private and compete in a market for public contracts and public funds. Within this new territory of exclusion, the social logics of welfare bureaucracies are replaced by new logics of competition, market segmentation and service management: the management of misery and misfortune can become, once more, a potentially profitable activity.

[...]

Risk, community and expertise

The notion of risk once more provides a useful point of entry into the revised relations of expertise taking shape on the territory of community. In part this is because the capacity for personal 'power', or the lack of it, which is the object of empowerment technologies is itself rethought in terms of the relations of risk and community which I discussed earlier: the risks posed to the individual themselves if they cannot adequately manage their life within the community, the risks the individual may pose to the community on account of their failure to govern themselves. It is also because the responsibilities of experts are themselves being reformulated in terms of risk and community. In a range of domains, social workers, psychiatrists, doctors and others have been allocated accountability not so much for the cure or reform of clients, patients and other problematic individuals, but for their administration according to a logic of risk minimization (cf. Castel 1991; Rose 1996a). The novel intellectual techniques of risk identification, risk assessment and risk management bring into existence a whole new set of professional obligations – the obligation that each individual professional should calculate and reduce the risk of their professional conduct, instruct the subjects of their authority in the riskiness of the practices and procedures in which they are engaged and manage their clients in the light of the imperative to reduce the risk they may pose to others – their children, members of 'the general public'. Experts are thus increasingly required to undertake not so much an identification of a condition but a calculation of the riskiness of an individual or an event, with the obligation to take (legal, moral, professional, financial) responsibility for the calculations that they make, the advice that they give and the success of the strategies that they put into place to monitor and manage that risk. This is only one of the ways in which the reconfiguring of the territory of government has been linked to new roles for experts in the government of the conduct of active individuals within their communities. [...] While the problems posed by experts were bemoaned over many years and from many different perspectives, a number of new technologies are currently being deployed through which experts can be linked into the devices for the conduct of conduct. Locales and activities that were previously part of the assemblages of the 'social' are being autonomized from the machinery of politics and novel devices are being used to govern the activities of those who work within them. In a plethora of quasi-autonomous units, associations and 'intermediate organizations', experts are allocated new responsibilities and new mechanisms are developed for the management of professional expertise 'at a distance' – that is, outside the machinery of bureaucracy that previously bound experts into devices for the government of 'the social'. Previously 'social' experts such as social workers, benefit officers, doctors, social service bureaucrats and others now operate within a whole variety of quasi-private regulatory organizations. [...] Three aspects are worth highlighting.

First, in the UK situation at least, there is a renewed emphasis upon the potential of a variety of legal and quasi-legal mechanisms to meet political obligations to address 'problems' – from discharged psychiatric patients to insider dealing – while refusing an extension of the politico-administrative machinery of the State. [—] The mechanisms of legal regulation are complex and fragmented. Politicians, professionals and consumer groups organize around the production of codes of professional conduct which specify various rights for users and clients. A new 'litigious mentality' ensures that 'the shadow of the law' becomes a means of managing professional activity through the self-regulation of decisions and actions in relation to such formally promulgated codes and standards. [...]

Perhaps even more significant has been the spreading of modes of financial calculation and budgetary obligations to areas which were previously governed according to bureaucratic, professional or other norms. The allocation of budgetary responsibilities to professionals – doctors, educationalists, civil servants, those working with excluded groups – requires them to calculate their actions not in the esoteric languages of their own expertise but by translating them into costs and benefits that can be given an accounting value. Coupled with the raft of other elements sometimes referred to as 'the new public management', this has transformed the governability of professional activity while, at the same time, apparently devolving more decisional power to those actually involved in devising and delivering services in local sites (cf. Hood 1991).
[...]

Conclusions

Many of the transformations to which I have drawn attention are themselves linked to a shift within the field of politics itself, in the ways in which political discourse itself configures the limits of the political and its relations with other domains. Confronted by supra-national associations and transnational ecological movements, rival nationalisms fighting across a single geographical terrain, federalism, the politics of ethnic, cultural and linguistic minorities, and multiculturalism, it is no longer easy for political thought to territorialize itself in an apparently 'natural' geo-political space in which the nation is coextensive with and delimited by a unified polity of social citizens (cf. Tully 1995). In the face of such 'strange multiplicities', to adopt Tully's term, in a variety of national contexts and from a variety of political positions, 'anti-political motifs' are on the rise within political discourse (Hindess 1994a). These motifs not only stress the corruption and ineffectiveness of the political classes but, more fundamentally, are based upon a sense of the limits of any politics that sees itself as omni-competent and articulates itself in terms of overarching political programs. These 'anti-political' motifs have recently alighted upon 'community' – which in recent years had been a part of the mundane vocabulary of social policy and sociological investigation, valorized only by a small band of communitarian political philosophers and romantic or eccentric activists – as the space in which powers and responsibilities previously allocated to politicians might be relocated. Each of these emergent political rationalities – civic republicanism, associationalism, communitarian liberalism – in its different way, seeks a way of governing, not through the politically directed, nationally territorialized, bureaucratically staffed and programmatically rationalized projects of a centrally concentrated State, but through instrumentalizing the self-governing properties of the subjects of government themselves in a whole variety of locales and localities – enterprises, associations, neighborhoods, interest groups and, of course, communities. Of course, it would be absurd to suggest that a politics of community is itself novel: as Tully points out, communitarianism may be regarded as one of the traditional themes of modern constitutional thought (along with nationalism and liberalism). But in these contemporary political rationalities, community is made calculable by a whole variety of reports, investigations and statistical enquiries, is the premise and objective of a range of governmental technologies and is to be acted upon in a multitude of authoritative practices and professional encounters. Community, that is to say, is to be governmentalized: it cannot be understood outside the other shifts to which I have tried to draw attention in this paper. What are of interest, therefore, are the problematizations through which collective existence has come to offer itself to thought in the form of community, and the new representations, techniques, powers and ethical relations that have been invented in the process.

It is too early to gauge the durability of these new ways of thinking about politics and government. For present purposes, their significance lies less in their success than in the evidence that they provide of an imperative felt at the heart of politics to fashion a revised way of governing, one which can, not only make itself consistent with the heterogeneity of the forms in which struggles are now carried out – nationalist, ethnic, religious, moral,

environmental – but also connect up with the new conceptions of subjectivity through which the subjects of government increasingly have come to
understand and relate to themselves. It is, of course, not a question of the
replacement of 'the social' by 'the community': the spatialization and territorialization of political thought does not proceed in such linear sequences.
None the less, the hold of 'the social' over our political imagination is
weakening. While the social has no doubt been seen as a zone of failure
since its birth, the solution to these failures is no longer automatically seen
to be reinvention of the social. While our political, professional, moral and
cultural authorities still speak happily of 'society', the very meaning and
ethical salience of this term is under question as 'society' is perceived
as dissociated into a variety of ethical and cultural communities with
incompatible allegiances and incommensurable obligations. [...]

Notes

1. This paper originated in comments prepared for a workshop on Radically
   Rethinking Regulation at Centre of Criminology, University of Toronto,
   16–17 April 1994. A version was also given at a conference to mark the tenth
   anniversary of the death of Michel Foucault held in London on 25 June 1994. My
   argument was intended to be open and speculative, and I have chosen to retain
   this in the written version. Barry Hindess helped me understand contemporary
   transformations in the government of 'the economy', but he is not responsible
   for my interpretation of his work. Thanks also to Mariana Valverde for perceptive
   criticisms of an earlier draft, to Clifford Shearing for insightful reader's comments, to Pat O'Malley for stimulating conversations on these topics and to
   Stephen Mugford for productive disagreements. The final version of the paper
   was prepared while I was a Visiting Research Fellow in the Political Science
   Program of the Research School of Social Sciences, Australian National University,
   and I would like to thank that institution for its support and hospitality.
   Comments from members of the *History of the Present* Research Network:
   especially Larry Barth, David Owen, Michael Power, Anne-Marie Singh and
   Grahame Thompson, helped me make some last minute revisions.
2. I take this phrase from Procacci (1989) but use it slightly differently.
3. Obviously there are similarities between this argument and that concerning the
   construction of nations and identities in the form of 'imagined communities',
   which cannot be discussed here (cf. Anderson 1991).
4. The term 'diaspora' which is sometimes employed here is interesting, implying
   that what is currently dispersed was once together – an essential unity scattered
   by the hand of fate or politics.
5. There are, of course, many other versions of this, most notably in the revival of
   civic republicanism. The 'advanced liberal' ethos of much contemporary civic
   republicanism is pointed out in Burchell (1995).

14

Governing the Unemployed Self in an Active Society*

Mitchell Dean

The possibility of a 'politics of identity' has been on the agenda for some time now. One thinks of all the contexts in which it has emerged in the last 20 years: not only in the motifs of identity politics and cultural pluralism, but also in those of multiculturalism, globalization and post-colonialism, in women's and gay movements, in the discussion of logics and strategies of resistance and contestation. It might be suggested that, far from providing a secure basis for all the strategies, programs and policies conducted in its name, the practice of a politics of identity invariably raises the fundamental question: what is identity and what has it got to do with politics?

This might be thought of as the background against which social and political thought has turned to a cluster of themes around the formation of identity, and notions of self, subject, person, individual and citizen. This has included attempts to reconsider the intersection between political, administrative and governmental processes and issues of 'self- and citizen formation.' Many of these developments recall Foucault's (1982: 208) retrospective characterization of his life-work over a decade ago as a concern with the different ways in which 'human beings are made into subjects'. Indeed, a concern with self-formation lies at the heart of not only his later volumes on sexuality and ethical practices but also his lectures and interviews on government, politics and liberalism (Foucault 1979, 1982, 1986c, 1988b, 1988c, 1989; Gordon 1991; Burchell 1993). The deliberation upon and use of the latter has proved helpful in illuminating aspects of our contemporary political and social life, particularly those concerning the means for the 'conduct of conduct'; or, more particularly, the relation between government and conduct.

The ensuing literature (e.g. Miller and Rose 1990; Rose and Miller 1992; Burchell, Gordon and Miller 1991) has been extremely valuable in its

* From *Economy and Society* 24(4) (1995): 559–83.

development of analytical frameworks for the investigation of what might be placed under the heading of 'governmentality'. It has first opened up a consideration of what might be called the techne of government. Here we find a search for analytical clarity concerning the techniques and instruments of government, the arts, skills and means by which rule is accomplished. It has also sought to examine in relation to these techniques the problem of the rationalities of government. Here lies the exploration of issues of the forms of expertise, knowledge, information and calculation that are the condition of government, its programmatic character, the language and vocabulary of rule, the formation of administrable objects and domains, and the changing forms and rituals of truth that authorize and are authorized by governmental practices and agents.

The analysis of these axes of government, however, is a necessary but not sufficient condition to define the ethos of various modalities and forms of government (i.e. their character, style, ideals, manner of self-problematization). It has become clear that the analytics of the techniques and rationality of government needs to be complemented by a fuller clarification and elaboration around a third axis, that, for want of a better term, we might call the 'axis of self-formation'. [...]

This is where the present paper stands or, indeed, falls. It certainly stands on this general terrain in which issues of politics and identity meet and intersect. However, it proposes an indirect route over it, a kind of thought experiment. This consists in seeking a clarification of the concepts necessary to analyse practices of self-formation from the perspective of the general concern for government and governmental practices. It then attempts to work these concepts by an analysis of a specific form of governmental practice, that concerning recipients of social security support, in particular the unemployed. Specific reference is made to the recent reform of social security and related practices in one national political territory, Australia. However, as we shall see, this reformation encompasses techniques and rationalities that are not peculiar to any nation-state and embodies a wider ethos, formula and rationale of government found in the rubric of an 'active society' as pronounced by no less an international authority than the Organization for Economic Cooperation and Development (OECD).

Foldings and selves

Let us start by noting that the general definition of government as the 'conduct of conduct' already implies the centrality of an axis of self-formation. Indeed, one way of thinking about what Nikolas Rose and Peter Miller (1992) call 'problematics of government' would be to regard the direction of conduct as absolutely central to them. To follow this line, as I shall do here, is to say that the regulation of things – from car exhaust emissions, the cleanliness of bathrooms, to national budgetary aggregates – is uninteresting except insofar as that regulation bears upon the regulation of human conduct. Government in this sense is distinguished from conventional notions of government in that it brings issues of the regulation of conduct into focus.

'Conduct' itself is somewhat difficult to define. It has a clear sense only in the first term of the phrase 'conduct of conduct'. In that instance, to conduct is to lead or direct. The latter sense of the term is harder to come to grips with. Perhaps it is stating the obvious to say that in this literature on government that conduct is human conduct, and that it is difficult to see how this could be contested. Given that, however, we might ask whether conduct is a synonym for all human action and behaviors. Does the notion of the government of conduct simply replicate the terms of a definition of power as 'a total structure of actions brought to bear upon possible actions' (Foucault 1982: 220)? Clearly there is some elision between power and government in this formulation such that action and conduct tend to become indistinguishable. While it might indeed be wise to resist a rigorous definition of conduct, given the kinds of problems raised by Weber's typology of social action (Dean 1994a), some greater specification is needed. For our purposes, government is distinguished as a form of power defined by the existence of some degree of calculation and conduct implies the possibility of acting otherwise, an observation that leads to a consideration of questions of freedom. At least in contemporary industrial democracies, the object of government is the conduct of the 'free subject; a term that, as we shall see, should be appreciated in its full irony and ambiguity. Government, then, is the more or less calculated means of the direction of human conduct. Conduct itself may be taken as a broad term encompassing all types of action and comportment, and styles and patterns of quotidian existence, involving some form of deliberation. It might be located as a region of action lying between the 'ideal types' of affective and habitual responses and rational action that does not exclude the possibility of an admixture of habit, emotion and calculation.[1] However, it does not necessarily presuppose a 'free subject' if by that is meant a self-determining being that exists as an autonomous center of consciousness, will and action. For example, one might want to regard late-medieval sumptuary laws that regulated behavior at church or in festivals, and prescribed the appropriate dress and behaviors for various ranks, as a form of the government of conduct (see Dean 1991). However, this sumptuary police sought to govern conduct without presupposing the agency of such self-standing individuals as might, say, contemporary employment contracts. It is thus useful to distinguish between government and liberal government.

While both concern the government of conduct, the latter presupposes, among other things, at least the possibility of a self-governing individual as the primary locus of conduct and as a norm through which to define the government of other categories which are held not to or only partially to possess the capacity of self-government (e.g. in certain instances, those considered insane, children, prisoners, paupers and wives). Perhaps we can say that the liberal government of conduct presupposes a free subject, if the latter term is read both as a free subject, one defined as a self-governing actor replete with a repertoire of choice, and a free subject, one whose subjection works through the promotion and calculated regulation of spaces in which choice is to be exercised. More generally, to delineate different forms of government it is necessary to examine the relations that inhere in them between those who are to be governed and their conduct. Such relations are enframed within different ways of thinking about the organization of the self, of which the self-determining individual is but one.

This brings us to our principal theme here: how to approach the question of an analytic of self-formation. We are used to thinking of the relation between the political and the ethical as separate domains, no doubt following Weber's conception of the separate departments or spheres of life in modern societies (1970). In contrast here I want to suggest that, while it is possible to make an analytic separation of these domains, they need not be separate in any given instance. In this paper, I address what I shall call governmental-ethical practices. This term seeks to underline the way in which what might loosely be called 'practices of government' come to depend upon, operate through and create relays and linkages with what might be called 'practices of the self'. These practices are, if one likes, hybrid ones in that it is often not clear where the locus or agency for the direction of conduct lies, and indeed which suggest rather elastic boundaries in processes of self-formation.

[...] To be precise, then, governmental self-formation concerns the ways in which various authorities and agencies seek to shape the conduct, aspirations, needs, desires and capacities of specified political and social categories, to enlist them in particular strategies and to seek definite goals; ethical self-formation concerns, practices, techniques and rationalities concerning the regulation of the self by the self, and by means of which individuals seek to question, form, know, decipher and act on themselves. The point that should be underlined is that this distinction cannot be an absolute one. To say that a practice is one undertaken by 'self upon self' is not to exclude the possibility that this practice is authorized by a particular agency, and transmitted and learnt within particular cultural forms. Indeed, to speak of techniques of the self is to treat self-formation as an historico-culturally transmitted set of practices. For example, the self-examination of conscience, or a technique of meditation, are practices of ethical self-formation transmitted through particular agencies and practices and learnt within the context of those agencies.

[...] If there is an equivalent of the philosophical notion of the subject here, it is a 'thin' conception of the subject as a human material that is composed of forces and endowed with capacities, and as such a space of conduct or action (Patton 1992). The organization of these capacities is not however immanent to such a subject. They are culturally and historically given and assembled through various practices and techniques encompassing a vast array of activities from corporeal training and discipline, the regulation of manners and civility, to spiritual exercises and ascetic forms, as the works of thinkers as otherwise diverse as Mauss (1978), Norbert Elias (1978), Pierre Hadot (1992), Peter Brown (1989) and others have shown. The self or subject is thus not a substance but a form, one that is not necessarily identical with itself (Foucault 1988a: 10). The capacities for political action and those of sexual conduct, for example, 'make up' different kinds of selves or subjects, despite the possibility of an overlapping or interference between them.

[...] Indeed, following Deleuze (1988: 99–103; 1993), one might think of this approach to self-formation by means of a spatial metaphor as involving the folding of relations of government and power to sculpt a domain that can act on and of itself but which, at the same time, is nothing more than a space marked out by that folding. We might further speak of a tissue of foldings by which one seeks to sculpt oneself in particular ways, e.g. as a beautiful and noble being or a self-legislating rational entity. Thus, practices of the disciplinary training of the body seek to 'enfold' forms of authority within a self-surveilling space, certain counseling techniques seek to enfold capacities of self-esteem and self-confidence, and practices of meditation seek to enfold powers of calmness, clarity and concentration. In all cases what is addressed is not the self and its capacities that are the putative terminal of these practices, but the practices of enfolding themselves, the forms of authority they seek to enfold, the material they seek to work with and upon, and the results they promise (cf. Rose 1994b). What is offered, then, is not a theory of subjectivity, but an analytic of diverse practices of enfolding.

[...] It is my contention that such a device need not be restricted to practices of the action of 'self on self' but can also be used to analyse governmental practices more narrowly conceived. Again I shall employ a well-known account from Foucault himself (1977: 16–31), that of modern punitive practices, to make my point. There the substance of the punishable element is less the criminal act than the 'soul' of the criminal – the circumstances, instincts, passions, desires and effects of environment or heredity. The work of punishment becomes one of the supervision, management and normalization of the individual. The criminal is subjectified as delinquent, deviant or maladjusted, as one capable or incapable of normalization. Finally, the telos of modern systems of punishment is not to be found in the history of criminal justice itself. Rather the telos refers to how the penalty is incorporated in a pattern of activities and knowledge leading to a specific end, mode of being or, as Weber would have put it, conduct of life. The telos of punishment, then, is discipline itself, the new 'political technology of the body' designed to operate on the body so that the subject will govern him or herself as a docile and useful individual. It is the telos of punitive practices that authorize the move beyond the history of punishment to that of discipline. Here, notions of a disciplinary society, far from being a totalizing description of a particular society, are simply the telos of such practices.

[...]

From social welfare to the active society

I shall now illustrate the form of analysis outlined above by reference to one sphere of the recent reform of the social security system in Australia, that of the income support for the unemployed, and by arguments for that reform, particularly those enunciated from within the international think-tank, the OECD. By regarding social security practices of income support as governmental-ethical practices, I hope to suggest their hybrid nature. On the one hand, they are called upon to fulfill various politico-administrative goals and ideals including those of income redistribution, alleviation of poverty and disadvantage, equity, efficiency and social justice; on the other, they involve practices of self-formation, practices concerned to shape the attributes, capacities, orientations and moral conduct of individuals, and to define their rights, obligations and statuses.

My argument is that these social security practices have taken a form that is relatively independent of goals such as the provision of income security or facilitating entry into the labor market, and that is irreducible to a concern with the universal rights and obligations of the citizen. I want to suggest that, cutting across such goals, contemporary practices of income support can be understood as ones concerned with the formation and reformation of the capacities and attributes of the self. In this respect, such practices are practices of self-formation in that they seek to define the proper and legitimate orientation and conduct of those who claim support. In short, as well as providing financial assistance for those excluded from employment, and attempting to enhance their job prospects, such practices seek to shape the desires, needs, aspirations, capacities and attitudes of the individuals who come within their ken. This, however, is not the entire story. These practices also engage 'clients' in their own government by demanding their complicity in these practices of self-shaping, self-cultivation and self-presentation. These practices become involved not simply in governmental practices but in ethical practices, and what emerges is a kind of governmental sponsorship and resourcing of certain kinds of ethical or ascetic practice.

The broad outlines of recent relevant social security policy history in this area in Australia are as follows. During the mid-1980s the Minister for Social Security established a major review of the Australian system. The review focused on four major aspects of policy: income support for families with children; income security for the aged; income support for the disabled; and income security programs for those in the labor force, i.e. those who had hitherto been called 'unemployed'. The review produced 31 Research and Discussion Papers and six Issues Papers. The latter put forward options for reform of the existing system. Pertinent to our present concerns is Issues Paper No. 4, Income Support for the Unemployed in Australia: toward a more active system, published in 1988. That paper put forward a radical reorganization of the administrative terrain earlier covered by the 'unemployment benefit' and argued for the integration of income support with labor-market programs and training of various kinds. To do so, it used a language concerning 'an active system of income support' that was broadly consonant with more general social policy pronouncements made by the OECD at the time, particularly its pamphlet, The Future of Social Protection (OECD 1988b), and a key article by the Director of Manpower Resources published in the OECD Observer, entitled 'Towards the active society' (Gass 1988). More recently, there has been a Green Paper (Committee on Employment Opportunities 1993) and a following White Paper on unemployment presented by the Australian Prime Minister on 4 May 1994 (Keating 1994). While the latter announces itself as a revolutionary statement of 'policies and programs' in this area designed to combat persistent and high levels of unemployment, it continues to refine and develop an active system of income support for the unemployed, particularly in its emphasis on what the active system problematizes, those 'at risk' of long-term unemployment and welfare dependency.

Now the relation of the review to the structural reform of the social security system was somewhat less than one of full implementation. However, key aspects of the issues paper found their way into legislation with the social security reforms of 1991. In particular, the notion of the active system was carried into the language of the reforms, including the replacement of the old 'work test' with an 'activity test'; the integration of income support with labor market and job-retraining programs provided by or brokered through the Commonwealth Employment Service (CES), and the abolition of the unemployment benefit and its replacement with a differentiated structure of benefits tailored to fit the particular requirements of various groups of the unemployed. The focus of problematization in these reforms was an emergent administrable domain, that of the 'long-term unemployed' or, more precisely, those 'at risk' of long-term unemployment. However, where the review had envisaged a more differentiated system of four new programs, the 1991 legislation resolved it into two programs, Job Search and Newstart.

These two programs gave institutional form to this problem of long-term unemployment. The Job Search Allowance (JSA) applies to all 16–17-year-olds and those over 18 years during the first 12 months of unemployment, while the Newstart Allowance (NSA) applies to those over 18 years who have been unemployed for 12 months or longer. The purpose of the former, to use the words of the 1990–1991 Annual Report of the Department of Social Security (DSS 1991: 105), 'is to support and require active job search, combined with appropriate training or other job preparation activities where there is an identified risk of long-term unemployment'; while the latter 'recognises the special and intractable problems facing the long-term unemployed and the need for a different approach to client contact, assistance and obligations'. The NSA introduced agreements between the client and the CES on 'appropriate job search, employment and/or training activities designed to improve their chances of returning to the paid workforce' (DSS 1991: 105). In both cases, the old 'work-test' of the system of unemployment benefits was replaced by an 'activity test' that required the recipient to fulfill a variety of obligations including appropriate job search, employment, education and training activities.

The recent White Paper announced the abolition of JSA for those under 18 and its replacement with a youth training allowance coupled with intensive case-management leading to placement in work, training or education. For others it placed the assessment of 'risk of long-term unemployment' at the moment of registration with the CES to determine those who are 'job-ready' and those at risk. The latter, like those under 18, would be assigned a CES or private case manager. After 18 months, NSA recipients are to be offered a subsidized job, mainly in the private sector, under a new Job Compact. [...]

Practices and techniques of government

[...] Practices of government, then, exist in various relations to particular knowledges, forms of expertise, discourses and rationales of government but in no way should be understood as a realization of them. These practices are rationalized and regulated according to such knowledges and discourses to varying and investigatable extent. It is important to emphasize, however, that the practical arts of government, no matter how apparently mundane, routine and technical, always coexist with, contain a dimension of 'thought'. The analysis of such arts, then, can never be reduced to an empirical description of the actuality of such practices.

Given what has been said so far, I want simply to note several arenas that such a form of analysis might explore concerning the practices under investigation here. These would include:

1. plans concerning the administrative structure and forms of integration of the various departments and agencies – in the Australian case, the Department of Social Security, the Commonwealth Employment Service and the providers of training programs;
2. schemata for the training of civil servants and the forms of expertise required of them in the administration of programs;
3. the means for the collection, collation, storage and retrieval of information about both the unemployed population and individual cases;
4. the planning of the design, layout and location of offices of these departments and agencies;
5. the various rationales for the procedures of the reception of clients, methods of queuing, interviewing and assessing them;
6. the use of assets tests, eligibility criteria, waiting periods, certification by former employers (in Australia known as Employment Separation Certificates), and application forms, to regulate the movement of clients into and out of benefits; and
7. the use and spatial placement of wall charts, information pamphlets, advertisements and other types of publicity.

Several points can be made regarding further avenues of investigation. First, various statements of policy deliberation and direction can be analysed according to the degree of attention to the practical and technical aspects of the arts of government. Thus the Australian Social Security Review compares unfavorably with the recent White Paper on a scale of degree of examination of the questions of the internal governance and organization of relevant departments, of issues of training and expertise, information management and intellectual technologies.

Second, by focusing on points 4 to 7 it would be possible to map the governmental biography of the social security client within the spatial and temporal coordinates of these practices. Governmental-ethical self-formation could be understood through the plans, diagrams, charts and other means which seek to describe and materially organize conduct in time and space. This point is developed later.

Finally, the means of government of the unemployed are not simply formally located within the institutions and practices of local, regional, national or transnational states. They consist, rather, in the complex linking of state bodies with heteromorphic practices, authorities, agencies and institutions. Thus businesses, employers, consultants, academics, community associations, technical colleges (in Australia, Technical and Further Education Colleges) and so on are employed in a variety of ways to fulfill the objectives of labor-market and job-retraining programs, to define and bring into play domains of expertise, to be involved in the training of civil servants, to undertake the review and evaluation of existing programs, etc. The government of the unemployed is undertaken by the complex linking of agencies and authorities within and without the boundaries of the state, the use of legal, financial and regulatory powers and resources, and the employment of myriad means of rule, only some of which are mentioned above. [...]

The virtue of this analytic of government for our purposes is that it directs attention to the conditions of operation of particular social security practices so that, at a minimum, such practices cannot be reduced to emanations of a particular ideology, policy perspective or even welfare-state regime. The analysis of social security measures as practices of government reveals the dependence of social policy on particular technical conditions of existence, routines and rituals of bureaucracy, forms of expertise and intellectual technologies and the enlistment of agencies and authorities both within and outside the boundaries of the state. It reveals, moreover, that governmental practices exist within, and are saturated by, the element of thought. In brief, in displacing attention from both the constitutional state and the analysis of ideology, the analytic of government reveal the complex and irreducible domain of practices and techniques that form the conditions of social policy. Such an analysis thus directs our attention to the need for the analysis and description of the practical rationalities and minor 'arts of government' that are the conditions of existence of a social security system.

This, however, is not the principal merit of these analyses of government from the perspective of our present concerns. What they have to offer is a concern with the ways in which these practices and techniques provide the horizon for the problematization of the self-formation and self-relation of the unemployed. It is this angle that I develop in the rest of this paper.

Practices of self-formation

[...] [T]here are four dimensions or types of questions we might pose to any governmental-ethical practice as a practice concerned with the direction of conduct and the relation of 'self to self'. I want now to deal with [...] those concerning the material or substance to be governed, the work of government and the governable subject. I leave the consideration of the telos of government to a final section that seeks to explore the general political rationality in which these practices of self-formation are imbricated.

Let us then see whether we can fruitfully use this schema to analyse the social security practices I have mentioned. What do they seek to govern? The answer here seems self-evident: unemployment. These practices certainly do this if by that is meant the condition occasioned by involuntary exclusion from the labor-market. It is true that the Australian policy formulations have placed great stress on the provision of adequate levels of income support and the removal of disincentives to paid work, and that the different allowances may be judged to be more or less adequate in these respects. However, from the vantage point of a concern with practices of self-formation, these practices also seek to govern what they consider the social and personal effects of unemployment (Cass 1988: 129–38). These include the erosion of self-esteem, the effects on physical and mental health, the isolation of the unemployed from social networks, their marginalization from the labor market, their potential for criminality and lawlessness, their poor morale and motivation, their attitude to the labor market, their boredom and their loss of social obligation. In other words, an 'active system' of income support for the unemployed not only acts upon the financial plight of the unemployed, and upon their job prospects, but also upon those attitudes, affects, conduct and dispositions that present a barrier to the unemployed returning to the labor market, and alienate them from social networks and obligations.

Of particular salience here are two ways in which this cluster of dispositions and conduct are conceived. The first is the attribute of 'job readiness' or 'work readiness' of the unemployed (Committee on Employment Opportunities 1993: 97; OECD 1990). The Australian Green Paper argued that higher rates of economic growth will bring more jobs but it is necessary to increase the job-readiness of the unemployed to ensure that the long-term unemployed attain a greater share of them and to prevent high unemployment coexisting with high levels of vacancies. In this it follows the OECD arguments (1990: 62–3) that social protection solely in the form of income support carries the risk of discouraging re-entry into the labor market and that maintaining job-readiness by active labor market programs can actually lead to a reduction in the total cost of support.

Second, there is the potential of a 'risk of dependence': by analysing the different subjective phases of unemployment, it is possible to identify the point at which the unemployed person risks falling into a cycle of long-term dependence on welfare benefits (Cass 1988: 132–3). What these systems seek to govern, then, are all those attitudes, feelings and conducts decreasing the job-readiness of the unemployed and constituting the risk of dependence. Indeed, the very fact of addressing this risk distinguishes an active system of income support from a merely passive system of benefits (e.g. Cass 1988: 4; OECD 1988b: 7–8).

The innovation of the recent White Paper is that it uses these two versions of the 'governed substance' to regulate the flow of clients through the system of employment services. At registration, clients are distinguished into those already 'job-ready' and those 'at a high risk of long-term unemployment'. The assessment takes into account factors such as skill levels, English language ability, age and whether the client belongs to a disadvantaged group such as aboriginal people, sole parents, people with disability and those absent from the workforce for a long period (Keating 1994: 111). At particular points – e.g. at a six-month assessment – those formerly designated 'job-ready' can be judged to have become 'at risk' and their status changed accordingly.

Let us turn to our second question concerning the means by which this complex of factors making up the 'risk of dependency' and 'job-readiness' is to be governed. The key here is the administrative practice known as the 'activity test' that replaces the old 'work-test' of the system of unemployment benefit (Cass 1988: 6, 141–7). This change is justified in terms of a particular historical narrative that runs as follows. In the post-war period of full employment, unemployment benefit could be regarded as a short-term measure to cover temporary contingencies of those between jobs or entering the workforce. The offer of work, or the search for employment on the part of the unemployed, was sufficient to test the legitimacy of the claimant's status as unemployed. However, in a period of high unemployment, and growing long-term unemployment, and the incapacity of the labor market to supply jobs to those wanting them, the notion of a work-test is extremely hard to sustain. On the one hand, there simply aren't the jobs to provide such a test. The test itself becomes increasingly meaningless and redundant. On the other, particularly for the long-term unemployed, the task itself is held to be as personally debilitating and demoralizing as it is fruitless. The work-test by itself could then be viewed as contributing to the very risk of dependency identified as the substance that income support should be combating. Thus what is required is a test that attacks this risk of dependency.

The review thus argued for, and the reforms implemented, an activity test by which the claimant must demonstrate not only active job-search but also training and job-preparation activities. In the case of the long-term unemployed, those on NSA, this activity test takes the form of an agreement between the client and the CES on what constitutes appropriate job-search, employment and training activities. Included in the activity test, then, is not only active job-search but participation in a wide range of other activities deemed to be, or even agreed to be, useful in promoting job re-entry. These might include: English language courses, linguistic and numeracy competency courses, short courses on particular skills, participation in 'Job Clubs; on-the-job training and training courses, part-time or short-term work, courses and counseling to improve confidence, motivation and presentation, and participation in voluntary work [...].

Fundamental to both the activity test and the Newstart Agreements is the notion of *reciprocal obligation* articulated by DEET (1992: 21–2) in the following way: 'if the Government is providing income support, labor market programs and other services, it is only fair that clients take up any reasonable

224 Globalization and Welfare

offer of assistance and do whatever they can to improve their employment prospects' (cf. Cass 1988: 1520. Benefits are not granted, then, as a right of citizen or taxpayer but as a part of mutual exchange or contract between the individual and the state in which both parties accept a new pattern of obligation. This is evidenced by a shift in language. Instead of granting a claimant her/his rightful benefit, the state provides an allowance and services on the condition that the client engages in job-search activities. Instead of a system of benefits for the unemployed, we have a complex of services and allowances for the job-seeker. One might think of all these practices, then, as administratively governed ascetic practices in contrast to the religiously governed asceticism of the famous Protestant ethic.

An excellent example of this administrative asceticism is the Job Search Kit provided by the CES. Included in it is a Job Search Workbook containing information on preparing a resume, writing applications, telephoning employers and doing interviews. It also recommends that the client makes up a 'job folder' containing job leads, application letters, written references, copies of qualification certificates, work samples, school reports and so on. The workbook contains pages for recording job leads and notes for following up such leads. The kit also includes a break-down of job-search into a detailed step-by-step set of activities that the client is advised to undertake. One might like to think of this as a kind of 'Taylorization' of the activity of being unemployed. These forms of asceticism are, needless to say, backed up by sanctions. Failing an activity test, breaking an agreement, failing to respond to correspondence or to report for an interview incurs cancellation of the allowance for varying periods for various groups of the unemployed.

New agents and forms of expertise are formed in relation to this governing work of the supervision of the various categories of the unemployed. Thus one of the initiatives foreshadowed by the 1994 White Paper concerns the resourcing, functions and training of a new agent, the case manager. Such case managers are to operate both in public and private employment services and are to assist all those at risk of long-term unemployment or the long-term unemployed. The case manager operates in what we can no doubt recognize, following Foucault (1982, 1988c), as a pastoral role, assessing the needs of clients, helping them prepare a plan to return to work and directing them towards the activities that enhance their job-readiness (e.g. vocational and remedial training, employment programs, counseling, voluntary work, placements under the job Compact), and reporting breaches of agreements and conditions of allowances (Keating 1994: 110–18). The case manager acts as a position of relay between the unemployed, local employers and appropriate services and agencies. In order to foster 'healthy competition; private and voluntary case managers are to compete with public ones, with their activities monitored and accredited by a new Employment Service Regulatory Agency (Keating 1994: 129–30).

This case-management approach appears as a refinement of the function of employment services outlined by the OECD (1990: 32–3). It describes the work of the public employment services as a set of 'Chinese boxes': the job-seeker's first contact may be simply the receptionist and vacancy list. Later a placement officer may be necessary. After this, the client may need contact with more specialized staff, counseling about alternative job-search strategies and so on. Finally, long-term unemployed people may require participation and counseling in 'self-help' groups known in Australia, France and the United Kingdom as 'job-clubs' and in Austria as 'help yourself groups'. The OECD (1990: 33) notes the use of interviews at particular intervals of unemployment in particular countries and advises that '(a)s a principle, targeted counselling and remotivation to strengthen job search always appears justified when there is a risk that certain persons will lose contact with the labor market'. The administrative biography of the unemployed has a spatial as well as temporal dimension. The first contact is with the receptionist at the front desk, more specialized services are undertaken further back in the office, while highly intensive support and training are provided outside the confines of the ordinary employment office.

What is at stake in my argument is not the question of the reasonableness, fairness, adequacy or effectiveness of the various practices mentioned here or the labor market programs offered or brokered by public, private or community employment services or the case managers. Rather, I wish to stress that such pastoral activities amount to a kind of interface between governmental activities of the state (the provision of allowances and services, etc.) and what might be thought of as a set of ascetic practices (self-examination, counseling, self-help groups, working on oneself to improve one's job-readiness, self-esteem, motivation levels, etc.). These ascetic practices seek ethical effectivity in the shaping of the relation of self to self. In short, through these practices the individual no longer claims a benefit but becomes a client of various agencies, seeking and obeying the directions of pastoral agents, and receiving an allowance conditional on establishing a particular relation to the self.

This, then, brings us to the mode of subjectification of the individual, what these practices hope to produce and the type of self-relation they promote. That relation is firstly one in which the individual is the proprietor and marketer of his or her skills, qualifications and even physical and psychological attributes. We might call this the 'active subject; in line with the language of the Review, the reforms and the OECD. The particular mode of obligation for an active but unemployed subject is that of the job-seeker. The job-seeker is opposed to the individual rendered dependent by the old passive system of unemployment benefit. To be an active subject is to take an active role in the management and presentation of the self, to undertake a systematic approach to the search for a job, and, ultimately, if possible, to participate in the labor-force. If the latter is not possible, the job-seeker as active subject participates in activities that enhance his or her prospects of entering or returning to paid work, while at the same time remaining bound to social networks and engaging in practices that overcome those attributes (fatalism, boredom, loss of self-esteem) which constitute the 'risk of dependency'. Moreover, by instaling the notion of contract in the Newstart agreements, the job-seeker is asked to become the active subject of his or her own destiny at least as far as the labor-market is concerned. If disciplinary practices attempt to render the individual docile and useful, and certain Christian religious practices aim to create a pure and immortal soul, these social security practices are concerned to remake the individual as an active entrepreneur of his or her own self, ready and able to take up such opportunities that the labor market, social provision, education and social networks may provide, and thus able to combat the risk of dependency.

These practices, then, do not simply relieve. They assess each individual as a case to be managed, they supervise the individual's relation with him or herself, they neutralize dependency by identifying certain risks in his or her relation to self and they seek to promote the various qualities encapsulated in the notion of 'job-readiness'. Further, by entering into agreements and undertaking the obligations imposed by the activity test, the client is to be made into the subject of his or her destiny, responsible for undertaking the type of activity determining that destiny. In so far as active subjects are obliged to agree to these practices of self-formation, it is difficult to distinguish them from the neoliberal figure of the 'enterprising self' (Rose 1992).

Consider, finally, the similarities between this active subject and the revamped *homo oeconomicus* of human capital theorists of the Chicago School of Economics, in which the individual seeks to use his or her own biologically endowed and socially acquired attributes as a form of capital presenting returns in the form of satisfactions (Gordon 1991: 41–4; Foucault 1989: 118–19). Indeed the language of investing in human capital and human resource management is pervasive in the OECD policy literature (e.g. 1990). In terms of one of our four dimensions, that of the governable subject, it is difficult to distinguish the objectives of active income support practices from many contemporary variants of neoliberalism. The active subject is the entrepreneur of his or her own capacities, skills, talents and so on. Yet one must be careful here. It may be possible to distinguish the active system along other dimensions. In terms of the work of government, the 'active system' of income support recognizes a pattern of 'reciprocal obligation' envisaging a role for state agencies in job-search, training and case-management far beyond that countenanced by the rhetoric of contemporary Anglo-American neoliberalism and conservative parties in Australia and elsewhere. In this regard, the active system would appear closer to post-war German neoliberalism and the work of the *ordoliberalen*

(Foucault 1989: 117–18) with its institutionalist emphasis on the juridical and policy conditions under which citizens are required to play the game of competitive freedom. In the Australian case, the national state takes it upon itself to coordinate and structure the institutional means by which disadvantaged groups, such as youth, the long-term unemployed, non-English speakers, aboriginal populations, sole parents and all those at risk of welfare dependency, can augment their human capital to take up the opportunities that markets and civil society provide. At a minimum, our investigation demonstrates that there is certainly more than one formula of 'advanced liberalism'; a point to which I shall return later.

The active society

The final dimension of the present analysis of these governmental-ethical practices is to question the kind of society or forms of existence they seek to engender, or the kind of world they would like to create. This is to address the telos of such practices. To do this is to address the points where the administrative and utopian dimensions of these practices meet. This is a more difficult, and somewhat more speculative, task than that undertaken so far. To do this, I refer to more general policy pronouncements of the OECD on the desirability of what it calls an active society.

[...] Importantly, the notion of an active society emerges as a more general way of addressing the Social Security Review's paradox of the maintenance of the provision of work as a central social value and governmental objective during a time of the decreased availability of full-time paid employment. Where the review, and the ensuing reforms, resolve this paradox practically by a shift from a work-test to an activity-test, the OECD seeks to transform the significance of work by placing it within the category of 'socially useful activity' (Gass 1988: 7). The problem is hence to displace the expectation of full employment underwritten by a welfare state, and the assumption that work is full-time wage-labor for all adults up to retirement age, with a society that guarantees access to a range of opportunities over the life-cycle of the individual (Gass 1988: 5). Thus the active society is one that ensures people can work, and enables them to do so, but also encourages activities outside the sphere of paid employment. An active society includes not only participation in the labor-market but also participation in education and training, in voluntary associations, in part-time work or periods of domestic work, in hobbies, travel and so on, or combinations of these, depending on individual preference and the point reached in the individual's life-cycle (Gass 1988: 5–7). Active societies are said to lead to 'a more ambitious and realistic form of full employment, which will require a variety of combinations of working time, education and other activities, in accordance with individual preference and family circumstance' (Gass 1988: 7).

[...] I would like to note a double move around this ideal of an active society that can be elucidated by what is excluded, left behind or opposed by such an ideal. On the one hand such a society is characterized by active income support policies rather than the passive form of benefits believed to have been characteristic of the welfare state. On the other, it promotes an active population that is able to take up the opportunities presented by the labor market, education, social provision and, indeed, social existence more generally. Such a population is defined in opposition to a dependent population, i.e., to the population rendered dependent upon the welfare state by the merely passive system of benefits (OECD 1988b: 21; Gass 1988: 6). The concept of an active society allows this form of rationality to attach a critique of an image of the welfare state as a merely passive system of handouts to the image of long-term dependency among the population.

[...] To suggest that the fear of the creation of this permanent underclass is one rationale for an active system of income support is neither to praise nor to decry the objectives and means of such a system. It is merely to make clear what it is that these systems have come to crystallize as the social problem for the 1990s and to suggest that this fear provides a certain justification for our elaborate systems of labor-market programs, retraining, and those 'ascetic' practices of the self that have come to characterize the experience of being a client of social security. The point to be made is that the concern for disadvantage and for social justice has become linked to a fear of long-term welfare dependency and its consequences. To prevent the formation of such an underclass our governmental-ethical practices of social security demand that clients work upon themselves so that they may be ready and able to work when opportunities are available. If neoliberalism today dreams of an enterprise culture, contemporary social policy has devised a range of institutional conditions and governmental means by which the active subject could be formed, and could form him or herself, in relation to such a culture. [...]

Conclusion

The advocacy and attempted implementation of an active system of administering the unemployed raises many issues. First, it is worth considering the implications of the related notions of 'at risk' groups and indices of disadvantage. It does not seem to me to go too far to consider the whole panoply of active measures as constituting a specific kind of 'risk technology' and as sharing some of the features of the most recent generation of risk technologies (Castel 1991). Its grid of perception and evaluation shares with these technologies a division of the population into those who are capable of managing risk and those whose riskiness requires management under what might be called a 'tutelary' relationship. [...] Thus, the Australian reforms concern not so much the privatisation of risk, and the abandonment of social right, as the grafting of a particular version of individualized risk assessment into a system of public benefits. We might thus talk of the 'enterprization of public benefits' rather than – or at least, as well as the privatization of social insurance. In such a technology, indices of disadvantage become as much a way of isolating, dividing, and targeting populations in terms of their risk factors (aboriginality, non-English speaking backgrounds, gender, age, locality, and so on) as a manifestation of a concern for social justice for all.

Secondly, the active system challenges and forces a reformulation of our conception of advanced or neoliberal formulae of government (cf. Rose 1993c). Certainly arguments for active measures contain a critique of the welfare state in which the circuit of social protection is viewed as interfering with economic circuits of wealth production and growth, decreasing the job-readiness of the population and increasing their dependency quotient. [...] Yet we must be cautious about the assimilation of the active system to other characterizations of advanced or neoliberal modes of governing. As I have already noted, it is characterized by strategies not so much of a privatization of risk as an enterprisation of public benefits. It also envisages an expansion in the 'substantive' arenas of expertise to be brought to bear on the unemployed, and constitutes new authorities (from social policy analyst to job-seekers' case-manager) rather than simply subordinating older forms of expertise to a new formal rationality embodied in the calculative regimes of financial management and accounting. Similarly, while we witness a pluralization of the social powers brought to bear on the unemployed, the notion of a 'reciprocal obligation' between the active subject and the national government attempts to create an assemblage of these powers in which, the national government acts as a kind of 'obligatory passage point' (Callon 1986: 196). This is to say that agencies within the national state, such as public employment services, enrol other associations, agencies and authorities in the government of the unemployed in such a way as to constitute themselves as 'turnstiles' through which the unemployed must pass into such an assemblage. The active system obliges the active subject to exercise choice, and to undertake an intensive work on the self, as it undertakes to ensure that the social technologies exist to enable that work on self to be performed. All of this says nothing about the capacities of national governments, and various other agencies and authorities, to fulfill such an undertaking.

A full appreciation of the analytic of governmental-ethical practices prevents the empiricist reduction of the analysis of technologies of government to the instruments of rule, to questions of the *how* of government, as is sometimes said. The present analysis suggests at the least that *what* is governed, *who* is to be governed and why are equally central questions. Technologies of government are not simply instruments but a frame in which questions of who we are or what we would like to become emerge, in which certain eventualities are to be avoided, and in which worlds to be sought and achieved appear.

If there is a normative question to be posed about such systems, it cannot be couched in terms of the rights of the citizen, an entity that is continually challenged and reshaped by these and other governmental-ethical practices, but in terms of the rights of those groups and individuals who, in any particular situation or for whatever set of reasons, constitute those to be governed.

Notes

1. A well-known example of these themes in general social theory is, of course, Giddens (1991). Of greater pertinence here however, is the way in which a range of thinkers, such as Mauss, Weber, Elias and Durkheim, have been taken up to consider social techniques and practices of self-formation, self-cultivation and self-stylization. Examples of this include the discussion of issues of how human attributes and capacities are used and assembled within various social relations (Hirst and Woolley 1982), of the relation between state-formation and the moral regulation of subjects (Corrigan and Sayer 1985), and of government and the educational cultivation of the self (Hunter 1990). For an extended criticism of Corrigan and Sayer and the ramifications of Foucault's work in this area, see Dean (1994b).
2. This is of course a very approximate way of locating a notion of conduct and certainly does not imply an endorsement of Weber's schema. See Chapter 4 of Dean (1994a).
3. I would caution against either making reflexivity a universal attribute of the subject or speaking of a 'reflexive project of the self' peculiar to modernity (Giddens 1991). Reflexivity for our purposes is to be conceived as a form of action upon the self that arises from specific problematizations of our sense of mental and corporeal individuality. I do not wish to take a position on the universality or otherwise of such forms. However, the marvellously rich work of Peter Brown (1989) on sexual renunciation in late antiquity reveals, at the least, that reflexivity is not a modern project.
4. Thomas Osborne's unpublished discussion paper (1992) set me on the path of thinking about the development of this formal analytic.

15

Compliant Subjects for a New World Order: Globalization and the Behavior Modification Regime of Welfare Reform*

Sanford F. Schram

There is an important debate about whether globalization needs to be taken seriously, especially in terms of its implications for social and economic life in the United States.[1] There is also another important debate about whether welfare reform's new behavior modification regime is more about imposing cultural values regarding family morality than enforcing labor discipline.[2] A third issue I would suggest is whether welfare reform is related to globalization. My thesis for the following analysis is that welfare reform's behavior modification regime is related to globalization in ways that are cultural as well as economic.

My argument is that globalization's undermining of social institutions requires the elaboration of surrogate means of social control to promote adherence to family as well as work values. Welfare reform therefore almost inexorably gets caught up in efforts to stave off the demise of the basic institutional structure of what various theorists have called the family-wage system, founded on a set of relationships between the traditional two-parent family, the market, and the state. Welfare reform in this sense is a critical component of the contradictory impulses of globalization. Economic processes of globalization create new forms of economic exploitation and domination, including the proliferation of new low-wage labor markets, heightened job insecurity, the increase in overwork, the rise in dual-earner families, and growing inequality between families that are benefiting financially from economic change and those who are not. In the process, the fabric of basic social institutions, including most especially the family, is worn increasingly threadbare.

---

* From *Praxis for the Poor: Piven and Cloward and the Future of Social Science in Social Welfare,* New York and London: New York University Press (2002): 218–89.

[...]

In other words, welfare reform reflects a series of antinomies that, upon closer examination, are more consonant than dissonant. Cultural versus economic, symbolic versus material, recognition versus redistribution, identity politics versus political economy, and even behavioral modification versus economic globalization: these are dichotomous distinctions that have been used to suggest that welfare reform is more about one side than the other of each divide. Yet, upon closer inspection one sees reasons to doubt that any of the distinctions holds much water. Instead, welfare reform indicates just how much one side of each divide is imbricated in the other. Welfare reform highlights its own hybridity as both a cultural and an economic policy that serves symbolic as well as material purposes. It is a policy that in the current period reflects an identity politics grounded in therapeutic interventions in service of economic globalization.

The 1996 law set strict time limits and work requirements for the receipt of aid. Yet, the first sentence of the law's preamble states that 'marriage is the foundation of a successful society.' In addition, the law included funding for abstinence – only education, 'illegitimacy bonuses' for states that reduced the number of children born outside of marriage, and options for states to limit assistance to children born to mothers while they were receiving welfare. Therefore, there is no surprise that there has been much debate about whether morality or economics has been the driving force behind the push to reform welfare and eliminate welfare dependency.[3] Was welfare reform primarily about work or about family? This debate took on heightened significance as the 1996 welfare reform law began to come up for reauthorization. Some groups had felt that welfare reform had in its first five years emphasized reducing welfare dependency by getting single mothers to take paid employment outside the home, and they felt that more emphasis now needed to be given to reducing welfare dependency by discouraging the formation of single-parent families.[4] Act I of welfare reform was work; Act II would be family. Economics was emphasized in the first round; in the second round morality would move to center stage.

[...] Welfare has never involved either strictly enforcing work or promoting family morality to the exclusion of the other. Instead, for much of the modern age, it involved reinforcing what Linda Gordon, Nancy Fraser, and others have called the 'family wage system,' which combines cultural issues of family morality with economic issues of work to reproduce the class, race, gender, and sexual hierarchies associated with the existing social order.[5] As Stephanie Coontz has emphasized, the traditional family was valorized as the foundation of society more in name than in fact since most families almost could never afford to conform to that ideal.[6]

The family wage system, founded as it was on this mythical ideal, is itself best seen as a cultural/economic hybrid. It is based on the relationship of the traditional two-parent family to the market and the state. This triad of family, market, and state is premised on the assumption that it will work best when these institutions are articulated smoothly. Their smooth articulation is premised on the idea that the implied subject position of this constellation of institutions is the male head of a traditional two-parent family. State social policies are primarily designed to insure the family against the temporary or permanent loss of income from the male breadwinner. Lineages of heteronormativity, as well as patriarchy and even white privilege, continue to run through this matrix even as it has had to adjust to changes that include women working outside the home, the emergence of dual wage-earning families, increased formation of alternative families, and other social changes.

[...] Today, welfare reform's highly invasive therapeutic regime intensifies this emphasis of the traditional family. It is a major example of how public policy works to reinforce both the cultural and economic dimensions of the family wage system in spite of the tumultuous social changes that have been talking place in work and family, at great cost of the well-being of low-income, mother-only families. In new ways, these families are being punished and forced to serve as denigrated examples to all other low-income families.

Therefore, while much is made of the idea that welfare encourages the formation of mother-only families, what is more often overlooked is that welfare does substantial cultural work reinforcing the traditional two-parent family ideal. The preoccupation with moral regulation of welfare recipients reinforces using the welfare population as a demonstration project for reinforcing the work and family values among the population more generally. By stigmatizing welfare recipients and holding them up for moral denigration, everyone else is reminded of the dangers of transgressing the standards of the family wage system. The regulation of welfare recipients sends the message to the whole low-income population that people in our society can only hope to be affirmed as full citizens if they play by the rules of the family wage system.

The relationship of regulating welfare recipients to reinforcing work and family values for the broader population points to another tie between the symbolic and the material. That is, there are larger symbolic purposes for regulating the population more generally that are served by the real material deprivation imposed on welfare recipients. For instance, the recent push toward the privatization of welfare administration includes allowing for-profit agencies to make large profits by placing welfare recipients in low-wage jobs.[7] This amounts to turning welfare recipients over to private corporations to be treated as commodities for making money. As a result, this privatization of welfare administration not only has real material consequences to welfare recipients in terms of how they are treated, it also demonstrates that welfare recipients can be treated as disposable commodities not worthy of being held onto and cared for by the state.

[...]

Globalization calls for new subjects, new workers, a new proletariat. Economic policies that facilitate an ever more rapid flow of capital across national borders are tied to welfare reform policies that participate in the refashioning of the acceptable self called for by the changing global economy. As the nature of work in the global order changes, especially at the lower rungs of the occupational structure, the need for new and different recruits emerges, and welfare reform is one way in which such recruits get made. In particular, the rise in low-wage service work, personal-care assistants, security workers, and related fields calls for grooming a new class of docile workers who can cheerfully work under the more privileged elements of the population while accepting low pay for demeaning work. [...]

Global knowledge regimes: decontextualizations

The ability to promote the cultural/economic behavior modification processes in service of the emerging global economy is facilitated by the proliferation of transactional knowledge regimes that articulate understandings of who people are and how they ought to behave in allegedly neutral terms decontexualized from considerations of culture and identity.[8]

[...]

The decontextualized abstract quality of welfare policy discourse parallels that of development discourse, which has for several decades already forged ahead as the pioneer in this respect, disseminating its allegedly neutral understandings of economic development to places far and wide. [...]

[...]

[...] The power of development discourse to manufacture problems and then impose solutions in ways that favor First World interests is masked under allegedly neutral technologies of development.

[...] The false neutrality of expert discourses are rampant domestically as well.[9] [...] Both legalization and medicalization constitute expert-dominated discourses that position women drug-users in ways that are disabling and denigrating.[10] Drug-using women are positioned in drug policy discourse in ways that ignore the role of poverty, inequality, discrimination, and other broad structural forces beyond personal behavior and psychological outlook.[11] Drug policy discourse replicates this injustice in many treatment programs that are excessively committed to attributing blame and personal irresponsibility to the person. Even when women get treatment, it is often in demeaning and stigmatizing ways that reinforce their designation as personally irresponsible individuals.

[...] Drug policy in both its soft therapies and hard punishments becomes focused on 'governing mentalities' at the expense of attending to the material practices that engender drug use.[12] Processes of class, race, and gender marginalization are ignored, while behavior and attitude are highlighted. Drug policy discourse becomes an agent in service of making social strain safe for the existing social order. People, not the social processes that grind them up, are the objects of treatment. Drug policy discourse puts these social processes beyond reach and out of sight, leaving the client as the only real object of concern.

[...] I want to suggest that there is merit in considering that the articulations of development and welfare reform discourses extend to helping create a frictionless global space when compliant populations are enlisted into an emerging global system. The power of expert discourse written in a decontextualized, abstract language of allegedly neutral science is that it can pretend to be without culture bias, even when it is profoundly biased. Now, as welfare reform discourse begins to spread from the United States across the First World, just as development discourse did a half-century ago across the Third World, there is even more reason to be alert to the operation of the behavior modification regime of welfare reform in reinforcing First World prejudices that consolidate privilege along class, race, and gender lines.

The false dawn of globalization

Detailing the economic processes of globalization and the therapeutic interventions of welfare reform still leaves them undertheorized about their connections. Several assumptions are necessary for theorizing one or another version of these connections. One set of assumptions is if globalization processes are actually occurring, and if so, how. John Gray has offered a nuanced reading of globalization that suggests it is indeed occurring but in a less than systematic and highly self-destructive way.[13] In its wake, globalization's helter-skelter disruption of social life creates an increased need for various forms of social control to substitute for the norm-enforcing effects of social institutions that are increasingly undermined by the processes of globalization. Gray sets himself against both the skeptics who deemphasize the significance of globalization and the proponents who glorify it as producing a new economic utopia.[14] He writes from the distinctive point of view of a 'radical-conservative,' deeply critical of global capitalism as destructive of traditional forms of life. For Gray, globalization is being promoted by a hegemonic, neoliberal ideology that glorifies the idea of a free, unregulated market on a grand scale, and does so in a way that is destructive of the very social institutions needed to sustain liberal democratic societies.

[...]
Gray's trenchant critique of globalization suggests that its unsystematic and even unpredictable character increases the need of enhanced forms of

social control that are not tied to, and can substitute for, the social institutions that globalization undermines. His analysis suggests that there is merit in theorizing welfare reform's behavior modification regime as part of more diffuse processes of promoting compliant subjects for the new world order.

I therefore want to build on Gray's vision of how the destructiveness of globalization creates needs for new forms of social control. I will suggest that this perspective indicates possible relationships between the therapeutic behavior modification regime of welfare reform and the economic processes associated with globalization. Yet, to do this, we may need to bracket his misleading statements about Michel Foucault. Foucault did not so much suggest that the new forms of power would be operating as some sort of centrally administered iron cage of bureaucracy.[15] Instead, his theorizing can be seen as more consistent with Gray's vision of the future, especially about articulations between microprocesses such as behavior modification in welfare reform and macroprocesses such as globalization. Theorists following Foucault's insights have suggested that globalization thrives on such diffuse networks of power relationships even as they develop without central coordination.[16]

We can relate Foucault's theorizing on new forms of power by focusing more explicitly on the terms 'macro' and 'micro.' These terms have long-standing relevance in the social work profession, but they also point to a way in which the work of Michel Foucault is directly related to concerns in that field.[17] Foucault emphasized that the sources of power had changed with the development of modern 'disciplinary society.' For Foucault, by the time we arrive at modern societies as they have developed since the 18th century, power becomes no longer headquartered in a central sovereign or authoritative source.[18] Instead, it is more dispersed, moving through the capillaries of the social organism more so than its main arteries. For much of his years in writing on this subject, Foucault emphasized how power operates at the microlevel, more through a 'micropolitics' of 'biopower' whereby individual human subjects self-police themselves by virtue of internalization of the dominant understandings of who they are and how they should behave. In this sense, disciplinary power is not so much repressive as it is productive, working from the bottom up, in and through subjectivities so that people engage in practices of self-production, thereby producing the good citizens that they are called upon to be by the social order. For Foucault, this sort of twist to the uses of power provides a new ironic meaning to the idea of 'self-governance.' In fact, Foucault was to use this irony to question the extent to which democracy created a social order that was truly one in which people were self-determining in a way that was reflective of real autonomy and liberation.

Foucault referred to the dissemination and maintenance of these practices of self-policing as the process of 'governmentality.'[19] Eventually he focused on what he called 'technologies of the self,' which were the practices to which individuals subjected themselves in order to refine their capacity to act as particular subjects of the social and political order.[20] Since these technologies of the self were forms of power, they could, for Foucault, then very much be sites of resistance. Ultimately, Foucault focused on the idea that taking ownership of these technologies as much as possible was the most important way that individuals could resist, be political and 'fight the power,' anonymous, impersonal, and diffused such as it is in all its polymorphous diversity and ambiguity.

Gilles Deleuze extended Foucault's concern about disciplinary power, suggesting that in the late-modern or even post-modern society that was emerging, the disciplinary institutions, such as the family, the school, the factory, the community, were breaking down and discipline was being eclipsed by control.[21] The post-modern societies of control did not need formal institutions of discipline that promulgated power relationships *via* punctuated applications of surveillance to encourage self-regulation by the compliant subject populations in question, whether they were children, students, workers, or law-biding citizens. Instead, these formal institutions were *passé*, given that new 'technologies of the self' were emerging that replaced periodic surveillance with continuous monitoring. The disciplined self was being surpassed by the continuously monitored self as the new preferred subject for the emerging post-modern societies of control.

Mitchell Dean has offered a novel extension of Foucault's concern about disciplinary social policies.[22] He has suggested, contrary to Gray, that the emerging forms of welfare policies in the globalizing era actually demonstrate the neoliberalism of the globalization ideology to be less the perfection than the perversion of the Enlightenment. For Dean, neoliberalism is its own counter-Enlightenment. The new welfare policies that emphasize disciplining the recipient population create new forms of compliance making 'targeted populations' synonymous with 'active citizens.' Creating 'active citizens' ironically by way of promoting abject, self-regulating subjects perverts the Enlightenment project the basic premises of humanism, and the ideals of the liberal contractual society. The idea that science and reason can be used to perfect society is overextended so that it turns back on itself, undermining the idea that they can serve the promotion of human freedom and self-actualization.

[...] There is one more source that effectively details these micropractices of welfare reform as integrally tied to the macroforces associated with the neoliberalism of the globalization ideology. Using the Foucauldian-inspired idea that post-modern power is lodged inside human subjects as they work to fashion identity and self, Michael Hardt and Antonio Negri have offered an ambitious attempt to theorize how this sort of 'self-governance' is critical to the formation of the brave new world order created by economic globalization.[23] Hardt and Negri put the micro/macro relationship front and center in their analysis of what is the new global system, how it came about, how it operates, and what sustains it. They see the contemporary processes associated with globalization as leading to the development of a post-modern, post-nation-state system of 'empire.' And for Hardt and Negri, the new post-modern transnational global empire is one that is built from the bottom up *via* the art of 'self-governance' and the politics of self-constitution associated with the systems of continuous monitoring and self-regulation as articulated by Foucault and Deleuze. The new world order is built on the back of the subjectivities of the people who populate it.

New subjects are needed for the new world order. In fact, what is new about the new world order is that it is one that is preoccupied with the creation of new subjectivities. It is an order of subjectivities. The new world order sustains itself through the people it creates. In particular, it thrives through the production of subjectivities that accept the need to make everything anew. In such a world, all is to be assimilated on its terms, even as those terms are constantly changing. The new systems of production are ones that emphasize artificiality, plasticity, the opportunity to remake things as needed, including people, their identities, and their self-understandings.

For Hardt and Negri, therefore, what is radically new about the new world order is that it represents the end of the 'outside.' The end of the outside implies the end of all that which is not incorporated into the systems of control operating within the new world order. This means the end of nature, the end of wilderness, the end of the primitive, the end of the uncivilized, the end even of the foreign, the alien, the unknown. The distinctiveness of the new world order lies in its break with the old binaries of the previous age. The symbolic/material, natural/cultural, the cultural/economic, the objective/subjective, the private/public, and so on, all dissolve in the face of the processes of incorporation. In place of the terms of inclusion and exclusion are the terms of incorporation promulgated by the systems of power operating to build and sustain the new world order.

These systems of power are also distinctive in a particularly post-modern way. Entirely consistent with Foucauldian theorizing, the power that fuels this system has no center and is not centralized in some sovereign source or central source of authority. Instead, it operates *via* networks that articulate relationships across a variety of nodes of communication and exchange. It works its way into social relations, including political and economic ones, *via* the arts of self-construction and the ways in which people are encouraged to fashion themselves as identifiable selves and subjects of the new world order, often in terms that do real violence to their lives, in particular by defining themselves as people who work more for less, and increasingly so. The empire of the new global economic order traverses national and cultural borders, cuts across social systems, and creates a smooth social space in which post-modern selves populate the new world order and arrive ready to fit into the emerging systems of global exchange. In its quest to conquer all by remaking it, the empire of the new global economic order creates its own 'world' here on earth.

For Hardt and Negri, these networks of self-construction are forms of cooperative production in the sense that people collaborate and actively participate in these networks of self-construction. This is then both a distinctive strength and a weakness, for collaboration implicates people in their own self-definition, making their own subjection as subordinated subjects of the new world order something they have chosen. For instance, the choice to see oneself as worthy exclusively in terms of one's productive contributions to the new order makes such a delimiting self-definition seem to be one that is not imposed *via* power exercised by others, but a result of one's own choosing and not a form of power at all. Yet, the idea that the subjected must be enlisted in their own subjection ups the *ante* for power requiring it to work through networks of cooperation in order to reproduce the social life that the new order calls for.[24]

Since the new world order develops an interest in not just the manufacturing of goods but the manufacturing of subjectivities, the affective dimensions of life become an important public issue. Hardt and Negri also emphasize how a power of subjectivity must of necessity also be a power of affectivity as well as effectivity. Once the power for reproducing society comes to involve self-construction, then sustaining the system involves both attending to issues of care as well as work. It involves the arts of reproduction as well as those of production. The bioproduction of life involves caring for the self and others, not only working for the self and others. The system of biopower therefore involves breaking down the distinctions between the public sphere of productive relations and the manufacturing of material goods on the one hand and the private sphere of reproductive relations and the attention to affective dimensions of social life on the other. The system of biopower involves creating compliant subjects for the new world order, socially and culturally as well as economically. And the ability to practice the arts of subject construction becomes itself a valued commodity. From personal care attendants to job coaches, the emerging order proliferates occupations in care of the self.

Hardt and Negri build on Foucauldian analysis to suggest that the biopower of the new forms of self-governance are very much tied to the new emerging systems of economic production. Yet, the new systems of production of post-modern society are very much the new post-industrial ones. Post-industrial society has been termed an 'informational society' where 'symbolic analysts' assume a critical role in producing new forms of communication and knowledge.[25] The new forms of power then are focused on language, communication, and intellectual power – the sources for information critical to the new central forces of production in the computerized post-industrial society.

Therefore, as Marxists have emphasized for the industrial system, power is still very much tied to the ability to dominate the systems of production. Yet, now production has changed and is critically driven by systems of communication and the production of knowledge. The bioproduction of life flows from this concern and engenders the populating of the smooth space of global capitalism with a striated social order based on people's abilities to participate in the informational society. The smooth space of the economic empire is segmented increasingly in terms of those who produce the critical communications and information needed and those who serve them. Increasingly, global flows of information and resources are matched by global flows of people so that an underclass of servants can support the information elites in their toils in the new system of production.

For Hardt and Negri, then, the people most likely to pose a threat to the bioproduction of life under this new system are those who end up with self-constructions least needed by the social order. The unassimilated parts of the First and Third Worlds, the communities and peoples passed over by the emerging economic empire become sites of social resistance. These poor and unpossessed selves, the dispossessed, become the basis for a new militancy that can enable 'the multitude' to constitute themselves as a new proletariat and resist their incorporation into the global economic empire and the hardship it implies for so many. Hardt and Negri remain optimistic that resistance to the emerging forms of self-governance can serve political ends:

> Militancy today is a positive, constructive and innovative activity. This is the form in which we and all those who revolt against the rule of capital recognize ourselves as militants today. Militants resist imperial command in a creative way. In other words, resistance is linked immediately with a constitutive investment in the biopolitical realm and to the formation of cooperative apparatuses of production and community. Here is the strong novelty of militancy today: it repeats the virtues of insurrectional action of two hundred years of subversive experience, but at the same time it is linked to a new world, a world that knows no outside. It knows only an inside, a vital ineluctable participation in the set of social structures, with no possibility of transcending them. This inside is the productive cooperation of mass intellectuality and affective networks, the productivity of post-modern biopolitics. This militancy makes resistance into a counterpower and makes rebellion into a project of love.[26]

Hardt and Negri provide us with a radical incrementalism for the new world order. For them, the resistance to domination by the macroprocesses of economic globalization begins with the resistance to the processes of micropolitics, biopower, and the production of life *via* the acts of subjectification built into the new forms of self-governance, self-regulation, and self-constitution called for by the new world order. Resisting the therapeutic interventions designed to get us to be the compliant subject of the new world order is the beginning of politics. Resisting such regimentation would be challenging the new forms of power at their most critical juncture. Micropolitics is macropolitics, and fighting therapeutic strategies to normalize the population is an important part of challenging globalization today.[27]

While there is much to debate about Hardt and Negri's ambitious analysis, they offer a rich perspective for examining how welfare reform's behavior modification program bears the traces of globalization. Welfare reform has heightened the emphasis on focusing on welfare recipients' behavior as the source of their poverty. It is reflective of a growing tendency in the culture to promote behavioral discipline as the source for achieving social and economic success and distinction. It echoes the concern that each family must find a way to be productive members of the emerging social order, relying as little as possible on assistance from the state. The first order of business is for all family heads to remake themselves in terms that will make them able to fit into the emerging system of production. If people cannot assume the role of privileged symbolic analysts, perhaps they can retrofit their identities to be seen as attractive for underlaborer positions in the service sector, whether it is as clerical assistants or personal-care attendants. We are all in recovery, and everyone is his or her own job coach.

[...]

Welfare reform therefore is not so much about disqualifying poor single mothers on welfare as undeserving of inclusion in the new world order as much as requiring all the poor to assume positions of inferiority in that order. Welfare reform works therefore on both these levels for the good of that new world order. Welfare reform provides aid and offers assistance to the needy on the basis of their willingness to make the transition to accepting positions of low-wage, servile work in the subordinate orders of the New Age economy, often slotting recipients into marginal positions in the service economy where they provide personal services for those who command the positions of privilege. This *quid pro quo* sends a signal across the economically marginal population more generally. As Peck himself aptly notes: 'Stripped down to its labor-regulatory essence, workfare is not about creating jobs for people that don't have them; it is about creating workers for jobs that nobody wants. In a Foucauldian sense, it is seeking to make "docile bodies" for the new economy: flexible, self-reliant, and self-disciplining.'[28]

[...]

Notes

1. See the debate between Frances Fox Piven and Richard A. Cloward and Ellen Meiksins Wood in Wood (1996): 21–39; and (1998): 24–43; Piven and Cloward (1998a): 11–24; and (1998b) 44–6.
2. See Piven (1998): 67–83.
3. For reviews of these debates, see Piven (1999): 32, and (1998): 67–83.
4. Rector (2001).
5. See Gordon (1994): 53–9; and Fraser (1994): 591–618.
6. See Coontz (1993).
7. See Schram (2000): 70–5.
8. On the value of decontextualized, abstract knowledge for purposes of domination that can be exported transnationally, see Peck (2001): 88–9.
9. See Edelman (1977).
10. *Ibid.*: 14–18.
11. See Currie (1993).
12. Campbell (2001): 33–54.
13. Gray (1998): 53–77.
15. See Foucault (1991): 87–104.
16. See Hardt and Negri (2000): 22–41.
17. See Chambon, Irving, and Epstein (eds) (1999).
18. For a poignant example of the disciplinary practices of the micropolitics of slavery, see Hartman (1997).
19. Foucault (1979): 87–104.
20. Martin *et al.* (1988).
21. Deleuze (1992): 4–6.
22. Dean (1998): 198–226.
23. Hardt and Negri (2000): 22–41.
24. For a related analysis, see Scott (1990).
25. The term 'symbolic analysts' was coined by Robert Reich. His ideas are discussed in Hardt and Negri (2000): 291–2.
26. *Ibid.*: 413.
27. The continuing importance of mass protest politics even on today's global stage is underscored by the diverse but coordinated efforts of the protesters of the World Trade Organization. See Hardt and Negri (2001): A18.
28. Peck (2001): 6.

16

Political Economies of Scale: Fast Policy, Interscalar Relations, and Neoliberal Workfare*

Jamie Peck

[...]

Despite its often abstract and metaphysical qualities, recent work on scale has drawn explicit attention to the way rescaling is achieved through, and subsequently entails, changing political-economic power relations, transformations in institutional capacities, and shifts in the parameters of political agency. Contrary to the prevailing neoliberal caricature of rescaling – which portrays an eviscerated national (welfare) state as a necessary and desirable outcome of economic globalization, conceiving appropriate responses in the narrow terms of privatized localism and individualized responsibility – the article makes the case for an explicitly politicized and transscalar conception of the processes of regulatory restructuring. There is a need to counter the pervasive naturalization of the global as the economically optimal scale of market forces and the local as the politically optimal scale of coping and adaptation. To do so, a relational and reflexive analysis of scale is necessary – one that is sensitive to geographic, historical, and institutional contingencies, rather than an absolutist and categorical approach in which political-economic functions are rigidly, exclusively, and unambiguously fixed at particular scales. Contingently scaled functions, such as those associated with the national welfare state, are not simply being moved around, they are undergoing a process of qualitative transformation through rescaling. And in the process, new rules or patterns of interscalar relations are emerging – for example, as nationally oriented systems of welfare policy formation are unevenly giving way to a combination of local program innovations; transnational policy narratives; and the proliferation of portable, technocratic policy tools that are designed to achieve 'reform at a distance' within a neoliberalized environment. Post-

---

* From *Economic Geography* 78(3) (2002): 331–60.

welfare politics seem to be becoming more global and more local at the same time, while in the gray space between, national states continue to exert important influences, albeit framed in terms of a narrative of powerlessness and an autocritique of past welfarist practices.

The field welfare/workfare restructuring offers some of the textbook instances of hollowing out – given that the emergence of global workfare discourses and the internationalization of active social-policy conventions have coincided with a marked devolution of welfare/workfare programming and conspicuous crises in numerous national welfare settlements. Yet, in other respects, the case of welfare reform/workfare illustrates the complex and contradictory ways in which regulatory discourses, institutional competencies, and political-economic functions are being rescaled in a multiscalar, rather than a unidirectional, fashion, and often in ways that provoke countertendencies and responses of a potentially path altering kind. For example, while stylized readings of local welfare reform models increasingly shape the terms of international policy debates ('America's great achievement' *The Economist* 2001; Peck and Theodore 2001), successful local programs remain both empirically rare and exceptionally difficult to replicate. Similarly, while the rhetoric of local experimentation and street-level innovation has been widely appropriated by neoliberal reformers, rule regimes and systems of metagovernance at the national and international scales are deeply implicated in guiding and orchestrating the (local) policy development process. The existence of these apparent scalar disconnects calls for a careful theorization of the relationship between local institutional changes and those extralocal rule regimes within which they are embedded – and through which they are partially constituted.

[...]

Thinking scale: relational conceptions and social constructions

[...]

By representing the globalized economy as an out-there phenomenon – as fickle and uncontrollable as the weather – neoliberal scalar narratives serve to disconnect the local from the global in political and analytical terms. It is almost as if capital and the market have 'jumped scale,' in Smith's (1993) evocative words, not only in the reach of national-state regulation, but also analytically, in the very theoretical plausibility of a territorially embedded, socially regulated, politically mediated economy. Such an abstract, idealized conception of the global economy is as theoretically misleading as it is politically disabling. Amin (1997: 129) insisted that globalization must 'not be misconstrued as or demonized as an "out there" phenomenon standing above, and set to destroy, the geography of territorial states, economies and identities.' Instead, along with Massey (1993), he highlighted the out-there/in-here qualities of the globalization process: the deepening interconnectedness of social, economic, and political life is resulting in an effective *hybridization* of scale. [...]

Politically, such hybridized conceptions of scale are potentially more empowering than the fatalistic scenarios associated with out-there readings of neoliberal globalization. Analytically, it may also be said that such a focus on inter-scalar connectivity (and the grounded nature of globalization) is more consistent with the kind of integral conception of the economy found in socio-economics and political economy. Instead of artificially separating the economic and the social or political and then sequestering them at different spatial scales, integral conceptions of the economy take it as axiomatic that, *inter alia*, the state is immanent in the operation of the economy; that markets and institutions have joint, conjunctural logics; and that processes of social regulation are normal and necessary, if contradictory and contingent (O'Neill 1997; Jessop 2001; Peck 2000). From this perspective, economic and extra-economic structures, imperatives, and dynamics maybe separable through abstraction, but they are organically connected in practice, being inescapably melded in ways that are both historically specific and geographically uneven. [...]

Rather than separate out the global as an all-determining and politically impervious 'metascale,' it is more appropriate to conceive scale, as Swyngedouw (1997a, 1997b) did, in relational terms. For Swyngedouw, ontological priority lies unequivocally with political-economic process, rather than scale *per se*, though he was at pains to emphasize that the operation of political-economic processes necessarily involves both the reproduction of scales and the reconstitution of scaled power relationships. Swyngedouw insisted that 'scale (at whatever level) is not and can never be the starting point for socio-spatial theory' – highlighting the folly of attempts to construct theories of globalization or localization *per se* – but that attention should be focused on the exploration of *'mechanisms* of scale transformation and transgression through social conflict and struggle' (1997b, 141, italics added).

[...] According to such relational views of scale, social and regulatory processes cannot be categorically assigned to specific scales and neither is the scalar constitution of these processes theoretically pre-given or historically fixed. Rather, the association between a particular scale and a specific social process – say, the privileging of the national scale as the primary site of regulation, economic management, and political struggle under the era of Keynesian-welfarism or the current neoliberal preoccupation with privatized localism and global deregulation – is historically and geographically contingent. Particular scale fixes are therefore political constructions that are subject to periodic contestation; they are not transcendentally determined. It follows that hegemonic power, in this context, is reflected in the control of scales and/or the assertion of a particular scalar fix in which certain sectional-political interests are privileged. Transformations in the pattern of power relations invariably result in shifts in scale relationships, often involving powerful actors, agents, and interests 'jumping scale' in order to acquire a tactical or strategic advantage. Perhaps the most often-quoted example of this phenomenon is the relationship between tendentially internationalizing capital and relatively place-bound labor: the wider locational reach of capital – often expressed as potential rather than actual mobility – is a key aspect of its asymmetrical power relationship with labor, which, by virtue of its social reproduction needs, tends to be more territorially dependent (Offe 1985; Storper and Walker 1989; Peck 1996). As Swyngedouw (1997a, 170) put it, 'Over the past decades, it has been mainly capital that jumped upwards [to the global scale], while in many cases (and with varying degrees of resistance) the regulation of labor moved downwards.' This does not mean that in all circumstances labor is a politically weak and place-bound social actor (Herod 2001). There is always space for social agency, while contextual conditions may also tip the balance of power away from capital (under tight job-market conditions, for instance). [...]

A further key advantage that actors who are organized at a higher scale typically possess – most clearly exemplified by the power of state and parastatal institutions operating at the national and international levels – is the ability to shape those extralocal rule regimes that constrain and channel the strategic options and tactical behavior of local actors. Many of the activities of entrepreneurial cities, for example, are strongly conditioned by such rule regimes, whether they are the formalized bidding systems and funding programs of national and transnational states, the dubious rituals of agencies like the International Olympic Committee, orchestrated competitions for inward investment (public or private), or the generalized pressure to make a distinctive mark in international 'image markets' (Harvey 1989; Brenner and Theodore 2002; Peck and Tickell 2002). Ironically, entrepreneurial city strategies are typically hailed by neoliberal ideologues as examples par excellence of local agency, in general, and elite vision, in particular. Of course, political agency is exercised at the urban scale, even if the outcomes – sports stadia, high-class shopping malls, waterfront redevelopments, and image rebranding – are so often depressingly similar and, in some respects, decidedly unlocal. Three implications follow. First, socio-regulatory processes operate across scales, rather than being confined to a particular scale, highlighting the need to consider the relative power of scale-based rule systems *vis-à-vis* that of scale-bound actors, agents, and institutional relationship that is often an asymmetrical if not a hierarchical one. Second, this process should be seen as one of scalar-structuration, in which the competitive (local) behavior of urban elites both reflects and reproduces the extralocal rule regimes that subsequently canalize and circumscribe local action (Jessop, Peck, and Tickell 1999). Third, it must also be acknowledged that there are institutionally enforced but not theoretically necessitated limits to local political agency, at least in the present context of deep neoliberalization; hence, there is a need to consider political and institutional processes that operate behind the backs or above the heads – of local actors (Peck 1995). Rule regimes embedded at higher spatial scales, such as the prevailing order of interurban competition or the nature of competitive funding systems, can be difficult to transform through unilateral local action. Meanwhile, the aggregate effect of such local actions can be the effective entrenchment and reproduction of these same relations of extralocal/scalar subordination. To fail to recognize this basic asymmetry in scalar power relations under conditions of neoliberalized competition – and the tendential scalar hierarchies that these entrenched yet institutionally specific conditions imply – is to run the risk of confusing theoretical correctness with political economic reality.

Taking extralocal rule regimes seriously means bringing the national state back into the center of the picture. And doing so, in turn, calls for the rejection of caricatured notions of the shrinking state. [...]

In Jessop's (1999) conception of the hollowing out of the national state... there is an explicit rejection of the shrinking-state thesis: while regulatory processes may be denationalizing, the national state retains crucial coordination functions, analogous to the headquarters operations of hollowed-out corporations. So, what is under way is a qualitative reorganization of state capacities, involving shifts in the structural form and strategic orientation of different tiers and levels of the state, and a complex reconstitution of state/market and government/governance relations. These developments certainly should not be mistaken for a rollback of the state in general, when they are actually centered on a critique and recomposition of a particular *historically and geographically specific form of state*, the KWS. So, as some institutions and regulatory capacities are being rolled back, others are being rolled forward – often, indeed, in the name of the market, business, and deregulation – albeit in radically different forms and with different purposes. [...]

Working scale: fast-policy workfarism

[...] The welfare/workfare transition thus represents an example of qualitative restructuring in state institutions and regulatory settlements. The rolling back of nationally constituted welfare states is occurring at the same rime as, and is partly being achieved through, the rolling forward of glocally constituted workfare regimes. Moreover, this is an asymmetrical and uneven process within which national welfare states are not so much being replaced as displaced through a complex combination of *in situ* restructuring, selective rollback, destabilization from above, and erosion from below. Crucially, this process of restructuring is being accomplished, to a substantial degree, through rescaling, but not so much through compartmentalized scale-discrete movements of regulatory functions or institutions. Instead, it involves strategies that explicitly tangle and confound scales. The workfare offensive is very much a multiscalar one, being prosecuted simultaneously through the internationalization of policy conventions, the reorganization of national-state roles and regulatory frameworks, the purposive animation of local delivery and policy development systems (along with their subsequent embedding in local labor markets), and the downloading both of socio-economic risks and the locus of regulatory control to the scales of the household and the poor body. [...]

[...] The workfare offensive is being married to, and pursued through, strategies of decentralization and downloading. Under the prevailing dynamic of downscaling, regulatory/financial responsibility and socio-economic risks are being downloaded (or dumped) from national states, not only to subnational and local states, but also to private corporations, agencies of the social economy, and individual workers and welfare recipients. As such, workfare strategies should be understood in the wider context of the localization, denationalization, and disorganization of labor regulation – coupled with the intensification of uneven spatial development and interlocal competition which has been a characteristic of recent decades (Burawoy 1985; Peck 1996). In the United States, the 'blockgranting' of residualized welfare/workfare functions to the 50 states in the Personal Responsibility and Work Opportunity Reconciliation Act of 1996, which effectively ruptured the federal entitlement status of welfare originally enshrined in the New Deal, represented a truly paradigmatic event in this respect (Handler and Hasenfeld 1997; Schram 2000; Peck 2001).

This prevailing downscaling dynamic should not be mistaken, however, for a straightforward downsizing of the national welfare state – in which the same basic set of pregiven regulatory functions are being dispensed, just in a way that is smaller, meaner, and tougher – for at least three reasons. First, these scalar movements entail far-reaching shifts in the functional roles, means, objectives, and discursive norms of the glocalizing welfare/workfare state, such that the income replacement/unemployment compensation/poverty alleviation logic of the welfare state is being unevenly displaced by a nascent workfarist logic, premised on the maximization of waged-labor force participation, the naturalization of contingent employment, and the rationing of residual welfare provisions and services according to criteria of employability. Second, the process of welfare/workfare restructuring must be understood as a multiscalar strategy, in which the downscaling dynamic is occurring at all levels below that of the national state and in ways that are critically connected to the reorganization of national and international regulatory frameworks, rule systems, policy conventions, and political norms, so that the only real way to appreciate the significance of 'local' workfare experiments is to place them in their national and international regulatory context. Third, considering these functional and scalar shifts in tandem, the downscaling of institutions and modes of intervention is fundamentally predicated on the reorganization of extralocal rule regimes, calling for an understanding of the increasingly cross-scalar constitution of restructuring strategies. [...]

The tangled scalar geographies of welfare retrenchment and workfarist institution-building cannot be collapsed into a single scalar narrative. [...] Rather, workfarism at a systemic level is associated with divergence, differentiation, and the proliferation of workfarist reform paths and strategies. In fact, the very unevenness of the emergent workfare regime is a source of innovation and energy, as translocal fast-policy transfers are being established as one of the principal means of policy development. In workfare discourse, much is made of localized learning, but ironically, what this term usually means in practice is the importation of off-the-shelf program techniques from other locations. One consequence is that a comparative approach to welfare reform is fostered, as local administrations benchmark their performance against that of other localities and frequently turn to consultants or to the evaluation literature to learn from the latest local success stories from which they may borrow, cafeteria-style (Theodore and Peck 1999). Perhaps the most hyped local reform program, in this context, is Wisconsin's W-2 model of work activation, the architect of which, former Governor Tommy Thompson, is the secretary of state for health and human services in the Bush administration – an embodiment of after-welfarist resealing, if ever there was one!

The destination of countless delegations of politicians and policymakers, Wisconsin has come to represent a potent symbol of workfarist reform at both the national and international scales (Peck and Theodore 2001), having been actively debated – if not emulated – in contexts as diverse as Germany; South Africa, the United Kingdom, Australia, the Netherlands, Canada, and Israel. For all its local shortcomings and failings – most notably the costs associated with displacing on-welfare poverty with in-work poverty – the Wisconsin model nevertheless continues to achieve extralocal traction in policy debates by virtue of its compelling fusion of a no-nonsense work message, an unequivocal institutional and political buy-in, contracted-out delivery, and, above all, falling welfare rolls (Berkowitz 2001; Piven 2001). The orthodox reading of the Wisconsin story is that its welfare-to-work successes should be attributed not to the growing economy of the 1990s, but to the fact that this state 'went furthest with [its] reform measures' ('America's great achievement', *The Economist* 2001: 26; Matthews and Becker 1998). Such processes of reform validation – given that workfare policies are only deemed effective, definitionally, when they are associated with falling welfare rolls – help account for the undue influence of the Wisconsin model in extralocal contexts such as federal rule systems and global policy conventions. In these latter contexts, of course,

W-2 is not merely a local program, but as a technocratically stylized reform signifier, it is associated with a decidedly out-here form of discursive authority, shifting the contours and the terms of debate and helping establish new metrics for the evaluation of effective policy. [...]

One of the deepest scalar paradoxes of the workfare offensive, however, is the stubbornly wide implementation gap that remains between the global visions of reform advocates, on the one hand, and the prosaic realities of local programming, on the other hand (Nathan 1993; Lurie 1996; Theodore and Peck 1999). Whereas the advocacy of workfare policy is increasingly taking on a transnational form, as an object of consensus among international policy elites, the delivery of workfare is, in many ways, a local matter, given the need to operate programs close to the local labor market and the associated imperative of micromanaging the domestic and job-search behaviors of welfare recipients. [...]

In this respect, the recursive restructuring of labor markets has been important, too. More now than just an impractical obsession of right-wing politicians, there are indications that workfarism may be exhibiting a nascent economic rationality. Even though the initial impetus for workfarism may have been primarily derived from (low) political motives, in its more mature manifestations, it is beginning to show signs of evolving a *post hoc* kind of economic logic as the system treads down into and interacts with (simultaneously restructuring) flex-labor markets. In functional terms, workfare naturalizes and normalizes such job market conditions. First, it explicitly socializes welfare recipients for unstable, contingent jobs, reconciling (in a downward direction) the needs and aspirations of welfare recipients in accordance with the realities of low wage employment in local labor markets. Second, the generation of administrative pressures to enter the first available job self-evidently erodes the capacity of labor to wait for more favorable employment opportunities, while intensifying competition for entry-level positions. Third, it effectively market-tests access to residual welfare services, rationing these services according to the criterion of employability (Peck and Theodore 2000). Yet workfare was not a spontaneous outcome of labor-market requirements, nor can the restructuring of flex-labor markets be fully explained in terms of the state's changing regulatory roles. Nevertheless, the economic and political moments of the workfarist regulatory process are connected, albeit in complex, temporally lagged, and geographically specific ways. Because the expansion of contingent labor demand and flexibilized labor markets helps realize workfare strategies in a practical sense and underpins their tendential legitimacy in a political sense, the stage is set for complex and scale-contingent interactions to take place between economic and political moments of the reform process. [...]

The hegemonic power of workfarism is therefore substantially rooted in the capacity not just to construct a compelling reform discourse, validated by expert nodes in centers of persuasion like Washington, D.C. and London, but to project and realize this reform narrative at a distance-across both space and scale. And this is where the confident rhetoric of fast-policy solutions and the conviction-speak of neoliberal politicians collide with the prosaic realities of slow (and uncertain) delivery. Workfare policy systems are territorially embedded in ways that the translocal, technocratic discourse of workfarism seeks explicitly to deny. Economically, workfare systems tend to be more effective in areas where the labor market is either buoyant or at least dynamic, given that tire methodology of work enforcement presupposes the ready availability of entry-level jobs. Institutionally, they tend to be more effective in the hands of single-minded administrators with a substantial degree of organizational flexibility and relatively small welfare caseloads, which usually means that they do not work in overloaded, pressurized, big-city administrations. Hence, the isolated local success stories of workfare tend to be contingent by-products of a whole series of conjunctural conditions, including a favorable extralocal regulatory environment, facilitative local institutional arrangements, and supportive local economic circumstances. The causal specificities that lie behind local outcomes are acknowledged, to a certain extent, in the orthodox policy-evaluation literature, though invariably it narrowly privileges (malleable) local institutional factors over contextual economic and political conditions. In their advocacy of high-performance welfare-to-work strategies like the much-vaunted Riverside, California, GAIN program, for example, proponents typically draw attention to the following features: prioritizing the program among top officials; a strong commitment and adequate resources to serve the full mandatory population; a pervasive emphasis on getting a job quickly, even a job that is relatively low paying; a strong focus on motivational training and job search, rather than on the provision of education and skills training; close case management of participants; the active use of job developers to establish close links with private-sector employers and to help recipients locate work; the willingness to use benefit sanctions to enforce the mandates of participation; tight administration, including a cost conscious approach oriented to the imperative of moving participants quickly into employment; and an outcomes-focused management style, including job placement standards for case managers (Gueron 1995; Mead 1995). [...]

What is crucial is that 'the dominant neoliberal responses to this problem of patchy, economically contingent, and unpredictable outcomes are basically twofold, both of which entail tire speedup of policy-development systems and both of which are manifest in scalar terms. First, policy advocates, consultants, and evaluators foster and circulate essentialized readings of effective local programs in which a small number of supposedly decisive (and potentially replicable) design features are privileged and promoted. In the process, complex and locally embedded interventions are rendered as simplified, disembedded, and reproducible administrative routines, related to such features as caseload management systems, rules of participation, the sequencing of services, the components of programs, reform and leadership philosophies, and even slogans. This disembedding process establishes the basis for a national and international market in transferable policy lessons and strategies, the unpredictable and inescapably slow process of institutional learning having been reduced to a technocratic process of administrative cloning. Somewhat paradoxically, the neoliberal preoccupation with local success stories is complemented with a mode of policy formation that aggressively disembeds, essentializes, and, in key respects, delocalizes the process of policy formation. The diffusion of the ascendant method of workfirst programming, for example, the conspicuous successes [in] which have been extremely sparse and localized, has been facilitated not only by the work of armies of consultants and policy advocates, but also by the circulation of 'transferability packages' and how-to manuals (Riverside County DPSS 1994; Brown 1997). In this fast-policy regime, then, new 'agents of persuasion' seek explicitly to disembed and circulate suggestive and loaded policy signifiers and reform texts, decoupling the moment of reform from the rationalist preoccupation with *results*, in favor of a commitment to technocratic emulation and rolling reform.

Second, channels of policy learning, transfer, and networking are increasingly being structured in transnational- and, more particularly, translocal-terms as new knowledge communities, intermediary agencies, global consultancy and evaluation houses, and multilateral partnerships are established to facilitate and foster the process of fast-policy transfer. The importation of off-the-shelf policy fixes becomes a way of shortening the development phase of new programs, while a new emphasis on systemic innovation and almost perpetual reform ensures that the turnover time of policy cycles is accelerated. On this basis, for example, the British welfare-to-work regime has been fundamentally redesigned by the Blair government, consideration of reform options having been substantially foreshortened and truncated by the suggestive and/or forceful promotion of 'ideas that work,' particularly from the United States (Deacon 1997; Rogers 1997; Matthews and Becker 1998; Walker 1998; Prideaux 2001). It is significant that local reform models suitably disembedded and stripped down to their methodological essentials – increasingly define the terms of national and international policy discourses as extralocal regulatory frameworks are fashioned in such a way as to be selectively responsive to new programming and case-management techniques. Under this fast-policy environment, then, local institutional systems and reform processes are much more reflexive and externally oriented than was previously the case. [...]

It is in this context that local reform models like Wisconsin's W-2 and the Riverside GAIN program acquire their extralocal salience: what begins as a territorially embedded and place-specific program is discursively deterritorialized through its translation into a politically loaded policy message. This speaks to the distinctive way in which the local is taken up into neoliberal restructuring strategies. Eschewing notions of policy learning and development as a socially structured, grounded, and organic process, neoliberalism constructs the local scale as a space of flux and continual adjustment, and localities as agentic nodes within competitive policy networks, restlessly searching for new ideas. The workfare reform process is animated by this environment of creative institutional destruction: the pursuit of policy innovation is continuous, since programs themselves are repeatedly churned in the search for elusive improvements in performance and credibility. [...]

If the present macroinstitutional conjuncture can be understood, in Brenner's (1998b) terms, as a form of 'crisis-induced restructuring,' then the apparent scalar paradox represented by the coincidence of the endemic failure of workfare policy at the local level and a deepening of the workfarist policy consensus at the international level can be seen to reflect a brutal, if contradictory, logic. Fast-policy regimes help secure a clumsy form of crisis displacement through space and across scales as macrolevel problems of underemployment and poverty are rescripted as matters of local institutional determination, if not personal failure, while local policy failures are managed through a combination of interlocal competition, technocratic translation, and serial emulation. The dynamic and destabilizing regimes that workfare systems impose on their 'clients' welfare can no longer be 'a way of life,' learn to accept that 'any job is a good job,' search for work purposefully and continuously consequently have suggestive echoes in the workfare policy process itself. Both participants and program managers are on tread mills of someone else's making, coerced and constrained by a combination of competitive relations and superordinate rule systems. [...]

The emergent neoliberal market for portable policy fixes is neither chaotic nor perfectly competitive; rather, it is institutionally and politically structured in important ways. While neoliberal rhetoric (and its softer variant in the shape of Third-Way pragmatism) privileges the local – at least discursively – as the most significant scale of innovation, dynamism, and front-line policy learning (while presenting autocritiques of big government, social and spatial redistribution, tax-and-spend interventionism, and federal/national welfarism), in reality national states continue to perform critical roles as arm's-length managers of the workfarist policy process. Emphatically, the process of welfare/workfare restructuring cannot be reduced to one of national state withdrawal or to some benign process of zero-sum resealing. Rather, in the course of the restructuring process, new institutional and regulatory structures are rolled out, while national states typically retain or acquire key functions as orchestrators of ostensibly devolved policy systems.

[...] In the post-1996 era, extralocal rule systems are not only being remade through such conventional lobbying strategies. They are also being reshaped through their complex interactions with the reanimated local policy development process. The wider ideological salience of models like W-2 and GAIN derives more from the ways in which they chime and resonate with these extralocal rule regimes and their technocratically induced velocity in fast-policy markets than it does from the energy and innovation of local policymakers. True, national and federal frameworks are increasingly porous to locally derived (or inflected) policy lessons, but only in a spatially selective and institutionally structured way (Jones 1997). In this sense, the issue of which policy lessons are incorporated into a wider policy discourse (and which are not) is closely bound with the way that new channels of interlocal and cross-scalar policy learning and transfer are being constituted. [...] Dominant evaluation methods, for example, which are based on quantitative, control-group studies, have played a role not only in generalizing decontextualized and essentialized policy knowledges about workfare programs and their rationally-acting participants, but also in privileging assessment metrics oriented to short-term outcomes and the minimization of costs (Schram 1995; Epstein 1997). The macropolicy environment of workfarism is structured so as to encourage the shallow emulation and serial reproduction of work-first programming techniques, not the kind of deep learning that may otherwise generate strategies outside the narrow repertoire of neoliberal workfarism.

In this way, as in others, the process of fast-policy transfer is profoundly contradictory, reproducing short-term responses and institutionally 'thin' strategies. So, one of the perverse consequences of the extensive process of contracting out welfare/workfare functions to private companies at the local level has been a corresponding partial privatization of channels of policy transfer. In Wisconsin, for example, the state's two largest for-profit providers, Maximus and Employment Solutions, have both been embroiled in a series of scandals related to operational and financial irregularities, including (perhaps most controversially) the diversion of W-2 funds into the solicitation of welfare contracts from other states (Berkowitz 2001; State of Wisconsin Legislative Audit Bureau 2000, 2001). Meanwhile, in the United Kingdom, some private providers are seeking to claim proprietary rights over programming innovations, despite the Blair government's efforts to create a learning network around its New Deal welfare-to-work program (Peck and Theodore 2001). By the same token, however, would-be local innovators are induced to market (and indeed sell) their wares through financial incentives like funding (from national governments or private foundations) for trials, prototypes, and demonstration projects.

[...] The politics of workfare resistance also tend to be highly localized, emerging most often out of city-level campaigns and organizing drives (Gilbert 2001). The national bases of welfare and anti-poverty advocacy having been deliberately undermined, the map of political resistance to workfare is sparse. Local opposition is critically dependent on the extent and nature of prior community/labor union organizing and tends to be contingent upon (and therefore constrained by) the particular form of workfare that is being rolled out locally. So far at least, localized anti-workfare campaigns have shown few signs of 'jumping scale' to the national or international level, although there have been some suggestive attempts at cross-locality networking among oppositional groups in places like New York and Toronto. But many, local anti-workfare movements bear the hallmarks of the kind of 'militant particularism' described by Harvey (1996) and Swyngedouw (1997a), in which the localization and specificity of oppositional forces can undermine the potential for cross-locality alliance building or scaling up. In many respects, processes of political contestation have been downloaded along with the programs, such that the scope for adequate responses to the multiscalar workfare offensive has – so far at least – been decisively curtailed.

[...]

Acknowledgments

The arguments in this article were shaped by joint work developed with Bob Jessop, Nik Theodore, and Adam Tickell. Although I like to believe that I retain some capacity for independent thought, I want to acknowledge these influences, while absolving my collaborators for the specific claims made here. The article also benefited from discussions at Clark University's Geographies of Global Economic Change Conference, 12–14 October 2001, as well as comments from Neil Brenner, Dick Peet, Bob Sack, and three anonymous *Economic Geography* reviewers.

References

Abercrombie, N. Hill, S. and Turner, B.S. (1980) *The Dominant Ideology Thesis,* London: George Allen & Unwin.

Abercrombie, N. and Warde, A. (eds) (2000) *Contemporary British Society,* Cambridge: Polity Press.

Abramson, J. and Greenhouse, S. (1997) 'Trade Bill's Fate Underlines Labor's Muscle', *International Herald Tribune,* 13 November.

Ad Hoc Working Group on the MAI (n.d.) *The MAI-Democracy for Sale?* New York: The Apex Press.

Agamben, G. (1998) *Homo Sacer: Sovereign Power and Bare Life,* Stanford: Stanford University Press.

Agence France-Presse (1998) 21 October in <infoweb@newsbank.com>

Alber, J. (1988) 'The west German welfare state in transition', in R. Morris (ed.) *Testing the Limits of Social Welfare,* Hanover: Brandeis University Press.

—— (1989) *Der Sozialstaat in der Bundesrepublik 1950–1983,* Frankfurt: Campus.

—— (1994) 'The Debate over Long-Term Care Insurance in Germany', contribution to an OECD seminar on the Care of the Elderly, Paris: OECD.

Alesina, A. (1989) 'Politics and business cycles in industrial democracies', *Economic Policy* 4(1): 1–30.

Alesina, A. and Gatti, R. (1995) 'Independent central banks: low inflation at no cost?', *American Economic Review* 85(2): 196–200.

Alesina, A. and Perotti, R. (1997) 'The welfare state and competitiveness', *American Economic Review* 87(5): 921–39.

Allmendinger, J. and Hinz, T. (1998) 'Occupational careers under different welfare regimes: West Germany, Great Britain and Sweden', in L. Leisering and R. Walker (eds) *The Dynamics of Modern Society: Poverty, Policy and Welfare,* Bristol: Policy Press.

Alvarez, R.M., Garrett, G. and Lange, P. (1991) 'Government partisanship, labor organization and macroeconomic performance', *American Political Science Review* (85): 541–56.

Altvater, E. (1992) 'Fordist and post-Fordist international division of labor and monetary regimes', in M. Storper and A.J. Scott (eds) *Pathways to Industrialization and Regional Development,* London: Routledge.

Amin, A. (1997) 'Placing globalization,' *Theory, Culture & Society* 14(2): 123–37.

—— (1999) 'An institutionalist perspective on regional economic development', *International Journal of Urban and Regional Research* 23: 365–78.

Amin, A. and Robins, K.L. (1990) 'The re-emergence of regional economies? The mythical geography of flexible accumulation', *Environment and Planning D: Society and Space* 8(1): 7–34.

Anderson, B. (1991) *Imagined Communities,* London: Verso.

Andrews, D. (1994) 'Capital mobility and state autonomy: toward a structural theory of international monetary relations', *International Studies Quarterly* 38.

Arnold, M. (1969) *Culture and Anarchy,* Cambridge: Cambridge University Press.

Arestis, P. and Sawyer, M. (2001) 'The economic analysis underpinning the "Third Way"', *New Political Economy* 6(2): 255–78.

Arsneault, S. (2000) 'Welfare policy innovation and diffusion: Section 1115 waivers and the federal system', *State and Local Government Review* 32: 490.

Ashley, Richard K. (1983) 'Three Modes of Economism', *International Studies Quarterly* 27(4): 463–96.

Arthur, W.B. (1989) 'Competing technologies, increasing returns, and lock-in by historical events', *Economic Journal* 99: 116–31.

Atkins, R. (1998) *Financial Times* 'Lafontaine says workers should benefit from Tax Co-ordination' (December 9): 1

Atkinson, D. (1994) *The Common Sense of Community*, London: Demos.

Auerbach, A. and Slemrod, J. (1997) 'The economic effects of the tax reform act of 1986', *Journal of Economic Literature* 35: 589–632.

Axford, B. (1995) *The Global System: Economics, Politics and Culture*, Cambridge: Polity Press.

Baeten, G. (2001) 'The Europeanization of Brussels and the Urbanization of "Europe": Hybridizing the city, empowerment and disempowerment in the EU district', *European Urban and Regional Studies* 8: 1170.

Bairoch, P. (1993) *Economics and World History: Myth and Paradoxes*, Chicago: University of Chicago Press.

Baistow, K. (1995) 'Liberation and regulation? Some paradoxes of empowerment', *Critical Social Policy* 42: 34–46.

Ballard, J. (1992) 'Sexuality and the State in time of epidemic', in R.W. Connell and G.W. Dowsett (eds) *Rethinking Sex: Social Power and Sexuality*, Melbourne: Melbourne University Press.

Balls, E. (1998) 'Open macroeconomics in an open economy', *Scottish Journal of Political Economy* 45(2): 113–32.

Balls, E. and O'Donnell, G. (eds) (2002) *Reforming Britain's Economic and Financial Policy*, London and Basingstoke: HM Treasury and Palgrave.

Barro, R. and Sala-I-Martin, X. (1995) *Economic Growth*, New York: Macmillan.

Barry, A. (1996) 'Lines of communication and spaces of rule', in A. Barry, T. Osborne and N. Rose (eds) *Foucault and Political Reason: Liberalism, Neo-Liberalism and Governmentality*, London: UCL Press.

Bartos, M. (1994) 'Community vs. population: the case of men who have sex with men', in P. Aggleton, P. Davies and G. Hart (eds) *AIDS: Foundations for the Future*, London: Taylor & Francis.

Baudrillard, J. (1983) *In the Shadow of the Silent Majorities or 'The Death of the Social'*, New York: Semiotext(e).

Bauman, Zygman (1998) *Globalization: The Human Consequences*, Cambridge: Cambridge University Press.

Baumol, W. (1967) 'The macroeconomics of unbalanced growth', *American Economic Review* 57: 415–26.

Bayoumi, T. (1990) 'Savings-investment correlations', IMF Staff Papers, 37: 360–87.

Beck, U. (1992) *Risk Society: Towards a New Modernity*, London: Sage.

—— (2000) *What is Globalization?* Trans. Patrick Camiller, Malden, Mass.: Polity Press.

Beiner, R. (ed.) (1995) *Theorizing Citizenship*, New York: State University of New York Press.

Bell, E. (1993) 'Social Policy and Economic Reality', *OECD Observer* 183: 14–17.

Benton, T. (1989) 'Marxism and natural limits: an ecological critique and reconstruction', *New Left Review* (November/December) 51–86.

Berkowitz, B. (2001) 'Welfare privatization: Developing a poverty-industrial complex', *Z Magazine* (July–August): 49–57.

Beveridge, W. (1942) *Social Insurance and Allied Services* (Cmd. 6404), London: HMSO.
—— (1944) *Full Employment in a Free Society*, London: Allen & Unwin.
—— (1948) *Voluntary Action*, London: Allen and Unwin.
Bhagwati, J. (1989) *Protectionism*, Cambridge: MIT Press.
Blackburn, R. (1997) *The Making of New World Slavery: From the Baroque to the Modern*. Verso: New York and London.
—— (1998) 'The European Left, Pension Reform and Complex Socialism' (unpublished paper).
Blair/Field Green Paper (1998) 'New Ambitions for Our Country – A New Contract for Welfare' (26 March) http://www.dss.gov.uk/hq/wreform/foreword.html
Block, F. (1994) 'The roles of the state in the economy', in N.J. Smelser and R. Swedberg (eds) *The Handbook of Economic Sociology*, Princeton: Princeton University Press.
Bloom, H.S. and Price, D. (1975) 'Voter response to short-run economic conditions: the asymmetric effect of prosperity and recession', *American Political Science Review* 69.
Blyth, M. (2002) *The Great Transformations*, Cambridge: Cambridge University Press.
Brennan, T. (1993) *History After Lacan,* London: Routledge.
—— (2000) *Exhausting Modernity: Grounds for a New Economy*, London: Routledge.
—— (2001) 'Which Third Way?', *Thesis Eleven* 64: 39–64.
Brenner, N. (1998a) 'Between fixity and motion: Accumulation, territorial organization and the historical geography of spatial scales', *Environment and Planning D: Society and Space* 16: 459–81.
—— (1998b) 'Global cities, glocal states: Global city formation and state territorial restructuring in contemporary Europe', *Review of International Political Economy* 5: 1–37.
—— (1999a) 'Globalisation as reterritorialisation: The re-scaling of urban governance in the European Union', *Urban Studies* 36: 431–51.
—— (1999b) 'Beyond state-centrism? Space, territoriality, and geographical scale in globalization studies', *Theory and Society* 28: 39–78.
—— (2001) 'The limits to scale? Methodological reflections on scalar structuration', *Progress in Human Geography* 25: 591–614.
Brenner, N. and Theodore, N. (2002) 'Cities and the geographies of "actually existing neoliberalism"', *Antipode* 34: 349–79.
Bretherton, C. (1996) 'Introduction: global politics in the 1990s', in C. Bretherton and G. Ponton (eds) *Global Politics: An Introduction*, Oxford: Blackwell.
Brittain, S. (1998) 'Foot on the Ladder', *The Financial Times*.
Brockes, E. (2000) 'Spot the difference', *The Guardian* (23 February).
Broder, J.M. (1997) 'Clinton Offers Workers Aid in Bid to Win Trade Battle', *International Herald Tribune* (7 November): 3.
Brodkin, E.Z. and Kaufman, A. (1998) 'Experimenting with welfare reform: The political boundaries of policy analysis', *JCPR Working Paper No. 1*, Chicago: Joint Center.
Brown, A. (1997) *Work First: How to Implement an Employment Focused Approach to Welfare Reform*, New York: Manpower Demonstration Research Corp.
Brown, K., Kenny, S. and Turner, B.S. (2000) *Rhetorics of Welfare. Uncertainty, Choice and Voluntary Associations*, Basingstoke: Macmillan.
Brown, P. (1989) *The Body and Society: Men, Women and Sexual Renunciation in Early Christianity*, New York: Columbia University Press.
Brown, W. (1995) *States of Injury: Power and Freedom in Late Modernity*, Princeton, N.J.: Princeton University Press.

Burchell, B., Gordon, C. and Miller, P. (eds) (1991) *The Foucault Effect: Studies in Governmentality with Two Lectures by and an Interview with Michel Foucault*, Chicago: Chicago University Press.

Buck-Morss, S. (1994) 'Fashion in Ruins: History after the Cold War', *Radical Philosophy* (Autumn) 68: 10–17.

Burawoy, M. (1985) *The Politics of Production: Factory Regimes Under Capitalism and Socialism*, London: Verso.

Burchell, D. (1995) 'Genealogies of the citizen: virtue, manners and the modern activity of citizenship', *Economy and Society* 24(4): 540–58.

Burchell, G. (1993) 'Liberal government and techniques of the self', *Economy and Society* 22(3): 267–82.

Burchell, G., Gordon, C. and Miller, P. (eds) (1991) *The Foucault Effect: Studies in Governmental Rationality*, Brighton: Harvester Wheatsheaf.

Burnham, P. (2001) 'New Labour and the politics of depoliticisation', *British Journal of Politics and International Relations* 3: 127–44.

Butler, S.M. and Kondratas, A. (1987) *Out of the Poverty Trap: A Conservative Strategy for Welfare Reform*, New York: Free Press.

Callon, M. (1986) 'Some elements of a sociology of translation', in J. Law (ed.) *Power, Action and Belief. A New Sociology of Knowledge?*, Sociological Review Monograph 32, London: Routledge & Kegan Paul.

Campbell, N.D. (2001) *Using Women: Drug Policy and Social Justice*, New York: Routledge.

Cameron, D.R. (1978) 'The expansion of the public economy: a comparative analysis', *American Political Science Review*, 72: 1243–61.

—— (1984) 'Social democracy, corporatism, labour quiescence and the representation of economic interest', in J. Goldthorpe (ed.) *Order and Conflict in Contemporary Capitalism*, Oxford: Oxford University Press, 1984.

Cantwell, J. (1989) *Technical Innovations in Multinational Corporations*, London: Blackwell.

Carr, E.H. (1965) [1945] *Nationalism and After*, London: Macmillan.

Cart, W.L. (1974) 'Federalism and corporate law: reflections upon Delaware', *The Law Journal* 83.

Cass, B. (1988) *Income Support for the Unemployed in Australia: Towards a More Active System*, Canberra: Australian Government Publishing Service.

Castel, R. (1991) 'From dangerousness to risk', in G. Burchell, C. Gordon and P. Miller (eds) *The Foucault Effect: Studies in Governmentality*, Hemel Hempstead: Harvester Wheatsheaf.

Castells, M. (1997) 'The end of Patriarchalism', in *The Information Age: Economy, Society, and Culture*, vol. II Oxford: Blackwell.

Caves, R.E. (1996) *Multinational Enterprise and Economic Analysis*, 2nd edn. New York: Cambridge University Press.

Cerny, P. (1997) 'Paradoxes of the competition state: the dynamics of political globalization', *Government and Opposition*, 32(2): 251–74.

Chait, J. (1998) 'The Slippery Center', *The New Republic* (16 November).

Chambon, A.S., Irving, A. and Epstein, L. (eds) (1999) *Reading Foucault for Social Work*, New York: Columbia University Press.

Chang, Ha-Joon (2002) 'Breaking the mould: an institutionalist political economy alternative to the neo-liberal theory of the market and the state', *Cambridge Journal of Economics* 26: 539–59.

Clarke, P. (1979) *Liberals and Social Democrats*, Cambridge: Cambridge University Press.

260   *References*

Cochrane, A. (1992) 'Is there a future for local government?', *Critical Social Policy* 32.

Cohen, J. and Rogers, J. (eds) 1995 *Associations and Democracy*, London: Verso.

Collini, S. (1979) *Liberalism and Sociology*, Cambridge: Cambridge University Press.

Collier, R. (1997) 'NAFTA Labor Problems Haunt New Trade Debate', *San Francisco Chronicle* (10 September).

Commission on Social Justice (1994) *Social Justice: Strategies for National Renewal*, London: Vintage.

Commission on Global Governance (1995) *Our Global Neighbourhood*, Oxford: Oxford University Press.

Committee on Employment Opportunities (1993) *Restoring Full Employment: A Discussion Paper*, Canberra: Australian Government Publishing Service.

Community Justice Center (1999) 'Unlocking the Prison-Industrial Complex', pamphlet, Boston.

Conlan, T. (1988) *New Federalism: Intergovernmental Reform from Nixon to Reagan*, Washington, D.C.: Brookings Institution.

Cook, L. and Barret, E.J. (1992) *Support for the American Welfare State*, New York: Columbia University Press.

Cooke, W.N. and Noble, D.S. (1998) 'Industrial relations systems and US foreign direct investment abroad', *British Journal of Industrial Relations* 36(4): 581–609.

Coontz, S. (1993) *The Way We Never Were: Family and the Nostalgia Trap*, New York: Basic Books.

Cooper, Melinda (2004) 'Insecure Times, Tough Decisions: The Nomos of Neoliberalism', *Alternatives* 29(5): 515–33.

Corden, W.M. (1974) *Trade Policy and Economic Welfare*, Oxford: Clarendon Press.

Corporate Europe Observatory: http://www.xs4all.nl/~ceo/mai/eu/113invest.html

Corrigan, P. and Sayer, D. (1985) *The Great Arch: English State Formation as Cultural Revolution*, Oxford: Blackwell.

Corsetti, G. and Roubini, N. (1991) 'Fiscal deficits, public debt and government insolvency', *Journal of Japanese and International Economies*, 5: 354–80.

—— (1995) 'Political Biases in Fiscal Policy', in B. Eichengreen, J. Frieden and J. von Hagen (eds) *Monetary and Fiscal Policy in an Integrated Europe*, New York: Springer.

Coyle, D. (1998) *The Independent*, 19 March.

Cox, K.R. (1995) 'The local and the global in the new urban politics: A critical review', *Environment and Planning D: Society and Space* 11: 433–48.

Cox, R. (1987) *Production, Power and World Order: Social Forces in the making of History*, New York: Columbia University Press.

—— (2004) 'Beyond Empire and Terror: Critical Reflections on the Political Economy of World Order', *New Political Economy* 9(3): 307–23.

Crowley, J. (1998) 'The national dimension of citizenship in T.H. Marshall', *Citizenship Studies* 2(2): 165–79.

Cruikshank, B. (1993) 'Revolutions within: self-government and self-esteem', *Economy and Society* 22(3): 327–44.

—— (1994) 'The will to empower: technologies of citizenship and the war on poverty', *Socialist Review* 23(4): 29–55.

—— (1999) *The Will to Empower: Democratic Citizens and Other Subjects*, Ithaca: NY: Cornell University Press.

Cummins, J.G., Hassett, K.G. and Hubbard, R.G. (1995) 'Tax reforms and investment: a cross country comparison', NBER Working Paper Series No. 5232.

Currie, E. (1993) *Reckoning: Drugs, the Cities and the American Future*, New York: Hill and Wang.

Cutler, T. and Waine, B. (1997) *Managing the Welfare State: the Politics of Public Management,* Oxford, Providence: Berg.

DEET (1992) *Department of Employment, Education and Training Annual Report 1991–92,* Canberra: Australian Government Publishing Service.

DSS (1991) *Department of Social Security Annual Report 1990–91,* Canberra: Australian Government Publishing Service.

Dasgupta, P. and Serageldin, I. (eds) (2000) *Social Capital. A Multifaceted Perspective,* Washington: The World Bank.

David, P. (1985) 'Clio and the Economics of QWERTY', *American Economic Review* 75.

De Angelis, M. (1997) 'The autonomy of the economy and globalization', *Common Sense,* 21: 41–59.

de Tocqueville, A. (1955) *The Old Regime and the French Revolution,* New York: Doubleday Anchor Books.

Deacon, A. (ed.) (1997) 'From welfare to work: Lessons from America', *Choice in Welfare* 39. London: Institute of Economic Affairs.

Deacon, B. (1995) 'The globalization of social policy and the socialization of global politics', in J. Baldock and M. May (eds) *Social Policy Review* 7, Social Policy Association.

—— (1999) 'Towards a Socially Responsible Globalization: International Actors and Discourses', GASPP Occasional Papers, STAKES: Finland.

Deacon, B. and Hulse, M. (1996) *The Globalization of Social Policy,* Leeds: Leeds Metropolitan University.

Deacon, B. with Stubbs, P. and Hulse, M. (1997) *Global Social Policy: International Organizations and the Future of Welfare,* London: Sage.

Dean, M. (1991) *The Constitution of Poverty: Toward a Genealogy of Liberal Governance,* London: Routledge.

—— (1994a) *Critical and Effective Histories: Foucaults' Methods and Historical Sociology,* London: Routledge.

—— (1994b) '"A social structure of many souls": moral regulation, government and self-formation', *Canadian Journal of Sociology* 19(2): 145–68.

—— (1995) 'Governing the unemployed self in an active society', *Economy and Society* 24(4): 559–83.

—— (1998) 'Neo-Liberalism as Counter-Enlightenment Cultural Critique', in S. Hänninen (ed.) *Displacement of Social Policies,* Jyvaskyla, Finland: SoPhi.

—— (1999) *Governmentality: Power and rule in modern society,* London: Routledge.

Defert, D. (1991) '"Popular life" and insurance technology', in G. Burchell, C. Gordon and P. Miller (eds) *The Foucault Effect: Studies in Governmentality,* Hemel Hempstead: Harvester Wheatsheaf.

Deleuze, G. (1979) 'Introduction', to Jacques Donzelot *The Policing of Families: Welfare versus the State,* London: Hutchinson.

—— (1988) *Foucault,* trans. S. Hand, Minneapolis: University of Minnesota Press.

—— (1992) 'Postscript on the Societies of Control', *October 59* (Winter): 4–6.

—— (1995) 'Postscript on control societies', in *Negotiations,* New York: Columbia University Press.

Deleuze, G. and Parnet, C. (1987) *Dialogues,* London: Athlone.

—— (1993) *The Fold: Leibniz and the Baroque,* trans. T Conley, Minneapolis: University of Minnesota Press.

Demirovic, A. *et al.* (eds) (n.d.) *Akkumulation, Hegemonie und Staat,* Muenster: Westfaelisches Dampfboot Verlag.

Dennis, N., Henriques, F.M. and Slaughter, C. (1962) *Coal is Our Life,* London: Eyre and Spottiswoode.

DeParle, J. (1999) 'As Welfare Rolls Shrink, Load on Relatives Grows', *New York Times* 21 February.

Deutsch, K. and Eckstein, A. (1960/61) 'National Industrialization and the Declining Share of the International Economic Sector, 1890–1959', *World Politics* 14: 267–99.

Dicken, P., Peck, J. and Tickell, A. (1995) 'Postscript on control societies', in *Negotiations*, New York: Columbia University Press.

—— (1997) 'Unpacking the global', in R. Lee and J. Wills (eds) *Geographies of Economies*, London: Arnold.

Dooley, M., Frankel, J. and Mathieson, D. (1987) *International capital mobility: what do savings-investment correlations tell us?*, IMF Staff Papers, 34: 503–30.

Donzelot, J. (1979) *The Policing of Families: Welfare versus the State*, London: Hutchinson.

—— (1984) *L 'Invention du Social*, Paris: Vrin.

Downs, A. (1957) *An Economic Theory of Democracy*, London: HarperCollins.

Dowty, A. (1987) *Closed Borders: The Contemporary Assault on Freedom of Movement*, New Haven, CT: Yale University Press.

Duchacek, I.D., Latouche, D. and Stevenson, G. (eds) (1988) *Perforated Sovereignities and International Relations: Trans-Sovereign Contacts of Subnational Governments*, New York: Greenwood Press.

Dunning, J.H. (1988) *Multinationals, Technology and Competitiveness*, Boston: Unwin Hyman.

Durkheim, E. (1992) *Professional Ethics and Civic Morals*, London: Routledge.

Dyson, K.W. (ed.) (1989) *Local Authorities and New Technologies: the European Dimension*, London: Croom Helm.

Eckes, A.E. (1995) *Opening Up America's Market: U.S. Foreign Trade Policy Since 1776*, Chapel Hill: University of North Carolina Press.

The Economist (1996) 'A Survey of the world economy: the hitchhiker's guide to cybernomics', 29 September.

The Economist (1996) 'A survey of the world economy: the hitchhiker's guide to cybernomics', 28 September.

The Economist (1998) 'Finance and Economics: The Sinking of the MAI'(March 14): 81–2, London.

The Economist (2001) 'America's great achievement', 25 August: 25–7.

Economic Policy Institute, Institute for Policy Studies, International Labor Rights Fund, Public Citizen's Global Trade Watch, Sierra Club and United States Business and Industrial Council Educational Foundation (1999) 'The Failed Experiment: NAFTA at Five Years', http://www.citizen/pctrade/epijoint.html

Edelman, M. (1977) *Political Language: Words that Succeed and Policies that Fail*, New York: Academic Press.

Edelman, P. (1997) 'The worst thing Bill Clinton has done', *Atlantic Monthly*, March: 43–58.

Ehrenreich, B. (1997) 'When Government Gets Mean: Confessions of a Recovering Statist', *Nation*, 17 November.

Eichengreen, B. (1996) 'Institutions and Economic Growth after World War II', in N. Crafts and G. Toniolo *Economic Growth Since 1945*, Cambridge: Cambridge University Press.

—— (1997) *EMU Up in the Air*, Stanford: Center for Advanced Studies in the Behavioral Sciences.

Eichengreen, B., Rose, A. and Wyplosz, C. (1995) 'Exchange market mayhem', *Economic Policy* 21: 249–312.

Elias, N. (1978) *The Civilising Process*, vol. I: *The History of Manners*, trans. E. Jephcott, New York: Urizen; and (1982) vol. II: *Power and Civility*. New York: Pantheon Books.

Ellis, V. (1998) *Los Angeles Times*, 27 May.

Epstein, W.M. (1997) *Welfare in America: How social science fails the poor*, Madison: University of Wisconsin Press.

Esping-Andersen, G. (1985) *Politics Against Markets: The Social Democratic Road to Power*, Princeton: Princeton University Press.

—— (1990) *The Three Worlds of Welfare Capitalism*, Princeton: Princeton University Press.

—— (1992a) 'Postindustrial cleavage structures: A comparison of evolving patterns of social stratification in Germany, Sweden, and the United States', in F.F. Piven (ed.) *Labor Parties in Postindustrial Societies*, Oxford: Polity Press.

—— (1992b) 'The emerging realignment between labour movements and welfare states', in M. Regini (ed.) *The Future of Labour Movements*, London: Sage.

—— (ed.) (1996) *Welfare States in Transition: National Adaptations in Global Economics*, London: Sage.

—— (2000) 'The sustainability of welfare-states into the twenty-first century', *International Journal of Health Services* 30(1): 1–12.

Etzioni, A. (1993) *The Spirit of Community*, New York: Crown.

European Commission (1994) *European Social Policy: a Way Forward for the Union: a White Paper*, Luxembourg: Office for Official Publications of the European Communities.

Evans, J. (n.d.) 'Economic Globalization: the Need for a Social Dimension', discussion paper, TUAC, Paris.

Evans, P. (1997) 'The Eclipse of the State? Reflections on Stateness in an Era of Globalization', *World Politics* 50(1): 62–87.

Ewald, F. (1991) 'Insurance and risk', in G. Burchell, C. Gordon and P. Miller (eds) *The Foucault Effect: Studies in Governmentality*, Hemel Hempstead: Harvester Wheatsheaf.

Falk, R. (1997) 'Resisting globalization-from-above' through 'globalization-from-below', *New Political Economy* 2(1): 17–24.

Feldstein, M. and Horioka, C. (1980) 'Domestic savings and international capital flows', *The Economic Journal* 90: 314–29.

Ferner, A. and Hyman, R. (eds) (1992) *Industrial Relations in the New Europe*, Oxford: Blackwell Business.

Field, F. (1998) 'A Hand-up or a Put-down for the Poor', *New Statesman* (27 November).

Financial Times (1998) Editorial: 'A Case of MAI culpa' (20 October).

Financial Times (1999) (25 January), title? London, p. 13.

Finch, J. (1989) *Family Obligations and Social Change*, Cambridge: Polity Press.

Finder, A. (1998) 'Evidence Is Scant That Workfare Leads to Full-Time Jobs', *New York Times* (12 April): B1, B30.

Flora, P. (1989) 'From industrial to postindustrial welfare state' in *The Advanced Industrial Societies in Disarray: What Are the Available Choices?* Tokyo: University of Tokyo, Institute of Social Science [Special issue of the Annals of the Institute of Social Science].

Flora, P. and Heidenheimer, A.J. (eds) (1982) *The Development of Welfare States in Europe and America*, New Brunswick, N.J.: Transaction.

Fosler, R.S. (ed.) (1988) *The New Economic Role of American States*, New York: Oxford University Press.

Foucault, M. (1977) *Discipline and Punish*, trans. A. Sheridan, London: Allen Lane.

—— (1979) 'Governmentality', *I & C* 6: 5–21.

—— (1982) 'The subject and power', in H. Dreyfus and P. Rabinow *Michel Foucault – Beyond Structuralism and Hermeneutics*, Brighton: Harvester.

—— (1985) *The Use of Pleasure*, trans. R. Hurley, New York: Pantheon.

—— (1986a) *The Care of the Self*, trans. R. Hurley, New York: Pantheon.

—— (1986b) 'On the genealogy of ethics: an overview of the work in progress', in P. Rabinow (ed.) *The Foucault Reader*, Harmondsworth: Penguin.

—— (1986c) 'Politics and ethics: an interview', in P. Rabinow (ed.) *The Foucault Reader*, Harmondsworth: Penguin.

—— (1988a) 'The ethic of the care of the self as a practice of freedom', in J. Bernauer and D. Rasmussen (eds) *The Final Foucault*, Cambridge, Mass.: MIT Press.

—— (1988b) 'The political technology of individuals', in L.H. Martin, H. Gutman and P.H. Hutton (eds) *Technologies of the Self – A Seminar with Michel Foucault*, London: Tavistock.

—— (1988c) 'Politics and reason', in L.D. Kritzman (ed.) *M. Foucault: Politics, Philosophy, Culture*, New York: Routledge.

—— (1988d) 'Technologies of the self', in L.H. Martin, H. Gutman and P.H. Hutton (eds) *Technologies of the Self – A Seminar with Michel Foucault*, London: Tavistock.

—— (1989) *Resume Descours 1970–1982*, Paris: Juilliard.

—— (1991) 'Governmentality', in G. Burchell, C. Gordon, and P. Miller (eds) *The Foucault Effect: Studies in Governmentality with Two Lectures by and an Interview with Michel Foucault*, Chicago: University of Chicago Press.

—— (1993) 'About the beginnings of the hermeneutics of the self', *Political Theory* 21(2): 198–227.

Finger, J.M., Ingco, M. and Reincke, U. (1996) *The Uruguay Round: Statistics on Tariff Concessions Given and Received*, Washington DC, World Bank.

Frankel, J. (1991) 'Measuring international capital mobility: a review', *American Economic Review: AEA Papers and Proceedings*, 82: 197–202.

—— (1993) *On Exchange Rates*, Cambridge: MIT Press.

Frankel, J. and Romer, D. (1996) 'Trade and growth: an empirical investigation', NBER Working Paper Series No. 5476.

Franks, S. (1999a) 'Vital Statistics', *Guardian*, 11 January: 7.

—— (1999b) *Having None of It: Women, Men, and the Future of Work*, London: Granta.

Fraser, N. (1994) 'After the family-wage: gender equity and the welfare state', *Political Theory* 22: 591–618.

Fraser, N. and Gordon, L. (1997) 'A geneology of "Dependency": Tracing a keyword of the US welfare state', in N. Fraser *Justice Interruptus: Critical Reflections on the 'Postsocialist' Condition*, New York: Routledge.

French, K. and Poterba, J. (1991) 'International diversification and international equity markets', *American Economic Review*, Papers and Proceedings, 81: 222–6.

Frey, B.S., Pommerehne, W., Schneider, F. and Gilbert, G. (1984) 'Consensus and Dissensus Among Economists: An Empirical Inquiry', *American Economic Review* 74: 986–94.

Frieden, J. and Rogowski, R. (1996) 'The Impact of the International Economy on National Policies: An Analytical Overview', in R.O. Keohane and H.V. Milner (eds) *Internationalization and Domestic Politics*, Cambridge: Cambridge University Press.

Friedman, T.L. (1997) 'Plotting Politics on the New Globalization Graph', *International Herald Tribune*, 14 November: 8.

Galaskiewicz, J. and Bielefeld, W. (1998) *Nonprofit Organizations in an Age of Uncertainty. A Study of Organizational Change*, York: Aldine de Gruyter.

Gamble, A. (1988) *The Free Economy and the Strong State*, London: Macmillan.

Garrett, G. (1993) 'The Politics of Structural Reform: Swedish Social Democracy and Thatcherism in Comparative Perspective', *Comparative Political Studies*, 25.

—— (1995) 'Trade, capital mobility and the politics of economic policy', *International Organization* 49: 657–87.

—— (1997) 'Capital flows, capital mobility and capital taxation', presented at the Annual Meeting of the American Political Science Association, Washington, DC.

—— (1998) *Partisan Politics in the Global Economy*, Cambridge: Cambridge University Press.

Garrettt, G. and Lange, P. (1991) 'Political responses to interdependence: what's "left" for the Left?', *International Organization*, 45: 539–64.

—— and —— (1995) 'Internationalization, institutions and political change', *International Organization*, 49: 627–55.

Gass, J. (1988) 'Towards the "active society"', *OECD Observer*, 152: 4–8.

Gebhardt, T. (1997) *Ending Welfare as We Know It: Die US-amerikanische Sozialhilfereform 1993–1996*, Bremen: Universität Bremen, Zentrum für Sozialpolitik.

Geyer, R. (1998) 'Globalization and the (non-)defence of the welfare state', *West European Politics*, 21(3): 77

Giddens, A. (1984) *The Constitution of Society: Outline of the Theory of Structuration*. Cambridge: Cambridge Polity Press.

—— (1991) *Modernity and Self-Identity*, Cambridge: Polity.

—— (1998) *The Third Way*, Cambridge: Polity Press.

—— (2000) *A Third Way and Its Critics*, Cambridge, Polity Press.

Gilbert, B. (1966) *The Evolution of National Insurance in Great Britain*, London: Michael Joseph.

Gilbert, M.R. (2001) 'From the "Walk for Welfare" to the "March of Our Lives": Welfare fights organizing in the 1960s and 1990s', *Urban Geography* 22: 440–56.

Gilpin, R. (1987) *The Political Economy of International Relations*, Princeton, NJ: Princeton University Press.

Giner, S. and Sarasa, S. (1996) 'Civic altruism and social policy', *International Sociology* 11(2): 139–59.

Gold, D.B. (1971) 'Women and volunteerism', in V. Gornick and B.K. Moran (eds) *Woman in Sexist Society: Studies in Power and Powerlessness*, New York: Basic Books.

Goodhart, C. (1995) 'The political economy of monetary union', in P. Kenen (ed.) *Understanding Interdependence*, Princeton: Princeton University Press.

Goodman, J. and Pauly, L. (1993) 'The obsolescence of capital controls? Economic management in an age of global markets', *World Politics* 46.

Gordon, C. (1991) 'Introduction', in G. Burchell, C. Gordon and P. Miller (eds) *The Foucault Effect: Studies in Governmental Rationality*, Brighton: Harvester Wheatsheaf.

—— (1994) *New Deals: Business, Labor, and Politics in America, 1920–1935* Cambridge: Cambridge University Press.

Gordon, D. (1988) 'The global economy: new edifice or crumbling foundations?', *New Left Review* 168 (March–April).

Gordon, L. (1989) *Heroes of their Own Lives: The Politics and History of Family Violence*, London: Virago.

—— (1994) *Pitied but not Entitled: Single Mothers and the History of Welfare*, New York: Free Press.

Gordenker, L. and Weiss, T.G. (1996) 'Pluralizing global governance: analytical approaches and dimensions', in T.G. Weiss and L. Gordenker (eds) *NGOs, the UN, and Global Governance*, London: Lynne Reinner.

Götting, U., Haug, K. and Hinrichs, K. 'The Long Road to Long-Term Care Insurance in Germany: A Case Study in Welfare State Expansion', Paper presented at the World Congress of Sociology, Bielefeld, July 1994.

Gramsci, A. (1971) *Selections from the Prison Notebooks*, London: Lawrence and Wishart.

Gray, J. (1998) *False Dawn: The Delusions of Global Capitalism*, London: Granta Books.

Green, A. (1997) *Education, Globalization and the Nation State*, Basingstoke: Macmillan.

Greenstein, R. (1991) 'Universal and Targeted Approaches to Relieving Poverty', in C. Jencks and P. Peterson (eds) *The Urban Underclass*, Washington, D.C.: Brookings Institution.

Greider, W. (1997) *International Herald Tribune*, 25 February: 9.

Grey, J. (1996) *After Social Democracy*, London: Demos.

Guardian (1997) 'Midwives to look for abuse of women', 29 December.

Gueron, J.M. (1995) Labor impact of welfare revisions. Federal Document Clearing House Congressional Testimony, 28 February.

Hacker, J. (1997) *The Road to Nowhere: The Genesis of President Clinton's Plan for Health Security*, Princeton, NJ: Princeton University Press.

Hacking, I. (1991) *The Taming of Chance*, Cambridge: Cambridge University Press.

Hadot, P. (1992) 'Reflections on the notion of the "cultivation of the self"', in T.J. Armstrong (ed.) *Michel Foucault Philosopher*, Hemel Hempstead: Harvester Wheatsheaf.

Hall, P.A. (1993) 'Policy paradigms, social learning and the state: the case of economic policy-making in Britain', *Comparative Politics* 25: 175–96.

Hallerberg, M. and Basinger, S. (1998) 'Internationalization and changes in taxation policy in OECD countries: the importance of domestic veto players', *Comparative Political Studies* 31(3): 321–52.

Handler, J.F. and Hasenfeld, Y. (1997) *We the Poor People: Work, Poverty, and Welfare*. New Haven, Conn.: Yale University Press.

Hardt, M. and Weeks, K. (eds) (2000) *The Jameson Reader*, Oxford, U.K.: Malden, Mass.: Blackwell.

Hardt, M. and Negri, A. (2000) *Empire*, Cambridge, Mass.: Harvard University Press.

—— and —— (2001) 'What the protesters in Genoa want', *New York Times*, July 20: A18.

Hartman, S.V. (1997) *Scenes of Subjection: Terror, Slavery and Self-Making in Nineteenth Century America*, New York: Oxford University Press.

Harvey, D. (1989) *The Condition of Postmodernity: An Enquiry into the Origins of Cultural Change*, Oxford and New York: Basil Blackwell.

—— (1996) *Justice, Nature and the Geography of Difference*, Oxford, U.K.: Blackwell.

Hay, C. (1996) *Re-Stating Social and Political Change*, Buckingham: Open University Press.

—— (1998) 'Globalization, welfare retrenchment and the "logic of no alternative"; why second best won't do,' *Journal of Social Policy* 24(4): 525–32.

—— (1999a) *The Political Economy of New Labour*, Manchester: Manchester University Press.

—— (1999b) 'Crisis and the structural transformation of the state: interrogating the process of change', *British Journal of Politics and International Relations* 1(3): 317–44.

—— (2000) 'Globalization, social democracy and the persistence of partisan politics: a commentary on Garret', *Review of International Political Economy* 7(1): 138–52

—— (2001) 'The crisis of Keynesianism and the rise of neoliberalism in Britain: an ideational institutionalist approach', in J.L. Campbell and O.K. Pedersen (eds) *The Rise of Neoliberalism and Institutional Analysis*, Princeton, NJ: Princeton University Press.

—— (2003a) 'Political participation and social capital in disaffected democracies: a problem of supply or demand?', in E. Page (ed.) *NGOs, Democratisation and the Regulatory State*, London: European Policy Forum.

—— (2003b) 'Macroeconomic policy coordination and membership of the Single European Currency: another case of British exceptionalism?', *Political Quarterly* 74(1): 91–100.

—— (2004a) 'Credibility, competitiveness and the business cycle in "Third Way" political economy: a critical evaluation of economic policy in Britain since 1997', *New Political Economy* 9(1): 39–56.

—— (2004b) 'Theory, stylised heuristic or self-fulfilling prophecy? The status of rational choice theory in public administration', *Public Administration* 82(1): 39–62.

—— (2004c) 'The normalizing role of rationalist assumptions in the institutional embedding of neoliberalism', *Economy and Society*, 33(40): 500–27.

—— (2005) 'Globalization's impact on states', in J. Ravenhill (ed.) *Global Political Economy*, Oxford, NY: Oxford University Press.

Heclo, H. (1988) 'Generational Politics', in J. Palmer, T. Smeeding, and B.B. Torrey (eds) *The Vulnerable*, Washington, D.C.: Urban Institute Press.

Hegel, G.W.F. (1952) *Hegel's Philosophy of Right*, trans. T.M. Knox, Oxford: Oxford University Press.

Heidegger, M. (1977) *The Question Concerning Technology and Other Essays*, New York: Harper and Row.

—— (1978) *Basic Writings*, ed. D. Krell, London: Routledge & Kegan Paul.

Held, D. and McGrew, A. (2002) *Globalization/Anti-Globalization*, Cambridge: Polity Press.

Henwood, D. (1996) 'Post What?', *Monthly Review* 48(4).

—— (1997) 'Talking about work', *Monthly Review* 49(3).

Herod, A. (2001) *Labor Geographies*, New York: Guilford Press.

Heron, L. (1985) *Truth, Dare, or Promise: Girls Growing Up in the Sixties*.

Hindess, B. (1993) 'Liberalism, socialism and democracy', *Economy and Society* 22(3): 300–13.

—— (1994a) 'Politics without politics: anti-political motifs in Western political discourse', paper delivered to Vienna Dialogue on Democracy, July.

—— (1994b) 'Governing what economy?', paper delivered to Governing Australia Conference, Sydney, November.

Hines, J.R. (1997) 'Altered states: taxes and the location of foreign direct investment in America', *American Economic Review* 86: 1076–94.

Hinrichs, K. (1993) 'Public Pensions and Demographic Change: Generational Equity in the United States and Germany', *Centre for Social Policy Research Working Paper no. 16/93*, Bremen: University of Bremen.

Hirschman, A.O. (1980) [1945] *National Power and the Structure of Foreign Trade*, Berkeley and Los Angeles: University of California Press.

Hirschman, A. (1991) *The Rhetoric of Reaction*, Cambridge, Mass.: Belknap Harvard.

Hirst, P. and Thompson, G. (1992) 'The problem of "globalization": international economic relations, national economic management and the formation of trading blocs', *Economy and Society* 21(4): 357–96.

—— (1996a) *Globalization in Question: the International Economy and the Possibility of Governance*, Cambridge: Polity Press.

—— (1996b) 'Globalization: Ten frequently asked questions and some surprising answers', *Soundings* 4.

Hirst, P. and Woolley, P. (1982) *Social Relations and Human Attributes*, London: Tavistock.

Hirst, P.Q. (1994) *Associative Democracy*, Cambridge: Polity.

Hoggarth, R. (1958) *The Uses of Literacy*, Harmondsworth: Penguin.

Hood, C. (1991) 'A public management for all seasons', *Public Administration* 69(1): 3–19.

Holton, R. (1996) 'Has class analysis a future?', in D. Lee and B.S. Turner (eds) *Conflicts about Class. Debating Inequalities in Late Industrialism*, London: Longman.

Holton, R.J. (1998) *Globalization and the Nation-State*, Basingstoke: Macmillan.

House Ways and Means Committee (1994) *Background Material on Programs within the Jurisdiction of the Committee on Ways and Means*, Washington, D.C.: GPO.

Huag, M. (1999) 'The anti-nuclear power movement in Taiwan: claiming the right to a clean environment', in J.A. Bauer and D.A. Bell (eds) *The East Asian Challenge for Human Rights*, Cambridge: Cambridge University Press.

Huber, E. and Stephens, J. (1996) 'Political power and gender in the making of the social democratic service state', Research Committee 19, *International Sociological Association*, ANU, August 19–23.

Hunter, I. (1990) 'Personality as a vocation: the political rationality of the humanities', *Economy and Society* 19(4): 391–430.

Hutton, Will (1995) *The State We're In*, London: Cape.

Irwin, D.A. (1996) *Against the Tide: An Intellectual History of Free Trade*, Princeton, NJ: Princeton University Press.

Isin, E.F. and Wood, P.K. (1999) *Citizenship and Identity*, London: Sage.

Iversen, T. (1996) 'Power, flexibility and the breakdown of centralized wage bargaining', *Comparative Politics* 28: 399–436.

Jacobs, H. (1997) *Zwischen Mißbrauch und Arbeitspflicht-Die Diskussion um die Sozialhilfe und die Novellierungen des BSHG 1993*, Bremen: Universität, Zentrum für Sozialpolitik.

James, H. (1996) *International Monetary Cooperation Since Bretton Woods*, Washington, DC: International Monetary Fund, and New York: Oxford University Press.

Jameson, F. (2000) 'Globalization and political strategy', *New Left Review* 4: 49–68.

Janowitz, M. (1976) *Social Control of the Welfare State*, Chicago: University of Chicago Press.

Jellin, E. (2000) 'Towards a global environmental citizenship', *Citizenship Studies* 4(1): 47–63.

Jessop, B. (n.d.) "Regulation und Politik: 'Integral Economy' and 'Integral State'", in A. Demirovic *et al.* (eds) *Akkumulation, Hegemonie und Staat*, Muenster: Westfaelisches Dampfboot Verlag.

—— (1991) 'The welfare state in the transition from Fordism to post-Fordism', in B. Jessop *et al.* (eds) *The Politics of Flexibility*, Aldershot: Edward Elgar.

—— (1992a) *State Theory: Putting Capitalist States in their Place*, Cambridge: Polity.

—— (1992b) 'Fordism and post-fordism: a critical reformulation', in A.J. Scott and M.J. Storper (eds) *Pathways to Regionalism and Industrial Development*, London: Routledge.

—— (1999) 'Narrating the future of the national economy and the national state? Remarks on remapping regulation and reinventing governance', in G. Steinmetz (ed.) *State/Culture: State Formation after the Cultural Turn*, Ithaca, N.Y.: Cornell University Press.

—— (2001) 'The social embeddedness of the economy and its implications for economic governance', in F. Adaman and P. Devine (eds) *Economy and Society*, Montreal: Black Rose Books.

Jessop, B. and Peck, J. (2000) 'Fast policy/local discipline: The politics of time and scale in the neo-liberal workfare offensive', Unpublished manuscript, Department of Sociology, University of Lancaster, Lancaster, U.K.

Jessop, B., Peck, J. and Tickell, A. (1999) 'Retooling the machine: Economic crisis, state restructuring, and urban polities', in A.E.G. Jonas and D. Wilson (eds) *The Urban Growth Machine: Critical perspectives two decades later*, Albany: State University of New York Press.

Jessop, B. and Sum, N.G. (2000) 'An entrepreneurial city in action: Hong Kong's emerging strategies in and for (inter)urban competition', *Urban Studies* 37: 287–14.

Jones, M.A. (1982) *American Immigration*, Chicago: University of Chicago Press, 2nd ed.

Jones, M.R. (1997) 'Spatial selectivity of the state? The regulationist enigma and local struggles over economic governance', *Environment and Planning A* 29: 831–64.

Jordan, B. (1998) *The New Politics of Welfare*, London: Sage.

Joseph Rowntree Foundation (1995) *Enquiry into Income and Wealth*, 2 Vols, York: Joseph Rowntree Foundation.

Joyce Foundation. (2002) *Welfare to Work: What Have We Learned?* Chicago, Ill.: Joyce Foundation.

Kahneman, D. and Tversky, A. (1979) 'Prospect theory: an analysis of decision under risk', *Econometrica* 47.

—— (1984) 'Choices, values and frames', *American Psychologist* 39.

Kaiser, M.S. (1996) 'Sozialpolitik nach dem Ende des Ost- West-Konflikts', in H. Dittgen and M. Minkenberg (eds) *Das amerikanische Dilemma: Die Vereinigten Staaten nach dem Ende des Ost-West-Konflikts*, Paderborn: Schöningh.

Katz, M.B. (1993) *The 'Underclass' Debate: Views From History*, Princeton, NJ: Princeton University Press.

Katzenstein, P. (1985) *Small States in World Markets*, Cornell University Press, Ithaca, N.Y.

Kaufmann, F.X. (1997) *Herausforderungen des Sozialstaates*, Frankfurt: Suhrkamp.

Keating, P. (1994) *Working Nation: Policies and Programs*, Canberra: Australian Government Publishing Service.

Kernell, S. (1977) 'Presidential popularity and negative voting: An alternative explanation of the midterm congressional decline of the President's party', *American Political Science Review* 71.

Kendall, J. and Knapp, M. (1996) *The Voluntary Sector in the United Kingdom*, Manchester: Manchester University Press.

Kent R. (1981) *A History of British Empirical Sociology*, Aldershot: Gower.

Kindleberger, C. (1996) *World Economic Primacy 1500–1990*, New York: Oxford University Press.

King, A. (1975) 'Overload: problems of governing in the 1970s', *Political Studies* 23(2/3): 284–96.

King, D.S. (1987) *The New Right*, London: Macmillan.

Kohl, J. (1981) 'Trends and problems in postwar public expenditures development in Western Europe and North America', in Flora, P. and Heidenheimer, A.J. (eds), *The Development of Welfare States in Europe and North America*, Somerset NJ.: Transaction.

Korpi, W. (1983) *The Democratic Class Struggle*, London: Routledge and Kegan Paul.

Krasner, S.A. (1989) 'Sovereignty: An Institutional Perspective', in J.A. Caporaso (ed.) *The Elusive State: International and Comparative Perspectives*, Newbury Park, Calif.: Sage Publications.

Kratke, S. (1999) 'A regulationist approach to regional studies', *Environment and Planning A* 31: 683–704.

Krugman, P.R. (1991) *Geography and Trade*, Cambridge: MIT Press.

Kuhn, T.S. (1962) *The Structure of Scientific Revolutions*, Chicago, IL: University of Chicago Press.

Kuttner, R. (1988) 'Reaganism, Liberalism, and the Democrats', in S. Blumenthal and T.B. Edsall (eds) *The Reagan Legacy*, New York: Pantheon.

Kydland, F.E. and Prescott, E.C. (1977) 'Rules rather than discretion: the inconsistency of optimal plans', *Journal of Political Economy* 85(3): 473–92.

Laffer, A.B. (1981) 'Government exactions and revenue deficiencies', *The Cato Journal* 1: 1–21.

Lang, T. and Hines, C. (1993) *The New Protectionism: Protecting the Future Against Free Trade*, New York: The New Press.

Larner, W. and Walters, W. (2004) 'Globalization as governmentality', *Alternatives* 29(5): 495–514.

Lash, S. and Urry, J. (1994) *Economies of Signs and Spaces*, London: Routledge.

Lau, R.R. (1985) 'Explanations for negativity effects in political behavior', *American Journal of Political Science* 29.

Leibfried, S. and Pierson, P. (1995) 'Semisovereign welfare states: Social policy in a multitiered Europe,' in S. Leibfried and P. Pierson (eds) *European Social Policy: Between Fragmentation and Integration*, Washington, D.C.: Brookings Institution.

—— and —— (1996) 'Social Policy', in H. Wallace and W. Wallace (eds) *Policy-making in the European Union*, Oxford: Oxford University Press.

Lepsius, M.R. (1979) 'Soziale Ungleichheit und Klassenstrukturen in der Bundesrepublik Deutschland,' in H.U. Wehler (ed.) *Klassen in der europäischen Sozialgeschichte*, Göttingen: Vandenhoeck und Ruprecht.

Levenstein, H. (1993) *Paradoxes of Plenty: A Social History of Eating in Modern America*, New York: Oxford University Press.

Levering, J. (1999) 'Theory led by policy: The inadequacies of the "new regionalism" (illustrated from the case of Wales)', *International Journal of Urban and Regional Research* 23: 379–95.

Levi, M. (1996) 'Social and unsocial capital: a review essay of Robert Putnam's *Making Democracy Work*', *Politics and Society* 24(1): 4–55.

Levine, D.P. (2001) *Normative Political Economy: Subjective Freedom, the Market, and the State*, London: Routledge.

Levitas, R. (1996) 'The concept of social exclusion and the new Durkheimian hegemony', *Critical Social Policy* 16(1): 5–20.

Light, P. (1985) *Artful Work: The Politics of Social Security Reform*, New York: Random House.

Lindbeck, A. (1988) 'Consequences of the Advanced Welfare State', *World Economy* 11: 19–37.

—— (1995) 'Welfare State Disincentives with Endogenous Habits and Norms', *Scandinavian Journal of Economics* 97: 477–94.

Lipietz, A. (1982) 'Toward global Fordism', *New Left Review* 132: 33–47.

Little, D.L. (1999) 'Independent workers, dependable mothers: Discourse, resistance, and AFDC workfare programs', *Social Politics* 6: 161–202.

Lockwood, D. (1996) 'Civic integration and class formation', *British Journal of Sociology* 47(3): 531–50.

Lurie, I. (1996) 'A lesson from the JOBS program: Reforming welfare is both dazzling and dull', *Journal of Policy Analysis and Management* 15: 572–86.

MacGregor, S. (1999) 'Welfare, Neoliberalism, and New Paternalism: Three Ways for Social Policy in Late Capitalist Societies', *Capital and Class* 67: 91–118.

MacLeod, G. and Goodwin, M. (1999) 'Space scale and state strategy: Rethinking urban and regional governance', *Progress in Human Geography* 23: 503–27.

Mansion, S.A. (2000) 'The social construction of scale', *Progress in Human Geography* 24: 219–42.

Marcuse, P. (2000) 'The Language of Globalization', *Monthly Review* 52(3): 23–7.

Marshall, T.H. (1963) [1949] 'Citizenship and social class', lecture given in 1949, in *Sociology at the Crossroads*, London: Heinemann.

—— (1950) [1964] *Citizenship and Social Class and Other Essays*, Cambridge: University of Cambridge Press. [This work was later published in 1964 as *Class Citizenship and Social Development*, 1964, London: Heinemann].

—— (1975) *Social Policy*, London: Hutchinson.

Marston, R. (1995) *International Financial Integration*, New York, Cambridge University Press.

Martin, C.J. (1995) 'Nature or nuture? Sources of firm preference for national health reform', *American Political Science Review* 89.

Martin, L.H., Gutman, H. and Hutton, P.H. (1988) *Technologies of the Self: A Seminar with Michel Foucault*, Amherst: University of Massachusetts Press.

Marx, K. (1954) *Capital*, Vol. 1, trans. S. Moore and E. Aveling, Moscow: Progress Publishers.

Massey, D. (1985) 'New directions in space,' in D. Gregory and J. Urry (eds) *Social Relations and Spatial Structures*, Basingstoke, U.K.: Macmillan.

—— (1993) 'Power-geometry and a progressive sense of place', in J. Bird, B. Curtis, T. Putnam, G. Robertson, and L. Tickner (eds) *Mapping the Futures*: *Local Cultures, Global Change*, London: Routledge.

Matheson, J. and Summer, C. (eds) (2000) *Social Trends 30*, London: The Stationary Office.

Matthews, M. and Becker, K.A. (1998) *Making Welfare Work: Lessons from the Best and Worst State Welfare Reform Programs*, London: Adam Smith Institute.

Mauss, M. (1978) *Sociology and Psychology*; London: Routledge and Kegan Paul.

Mayer, K.U. and Müller, W. (1986) 'The State and the Structure of the Life Course', in A.B. Sorensen, F.L. Weinert, and L.R. Sherrod (eds) *Human Development and the Life Course: Multidisciplinary Perspectives*, Hillsdale, NJ: M.E. Sharpe.

—— (1989) 'Lebensverläufe im Wohlfahrtsstaat," in A. Weymann (ed.) *Handlungsspielräume: Untersuchungen zur Individualisierung und Institutionalisierung von Lebensverläufen in der Moderne*, Stuttgart: Enke.

McDowell, L. (2001) 'Linking scales: Or, how research about gender and organisations raises new issues for economic geography', *Journal of Economic Geography* 1: 2270.

McFate, K., R. Lawson, and W.J. Wilson (eds) (1995) *Poverty, Inequality and the Future of Social Policy*, New York: Russell Sage.

McIntosh, M. (1998) 'Dependency Culture? Welfare, Women, and Work', *Radical Philosophy*, 91.

McKenzie, R. and Lee, D.R. (1991) *Quicksilver Capital: How the Rapid Movement of Wealth Has Changed the World*, New York: Free Press.

Mclennan, G. (2004) 'Travelling with vehicular ideas: the case of the Third Way', *Economy and Society* 33(40): 484–99.

Mead, L.M. (1995) 'Senate finance welfare revision', Federal Document Clearing House Congressional Testimony, 9 March.

Mead, L. (ed.) (1997) *The New Paternalism: Supervising Approaches to Poverty*, Washington, D.C.: Brookings Institute Press.

Meehan, E. (1992) *Citizenship and the European Community*, London: Sage.

Meeker-Lowry, S. (1996) 'Community, money: the potential of local currency', in J. Mander and E. Goldsmith (eds) *The Case Against the Global Economy and for a Turn Toward the Local*, San Francisco: Sierra Club Books.

Meuret, D. (1981) 'Political economy and the legitimation of the state', *I & C* 9: 29–38.

Miller, P. (1992) 'Accounting and objectivity: the invention of calculating selves and calculable spaces', *Annals of Scholarship* 9(1/2): 61–86.

Miller, P. and Rose, N. (1990) 'Governing economic life', *Economy and Society*, 19(1): 1–31.

—— and —— (1991) 'Programming the poor: poverty, calculation and expertise', in J. Lehto (ed.) *Deprivation, Social Welfare and Expertise*, Helsinki: National Agency for Welfare and Health.

—— (1995) 'Production, identity and democracy', *Theory and Society* 24: 427–67.

Minson, J. (1993) *Questions of Conduct: Sexual Harassment, Citizenship and Government*, London: Macmillan.

Moi, T. (1994) 'Psychoanalysis, feminism, and politics: a conversation with Juliet Mitchell', *South Atlantic Quarterly* 93.

Moody, K. (1997) *Workers in a Lean World*, London: Verso.

Moore, B. (1966) *Social Origins of Dictatorship and Democracy*, Boston: Beacon Press.

Montgomery, D. (1993) *Citizen Worker: The Experience of Workers in the United States with Democracy and the Free Market during the Nineteenth Century*, Cambridge: Cambridge University Press.

Morales, R. and Quandt, C. (1992) 'The new regionalism: developing countries and regional collaborative competition', *International Journal of Urban and Regional Studies* 16(3): 462–75.

Moran, M. and Wood, B. (1996) 'The globalization of health care policy?', in P. Gummett (ed.) *Globalization and Public Policy*, Cheltenham: Edward Elgar.

Moravcsik, A. (1994) 'Why the EC Strengthens the State', Manuscript.

Moulaert, F., Swyngedouw, E. and Wilson, P. (1988) 'Spatial responses to Fordist and post-Fordist accumulation and regulation', *Papers of the Regional Science Association* 64(1): 11–23.

Mueller, T. (2001) 'Globalisation, Legitimacy, and Pacification: The Emergence of a Global Welfare Regime', *New Political Science* 23(2): 241–65.

Myles, J. and Quadagno, J. (2000) 'Envisioning a Third Way: the welfare state in the twenty-first century', *Contemporary Sociology* 29(1): 156–67.

Nader, R. and Wallach, L. (1996) 'GATT, NAFTA and the subversion of the democratic process', in J. Mander and E. Goldsmith (eds) *The Case Against the Global Economy and for a Turn Toward the Local*, San Francisco: Sierra Club Books.

Nancy, J.L. (1991) *The Inoperative Community* (ed.) P. Connor, trans. P. Connor, L. Garbus, M. Holland and S. Sawhney, Minneapolis: University of Minnesota Press.

Nathan, R.P. (1993) *Turning Promises into Performance: The Management Challenge of Implementing Workfare*, New York: Columbia University Press.

National Conference of State Legislatures (1998) 'Tracking Recipients After They Leave Welfare: Summaries of State Follow-up Studies (Welfare Reform Project)' (February) http://vcvw.ncsl.org/statefed/welfare/followup.html.

National Governors' Association (2001) *Policy Positions*, Washington, D.C.: National Governors' Association.

Navarro, V. (ed.) (2002) *The Political Economy of Social Inequalities*, Amityville, NY: Baywood.

Nelson, D.D. (1998) *National Manhood: Capitalist Citizenship and the Imagined Fraternity of White Men,* Durham and London: Duke University Press.

Newby, H. (1996) 'Citizenship in a green world: global commons and human citizenship', in M. Bulmer and A.M. Rees (eds) *Citizenship Today. The Contemporary Relevance of T.H. Marshall,* London: UCL Press.

Norberg-Hodge, H. (1996) 'Shifting direction: from global dependence to local interdependence', in J. Mander and E. Goldsmith (eds) *The Case Against the Global Economy and for a Turn Toward the Local,* San Francisco: Sierra Club Books.

North, D.C. (1990) *Institutions, Institutional Change, and Economic Performance,* Cambridge: Cambridge University Press.

Ohmae, K. (1991) *The Borderless World,* New York: HarperCollins.

OECD (1988a) OECD's Directorate for Financial, Fiscal and Enterprise Affairs, 'The MAI Negotiating Text', 24 April, OECD, Paris.http://www.citizen.org/pctrade/mai.html

―― (1988b) *The Future of Social Protection,* OECD Social Policy Studies No. 6, Paris.

―― (1988c) *Ageing Populations,* Paris: OECD.

―― (1990) *Labour Market Policies for the 1990s,* Paris: OECD.

―― (1994) *The OECD Jobs Study: Facts, Analysis, Strategies,* chart 16, Paris: OECD.

―― (1996) *Literacy and the Economy,* Paris: OECD.

―― (1996) *Economic Outlook 59,* Paris: OECD.

―― (1997) *Consumption Tax Trends,* 2nd edn. Paris: OECD.

Offe, C. (1985) *Disorganized Capitalism,* Cambridge, U.K.: Polity Press.

―― (1991) 'Smooth consolidation in the West German welfare state: structural change, fiscal policies, and populist politics', in F.F. Piven (ed.) *Labor Parties in Postindustrial Societies,* Oxford: Polity Press.

Oliker, S.J. (1994) 'Does workfare work? Evaluation research and workfare policy', *Social Problems* 41: 195–213.

Oliver, M.J. (1997) *Whatever Happened to Monetarism? Economic Policymaking and Social Learning in the United Kingdom since 1979,* Aldershot: Ashgate.

Olson, M. (1973) *The Logic of Collective Action: Public Goods and the Theory of Groups,* Cambridge: Harvard University Press.

O'Malley, P. (1992) 'Risk, power and crime prevention', *Economy and Society* 21(3): 252–75.

―― (1995) 'The prudential man cometh: life insurance, liberalism and the government of thrift', Paper presented to the Annual Meeting of the Law and Society Association, Toronto, June.

O'Neill, P.M. (1997) 'Brining the qualitative state into economic geography,' in R. Lee and J. Wills (eds) *Geographies of Economies,* London: Arnold.

Osborne, T. (1992) 'Techniques of the self,' an unpublished discussion paper for the History of the Present Research Network.

Paccione, M. (1997) 'Local exchange trading systems as a response to the globalization of capitalism', *Urban Studies,* 34(8): 1179–99.

Palmer, J. and Sawhill, I. (eds) (1982) *The Reagan Experiment,* Washington, D.C.: Urban Institute Press.

Palmer, J.L., Smeeding, T. and Boyle, B. (eds) (1988) *The Vulnerable,* Washington, D.C.: Urban Institute Press.

Parker, J. (1998) *Citizenship, Work and Welfare Searching for the Good Society,* Houndmills: Macmillan.

Patel, P. and Pavitt, K. (1991) 'Large firms in the production of the world's technology: an important case of non-globalization', *Journal of International Business Studies,* First Quarter: 1–21.

Patton, P. (1992) 'Le sujet de pouvoir chez Foucault', *Sociologie et Societes* 24(1): 91–102.

Pearce, J.L. (1993) *Volunteers: The Organizational Behavior of Unpaid Workers*, London and New York: Routledge.

Peck, J. (1995) 'Moving and shaking: Business elites, state localism and urban privatism', *Progress in Human Geography* 19: 16–46.

—— (1996) *Work-place: The Social Regulation of Labor Markets*, New York: Guilford Press.

—— (2000) 'Doing regulation', in G.L. Clark, M.S. Gentler and M. Feldman (eds) *The Oxford Handbook of Economic Geography*, Oxford, U.K.: Oxford University Press.

—— (2001) *Workfare States*, New York: Guilford Press.

Peck, J. and Theodore, N. (2000) 'Work First: Workfare and the Regulation of Contingent Labour Markets', *Cambridge Journal of Economics* 24: 119–38.

—— and —— (2001) 'Exporting Workfare/Importing Welfare-to-Work: Exploring the Politics of Third Way Policy Transfer', *Political Geography* 20: 427–60.

Peck, J. and Tickell, A. (2002) 'Neoliberalizing space', *Antipode* 34: 380–404.

Pedersen, S. (1989) 'The failure of feminism in the making of the British welfare state', *Radical History Review* 43.

Peet, R. (2001) Geographies of policy formation: Hegemony, discourse and the conquest of practicality. Paper presented at the Geographies of Global Economic Change Conference, Clark University, Worcester, Mass., 12–14 October.

Perraton, J., Goldblatt, D., Held, D., and McGrew, A. (1997) 'The globalization of economic activity', *New Political Economy*, 2, 2.

Peterson, P.E. (1988) 'The Rise and Fall of Special Interest Politics', *Political Science Quarterly* 105, Washington, D.C.: Brookings Institution, 1988), 95–238. Winter 1990–91.

Petrella, R. (1996) 'Globalization and internationalization: the dynamics of the emerging world order', in R. Boyer and D. Drache (eds) *States against Markets: the Limits of Globalization*, London: Routledge.

Pfaff, W. (1997) 'Don't forget that globalization creates losers too', *International Herald Tribune*, 13 November.

Pharr, S.J. and Putnam, R.D. (eds) (2000) *Disaffected Democracies: What's Troubling the Trilateral Countries?* Princeton, NJ: Princeton University Press.

Pierson, C. (1998) *Beyond the Welfare State: the New Political Economy of Welfare,* 2nd edn., Cambridge: Polity Press.

Pierson, P. (1992) 'Policy feedbacks and political change: contrasting Reagan and Thatcher's pension-reform initiatives', *Studies in American Political Development* 6.

—— (1993) 'When Effect Becomes Cause: Policy Feedback and Political Change', *World Politics* 45.

—— (1994) *Dismantling the Welfare Stale? Reagan, Thatcher and the Politics of Retrenchment in the US and UK*, Cambridge: Cambridge University Press.

—— (1996) 'The new politics of the welfare state', *World Politics* 48: 143–79.

Pierson, P. and Leibfried, S. (1995) 'Multitiered institutions and the making of social policy', in S. Leibfried and P. Pierson (eds), *European Social Policy: Between Fragmentation and Integration*, Washington DC: Brookings Institution.

Pissarides, C. (1980) 'British government popularity and economic performance', *Economic Journal* 90: 569–81.

Piven, F.F. (1999) 'The welfare state as work enforcer', *Dollars & Sense* (September).

Piven, F.F. (1991) *Labor Parties in Postindustrial Societies*, Oxford: Polity Press.

—— (ed.) (1998) 'Welfare and work', *Social Justice* 25: 67–83.

—— (2001) 'Thompson's easy ride', *The Nation* 26 February.

Piven, F.F. and Cloward, R.A. (1985) *The New Class War*, New York: Pantheon Books.

—— and —— (1998a) 'Eras of Power', *Monthly Review* 49: 11–24.

—— and —— (1998b) 'A reply to Ellen Meiskins Wood', *Monthly Review* 44–6.

Plant, S. (1997) *Zeroes and Ones: Digital Women and the New Technoculture*, London: Fourth Estate.

Plaschke, J. (1994) 'Die Sozialpolitik in den Monaten November Dezember 1993 und ein sozialpolitischer Rückblick auf das Jahr 1993', *Nachrichtendienst*, 2.

Polanyi, K. (1957) [1944] *The Great Transformation*, Boston: Beacon Press.

Pontusson, J. and Swenson, P. (1996) 'Labor markets, production strategies and wage-bargaining institutions: the Swedish employers' offensive in comparative perspective', *Comparative Political Studies* 29: 223–50.

Posen, A. (1993) 'Why central bank independence does not cause low inflation: there is no institutional fix for politics', in R. O'Brien (ed.) *Finance and the International Economy 7*, Oxford: Oxford University Press.

Price, S. and Sanders, D. (1993) 'Modelling government popularity in postwar Britain: a methodological example', *American Political Science Review* 37(1): 317–34.

Prideaux, S. (2001) 'New Labor, old functionalism: the underlying contradictions of welfare reform in the U.S. and the U.K.', *Social Policy and Administration* (35): 85–115.

Procacci, G. (1989) 'Sociology and its poor', *Politics and Society* 17: 163–87.

Putnam, R.D. (1993) *Making Democracy Work. Civic Traditions In Modern Italy*, Princeton, NJ: Princeton University Press.

—— (1995) 'Bowling alone: America's declining social capital', *Journal of Democracy* 6(1): 65–78.

—— (2000) *Bowling Alone: The Collapse and Revival of American Community*, New York: Simon & Schuster.

—— (2002) *Democracies in Flux: The Evolution of Social Capital in Contemporary Society*, Oxford: Oxford University Press.

Quinn, D. (1997) 'The correlates of change in international financial regulation', *American Political Science Review* 91: 531–52.

Reich, R. (1992) *The Work of Nations: Preparing Ourselves for 21st Century Capitalism*, New York: Vintage.

—— (1999) 'We are all Third Wayers now', *The American Prospect* 43 (March 1): 46–51.

Rector, R. (2001) 'Implementing welfare reform and restoring marriage', in S.M. Butler and K.R. Homes (eds) *Priorities for the President*, Washington, D.C.: Heritage Foundation.

Rector, R., and Butterfield, P. (1987) 'Reforming welfare: The promises and limits of workfare', Backgrounder No. 585. Washington, D.C.: Heritage Foundation.

Regini, M. (ed.) (1992) *The Future of Labour Movements*, London: Sage.

Rhodes, M. (1996) 'Globalization and West European welfare states: a critical review of recent debates', *Journal of European Social Policy* 6.

Richardson, D. (2000) *Re-Thinking Sexuality*, London: Sage.

Riverside County DPSS (Department of Public Social Services) (1994) *Transferability Package for High Output Job Placement Results*, Riverside, Calif.: Riverside County DPSS.

Robinson, W. (1996) 'Globalization: nine theses on our epoch', *Race and Class*, 38.

Rodrik, D. (1997) *Has Globalization Gone Too Far?* Washington, DC: Institute for International Economics.

Rogers, H.R. (2000) *American Poverty in a New Era of Reform*, Armonk N.Y.: M.E. Sharpe.

Rogers, J.J. (1997) 'Making Welfare Work', *New Statesman* August 29: 17–20.

Rogowski, R. (1989) *Commerce and Coalitions: How Trade Affects Domestic Political Alignments*, Princeton, NJ: Princeton University Press.

Rojek, C. and Turner, B.S. (eds) (1993) *Forget Baudrillard?* London and New York: Routledge.

Rose, N. (1990) *Governing the Soul: The Shaping of the Private Self*, London: Routledge.

—— (1992) 'Governing the enterprising self'', in P. Heelas and P. Morris (eds) *The Values of the Enterprise Culture: The Moral Debate*, London: Routledge.

—— (1993a) 'Eriarvoisuus ja valta hyvinvointivaltion jalkeen' (Finnish translation of 'Disadvantage and power "after the Welfare State")', *Janus* (Journal of the Finnish Society for Social Policy) 1: 44–68.

—— (1993b) *Towards a Critical Sociology of Freedom*, London: Goldsmiths' College.

—— (1993c) 'Government, authority and expertise in advanced liberalism', *Economy and Society* 22(3): 283–99.

—— (1994a) 'Expertise and the government of conduct', *Studies in Law, Politics and Society* 14: 359–67.

—— (1994b) 'Authority and the genealogy of subjectivity', in P. Heelas, P. Morris and S. Lash (eds) *De-Traditionalization: Authority and Self in an Age of Cultural Uncertainty*, Oxford: Blackwell.

—— (1996a) 'Psychology as a political science: advanced liberalism and the administration of risk', *History of the Human Sciences* 9(2): 1–23.

—— (1996b) *Inventing Our Selves: Psychology, Power and Personhood*, New York: Cambridge University Press.

—— (1996c) 'The death of the social? Refiguring the territory of government', *Economy and Society* 25(3): 327–46.

Rose, N. and Miller, P. (1992) 'Political power beyond the state: problematics of government', *British Journal of Sociology* 43(2): 173–205.

Rosen, S. (1994) 'Public employment and the welfare state in Sweden', *Journal of Economic Literature* 34: 729–40.

Rosenberg, J. (2000) *The Follies of Globalisation Theory: Polemical Essays*, London: Verso.

Rosenberry, S.A. (1982) 'Social Insurance, Distributive Criteria and the Welfare Backlash: A Comparative Analysis', *British Journal of Political Science* 12.

Rowbotham, S. and Millen S. (eds) (1994) *Dignity and Daily Bread: New Forms of Economic Organizing Among Poor Women in the Third World and the First*, London: Routledge.

Rub, F. and Nullmeier, F. (1991) 'Alterssicherungspolitik in der Bundesrepublik', in B. Blanke & H. Wollman (eds) *Die alte Bundesrepublik: Kontinuit at und Wandel*, Opladen: Westdeutscher Verlag.

Rubin, L.B. (1976) *Worlds of Pain: Life in the Working-Class Family*, New York: Basic Books.

Ruggie, J. (1983) 'International regimes, transactions and change: embedded liberalism in the postwar economic order', in S.D. Krasner (ed.) *International Regimes*, Ithaca: Cornell University Press.

Ruigrok, W. and Van Tulder, T. (1995) *The Logic of International Restructuring*, London: Lawrence and Wishart.

Sabel, C.F. (1989) 'Flexible specialisation and the re-emergence of regional economies', in P. Hirst and J. Zeitlin (eds) *Reversing Industrial Decline*, London: Routledge.

Salamon, L. and Anheier, H. (1996) *The Emerging Non-Profit Sector*, Manchester, England: University Press.

Sanger, M. (1998) 'MAL Multilateral Investment and Social Rights', Paper presented to the GASPP seminar on International Trade and Investment Agreements and Social Policy, Sheffield, December.

Schmahl, W. (1992) 'Die finanzierung der rentenversicherung im vereinten Deutschland', *Wirtschaftsdienst* 1.

Schmid, G. (1997) 'Beschaftigungswunder Niederlande? Ein Vergleich der Beschaftigungssysteme in den Niederlanden und Deutschland', *Leviathan* 25: 302–37.

Scholte, Jan Art (2000) *Globalization: A Critical Introduction*, Basingstoke: Palgrave.

Schor, J.B. (1991) *The Overworked American: The Unexpected Decline of Leisure*, New York: Basic Books.

—— (1998) WFD/Management Today Survey, London.

Scott, J.C. (1999) *Seeing Like a State: How Certain Schemes to Improve the Human Condition Have Failed*, New Haven: Yale University Press.

Schram, S.F. (1995) *Words of Welfare: The Poverty of Social Science and the Social Science of Poverty*, Minneapolis: University of Minnesota Press.

—— (2000) *After Welfare: The Culture of Postindustrial Social Policy*, New York: New York University Press.

—— (2002) *Praxis for the Poor: Piven and Cloward and the Future of Social Science in Social Welfare*, New York: New York University Press.

Schumpeter, J. (1950) *Capitalism, Socialism and Democracy*, New York: Harper and Row.

—— (1991) 'The crisis of the tax state', in R. Swedberg (ed.) *Joseph A. Schumpeter: The Economics and Sociology of Capitalism*, Princeton: Princeton University Press.

Schwartz, H. (1994) 'Small states in big trouble: state reorganization in Australia, Denmark, New Zealand, and Sweden in the 1980s', *World Politics* 46.

Seeleib-Kaiser, M. (1996) 'Sozialpolitik nach dem Ende des Ost-West-Konflikts', in H. Dittgen and M. Minkenberg (eds) *Das amerikanische Dilemma: Die Vereinigten Staaten nach dem Ende des Ost-West-Konflikts*, Paderborn: Schöningh.

Segal, L. (1994) *Straight Sex: Rethinking the Politics of Pleasure*, Berkeley: University of California Press.

Segal, L. and McIntosh, M. (eds) (1992) *Sex Exposed: Sexuality and the Pornography Debates*, New Brunswick, N.J.: Rutgers University Press.

Shapiro, R.Y. and Young, J.T. (1989) 'Public opinion and the welfare state: the United States in Comparative Perspective', *Political Science Quarterly* 104.

Shaw, L. (1996) *Social Clauses*, London: Catholic Institute for International Relations.

Shearing, C. (1995) 'Reinventing policing: police as governance', in O. Marenin (ed.) *Policing Change: Changing Police*, New York: Garland Press.

Sheth, D.L. and Nandy, A. (eds) (1996) *Multiverse of Democracy: Essays in Honor of Rajni Kothari*, New-Delhi: Thousand Oaks, Sage.

Shragge, E. (ed.) (1997) *Workfare: Ideology for a New Underclass*. Toronto: Garamond Press.

Sinn, H.W. (1986) 'Risiko als Produktionsfaktor', *Jahrbücher für Nationalökonomie und Statistik* 201: 557–71.

—— (1996) *Social Insurance, Incentives and Risk Taking*, München: Center for Economic Studies, 1996, Working Papers no. 102.

Skinner, Q. (1991) 'Thomas Hobbes: Rhetoric and the Construction of Morality', *Proceedings of the British Academy* 76: 1–61.

Sklair, L. (1998) 'Competing conceptions of globalization', paper presented to World Congress of Sociology, Montreal, July.

Slemrod, J. (1995) 'What do cross-country studies teach us about government involvement, prosperity and economic growth?', *Brookings Papers on Economic Activity* 2: 373–431.

Smith, A.M. (1997) 'Feminist Activism and Presidential Politics Theorizing the Costs of the 'Insider Strategy', *Radical Philosophy* (83): 25–35.

Smith, N. (1993) 'Homeless/global: Scaling places', in J. Bird, B. Curtis, T. Putnam, G. Robertson, and L. Tickner (eds) *Mapping the Futures – Local Cultures, Global Change*, London: Routledge.

Somary, F. (1929) *Wandlungen der Weltwirtschaft seit dem Kriege*, Tübingen: J.C.B. Mohr.

Soskice, D. (1997) 'Divergent production regimes', in H. Kitschelt, P. Lange, G. Marks and J. Stephens (eds) *Continuity and Change in Contemporary Capitalism*, New York: Cambridge University Press.

Spahn, P.S. and W. Fottinger (1997) 'Fiskalische Disziplin und institutionelle Budgetkoordinierung Erfahrungen und ihre Bedeutung fur die Europaische Union,' in T. Konig, E. Rieger and H. Schmitt (eds) *Europaische Institutionenpolitik*, Frankfurt: Campus.

Stacey, J. (1998) 'Families against the Family', *Radical Philosophy* 89: 1–2.

—— (1996) *In the Name of the Family: Rethinking Family Values in the Postmodern Age*, Boston: Beacon.

State of Wisconsin Legislative Audit Bureau (2000) *Administration of the Wisconsin Works Program by Maximus, Inc.*, Madison: Legislative Audit Bureau.

—— (2001) Administration of the Wisconsin Works program by Employment Solutions, Inc., and other selected agencies. Madison: Legislative Audit Bureau.

Steedman, C. (1992) 'Landscape for a good woman', in *Past Tense: Essays in Writing, Autobiography, and History*, London: Rivers Ocean.

Steinmo, S., Thelen, K. and Longstreth, F. (eds) (1992) *Structuring Politics: Historical Institutionalism in Comparative Analysis*, Cambridge: Cambridge University Press.

Stephens, H. and Ray, L. (1994) 'The welfare state in hard times', paper presented at the conference on the Politics and Political Economy of Contemporary Capitalism, University of North Carolina, Chapel Hill, September.

Stewart, M. (1984) *The Age of Interdependence: Economic Policy in a Shrinking World*, Cambridge MA: MIT Press.

Stiglitz, Joseph (2002) *Globalization and its Discontents*, Allen Lane: Penguin Books.

Storper, M. (1997) *The Regional World: Territorial Development in a Global Economy*. New York: Guilford Press.

Storper, M. and Walker, R.A. (1989) *The Capitalist Imperative*, Oxford, U.K.: Blackwell.

Strange, S. (1996) *The Retreat of the State: The Diffusion of Power in the World Economy*, Cambridge: Cambridge University Press.

Streeck, W. (1995) 'From market making to state building? Reflections on the political economy of European social policy', in S. Leibfried and P. Pierson (eds) *European Social Policy: Between Fragmentation and Integration*, Washington DC: Brookings Institution.

Stryker, R. (1998) 'Globalization and the welfare state', *International Journal of Sociology and Social Policy*, 18 (2/3/4): 1–49.

Swank, D. (1998) 'Funding the welfare state: globalization and the taxation of business in advanced market economies', *Political Studies* 46(4).

Swenson, P.A. (2000) *Capitalists against Markets*, Oxford: Oxford University Press.

Swyngedouw, E.A. (1996) 'Reconstructing citizenship, the re-scaling of the state and the new authoritarianism: closing the Belgian mines', *Urban Studies* 33: 1499–521.

—— (1997a) 'Excluding the other; the production of scale and scaled politics', in R. Lee and J. Wills (eds) *Geographies of Economies*, London: Arnold.

—— (1997b) 'Neither global nor local: "Glocalization" and the politics of scale', in K. Cox (ed.) *Spaces of Globalization*, New York: Guilford Press.

—— (1996) Neo-voluntarism: a new social policy regime?', in G. Marks, F.W. Seharpf, P.C. Schmitter and W. Streeck (eds) (1996) *Governance in the European Union*, London: Sage.

Tabb, W. (1997) 'Globalization is *an* issue, the power of capital is *the* issue', *Monthly Review* 49(2): 20–30.

Tanzi, V. (2001) 'Globalization without a net', *Foreign Policy* 125: 78–9.

Teeple, G. (1995) *Globalization and the Decline of Social Reform*, Toronto: Garamond Press.

Thain, C. (2000) 'Economic policy', in P. Dunleavy, A. Gamble, R. Heffernan and G. Peele (eds) *Developments in British Politics 6*, Basingstoke: Palgrave.

Thelen, K. (1993) 'West European labor in transition: Sweden and Germany compared', *World Politics* 46.

Theodore, N. and Peck, J. (1999) 'Welfare-to-work: National problems, local solutions?', *Critical Social Policy* 61: 485–510.

Thompson, G. (1986) *The Conservatives' Economic Policy*, London: Croom Helm.

Titmuss, R. (1962) *Income Distribution and Social Change: A Case Study in Criticism*, London: Allen and Unwin.

Townsend, P. and Donkor, K. (1996) *Global Restructuring and Social Policy: the Need to Establish an International Welfare State*, Bristol: Policy Press.

Tully, J. (1995) *Strange Multiplicities: Constitutionalism in an Age of Diversity*, Cambridge: Cambridge University Press.

Turner, B.S. (1990) 'Outline of a theory of citizenship', *Sociology* 24(2): 189–214.

——(1993) 'Outline of a theory of human rights', *Sociology* 27(3): 489–512.

—— (1997) 'Citizenship Studies: A General Theory', *Citizenship Studies* 1(1): 5–18.

—— (1999) *Classical Sociology*, London: Sage.

—— (2001) 'The erosion of citizenship', *British Journal of Sociology* 52(2): 189–209.

US Congress (1996) H.R.3734: Personal Responsibility and Work Opportunity Reconciliation Act, Section 103, Washington, DC.

U.S. Department of Health and Human Services (2002) 'President's TANF proposals good for families', *HHS News* 5 March.

—— (1999) (USDHHS) Administration for Children and Families 'Change in Welfare Caseloads Since Enactment of the New Welfare Law' (January) http://www.acf.dhhs.gov/news/stats/aug-sep.html

—— (1996) *Social Security Bulletin*, Annual Statistical Supplement. Washington, D.C.

van der Pijl, K. (1984) *The Making of the Atlantic Ruling Class*, London: NLB.

Van Hoogstraten, P. (1983) 'De ontwikkeling van het regionaal beleid in Nederland 1949–1977', Nijmegen: Stichting Politiek en Ruimte.

Visser, J. (1991) Trends in trade union membership, OECD Employment Outlook, Paris: OECD.

Voet, R. (1998) *Feminism and Citizenship*, London: Sage.

Wacquant, L. (1999) 'How penal common sense comes to Europeans: Notes on the transatlantic diffusion of the neoliberal *doxa*', *European Societies* 1: 319–52.

Wade, R. (1996) 'Globalization and its limits', in S. Berger and R. Dore (eds) *National Diversity and Global Capitalism*, Ithaca: Cornell University Press.

Wagner, A. (1883/1958) 'The nature of the fiscal economy', in R.A. Musgrave and A.R. Peacock (eds) *Classics in the Theory of Public Finance*, London: Macmillan.

Walby, S. (2001) 'From Community to Coalition: The Politics of Recognition as the Handmaiden of the Politics of Equality in an Era of Globalization', *Theory, Culture & Society* 18(2): 113–36.

Walker, R. (1998) 'The Americanization of British welfare: A case study of policy transfer', *Focus* 19: 32–40.

Walker, R.B.J. (1993) *Inside/Outside: International Relations as Political Theory*, Cambridge: Cambridge University Press.

Walters, W. (1994) 'Social technologies after the welfare state', paper delivered to London History of the Present Conference, Goldsmiths College, April.

—— (1996) 'The Demise of Unemployment?', *Politics and Society* 24(3): 197–219.

Walton, J. (1987) 'Urban protest and the global political economy: the IMF riots', in author? *The Capitalist City*, Oxford: Blackwell.

Wanniski, J. (1978) 'Taxes, revenues and the "Laffer curve"', *Public Interest* 50: 3–16.

Watts, P. (1994) 'Absolutely positive: AIDS, the self and the performance of community in the user discourses of the Body Positive organisation', paper given to London History of the Present Research Network, June.

Weaver, Kent (1986) 'The politics of blame avoidance', *Journal of Public Policy* 6.

Webber, D. (1988) 'Krankheit, geld und politik: zur geschichte der gesundheitsreform in Deutschland', *Leviathan* 16.

Weber, M. (1970) 'Religious rejections of the world and their directions', in H.H. Gerth and C.W. Mills (eds) *From Max Weber*, London: Routledge & Kegan Paul.

Western, B. (1995) 'Union decline in eighteen advanced capitalist countries', *American Sociological Review* 60(2).

White, J. and Wildavsky, A. (1989) *The Deficit and the Public Interest*, Berkeley: University of California Press.

Wilding, P. (1997) 'Globalization, regionalism and social policy', *Social Policy and Administration* 31(4): 410–28.

Williams, R. (1958) *Culture and Society 1780–1950*, London: Chatto & Windus.

Wilson, J.Q. (1973) *Political Organizations*, New York: Basic Books.

Wilson, W.J. (1973) *Power, Racism, and Privilege: Race Relations in Theoretical and Sociohistorical Perspectives*, New York: The Free Press.

—— (1987) *The Truly Disadvantaged: The Inner City, The Underclass, and Public Policy*, Chicago, IL: University of Chicago Press.

—— (1996) *When Work Disappears: The World of the New Urban Poor*, New York: Alfred A. Knopf.

Wiseman, M. (1996) 'Welfare Reform in the United States: A Background Paper', *Housing Policy Debate*, 7: 1–54

—— (1987) 'How workfare really works', *The Public Interest* 89: 36–47.

—— (1995) 'Fixing welfare waiver policy', *Public Welfare* 53: 10–6.

Witherell, W.H. (1997) 'Developing International Rules for Foreign Investment: OECD's Multilateral Agreement on Investment', *Business Economics* 32(1): 38–43.

Wolff, B. (1997) *Incentive-Compatible Change Management in a Welfare State: Asking the Right Questions in the German Standort-Debate*, Cambridge: Harvard University, Center for European Studies, Working Paper Series #6.4.

Wolin, S.S. (1961) *Politics and Vision. Continuity and Innovation in Western Political Thought*, London: George Allen & Unwin.

Wood, E.M. (1996) 'Modernity, postmodernity, or capitalism?', *Monthly Review* 48(3): 21–39.

—— (1998) 'Class compacts, the welfare state, and epochal shifts: A reply to Frances Fox Piven and Richard A. Cloward', *Monthly Review* 49: 24–43.

Yeates, N. (1999) 'Social politics and policy in a era of globalization: critical reflections', *Social Policy & Administration* 33(4): 372–93.

Yuval-Davis, N. (1998) *Gender and Nation*, London: Sage.

Zevin, R. (1992) 'Our world financial market is more open: If so, why and with what effect', in T. Banuri and J. Schor (eds) *Financial Openeness and National Autonomy: Opportunity and Constraints*, New York: Oxford University Press.

Zizek, Slavoj (1994) *Mapping Ideology*, London: Verso.

Zukin, S. (1991) *Landscapes of Power*, Berkeley, CA.: University of California Press.

Index

aboriginals, 48
accumulation regime, 22, 106, 108, 114, 115, 119
active society, 29, 213, 217–19, 227, 228
active subject, 7, 29, 225–6, 228, 229
advanced capitalism
    capitalist democracies, 1, 4, 21, 75, 101
AFDC (Aid to Families with Dependent Children), 150, 158
aged, 51, 52, 120, 132, 155, 188, 206, 218, 223, 227
agency, 12, 26, 94, 180, 214, 215, 224, 243, 246, 247
AIDS, 47
alterity, 8, 19
Anglophone democracies, 9, 88, 89, 90
Anglo-Saxon, 53
anti-statism, 5, 9, 10, 16, 17, 27, 184
Ashley, Richard, 11
'assemblages of risk', 205
associations, 40, 42, 43, 44, 45, 46, 54, 56, 59, 67, 68, 117, 209, 210, 220, 227, 229
Australia, 29, 43, 44, 45, 46, 59, 159, 172, 211, 213, 217, 220, 221, 225, 226, 227, 228, 229
Australian Green Paper, 218, 222
autonomy, 6, 27, 44, 67, 71, 112, 130, 161–74, 181, 184, 206, 236

Bank of England, 89, 98, 100
'basic needs', 2, 13, 15, 16, 18
Baudrillard, Jean, 196
Baumol cost disease, 55, 59
Beck, Ulrich, 2, 47
behavior modification, 30, 231–42
Beveridge, William, 39, 129, 206
biopower, 7, 16, 236, 239, 241
bioproduction, 239, 240
borderless economy, 61
borderless world, 5
bourgeois individual, 13
Brazil, 115, 116

Brown, W., 187, 191
budget(s), 7, 53, 56, 57, 65, 85, 94, 95, 96, 111, 122, 126, 129, 130, 150, 151–2, 153, 154, 157, 165, 168, 209, 214
budgetary crisis, 149, 156
bureaucracy, 32, 198, 209, 221, 236
business
    cycle, 76, 78, 98, 149, 167, 168

capital
    constant, 138, 139, 175
    financial, 110, 164
    footloose, 5
    mobility, 31, 50, 93, 100, 165, 171
    outflows, 165
    as a social relation, 3, 110, 176
    taxation of, 50, 77, 170, 172–3, 174
capitalism
    golden age of, 1
    late, 135
    logic of, 2–3
    longue duree, 2–3
    self-expanding, 3
    species of, 65, 67
capitalists, 77, 78, 166, 176, 179, 180
'category error', 3
Chicago School of Economics, 226
child-care, 2, 6, 40, 44, 52, 135, 142, 144, 187, 188, 189
Christian socialism, 76
churches, 39, 40, 43, 54, 214
citizen
    rights, 2, 8, 23, 83
    soldier, 19, 39, 41
citizenship
    active, 38, 40, 41, 42, 44, 201
    enactment of, 38
    environmental, 47, 48
    multiple, 38
    national, 32, 38, 39
    passive, 38
    as process, 38–9
    social, 18–19, 26–7, 32, 39, 199

effect of, 3, 124, 129, 168
of finance, 162
financial, 19, 50, 51, 65
as a 'forcing mechanism', 120
of markets, 161, 162, 169, 173, 181
theory, 7, 20, 25, 60, 61, 62, 63, 189
globalization-from-above, 69
globalization-from-below, 70
global welfare regime, 18
Gordon, L., 184, 190, 232
governability, 21–2, 77, 209
government
advanced liberal programs of, 197
axes of, 213
through community, 198, 200
consumption expenditures, 167, 168
devices employed by authorities, 195
ethical practices, 29, 212, 215, 217,
218, 227, 228, 229, 230
governmentality (Foucault), 18, 27,
28, 29, 30, 195, 213, 236
growth, 167, 171
liberal, 197, 214, 215, 216
rationalities of, 200, 213
spending, 166, 167, 168, 169, 170
strategies, 197, 200, 201, 203, 204
subjects of, 198, 203–6, 210, 211
tactics, 28, 195
techniques, 10, 197, 202, 219–21
territory of, 198, 199, 200
Gramsci, Antonio, 9, 11, 106, 118
Gray, J., 67, 235, 236, 237, 242

Hardt, Michael, 30, 237, 238, 239, 240,
241, 242
health, 2, 15, 25, 29, 44, 48, 59, 63, 68,
76, 80, 82, 117, 126, 162, 173, 190,
199, 200, 202, 205, 206, 222, 224,
249
care, 6, 39, 52, 53, 54, 56, 163
insurance, 56, 81, 132, 205
system, 38
Hegel, G.W.F., 1
Hegelian idealism, 12
Hobsbawm, E., 178
homelessness, 135
household economy, 20, 52, 56, 57, 58,
59
households, 39, 52, 55, 56, 58, 66, 142
human capital, 25, 57, 125, 127, 226,
227

humanism, 237
human reproduction, 24, 41, 134, 136,
138, 141
human rights, 15, 19, 46, 47, 48, 49, 67
Hume, David, 124
hunger, 135
hybridity, 232

identity, 15, 39, 40, 42, 47, 48, 49, 92,
195, 200, 213, 234, 237
identity politics, 212, 232
ideology/ideological, 3, 6, 7, 23, 27, 29,
32–3, 60, 63, 64, 65, 68, 69, 70, 80,
81, 83, 87, 133, 140, 141, 144, 154,
180, 181, 186, 189, 190, 201, 221,
235, 237, 254
imperialism, 139
imperial state, 9
imports
competition, 124, 127
income
maintenance, 57, 21
security, 217, 218
transfer, 130, 162, 168, 169, 170
India, 70, 143, 164
individual, 1, 2, 5–6, 8, 9, 12, 13, 14, 15,
19, 21, 27, 28, 31, 37, 38, 40, 42,
43, 47, 53, 56, 58, 77, 81, 83, 109,
116, 124, 126, 171, 196, 197, 198,
199, 201, 202, 203, 205, 206, 207,
208, 212, 215, 216, 217, 220, 224,
225, 226, 227, 236, 248
individualism, 80, 174, 196
inequality, 1, 20, 55, 57, 58, 140, 170,
186, 231, 234
inequities, 44, 55, 57, 113, 176
inflation, 77, 78, 86, 93, 94, 97, 98, 99,
104, 157, 158, 163
institutional comparative advantage,
166
institutional path-dependency, 19, 52
interest groups, 7, 10, 18, 24, 127, 177,
188, 210
interest rates, 64, 98, 100, 163, 164, 165,
202
intermediary associations, 40
international lending agencies, 1
International Monetary Fund (IMF), 1,
5, 18, 31, 66, 67, 69, 94, 162
investment
disincentive to, 77, 78, 93, 222

neoliberalism
  global economic agenda, 1
  global imaginary, 7
  ideology, 32, 64, 92–4, 235, 246
  necessitarian, 1, 23, 92
  normative, 23, 89, 92, 97, 98, 103,
    105
  practices, 226
Nettl, J.P., 8
new globalized order, 61
New Labour, 93, 97, 98, 99, 100, 102,
    104, 105
new managerialism, 27, 186
new paternalism, 186
new prudentialism, 205
New Zealand, 48, 59, 159, 171, 195
NGOs (non-governmental
    organizations), 23, 67, 68
NHS (National Health Services), 38, 157
Nordic states
  model, 55
normalization, 23, 88, 89, 92, 97, 98,
    103, 104, 216, 217
normal science, 4, 9, 25, 90, 91
North America, 42, 51, 62, 107, 113
North American Free Trade Agreement
    (NAFTA), 134, 136, 140, 141, 143,
    144, 163
Norway, 168, 172

old international order, 61
ontological security, 48, 49
Organization of Economic Cooperation
    and Development (OECD), 5, 57,
    69, 70, 121, 133, 134, 136, 137,
    143, 159–60, 162, 163, 164, 165,
    167, 170, 172, 173, 174, 213, 217,
    218, 222, 225, 226, 227, 228
overaccumulation, 78

paradigm, 18, 37, 47, 88, 89, 90, 91, 92,
    94, 95, 96, 102, 103, 104, 105, 111,
    115, 119
Pareto-optimal, 57, 58
Pateman, Carole, 27
patriarchy, 233
Peck, Jamie, 30, 31, 241, 242, 243, 244,
    245, 246, 247, 248, 249, 250, 254
pensions, 2, 39, 53, 59, 127, 129, 143,
    149, 153, 155, 162, 188, 205
Pensions Reform Act, 153

perforated sovereignty, 114
Personal Responsibility and Work
    Opportunity Reconciliation Act of
    1996, 135, 248
philanthropy, 43, 45, 185
Philippines, 164
Polanyi, K., 7, 11, 21
political
  rationalities, 27, 197, 210
  technologies, 206, 217
poor relief, 176
population, 1, 10, 17, 20, 28, 32, 41, 47,
    51, 67, 79, 82, 124, 128, 129, 152,
    162, 195, 198, 201, 202, 206, 220,
    227, 228, 229, 233, 234, 235, 237,
    241, 251
postcolonialism, 212
post-Fordism, 108, 111, 114, 118, 175
post-Fordist
  production, 178
post-industrial
  proletariat, 55
  society, 50, 52, 239–40
post-materialism
  values, 84
postmodernity, 175
post-structural, 7, 10, 16, 27, 30
poverty
  alleviation, 29, 217, 248
  entrapment, 55
  wages, 57
power, 4, 5, 6, 7, 8, 9, 10, 12, 16, 17, 18,
    20, 26, 27, 28, 29, 30, 32, 33, 37,
    47, 48, 60, 61, 62, 64, 65, 66, 67,
    70, 75, 77, 78, 85, 86, 87, 89, 100,
    107, 112, 117, 121, 129, 134, 136,
    149, 150, 152, 155, 168, 169, 173,
    175–83, 208, 209, 210, 214, 216,
    218, 221, 229, 234, 235, 236, 237,
    238, 239, 240, 241, 243, 245, 246,
    247
price, 59, 95, 100, 122, 123
  stability, 97, 99, 162
privatization, 1, 2, 6, 20, 25, 53, 56,
    57, 65, 116, 154, 197, 229, 233,
    254
problem-solving approach, 4, 31
production
  cooperatives, 142
  multinationalization of, 161, 163,
    164, 166